THE CRISIS OF THE
MERITOCRACY

THE CRISIS

OF THE

MERITOCRACY

BRITAIN'S TRANSITION TO MASS EDUCATION SINCE THE SECOND WORLD WAR

PETER MANDLER

OXFORD
UNIVERSITY PRESS

OXFORD

UNIVERSITY PRESS

Great Clarendon Street, Oxford, OX2 6DP,
United Kingdom

Oxford University Press is a department of the University of Oxford.
It furthers the University's objective of excellence in research, scholarship,
and education by publishing worldwide. Oxford is a registered trade mark of
Oxford University Press in the UK and in certain other countries

© Peter Mandler 2020

The moral rights of the author have been asserted

First Edition published in 2020

Impression: 1

Published in the United States of America by Oxford University Press
198 Madison Avenue, New York, NY 10016, United States of America

British Library Cataloguing in Publication Data
Data available

Library of Congress Control Number: 2019956693

ISBN 978–0–19–884014–5

Printed and bound in Great Britain by
Clays Ltd, Elcograf S.p.A.

For Laura Carter and Chris Jeppesen

Acknowledgements

My interest in the recent history of education was first stimulated in the late 1990s when I began what turned out to be 20 years (off and on) of work on education policy for the Royal Historical Society, culminating in three years as Vice President for education policy and four years as President. I am grateful to Peter Marshall for inviting me into this work in the first place and to Colin Jones for asking me to return to it; to the staff and officers of the Society who did it alongside me, particularly Arthur Burns and Margot Finn; and to the many people from whom I have learnt in that work in a variety of roles, from civil servants in the Department for Education to the staff of the Historical Association to my colleagues in the Arts and Humanities Alliance to the staff of the British Academy. My preliminary ideas for this book were worked out in four presidential addresses to the Society, appearing in its *Transactions* in the years 2014–17 inclusive.

Serendipitously (or not—you can't escape the Zeitgeist), at about the time my work for the RHS came to a head, I also gained two collaborators who have made all the difference, first as students, now as colleagues. Laura Carter wrote an undergraduate dissertation with me on new methods of teaching history in the interwar period at the same time as Chris Jeppesen was writing a PhD dissertation under my supervision on career choice in the imperial civil service. Over time the three of us realized that in different ways we were all interested in the same thing—that is, mass education as a social and cultural (and not only a political) phenomenon. By around 2015 we were ready to prepare a joint project and in 2017 we were awarded a four-year research grant from the Economic and Social Research Council (Ref. ES/P010261/1), under the title, 'Secondary Education and Social Change in the United Kingdom since 1945' (SESC). The latter phases of the current book were completed with the support of that grant and I am very grateful to the ESRC for its support. I am even more grateful to Laura and Chris, sine qua non. If I had thanked them for every contribution they made to my thinking and writing, I'd be thanking them on every page;

instead, I have dedicated the book to them. There is much more to come from the SESC project: you can follow its work at sesc.hist.cam.ac.uk. If this book provides a 'bird's-eye view' of mass education in the postwar decades, SESC will provide the 'worm's-eye view', with a much greater emphasis on individual experiences, identities, and legacies, using wherever possible the voices of participants, and I hope with an even deeper (though ideally not incompatible) understanding of what difference education has made to people's lives over the last three generations.

In this book I have tried to pull together the disparate and often unconnected work of historians of education, sociologists, economists, and modern British historians; I hope my great debt to them is fully visible in the bibliography and the notes, even, or especially, where I have disagreed with them. But there are individuals who have gone out of their way to guide me through often unfamiliar disciplinary labyrinths. Amongst the historians of education, I'd like to thank especially Cathy Burke, Lottie Hoare, Gary McCulloch, and Stephanie Spencer. Among the sociologists, Mike Savage, Jane Elliott, and Lindsay Paterson have been absolute models in their continuous helpfulness and willingness to engage, well beyond the call of duty. Plamena Panatoyova invited me to join a conference on the history of sociology, which allowed me to explore further the teaching of a wide range of social studies subjects, and to draw on the expertise of John Goldthorpe and Geoff Payne among many others. The directors and staffs of the 1946, 1958, and 1970 birth-cohort studies—now in the care of the Medical Research Council (National Survey of Health and Development, 1946) and the Centre for Longitudinal Studies, University College London (National Child Development Study, 1958, and British Cohort Study, 1970)—have been indispensable to the SESC project, though they must often have been puzzled by the questions and approaches that we strange historians have adopted. Among the economists, Anna Vignoles has been patient and cogent, again well beyond the call of duty, in explaining to me how economists work, opening up new literatures, and engaging closely with my four original papers in ways that helped me understand more of what was at stake in the different disciplinary perspectives. Among the psychologists, Michelle Ellefson has provided another model, of how to be expert in your field and still keep channels open to others. Fortunately—thanks again to the Zeitgeist—my colleagues in modern British history have also recently taken a new interest in the social history of education and many of them have contributed profoundly to my thinking: special thanks for conversation and disputation to Jon Lawrence, Florence Sutcliffe-Braithwaite (who even convened a private tutorial for me, Chris and Laura), David Edgerton, Selina Todd, Laura Tisdall, Andrew Burchell, Helen Carr, Heidi Egginton (who also cracked open for me the treasures of the Churchill Archives Centre), Lawrence Black, Stefan Collini, and William Whyte. Gill Sutherland and Deborah Thom were there long before most. Miles Taylor invited me to join, more or less as a free rider, his project on the 'Utopian Universities' of the 1960s which exposed me to a wide range of new work on the history of higher education. Hannah Forsyth and Stuart Macintyre shared their expertise in helping me make comparisons with Australia.

I had a number of crucial opportunities, beyond the RHS lectures, to air my early ideas and to collect ideas and criticisms from much wider circles of expertise: lectures and seminars at St Anne's College, Oxford, Christ's, Queens', St John's, and Pembroke Colleges, Cambridge, the Raphael Samuel History Centre at the Bishopsgate Institute, the Universities of Bristol, Manchester, Warwick, St Andrews, Lancaster, Lincoln and Suffolk, Leeds Beckett, Columbia and Rutgers Universities, the School of Oriental and African Studies, the Schools History Project annual conference at Leeds Trinity University, the Historical Association annual conference at Chester, the annual conference of University English at the University of London, the A.B. Emden Lecture at St Edmund Hall, Oxford, the Ewen Green Memorial Lecture at Magdalen College, Oxford, the North American Conference on British Studies, the Institute of Historical Research, the University of Regensburg, Nanjing, Fudan, Beijing Foreign Studies and Shanghai International Studies Universities, Kyungpook National University, the Australian Historical Association, the Institute of Education at University College London, and the Society for the History of the Humanities at Somerville College, Oxford. The Permanent Secretary at the Department for Education organized a panel discussion for his senior staff on the legacies of the Butler Act 70 years later where I spoke alongside and learned from Michael Barber and Alison Wolf. Alison Wolf also invited me to contribute to a Radio 4 programme she masterminded on the history of secondary education, which embroiled me in controversy with Peter Hitchens. Marina Vaizey spoke to me about the work of John Vaizey; other contemporary witnesses are thanked in the notes at the specific points where their observations were most invaluable. Sam Haselby invited me to contribute to *Aeon*, and engaged critically with what I had to say. Since everyone has a story to tell about their own education, I learned a very great deal from talking to almost everyone I met over the last ten years but also to organized groups in Sheffield and at the Hay Festival.

Somewhat to my surprise, Twitter has been a crucial resource, not only for keeping me in touch with the latest research from think tanks and disciplines far beyond my own, but also in making more personal and direct connections with yet more sources of expertise—I should mention at the very least Chris Newfield, Mary Curnock Cook, Ben Schmidt, and Nick Hillman, some but not all of whom I have also got to know In Real Life.

Getting closer to home, my colleagues at Cambridge University and Gonville and Caius College have also obliged by telling me their own stories and listening tolerantly to my interpretations of them. The seminar in Modern Cultural History and the New York–Cambridge Collaboration in Twentieth-Century British History have been my intellectual and professional lodestars. My family—Ruth Ehrlich, Ben Mandler, Hannah Ehrlich—have provided yet more stories (not least about their own passages through schools and universities) and more intelligent testing of my half-baked ideas about them. My closest historian-friends have heard and read a lot more on this subject than they ought to have done—loving thanks especially to Deborah Cohen and Susan Pedersen, who heroically read the whole of the manuscript.

Finally, it's a pleasure to return to Oxford University Press which published my first book thirty years ago. Luciana O'Flaherty has been a consistently supportive and responsive editor and supplied two readers' reports on the original proposal which have helped guide me through the writing of the actual book. Kizzy Taylor-Richelieu shepherded the manuscript into print. Martin Noble was an unusually tactful copy-editor. Sinduja Abirami supervised the production process and Kate Shepherd and Kate Roche publicized the final product.

The writing is done now. From here onwards it's up to the readers.

Contents

List of Figures

List of Abbreviations

A-level   GCE Advanced Level (1951–87)
APR   Age Participation Rate, i.e. proportion of 18–19 year olds who progress to higher education
BTEC   Business and Technical Education Council (from 1984)
CAT   Colleges of Advanced Technology (England and Wales, 1956–66)
CCCS   Centre for Contemporary Cultural Studies
CEO   Chief Education Officer (of LEA)
CSE   Certificate of Secondary Education (England and Wales, 1965–87)
DES   Department of Education and Science (1962–92)
GCE   General Certificate of Education (England and Wales, 1951–87)
GCSE   General Certificate of Secondary Education (England and Wales, from 1988)
HEIPR   Higher Education Initial Participation Rate
Higher   SCE Higher Grade (1963–99)
LCC   London County Council (1889–1965)
LEA   Local Education Authority
LEO   Longitudinal Educational Outcomes
MASN   Maximum Aggregate Student Numbers
NAB   National Advisory Body (for Local Authority Higher Education, 1982–88)
NALT   National Association of Labour Teachers
O-E-D   Origins–Education–Destination
O-grade   SCE Ordinary Grade (1962–90)
O-level   GCE Ordinary Level (1951–87)
OECD   Organisation for Economic Co-operation and Development
PEP   Political and Economic Planning
QLR   Qualified Leaver Rate, i.e. proportion of school leavers who attain two A-levels and qualify for progress to higher education
QPR   Qualified Participation Rate, i.e. proportion of qualified leavers who participate in higher education

ROSLA   Raising of the School-Leaving Age
S-grade   SCE Standard Grade (1986–99)
SBTC   Skill-Biased Technological Change
SCE   Scottish Certificate of Education (1962–99)
SED   Scottish Education Department (1872–1999)
STEM   Science, Technology, Engineering and Mathematics
TEF   Teaching Excellence Framework
UGC   University Grants Committee (UK, 1919–89)
WEA   Workers' Educational Association

I

Meritocracy vs Democracy

Britain made its transition to a mass education system within living memory—not, as is often assumed, long ago in the Victorian period. Though elementary education was made free and compulsory in 1880—and, unlike in many other countries, was almost universally enforced—that elementary phase of education was terminal for the vast majority of the population at age 10, and was not patronized at all by more privileged groups that preferred private and charitable schools. There was no education system for all until after the Second World War. Before then elementary education was not aimed at providing a ladder of opportunity. It offered a minimum competency to the 80 per cent+ of the population that were expected to end their education at the elementary level. It was not a gateway to secondary education. The social elite did not send their children to elementary schools and had their own ladder that led to secondary and higher education. This system of educational apartheid—a system dominated by inherited privilege—was not much affected even when the school-leaving age was raised successively to 11, 12, and 14 between 1899 and 1921. A very small proportion won scholarships and made the leap to grammar school, but the vast majority simply remained confined to elementary schools for a few more years. In the last year before the Second World War, 80 per cent of the age-cohort still had no experience of secondary (still less of tertiary) education. There was no ladder of opportunity, no 'meritocracy', for the vast majority.[1]

It was only after the Second World War, when secondary school was made compulsory for all and further and higher education began to expand, that something like a universal education service such as we know today began to emerge. That universal service has become so taken for granted that it is easy to forget how recent is its origin. Most baby-boomers' parents did not go to secondary school, and only a tiny fraction of them went to university; in contrast, the baby boomers themselves all went to secondary school and nearly half of *their* children have continued in education beyond 18. In 1938 only about 14 per cent of the population of England and Wales progressed from state elementary to state secondary schools,[2] most of them dropping out before they received any qualifications, and fewer than 1 per cent of those educated in state schools got as far as university.[3] Today everyone goes to secondary school and nearly half the age cohort to university. This book recaptures the story of how and when this momentous change occurred and with what fateful consequences for the shape of the society we live in today.

In making this transition relatively recently Britain was not unusual among economically developed countries.[4] In fact if anything it was somewhat ahead of many of them, as one might expect of the great power that Britain then was. Some countries like Prussia and France decreed compulsory universal education much earlier but were unable to enforce it until much later, after Britain.[5] By 1938 Britain had more years of compulsory schooling—nine—than any other European country. Most other Northern European countries were not far behind, but Southern European countries required as few as three years of education, and found it difficult to enforce even that much.[6] The real outlier was the United States, which by 1940 was not only enrolling but graduating half of the age cohort from secondary school, well ahead of the rest of the world.[7] But all developed nations were heading in this direction by the time of the Second World War, and especially after 1945 the extension of compulsory education—including secondary education—accelerated.[8]

Why did this happen? A conventional explanation looks to economic growth, which was both the foundation of educational expansion—richer countries can afford more educational investment—and also vice versa—education is increasingly seen as providing the basis for economic growth.[9] Once nations began to compete with each other in economic growth, and to promise their citizenry ever higher standards of living, then education became an integral part of these nations' public policy. There is some truth in this explanation, but it only goes so far. Many nations began to extend their educational systems before their economies grew, some—the British Caribbean, the Philippines—even before they were independent nations. Conversely, Hong Kong and Singapore had high growth rates long before they prioritized education in public policy. While economic growth was part of the twentieth-century idea of what it meant to be modern, it was only part, and for a long time a subsidiary part—subsidiary to the deepening compact between the individual citizen and the state, which came with formal democracy and the idea of equal citizenship. Few nations were formal democracies before the end of the nineteenth century; Britain only enacted universal male suffrage in 1918, universal adult suffrage in 1928, one person, one vote in 1948. Even in formally democratic nations deference to established elites continued to rule for some time. Over time, however, the idea that for true equal citizenship to flourish the state needed to attend more closely to the civic equipment of all citizens established itself in all developed nations, whether formally democratic or not—to enable their participation in the state, but also to establish essential pre-conditions for individual development and human flourishing, indeed ultimately to allow everyone 'equal opportunity' to find their own place in society. In embracing this charge the state began gradually to displace and to secularize functions formerly monopolized by official religions. Even in states with religions still established by law—such as England—or with religious observance relatively unaffected by secularization—such as the United States—the state became the senior partner in education, using education as an instrument for making citizens, consumers, free and self-determining agents in society. Schools rather than churches became the principal site of socialization— where children learned to become adults—outside the family, and both equalization and standardization of schooling under the aegis of the state have become explicit aspirations of most developed or developing countries in the latter part of the twentieth century. Formal political equality and accompanying social rights (such as universal education) are every bit as important a definition of a 'modern' society as economic growth.[10]

Britain was not unusual in this, and certainly not backward, but its experience was distinctive. Like many of its European rivals, when it began to provide state elementary education towards the end of the nineteenth century it did so on a very limited and highly segregated basis. Secondary education was absolutely excluded from the province of the state, and therefore confined to private and charitable provision. State education was aimed at consolidating the social order rather than challenging it—equipping workers to be better workers, not to help them develop into something else. The Taunton Report of 1869, for example, which was charged with ensuring that Britain had enough educated workers to staff its professions and civil service, prescribed three kinds of schools (all charitable) for different sections of the upper and middle classes who were expected to stock them, and showed little interest in the 80 per cent of the population that was thereby excluded. In the words of an American sociologist, this was a regime of 'sponsored mobility', whereby only a steady trickle of fresh talent was admitted into the upper echelons of the system, enough to keep the gears of modern society moving, and on a basis strictly determined from on high.[11]

But already by 1900 two great forces began to challenge the rigidity of the system: we will call them 'meritocracy' and 'democracy'. 'Meritocracy' was a word not coined until the end of the 1950s, in telling circumstances to which we will return, but at the end of the nineteenth century its mean- ing was conveyed by a term that was then entering circulation, 'equality of opportunity'.[12] Meritocracy made no assumptions about who deserved high-status positions in life but argued that to ensure the best selection (or alternatively a degree of natural justice) everyone ought to be allowed to compete for them. Thus selection for education ought to be made not on the basis of class position, or not solely on that basis, but rather on some assessment of merit, usually a test, a system dubbed 'contest' in contrast to 'sponsored' mobility. It was widely felt that Scotland—with its smaller, less secure elite, and its long tradition of radical Protestant individualism—had already benefited from the workings of 'meritocracy' for a century or more, which explained the somewhat larger (though still small and still very socially selected) recruitment to secondary and even higher education in Scotland than in England.[13]

Meritocracy, a liberal principle that privileges ability over birth, remains a shibboleth in education today. There has long been a feeling in all classes that people ought to 'earn' their rewards through a combination of hard work and ability, and that access at least to higher levels of education ought to be controlled by a test of ability. Today admission to university is made in theory on a quasi-meritocratic basis—most people are assumed to be quali- fied, but not everyone is, and distinctions are made between different levels of qualification—and admission to postgraduate study is made, again in theory, on an almost wholly meritocratic basis, without controversy.

However, at just the same time that meritocracy went on the march at the end of the nineteenth century, so did a second force, which cut across or against it, that is, democracy. Formal democracy, attained by many devel- oped nations in the late nineteenth and early twentieth century, secured equal voting rights for adults, and 'equal opportunity' to participate in elec- tions, representation, and public debate. But it did not take long for other criteria to be attached to democracy to make formal democracy real, to ensure that all adults were equipped to exercise those civil rights, and secondary education—not for job training but for citizenship—was amongst the first of those criteria to be widely bruited. The meritocratic 'earning' of rewards, it has widely been felt, could only fairly begin from a democratic common platform (a 'level playing field' in recent parlance). Other forms of 'social security', which would also later be deemed essential for equal citizenship—minimum living standards in health, housing, subsistence— tended to come later. Though only later, when it had been retrospectively recognized as a social service, education became known as the 'senior social service', claiming the same precedence in civil affairs that the Navy claimed in the military.[14]

Democracy offered a different interpretation of 'equality of opportunity' that was in tension with, and often openly at odds with, the interpretation offered by meritocracy. The rise of democracy coincided with a growing realization that education, if not itself made more equal, at least through adolescence, would simply reproduce existing social inequities rather than providing 'equal opportunity'. If meritocratic competition were applied too early or too nakedly, then the inequalities embedded in society and economy would lead to unequal educational experiences and unequal social outcomes. Emile Durkheim and his students in France were from the 1880s demonstrating exactly how education worked to confirm rather than to disrupt existing inequalities, although even they were not always principally concerned to critique it.[15] This kind of sociological awareness was less common in Britain until the 1950s (when it suddenly became very common indeed), but democratic critics of meritocracy didn't need sociology to stake their claim. Other bases for claiming universal civil rights—radical Christianity, radical liberalism, ethical socialism—could easily spill over from the claim for formal democracy to the claim for more equality in education. 'Equality of outcome'—a redistributionist goal seeking more absolute social equality—was not often explicitly advocated, except by the far left, but neither was it the only alternative to a meritocratic idea of 'equality of opportunity'. 'Equality of provision' for basic rights, especially in formative or vulnerable stages of the life-course, was more widely advocated instead. Only more equal provision of education could lead to *true* 'equality of opportunity' in adult life. What the British sociologist T. H. Marshall dubbed in 1949 'social citizenship', a wider definition presented as a further development from or actualization of equal political citizenship, had in fact already been conceptualized (though not in so many words) at the dawn of political equality, as an essential component or 'a consumption right' of citizenship.[16]

Britain's achievement of equal citizenship came a little late. It was in fact one of the last countries in Europe to accord adult men equal political rights, though the transition happened everywhere in a matter of a few decades. By contrast, the demand for social citizenship, to make political equality real, came earlier and stronger, and it is this which makes Britain's transition to mass education particularly distinctive and instructive. Britain's slow transition to political equality had permitted the development of a richer set of mechanisms especially in local government, though also participatory political parties at the national level, to channel public opinion. Its liberal regime permitting free physical mobility, organization in civil society and self-expression encouraged the proliferation of lobbying and campaigning groups.[17] Its hostility to the central state's organization of individual conscience, which encouraged private, charitable, and local developments in education but not a centralized state system—though often seen as a 'backward' feature[18]—in fact prevented the early crystallization of a very hierarchical state system, as seen in France or Prussia. For most of the twentieth century it left the initiative in the hands of local education authorities (LEAs), who developed a bewildering diversity of local systems. In this respect, British education resembled more than is usually recognized the American system, which once it caught up with America in terms of formal democracy it increasingly sought to emulate.

All of these features combined in the mid-twentieth century when their force was greatly enhanced by the tremendous social and political upheavals of those decades. The 'people's war' of 1939–45 dramatically heightened most people's awareness of social inequality but also their appreciation of what could be achieved with greater social cohesion, and also greater state provision, if only at first on an emergency basis. In the immediate postwar decades, an even more consequential (though often overlooked) social upheaval created optimism and purposefulness about the chances for individual realization and development. Something like half the young people of these decades moved upward in the social scale, predominantly from manual (working-class) to non-manual (retail, office, service-sector) occupations. Instead of accepting their place, the rising postwar generations rejected deference to the established order and their inherited lot, and embraced great expectations. Real incomes across Western Europe boomed in what the French called the '*trente glorieuses*'—the glorious thirty years—which has been sadly denied its English catchphrase, though the great historian Eric Hobsbawm dubbed this 'the golden age'.[19]

These social and labour-market changes were in reality so powerful that they benefited people at all levels of educational attainment, but nevertheless the link in people's minds between education and employment remained strong and a more equal provision of education became firmly embedded in most British people's conceptualization of what had driven social change and what was needed to sustain it. The decentralized nature of the British education system meant that these changing attitudes registered from the bottom up and drove widening participation in education across the whole of the second half of the twentieth century. Meritocracy remained a powerful ideal but it was pushed later in life, as not only equal provision of secondary education or training—today compulsory to 18—but also equal access to higher education, or at least steadily widening access, became very widely embraced. The 'level playing field', which meritocracy had originally defined at birth—that is, background at birth shouldn't matter, only subsequent ability and hard work—had to be re-engineered on a more democratic basis. The meritocratic assumption prevalent around the time of the Second World War that 'selection' could fairly take place at age 11, identifying ability regardless of background, was immediately challenged by the majority of the democratic citizenry that didn't think it fair, either to themselves as individuals or to the public's civic rights as a whole, for the state to impose such an important decision on their children at such a tender age. Selection was postponed first to age 15 or 16 (when students self-selected to 'stay on' after compulsory education), then to age 18 (when staying on became nearly universal), and now perhaps to age 21 (when most people are expected to go to university). 'Equal opportunity' remained the ideal, but its previous, narrowly meritocratic definition—equal opportunity to advance up a social hierarchy based on intelligence as determined by state-sanctioned test at age 11—was challenged by new, more generous, and democratic definitions—equal opportunity to acquire intelligence, to keep one's options open as long as possible, to play a full role in society.[20] A good deal of this book will be devoted to showing how these new attitudes emerged, how they registered, and how this 'demand side' created a mass education system, often in defiance of the grudging 'supply side' of state education crafted by educationists and politicians.

Understanding Social Change in Postwar Britain

Unfortunately, historians have not been of much help in revealing the inter-play between meritocratic and democratic forces in the making of Britain's mass education system. For a long time historians have been in thrall to political history, because the archives of legislatures and executives are so richly and easily available, because the narrative of party politics with its electoral turning-points and heroes and villains provides such an appealing framework for breaking down long-term changes, and in truth because it flatters us to be the bards of the political establishment. So our narrative of the history of education has been tailored neatly to fit the political land-marks—the 1944 Education Act, the Wilson Government's 1965 decision to press for comprehensive education, the Thatcher Government's 'market' reforms of education in 1988. These are all 'supply side' landmarks. It is far from clear that any of them was decisive in determining who went to school or university, for how long, for what reasons, and with what outcomes. Although since the 1970s successive waves of younger historians have sought to broaden the scope of their discipline—with social, economic, cultural, and gender history—very few of these new departures have thought education worthy of scrutiny, though education is surely among the most important spheres for the operation of social, economic, cultural, and gender distinctions in our own time. In part this neglect arose because of the priority given to class in the new social history, itself revolving prin-cipally around work and community. The agencies of the state seemed to the social historians too remote and alien to most people's daily lives, despite the accumulating evidence that people have cared more and more about education with every passing decade. Even a welcome move to the history of gender relations and family still manages to relegate education to an afterthought.[21]

Even more surprisingly historians of education have often remained trapped within the same paradigm. Up until the 1970s or '80s in fact his-torians of education, in dialogue with sociologists, proved more open to embedding education in the process of social change. Olive Bank's early work of historical sociology, *Parity and Prestige in English Secondary Education: A Study in Educational Sociology* (1955), stands out for its willingness to see educational change as driven by social change rather than paralysed by political conservatism.[22] But mostly, and especially recently, historians of education—who are themselves usually educationists, lodged in university departments of education—have become just as addicted to the morality play of party politics as the mainstream historians.[23] Since the 1970s and '80s, they have felt increasingly disillusioned by the drift of party politics (as they see it, to the right) and what had up to that point been a celebratory story of widening participation has become a gloomy story of betrayal and exclusion, though in both cases with party politics still very much in the driver's seat. Their version is sometimes even less interested than that of the political historians in the values, attitudes and behaviours of ordinary people, who are seen as cowed by the oppressions of the political and social struc-ture, unable even to aspire to better.[24] Teachers and educational experts are instead the lonely visionaries of an idealized egalitarian society, and the villains—who are usually successful in thwarting their plans—are the party politicians of all stripes. As the long list of titles that spools out in the note at the end of this sentence indicates, we have had literally dozens of histories of education in the last generation that tell more or less this same story of crushing political failure over and over again, in ever more excruciating detail.[25] Even books overtly devoted to the 'social history of education' have tended to argue that the political structure of the educational system has remained so rigid as to be virtually 'inoculated against sweeping social changes', rather than in any way reflecting them.[26]

This now familiar narrative usually hinges on the theme of 'divided Labour', which bemoans the failure of the Labour party—the 'natural' party of the people—to promote genuinely egalitarian education, despite the best efforts of left-wing activists, teachers and educationists. Labour *was* divided between a meritocratic and a more democratic vision of how education should be organized, both of which could be defended on egalitarian grounds. But so were the Conservatives, if not in ideology at least in policy. And both parties were also under constant pressure from their grass-roots to extend educational provision. Even if Labour did for much of its history have a higher proportion of working-class and the Conservatives of lower-middle class voters, the latter were often just as keen to promote more equal educational provision as the former. It is not an 'irony' but rather an illus-tration of this essential truth that Conservative LEAs were as likely to move to comprehensive education in the late 1950s as Labour-controlled ones (discussed in Chapter 4); that the expansion of higher education was first authorized by a Conservative government (and set on a forty-year trajectory by the Robbins Report, which they commissioned, for which see Chapter 5); that Margaret Thatcher approved more comprehensive schools in the early 1970s than any other Secretary of State for Education

(Chapters 4 and 6); and that despite her ideological suspicions of mass higher education Thatcher flipped in the mid-1980s from a policy of restriction to an unprecedented expansion of higher education which has continued to this day (Chapters 6 and 7). A complementary narrative suggests that after some limited success by 'divided Labour' in setting up a comprehensive system between 1965 and 1979 (which I argue didn't happen) the Conservatives have been able to dismantle it since 1979, leading to the 'death of the comprehensive school' or even 'the death of secondary education' (which I argue hasn't happened either).[27] Because educationists have felt increasingly marginalized, not only by Conservative electoral success but also by what they see as New Labour's capitulation to selective education, their political narratives have if anything become more declinist and despairing. What Roderick Floud said about the history of education over 30 years ago rings even truer today: historians of education are 'obsessed...with chronicling administrative history rather than seeing education as a reflection of the society within which policy is formed', but with the passionlessness Floud detected now displaced by a white-hot political fury.[28]

It's not that politics doesn't matter, but only that the fixation on the political narrative has caused us to overlook some of the most powerful forces shaping society in modern Britain. These forces have often over-whelmed politicians and wrong-footed 'experts', and required them to dance along a highwire to maintain the pretence—or sometimes a tenuous reality over which they had little control—that their stated policies were still in operation. For example, in the 1960s and '70s when politicians were manifestly failing to engineer a 'swing to science' because the new entrants flooding into further and higher education were choosing to study other subjects, they tried persistently to pretend that the opposite was the case, until they just had to fall silent in the face of unbudgeable facts—inexplic-able facts, unless the new entrants and their aspirations were taken into account, which they have not been (and for which see Chapter 8). Even more clearly, politicians have often claimed that their specific educational policies were responsible for major shifts in social mobility when those pol-icies often only benefited from or most often had no impact whatsoever on the real social and economic drivers of social mobility (Chapter 9).

To get a handle on these powerful social forces, we ought to be able to turn to social scientists, who are less easily swayed by political narrative, and whose manifest subject matter is the individual and collective actions of the mass of the people in society. Much of what follows is deeply indebted to

works of social science, especially work done in the 'heroic age' of postwar
social science between the late 1940s and the late 1970s, when awareness of
expanding educational opportunity was at its peak. Unfortunately contemporary social science has not been quite as helpful. It has become more
specialized, less historical, more quantitative. Like the historians, social scientists increasingly aim to flatter the politicians, especially by indulging in
the fashion for 'evidence-based policy'. Who could be against this? But in
fact policy used to be more 'evidence-based' than it is now; it's only that a
new kind of evidence is now privileged, usually huge databases of quantitative evidence, subject to ever more sophisticated statistical manipulations.
One only has to look at the diminishing size and breadth of government
reports into educational questions, from the weighty tomes of the Crowther,
Newsom, Robbins, and Plowden Reports, with their vast apparatus of expert
testimony, social surveys and in-depth analysis, to the thin, flashy, determin-
istic, data-driven pamphlets of recent days, such as the Dearing and Browne
Reports. The result has been a move away from synthetic explanations of
human action, and certainly away from historical change, except where it
can be reduced to a longitudinal series of strictly comparable data-points. It
has also had the effect of fragmenting approaches, whereby sociologists
gather and analyse data on social structures (occupations, education, generation), economists on economic measures (income, wealth, 'human capital'),
and so on. They rarely read or comment on each other's findings, and
when they do a dialogue of the deaf often results.[29] Nevertheless, with a
dose of methodological eclecticism there is still a great deal a historian
can do to exploit and reconcile these seemingly incommensurable and
fragmentary findings.

Sociology has the longest and most distinguished tradition of considering
the role of education in supporting or reflecting or perhaps altering the
social structure. We have already noted the pioneering researches of the
Durkheimian sociologists in France, a perspective which began to trickle
into study of Britain in the 1930s, notably in the Sociology Department at
the London School of Economics, chaired by T. H. Marshall. Out of this
stable came a series of enquiries into the relationship between education
and social structure by the likes of David Glass and his students A. H. Halsey,
Jean Floud, Olive Banks and John Goldthorpe, whose egalitarian leanings—
they were mostly ethical socialists and supporters of the Labour party—
provoked a more critical view of education than had been common amongst
the Durkheimians.[30] Parallel tracks were followed at the same time by

sociological users of the birth-cohort studies and the Manchester School of educational sociology that drew on ethnographic approaches from anthropology. Though Goldthorpe is at the time of writing still active, and spawning students and new projects of his own, it is fair to say that this style of educational sociology has been in recent decades eclipsed by more purely quantitative and narrowly policy-oriented research, relatively uninterested in longer periods of historical change, and this trend is at least partly owing to the rising profile of economics in the social sciences.[31]

Economists had not typically been very much interested in education until the 1960s. They treated it (fairly enough) as a 'consumption good', which satisfies 'normal' needs and wants, but showed little curiosity about what constituted 'normal' and how these needs and wants varied over time. The casual assumption was just that more education would accompany more economic growth.[32] As we have noted, that correlation doesn't work very well in explaining the patterns of expansion of education over time and place.[33] It certainly doesn't penetrate very far into the thought processes of consumers, which may assign very different preferences to education in different phases of economic growth, depending on values, attitudes, experiences—but alas those are seen as the province of the sociologist. Then, in the late 1950s, partly as a result of government interest, partly as a result of the development of new quantitative measures, economists began to consider education more as an 'investment good'. In this view you could *increase* economic growth by investing more in education: it was an investment not in physical capital (machines or buildings) but in 'human capital' (smarter and thus more productive workers). Although by their own calculations sometimes education behaved more like a 'consumption good' and sometimes more like an 'investment good', because *theory* increasingly directed them towards the latter—and theory increasingly directed them towards the latter because it offered something immediately useful to policymakers— they tended to forego the more complicated questions involved in assessing 'consumption goods': why people chose more education and with what results.[34] Though lip service is still paid to education as a 'consumption good', human capital theory and its assumptions about investments in education are now virtually hegemonic in the economics of education, and although behavioural economics is supposed to be diverting economists' attention back to human motives there is still precious little evidence that economists are willing to consider any motive for education other than as investment in future earnings.

There is no doubt that the quantitative data marshalled by economists and quantitative sociologists can be a great boon to historians seeking to track the values and behaviours of the mass of the people, and not just political elites, experts, and activists. But a too purely quantitative approach, fashionable nowadays in these social sciences, has great pitfalls. It tends to be confined to things that can be easily measured, at times when they can be measured—thus men's contributions to family support rather than women's, income rather than wealth, occupation rather than status or identity. It tends to be very policy- and thus present-oriented. For the same reason, it shares the political historians' tendency to chop up long-term trends into short political segments—'Thatcherism', 'New Labour', 'the Coalition Government'—because it wants to test the efficacy of specific policy measures of individual governments.[35] Even when longitudinal, it privileges the present-day outcomes rather than the differences of the past. And as the explanatory mechanisms are almost entirely about correlation rather than causation—x accompanies y, without so much concern for why—the limitations of the data reproduce themselves in limitations of explanation.

Take the important early work of Christopher Pissarides, the labour economist who later won the Nobel Prize for his work in the field. In assessing who 'stayed on' in school after the school-leaving age and who went on further to university between the 1950s and the 1980s, unusually among economists he accepted that sometimes people behaved as if education was a consumption good—they took more of it just because they had more money—and sometimes as if it was an investment good—they took more of it when they would be rewarded by future returns. But he showed little or no interest in why they shifted back and forth in these ways—he was simply reporting a correlation between 'staying on', income and the labour-market value of qualifications. When (as others pointed out) none of these correlations worked any longer—indicating possibly some further reasons why people chose education—he simply lost interest.[36] I wouldn't want to do without Pissarides' evidence, but on its own it doesn't get us very far in determining why people consumed more and more education over time.

Other social scientists also follow their own disciplinary instincts—psychologists have suggested that educational choices are driven by the prevalence of certain personality types in a population, careers advisers naturally see choice as driven by careers advice, and so on.[37] What is an historian to do? Only to synthesize these various perspectives—the sociologists' care for social structures, the economists' for market behaviours, the historians' for political turning-points—and to bring to bear also some of the latest rethinkings of the great changes in values, attitudes, and experiences of the postwar era that the rising generation of social and cultural historians is helpfully producing. A heightened awareness of these great social and cultural changes sweeping through the postwar world can help breathe new life and meaning into the quantitative data assembled by social scientists which tend to tell us what is happening but very little about why.[38]

To get behind the narrative of party politics, and to bring into view the way that changing values, attitudes and experiences drive forward the transition to mass education, I adopt a promiscuous array of methods and sources drawing equally on the talents of historians and social scientists. As one of the most historically-minded of sociologists, Diego Gambetta, has ably argued, to understand the growing uptake of education we need to develop 'a dense combination of mechanisms', allowing for both demand and supply factors, assessments 'of what one can do, of what one wants to do and, indirectly, of the conditions that shape one's preferences and intentions'—to ask, in the felicitous title of his book, 'were they pushed or did they jump?' (Sadly, or perhaps happily for me, his book is about Italy, not Britain.)[39] On the demand side, we need to consider a host of demographic, social, and cultural factors. How is the age structure of the population changing? What do rising birth-rates tell us about optimism for the future and investment in children? How and why does appetite for education grow? What connections do people draw between education and future economic prospects, between education and civil rights, between education and democracy? What difference does it make when educational systems and labour markets formerly dominated by young men become populated also with young women? What are people's expectations of state provision and state welfare across the different spheres and phases of life? How does one generation's exposure to education affect the next? And then there are a complex network of supply-side considerations as well. How are changing values and behaviours registered by government, locally as much as centrally? How well do politicians understand their constituents' needs and wishes, and how do they respond to them? How well do educational provision and outcomes match up with those perceptible needs and wishes? What do people do instead when they can't get the education they want or need?

There is in addition an important generational element that is hard to capture because both 'older' needs and attitudes (those of the parents, and sometimes the teachers) and 'newer' ones (those of the students) are present at the same time, often in conflict. As we have noted, in the twentieth century schools and universities have become not only motors of economic growth and cockpits of citizenship but also the most important theatres of socialization outside the family. They stand, therefore, on the front line of social change. Often parents sense this and trust education to serve their children as the path to a better life or to fit them for new modes of living. Mothers, in particular, before married women's participation in the labour force took off later in the century, relied on schooling to complement their own familial efforts on behalf of their children at a time when fathers could still exercise more influence at least over their sons in facilitating their entry to the workplace. But in periods of rapid change—and as various forms of mobility widened the gap between parents and children—education could also be seen to rival or disrupt the transmission of familial values. In these circumstances, education became a site of conflict, intergenerational and often political. We will see this conflict in dramatic form in Chapter 6, on the 1970s, when rapid generational change raised questions about the place of education in the life course and, uniquely, for a time caused the demand for more and more education to falter. In both cases, when the generations agree and when they conflict, we can't understand the demand for education, the hopes invested in it, the uses made of it, or disagreements over it unless we contextualize it fully in contemporary social changes.

Fortunately portions of this story have been examined closely, particularly by historically minded social scientists. Thanks to Olive Banks, we can start out on a good footing by embedding the initial cry for 'secondary education for all' in the first half of the twentieth century in changes in social structure and social attitudes. Alan Kerckhoff and Eileen Byrne have, very unusually, peered into the wild diversity of local-government sub-cultures in England and Wales to explore how pressures from above (and, less so, from below) were mediated by local conditions and personnel, especially in the transition from selective to comprehensive education.[40] Andrew McPherson and his colleagues have similarly sought to open up the 'black box' of educational decision-making in Scotland to get a handle on the somewhat different 'dense combination of mechanisms' operating there.[41]

Ample social-science and historical materials exist to fill in the gaps and allow us to stitch together a more comprehensive and longer-term story. The quantitative social scientists have left us a legacy of hundreds of longitudinal studies of educational experiences and outcomes over the past half-century, often based on the famous British 'birth cohort studies' which have followed a representative sample of children born in 1946, 1958, and 1970 (and now 2000) throughout their lifetimes. Other social-survey material has received less attention because it is less susceptible to quantitative analysis, but all the more useful to us for that—newspaper and opinion research surveys, consumer reports, admissions statistics, examination results, and above all the surveys commissioned and analysed for those once-weighty government reports. Since the 1950s the Organization for Economic Cooperation and Development (OECD) has been surveying and comparing the educational systems of developed countries, often startling the British by challenging the myths of their own distinctiveness. The papers of central government, if read between the lines, can tell us about their tendency to follow rather than to lead trends, to respond to demand even if they only faintly perceived it.

This book is not a history of education in modern Britain; it is an argument about the transition to mass education specifically. It says little about the nitty-gritty of educational experience, except where that has a bearing on supply and demand, although there is a great deal more to be said about educational experience too, again reversing the usual top-down educational narrative.[42] It says very little about private education, which did not, needless to say, contribute at all to mass education; to the contrary, one of the astonishing and still under-explored facts about private education in Britain is that while it catered to a relatively high proportion of the school-age population—between 6 and 7 per cent—its share hardly changed for most of the period of spreading affluence since the 1960s.[43] The bulk of the evidence and argument applies to England and Wales, but an effort has been made at every stage to keep the interestingly similar (and interestingly different) experience of Scotland alongside, for comparative purposes and to ensure that this remains a British history. Northern Ireland (which is excluded from most of the birth-cohort studies) requires separate treatment.[44]

It would be easy to tell a 'Whig' story of inevitably ever-expanding access, and indeed that was once how the story was told, a golden age of meritocracy, with the 'ladder of opportunity' gradually bearing more and more of the population ever upwards.[45] As democratic forces appeared to triumph, however, seeking to make education more equal, at least up to a point, meritocratic explanations lost favour—or became elegies to a lost past of earned inequality. However, meritocracy and democracy do not form a sequence in the history of education; rather, they are always constantly in tension. There is a 'before and after' story—before 'education for all' became a reality—but it is not a story of meritocracy before and democracy after. As soon as meritocratic arguments appeared to call for equal opportunity, democratic arguments for equal provision were already making themselves felt.

2

Before the Butler Act

At the end of the nineteenth century a strictly segregated system of education—state education at primary level only, for strictly functional purposes, secondary and further education available only through charitable or private institutions—was operating in England and Wales. Though Welsh county councils were permitted to operate secondary schools from 1889, English authorities were forbidden to use the rates to pay for schooling after the age of 14.[1] Only in Scotland had there been since at least the eighteenth century a meritocratic place for the 'lad o' pairts', the clever rustic who had by dint of his inborn genius and hard work scrambled his way up from the parish school to university and the profession. Scotland and Wales shared a radical nonconformist tradition that privileged ability over birth and both lacked a substantial elite to develop and monopolize private secondary education. A single 'public' (that is, private) school in England, Eton, had a greater endowment than all the 54 fee-paying burgh schools and 5 universities in Scotland put together.[2] But Wales only enrolled 0.1 per cent of its age cohort in secondary education at the time. Opinion differs as to whether the myth of the 'democratic intellect' that prevailed in Scotland, and was spreading to Wales, made much difference at all, considering how few examples could be found of 'lads o' pairts', but at least the idea was defensible and increasingly defended.[3]

Such an idea made its belated appearance in England, where three-quarters of the population of the British Isles lived, in the last decades of the nineteenth century.[4] In its first, strongest version the critique of the segregated system was not even truly meritocratic, but simply an extension of the functional point of view that had finally necessitated compulsory primary education a decade earlier. Concerns that the private sector was unable to supply sufficient numbers of well-educated personnel to serve the functions of the state mounted as economic rivals with growing state educational systems—the United States, Japan, and, especially, Prussia—seemed to be surging ahead, and especially around 1900 when the great British state performed poorly in the Boer War. These concerns registered across all parties. The Conservatives, in power for much of this period, were probably most affected, as they had hitherto been relatively detached from questions of state education altogether, and concerns about 'national efficiency' marked their entry into educational policy. But Liberals and socialists were engaged too. Indeed Fabian socialists, who aspired to be the technocratic managers of an expanded state, and were relatively indifferent to the democratic equipment of the mass of the people, were among the leading voices in calls for very selective secondary education to build a skilled elite. Their chieftain Sidney Webb was opposed to doling out even elementary education 'to all and sundry'—that would be national inefficiency. He wanted the state to focus on recruitment of a class of 'New Samurai', as his Fabian colleague H. G. Wells dubbed them (the Japanese association was telling[5]), to catch special capacity or ability wherever it may be found and bring it to the aid of the state.[6]

Because Webb, unlike the Conservatives, thought the existing elite was not only inadequate but defective, based on accidents of birth, his support for selective education was about efficiency *and* meritocracy: only an elite selected *for* ability could serve the state properly.[7] Calls for the extension of state education in this early period often partook of both motivations. They were reflected in two closely-related yet subtly different ideas that filtered into public discourse from the 1890s. Concerns for national efficiency deplored the 'waste of talent' which a purely hereditary elite and its training system implied and which a nation in hot competition with rising powers like the U.S., Prussia and Japan could not afford.[8] At the same time, the provision of a 'ladder of opportunity', such as all-ability and all-age parish schools and universities offered to the 'lad o' pairts' in Scotland, could be seen as serving not only national efficiency but also social justice. No-one knew how 'ability' was distributed through the population—it could, as Tories often assumed, be heavily concentrated in existing elites—but people of all political stripes now started to see that providing at least an opportunity for hidden talent to flourish might be good for all sorts of reasons: economic, social, political.[9]

Furthermore, 'national efficiency' (or 'waste of talent') and 'meritocracy' (or a 'ladder of opportunity') did not exhaust the motives for expanding access to education in this period. At the same historical moment at the end of the nineteenth century, Britain was grappling with the problem of democracy—whether and how to extend the franchise to encompass all adult men, as many other European countries had already done, and then also to women. In this context, education began to be seen not only as a way of building the national economy or of unleashing 'hidden talent' but also as a prerequisite for a common citizenship—a 'consumption right of citizenship' (something to which citizens were entitled as citizens) or a necessary prerequisite for it (something which citizens needed to make them good citizens)—criteria which might be applied to women as well as men, unlike efficiency arguments which tended to dwell very narrowly on men, and men in technical and scientific education at that.

These more democratic sentiments manifested themselves in a number of different ways. Amongst liberal intellectuals, they often took the form of Idealism, a philosophical movement which emphasized the nurturing of a common citizenship, very often bolstered by a Christian commitment to the universal brotherhood of men under the fatherhood of God (gendered in precisely that way). While early Idealists like T. H. Green had couched their views in meritocratic language of the 'ladder of opportunity', by the 1890s later Idealists like the Liberal MP A. H. D. Acland were increasingly turning to the idea of common schooling as widely practised in America, with all classes joined together in a single, normally mixed-sex institution, even at secondary level (the 'high school'). The American model, with its emphasis on common citizenship, was much more sympathetic to this line of thinking than the Prussian model, with its emphasis on service to the state, favoured by Tories, mainstream Liberals and some Fabians.[10]

A convergent but distinctive line of thinking could be found in the labour movement. State education had previously been a controversial subject in the labour movement, both because of religious divisions—nonconformists were suspicious that state education would become a tool of the Church of England (with political effects, too, inculcating a priest-ridden deference to established authority)—and because working-class exclusion from the franchise had encouraged many to consider the state an alien imposition. As Britain moved to universal suffrage, attitudes on both fronts began to shift. The importance of securing truly equal citizenship began to eclipse both religious differences and fears of the state, at least among trade-union activists. It is very difficult in this early period to gauge mass popular opinion: there are no opinion polls and not even much social investigation (at least on educational matters) to call upon. Elite politicians often claimed that their constituents didn't want more education, but they rarely asked them.[11] However, we can say that the idea of universal free and compulsory elementary education from 1880, which was indeed initially resisted on both libertarian and economic grounds—parents didn't want to be told how to parent, nor have their children's wages denied them—was also gradually built into the routines of working-class life.[12] The period of compulsory education was extended three times between 1880 and 1900. The alleged hostility of working-class parents to education continued to be cited by elite politicians, who had their own reasons for slowing the pace of change—worries about cost, worries about 'Prussian' forms of state compulsion—though more surprisingly also by historians. A disproportionate amount of attention has been paid to the hostility to educational extension of the cotton textile unions, whose sector was hard-pressed and who relied to an unusual degree on adolescent labour.[13] But textile unionists were hardly typical. The Trade Union Congress as a whole voted for raising the school-leaving age to 15 in 1896 and to 16 in 1906, and for 'secondary education for all' in 1907. As with the Idealists, the American model of common schools was frequently cited. As early as 1894 a trade-union memorial to the Bryce Commission, appointed to consider a possible extension of state aid to secondary education, held that 'it would be highly beneficial to all classes of the community if their children were to attend a common school'.[14]

Over time, cooperation deepened between the Idealist and the trade unionist advocates of universal secondary education. The Workers' Educational Association, founded in 1903 to provide further education on a voluntary basis, operated not only as a provider but also as a lobby, bringing together intellectuals and workers' organizations. The Liberal intellectual J. A. Hobson became a hero of the Gasworkers' Union for his advocacy of universal secondary education and the social theorist and historian R. H. Tawney got drawn into educational activism through his work for the WEA, initially teaching pottery workers in Staffordshire.[15] Both groups more or less explicitly repudiated the 'ladder of opportunity' as too narrow. They preferred the language of the 'broad highway', along which not only talented individuals but whole classes could travel together. 'A ladder, after all, is a shaky thing by which people mount precariously, a step at a time', said the Liberal MP F. D. Acland in Parliament in 1918, 'It is a broad highway that we want from school to school, according to the real powers and abilities of the children concerned.'[16] How far they would travel together remained ambiguous, however, depending on your view of how 'real powers and abilities' were distributed, showing the continuing influence of meritocratic thinking about the centrality of 'ability' in education, even in the midst of growing democratic emphasis on more equal provision.

Although the Bryce Commission did recommend that local authorities be empowered to oversee and provide secondary education in their districts in 1895, these powers were not finally granted until 1902, when a Conservative government finally freed English local authorities (now organized into LEAs) to do so under the supervision of a central Board of Education. The 1902 Act thus brought England more or less into line with Scotland, where local school boards had been able to provide secondary education since 1872, and Wales, where county councils had been so empowered since 1889, and whose first secondary schools had been an important inspiration for the Idealists.[17] But of course having the ability to provide any secondary education was very far from having the ability or even the desire to provide secondary education for all. Instead, it is often argued, a very narrow and hierarchical ladder was erected by the 1902 'system' which set the seal on the development of state education for the next century. The skeleton of a 'tripartite' system was put into place which only perpetuated the existing system of educational apartheid, reproducing the existing class system which roped off 'academic' (mostly male and middle-class) children from 'vocational' (entirely male and mostly skilled working-class) children from 'unskilled' (mostly unskilled working-class children of both sexes).[18]

The charge is not completely without foundation, though it exaggerates both the uniformity of the 'system' and its rigidity in the face of local experimentation and massive social change. In its initial implementation, we can see some of the bare bones of a 'tripartite' system emerging from the 1902 Education Act. The guiding light at the new Board of Education, Robert Morant, who had links to the Idealists, placed special emphasis on the grammar schools. Grammar schools up to this point had been exclusively private or charitable institutions providing a secondary education in academic subjects mostly for the fee-paying middle classes. Morant's Free Place Regulations of 1907 offered the grammar schools a government subsidy to make 25 per cent of their places free of fees for selected pupils educated at state elementary schools. LEAs were also encouraged to open their own grammar schools, with both fee-paying and free places, and by 1911 there were in England 352 LEA grammar schools and 510 grant-aided grammar schools, over half of whose students had come from state elementary schools.[19] Still, this network of grammar schools only provided places for a tiny proportion of adolescents—3 per cent of 12-to-17-year olds. Beneath this thin stratum lay a growing variety of 'central schools' and 'junior technical schools', mostly in large urban authorities that could afford them such as London and Manchester, providing technical and vocational courses to age 15, aimed at skilled workers, particularly promoted by Morant's successor L. A. Selby-Bigge.[20] Beneath this stratum, however, lay the thickest layer—still the great majority of all adolescents—who never entered secondary school at all, but who were simply retained in elementary schools until the leaving age. As Albert Mansbridge of the WEA said in 1912, 'There are, indeed, educational ladders *in some places*. In many parts of England they do not rest upon the earth; when they do, the rungs are not infrequently missing.'[21] In Scotland, where there had been a longer tradition of state secondary education, there was some of the same drift, directed by Sir Henry Craik at the Scottish Education Department (SED), to emphasize the academic standards of a limited number of state secondaries, thus narrowing the opportunities for the 'lad o' pairts' to climb from parish to university.[22] Thus across Britain there has been detected in the first few decades of the twentieth century a growing centralization aimed at containing 'the democratic intellect' and setting up a tripartite system that carefully controlled access to high-quality education and high-status occupations, in accordance with the idea of 'sponsored mobility'.

On the other hand, neither public opinion nor educational thinking nor even educational provision were mainly left in the hands of central government; nor were they static. As public experience with secondary education began to extend, and also as expectation of government began to grow, democratic hopes for education burgeoned too. Especially around the First World War—when conscription for the first time bound all families close to the state, and state control of the economy reached unprecedented heights— even elite politicians used to depreciating public interest in education changed their tune. The war itself highlighted older arguments for educational extension based on national efficiency. 'An educated man is a better worker, a more formidable warrior, and a better citizen', as Lloyd George said in September 1918, perhaps in order of priority.[23] But combined with universal suffrage for men and partial suffrage for women the war also cemented belief in a higher universal standard of education for democracy. Rates of staying on past the school-leaving age jumped during the war, and more young men in their later teens moved almost seamlessly from state school to state army. There were many more applicants for free places in grammar schools than there were places, and revealingly the 'free placers' did better in exams than the fee-payers, indicating more severe selection for poorer than wealthier children in a supposedly meritocratic system. In the midst of war both the WEA and the trade-union movement redoubled their commitment to universal secondary education, the so-called 'Bradford Charter' for free and compulsory education to 16 was drawn up, and the Labour party adopted it as policy in 1917.[24] While Liberal and Tory MPs continued to deplore the working man's resistance to education, this argument began to lose traction, and some acknowledged the broadened horizons and expanded hopes for the state that were leading to calls for 'a better and more widely diffused education'.[25] Even the Tory politician Lord Eustace Percy recognized in retrospect that 'something was happening in the country which had hardly yet penetrated to the mind of any politician in Whitehall or Westminster. The demand for real "equality of opportunity" in education was becoming nothing less than the main popular motive for political action.'[26]

The principal voice emerging to trumpet this position was the WEA's R. H. Tawney, who was fast becoming the Labour party's leading educational thinker. In his first campaigning writings on education during the war, Tawney explicitly rejected the 'ladder of opportunity' as too narrow and joined the calls for a 'broad highway' and more, 'universal provision', that would recognize the brotherhood of man.[27] After the war Tawney became the publicist for the Labour party's new commitment to secondary education for all, deploring the system of selection being run by the Board of Education and demanding 'equality of educational provision' in a single system.[28] As has often been rightly pointed out, Tawney's own beliefs were not quite as egalitarian as his rhetoric. 'Equality of educational provision' did not for him mean 'identity of educational provision'. So long as everyone was educated to 16, he did not object to differentiation—which did of course amount to selection—on the basis of 'ability and aptitude'. His Christian Idealism deplored mass methods and demanded a focus on the individual; his understanding of psychology led him to believe that 'ability' was randomly distributed, as part of God's providence, and his poor understanding of sociology underplayed the role of class in the differential production of 'ability'.[29] In this way even Tawney's apparent egalitarianism can be seen as another endorsement of the tripartite system and meritocratic selection, rather than a true commitment to equal provision, a key component of the 'divided Labour' diagnosis of Britain's failure properly to democratize education.[30]

But if Tawney's was the Labour party's chosen voice for educational policy in this period, his was not the only voice in democratic circles. The Parliamentary debates around the Fisher Act in 1918, for example, offer a wider and richer selection of views—and not Tawney's, as he failed three times to win election to Parliament. The Fisher Act was the government's lukewarm response to the surge of public support for educational extension during the war. Fisher himself was a moderate Idealist chosen by Lloyd George to lead the Board of Education for his pious, emollient appeals to citizenship and community, but whose strongest arguments for reform tended to be more utilitarian, like Lloyd George's, urging on grounds of national efficiency a modestly elevated level of secondary education to match Prussia's.[31] His Act raised the school-leaving age from 13 to 14, but otherwise left the nascent tripartite system of the Board of Education pretty well intact. Most adolescents still remained in elementary schools, though now for an additional year. The only real extension was a provision for part-time vocational training in 'continuation schools' after 14 which was never implemented.[32]

Debate in Parliament over his proposals, however, revealed a swelling reservoir of political dissatisfaction with this meagre measure. A series of amendments moved by both Liberal and Labour MPs objected to selection for secondary education by ability as a 'class system', proposed secondary education not for those deemed to have 'ability and aptitude' but 'for all persons desirous of such education', advocated a liberal education for all without the vocational tracks of 'continuation schools', and would have permitted local authorities to raise the school-leaving age to 16 in order to provide secondary education for all. No fewer than 75 MPs voted for at least one of three amendments along these lines, including about half the Labour MPs, about a third of the Liberals, and over a third of all Welsh MPs.[33] They were led jointly by Liberal Idealists and trade unionists and indeed this finding of common cause proved a bridge over which some of the former crossed to join the Labour party in the next few years.[34] Their arguments were strongly democratic at the very least, against class-based selection, against separate vocational and liberal tracks, and very American. While it was still possible to make technocratic arguments for education based on rivalry with Germany—as Lloyd George did—it was in fact much easier in

1918 than before (and perhaps since) to deploy the American common school as a model, and leading speakers in the 1918 debates did just that.[35]

Changes in public opinion registered even more directly in local authorities than in Parliament, both because local authorities had long had wider franchises and were closer to the mass of their constituents—a point frequently made by critics of the Board and the SED—and because even under the limits imposed by the 1902 and 1918 Acts LEAs had considerable latitude to set their own policy. As the Fabians pointed out, LEAs could offer 'as much education as they choose, of whatever kind they choose, at such fees as they choose, up to whatever age they choose, with as many and as valuable scholarships as they choose, without distinction of sex or rank or wealth'—always depending on political will and available cash.[36] How narrow a ladder would be provided, with what audiences and goals in mind? Within those limits LEAs adopted a number of strategies. Many sought to increase the number of free places in their own grammar schools and/or to buy more free places in grant-aided grammar schools than the 25 per cent maximum provided by central government. Middlesbrough was able to provide free places to as many as 75 per cent of the boys in its grammar schools by 1938.[37] Welsh LEAs expanded their grammar schools so rapidly that they whooshed past England in the rate of transfer and by 1931 were educating a fifth of the age cohort in grammar schools, twice the English rate.[38]

Others, aware that grammar schools were only ever likely to admit an academic elite, focused on extending other forms of secondary education to wider tranches of student. Bradford did both; by 1926 it was providing free secondary places for over a quarter of the age cohort, one of the highest rates of secondary education provision in the country. Wallasey's was even higher.[39] Glamorgan aimed at 100 per cent. Welsh LEAs also championed common schools. Like exurban areas of Scotland they had practical reasons for this—a small middle class, a thinly dispersed population, resource constraints which made it difficult to provide two parallel school systems—but they were also seeking to develop their own version of the Scottish 'democratic intellect'. W. G. Cove, a president of the National Union of Teachers and from 1923 MP for Aberavon, was an early, vocal advocate of common schools. Even the Welsh Department of the Board of Education and the Welsh Schools Inspectorate saw the resource arguments for common schools, as well as Wales's 'democratic' claims. With their tolerance Anglesey became the first LEA to develop a plan for a single system of common schools from 1936.[40]

If these vigorous debates and innovations, stimulated by the war, have been since forgotten, it was because they were very quickly staunched by waves of depression and austerity that swept over Britain, and particularly over the most innovative Northern local authorities, from the early 1920s to the late '30s. Even the limited extensions of the Fisher Act were almost immediately overturned. The raising of the school-leaving age to 14 was postponed. Part-time continuation schools for 14-to-16-year-olds were axed. So were proposed maintenance grants to help 14-to-15-year-olds stay in school. Fatefully, as part of a renewed wave of cuts in the early 1930s, free places were subject to a means test, ending efforts by LEAs such as Glamorgan, Bradford, and Manchester to provide 100 per cent free places in their secondary schools, and associating state education with the hated means test applied to unemployment benefits. In perilous international and economic times, education dropped suddenly down the list of national priorities.[41]

Under these constraints a narrower, meritocratic 'ladder of opportunity' became a kind of consensus policy, including among formerly more democratic socialists and formerly more segregationist Tories. Threatened by cuts, Labour authorities were forced into defending features of the Fisher Act on which they had not previously been agreed. They fought hard to create as many free places as possible in their grammar schools, while secondary education for all, not to mention common schools, seemed to recede into the distance.[42] The proportion of free places at state secondary schools rose from a quarter to a half, but then fell back again after 1930. The proportion of all 11-year-olds in England and Wales who transferred to a secondary school rose slowly from about 10 per cent to not quite 15 per cent.[43] Not so much a bipartite or a tripartite as a unipartite system of free grammar-school places for a 'talented' minority was cemented into place. The painfully accumulated investment in these free places became a source of pride—individual pride for those who had won them, local pride for the authorities that had provided them, class pride for the labour movement. Although most upwardly mobile working-class children did *not* go to grammar school, those who did were the most visible and paraded, forming by definition 100 per cent of the working-class children who went into those few professions that required educational qualifications—primarily school-teaching and medicine. The most celebrated example is Ellen Wilkinson, the Minister for Education in the Attlee government, born into a working-class home in Manchester, who won scholarships to train as a teacher and then, even more unusually, to study history at the University of Manchester. She remained a lifelong advocate of the scholarship ladder, even under heated pressure from her left-wing Labour colleagues.[44] This ladder, if supported by free places for those who climbed it, was hailed as offering 'equal opportunity' for all those 'capable of profiting' from further education. Gradually the Conservatives too came to accept that the ladder would not waste money or destabilize the social order, but might increase national efficiency and salve some of the social divisions created by unemployment and inequality. 'Brains are the prerogative of no single class', pronounced the Tory-led National Government in its 1935 election manifesto, 'it is essential in the interest of the State, as well as of the individual, that they should be given every opportunity of development'.[45]

Advocates of secondary education for all did not fall silent. Tawney led a Labour party campaign under this banner and a short-lived Labour government in 1924 commissioned a report from the Board of Education's Consultative Committee under the chairmanship of Sir Henry Hadow to bring forward proposals for widening access to secondary education. This all-party committee, which included Tawney and Mansbridge of the WEA, did recommend secondary education for all, but in a form that perpetuated the tripartite ladder. They proposed to preserve and defend academic selection for grammar schools, but also to broaden access to other forms of secondary schools—which they called 'secondary modern' schools—focused on 'practical work and realistic studies' suited to the great majority of adolescents. Thus the 'segregation' between elementary and secondary education would give way to a much fairer process of 'selection' or 'differentiation' according to ability.

For Tawney and some of his fellow socialists, this plan met their democratic aspirations so long as the two types of school were granted 'parity of esteem' and did not divide along class lines. Thanks in part to the work of the Idealist Ernest Barker, who chaired the Hadow drafting committee, both types of secondary school were supposed to provide 'a general and humane education', while 'adjusted, as far as possible, to the interests and abilities of each range and variety', and with particular emphasis on suiting the education to the individual child.[46] Universal transfer to secondary education at age 11 would guarantee a fair selection, in which only intelligence and ability—assessed by test or other objective standard—rather than background or wealth would count. Again the reformers' psychological and sociological naivete told against them—they were not fully alive to the ways in which background and wealth defined and constructed 'intelligence' and 'ability', continuing to rely, as one LEA put it rather poetically, on 'a generous symmetry about nature' in the distribution of intelligence.[47] Selection on the basis of 'individual' qualities seemed to them like a rejection of 'class' segregation, and as long as most places were still assigned by ability to pay selection by 'native' ability seemed more egalitarian.[48] Only after fee-paying was abolished did it become clearer that selection on the basis of individual ability only had the effect of reinforcing 'class' segregation. Only then did it become clear how neatly access to grammar school correlated with social class (both before and after 'equal opportunity' was extended by abolishing fee-paying)—the higher your occupational status, the more likely you were to access grammar school in this period, and in the highest classes grammar school would have been nearly universal if so many of these classes weren't opting out of state-aided education altogether (see Appendix, Figure 2.1).

The Hadow Report therefore did further cement the idea of the meritocratic ladder of opportunity into public policy. It encouraged LEAs to employ more rigorous methods of selection—especially the adoption of the intelligence or IQ test—and to apply them to more children. After all, the evidence was that the bar was still much higher for poorer children than wealthier. Free placers continued to do better in school than fee payers and, astonishingly, to stay in school longer; thus, even by prevailing definitions of 'ability', less able fee payers were still being admitted in preference to more able free placers.[49]

Not many LEAs were able or willing to extend secondary education beyond grammar school by creating a widely available second tier of modern schools. There was so much ground still to be covered ensuring that even grammar schools were free and accessible to all, and renewed cuts in the early 1930s caused that ground to recede further. It was not clear what advantage their constituents had to gain from what seemed a purely formal reclassification of the higher grades of elementary school into 'secondary modern' schools. Grammar schools, in contrast, were looking more and more appealing. If educational policy was in the deep freeze in the 1920s and '30s, social change was not. Universal adult suffrage was introduced in 1928, raising new expectations of the relationship between state and people. If secondary education was becoming more problematic, with means-testing and highly variable levels of access, universal elementary education was becoming less problematic, as former inhibitions about accepting state aid were shed.[50]

Furthermore, despite the roller coaster of slump and mass unemployment, substantial portions of the population were now making better use of both state and market to stabilize and improve their standard of living and their welfare. Aspirations to move out of low-paid, wearying and often demeaning industrial employments, also hard hit by the slump, and into 'clean jobs' in the retail and clerical sectors were growing, especially for girls.[51] These were precisely the jobs to which a grammar-school education—even a few years of grammar school—was thought to lead, for all but a few very high flyers like Ellen Wilkinson.[52] From 1918, grammar schools were also offering a widely recognized 'School Certificate'—the forerunner of O-Levels—which would come to provide certification for a tier of higher-value jobs. 'Secondary modern' schools, where they existed, had a less obvious function, in terms either of civic or labour-market participation. Technical schools were not much more attractive; teachers and trade unionists feared that they would '[stamp] at an early and impressionable age, the idea of class and inferior status on the scholar, which it is the aim of a noble education to avoid'. While employers claimed to like them for the craft skills they imparted, in fact technical school graduates were more likely to end up in the same clerical and retail jobs that went to grammar school graduates; so why accept a second-class version? As Olive Banks argued, parents as much as anyone else knew how hollow was 'parity of esteem' and were already at this early point gravitating to grammar schools, when they could access them. Little wonder that LEAs worked so hard to secure the highest possible proportion of free grammar-school places for their constituents.[53]

In these circumstances, the call for 'common schooling' on the American model seems to have subsided, to be replaced by a compromise—however grudging in some quarters—based on selection and differentiation. Parents were encouraged to aspire to grammar-school education as the best form of state education on offer, even if not on offer to many—an aspiration that would have fateful consequences after the war. The idea of the common school did not disappear. Labour teachers, in the National Association of Labour Teachers (NALT) and in their union the National Union of Teachers (NUT), were pressing for 'multilateral' schools, in which children of all abilities and aptitudes were educated together, although not necessarily in the same classes.[54] Even Tawney worried about the emergence of a 'disastrous dualism' and 'a new class division' which might be brought about by too stark a divide between grammar and other secondary schools.[55] After all, Scotland had achieved higher rates of transfer to secondary education into common schools with a liberal curriculum than London had achieved with a combination of grammar schools and more vocational central and technical schools.[56] But until secondary education for all was again on the agenda, this call was highly theoretical, and outside the ken of most parents and adolescents. Grammar schools remained the only kind of secondary education with which most people were familiar, and grammar school remained out of reach of most parents unable to pay.[57] It would take the enormous social, economic and political changes of the 1940s, extending the claims of democracy to education and other social services, and raising expectations for full citizenship (including good jobs) for all, to bring about secondary education for all and raise more practically the questions of what kind of secondary education and for whom.

3

Crisis of the Meritocracy

The Butler Act of 1944 mandated English and Welsh LEAs to provide free secondary education for all. Enacted by a Conservative-dominated Parliament, under pressure from the demands of a 'people's war', it appeared (like the Beveridge Report) to represent the triumph of 'social citizenship' and the welfare state. But it also appeared to represent the triumph of meritocracy, setting up a 'tripartite' system much as envisaged by Hadow and as explicitly recommended by the wartime Norwood Report, with all pupils allocated at around age 11[1] to either a grammar, a technical, or a 'modern' school, according to their 'aptitudes and abilities'. Similar obligations were extended to Scottish Local Authorities under an Act of 1945. In the conventional political narrative, this now entrenched meritocratic system was only slowly and gradually critiqued by a valiant band of experts and socialists, who finally succeeded in 1965 in challenging the tripartite system with the ideal of a comprehensive system that would educate all secondary-age students in common schools. Yet this challenge came too little and too late, the standard narrative contends, and was successfully thwarted so that a comprehensive *system* never came into being.

This chapter and the one that follows will tell a very different story. I start by querying whether a tripartite system ever came into being. Meritocracy was tested by democracy from the outset. I then invert the usual sequence—which assumes that there was only a shallow, grudging, top-down reform of the system—by looking at social and economic changes and accompanying changes in attitudes to education in public opinion before considering political, institutional change. Viewed this way, the awakening of the experts—and, especially, Labour leaders—*did* come late but was underpinned by powerful social changes that were not easily ignored or burked—even by Conservative policymakers. These changes registered first in local government, which was closer to grass-roots opinion and also of course in the case of education had statutory responsibility, and only later in central government. By the time that the Wilson government had plumped for comprehensive education in 1965, most LEAs had moved decisively in that direction already. The result was a system much more firmly rooted in the experiences and values of the great mass of the people than a top-down analysis (either of that system's construction or of its alleged destruction after the 1970s) can compass.

The Triumph of the Meritocracy?

In both the popular and the academic imagination, the Education Act of 1944—skilfully steered through a coalition government by R. A. Butler, the Conservative President of the Board of Education—represents the triumph of the meritocratic ideal of 'equal opportunity' that had been brewing in state grammar schools throughout the first half of the twentieth century. From its late 1940s implementation, and with the raising of the school-leaving age to 15, the Butler Act assessed not just a talented minority but *all* 11-year-olds, increasingly on the basis of 'objective' IQ tests, to determine their 'abilities and aptitudes', and allocated them accordingly to either secondary modern schools, technical schools or grammar schools—the 'tripartite system'. Thus was 'secondary education for all' achieved, and a secondary education based not on ability to pay, or on birth or upbringing, but on merit.[2]

It is true that most of the architects of the Butler Act saw it this way. But that is not the way it played out in practice, unsurprisingly since the education system remained fragmented, under local control, and driven essentially by changes at the local level that were hardly detected by policy-makers until the late 1950s. Butler was immensely proud of his Act, as a far-sighted piece of Conservative policy-making, and the Conservatives eventually came to see it as theirs too. The Butler Act was a rare piece of 'welfare state' legislation actually brought to fruition by the Conservative-dominated coalition, before Labour's victory in 1945. It therefore reflected not only Labour's ambitions for a 'New Jerusalem' of equal citizenship and social justice, but also—perhaps more so—quintessentially Conservative adjustments to the new social order, heralded by a 'people's war', cross-class solidarities and promises for social reconstruction in popular documents such as the Beveridge Report. Most Conservative MPs had little interest in state education; their gut ideological concern, if they had one, was to ensure that the Church of England's interests were protected in any move to universal secondary education. Butler addressed these concerns by bringing most religious schools into two new classes of 'state' school, voluntary-aided and voluntary-controlled (both mostly grammar schools), which gave the churches a share of control over the management of their schools—such as curriculum, about which they cared the most—while relieving them of some or all of the cost of running their schools and thus of the need to charge fees.[3] He also perpetuated a third, amphibious class of 'direct grant' schools which were allowed to continue charging fees and to retain even more autonomy, in return for offering at least 25 per cent (and often 50 per cent or more) of free places for purchase by the state. This status was granted to a relatively small number of schools, mostly highly prestigious grammar schools and much poorer Catholic schools, both of which had grounds for defending more jealously their independence from the state.[4]

Still, the Butler Act did also legislate for free secondary education for all, an enduring demand from the left; how was that achieved? To begin with, most Tory MPs—who formed the vast majority of all MPs in a Parliament left over from the General Election of 1935—were not personally much touched by state education. A large majority had been educated in public schools, a third at Eton and Harrow, and even in 1950 public-school edu-cated Conservative candidates outnumbered state-educated ones 2-to-1.[5] No reorganization of secondary education envisaged at this time would have endangered their 'opt out'. More to the point, Butler convinced them that free and universal secondary education would not endanger, but might bolster the established social order. The preservation and extension of Christian education was part of that formula; in addition to the religious schools, Christian worship was now for the first time required in all state schools.[6] But another part was the dawning realization that meritocracy and inherited privilege were not necessarily at odds. It was not only that the Butler Act preserved the opt-out to the independent sector. Increasingly Conservatives also relied upon the way in which family investments in chil-dren outside the educational sector were an integral part of the educational system, especially when academic selection was universally applied as early as 10 years of age.[7] If privileged parents invested in their children, either through private education or in preparing them for success at the 11+, that was to be celebrated. The 11+ thus put the seal on the social order, rather than disrupting it. Conservatives still displayed signs of uneasiness. When the Conservative Shadow Education Minister in 1951, Florence Horsbrugh, defended the tripartite system as a means of acknowledging differences between children, she was challenged to confirm that this did not mean embedding privileges, but she bridled: 'I would infinitely rather have privilege than have children all of one sort.'[8] But in the 1950s the tripartite system was generally defended by reference to 'ability and aptitude', not privilege.[9]

For their part, Labour—still only thinly represented in Parliament, but central to the governing coalition—seemed satisfied with free secondary education for all, which after all had been its principal demand under Tawney's guidance since the Great War. The Butler Act in fact made no stipulation as to tripartism; it only required local authorities to provide for all pupils over the age of 11 'such variety of instruction and training as may be desirable in view of their different ages, abilities, and aptitudes'.[10] Critics of tripartism, of which there were many in the constituency Labour parties and in the trade unions, were confidently assured that LEAs would be able to develop along alternative lines if they chose. Chuter Ede, the party's principal spokesperson on education, was in theory a supporter of common schools and insisted on keeping out of the Butler Act specific mention of tripartism to give LEAs maximum latitude.[11] Advocates of grammar schools, of which there were many in the Parliamentary party, were assured likewise that LEAs would be able to preserve and develop them where local needs and demands required. Some of them were Fabians, more concerned about national efficiency than about equality,[12] but some like Ellen Wilkinson (who became Labour's first Minister of Education in 1945) came from the left of the party. The traditional left was not much engaged in debates about education. Its focus was on control of the economy and especially on nationalization. It could thus be very industrial and producerist in character, and even dismissive of aspirations to grammar school on the part of those large sections of the population who were (and had to be) industrial workers. As Wilkinson put it, 'coal has to be mined and fields ploughed'; she didn't wish to focus too much attention on those (like her) who could and did pass exams; and like many Conservatives she approved of an educational system that promoted 'distinctions', though not one which perpetuated privilege.[13] For those like her, social equality required not common schools but 'parity of esteem' between the different schools in the tripartite system.[14]

Different sections of the party thus had (reasonably) different expectations. So did different LEAs. Given their diversity of reactions—and also the conditions under which they advanced their development plans (initially, demographic decline; enormous pressure on public funds; close scrutiny from the Ministry of Education, as the Board for England and Wales was now called, and the Scottish Education Department)—there was never likely to be anything approaching a tripartite 'system'. One spanner thrown in the works of the putative system from the start was the resistance of most LEAs to opening or expanding technical schools, the middle term in the tripartite system.

This resistance to technical schools has often been taken as a retrograde sign of the anti-industrial bent in British culture and of 'academic drift' caused by obeisance to the grammar schools.[15] But that is to misunderstand both the nature of the resistance and its effects. As we have seen, many LEAs had already experienced parental indifference to technical schools before the war: they seemed second-rate next to grammar schools, they offered no obvious advantages in the labour market, and allocation to them seemed like just another means test to separate the privileged from the not.[16] In Scotland, one observer of the postwar system commented, to many parents 'the fact that a boy or girl is being given a technical or domestic or commercial course is *ipso facto* a declaration that the pupil has no academic ability. Resistance is automatic ... there is a national prejudice against vocational education'.[17]

'Parity of esteem' was thus doomed from before the start. Grammar schools were in any case very scientific in orientation, and became more so after the war. The new General Certificate of Education that replaced the School Certificate—offered at 16 ('Ordinary' or 'O' level) and 18 ('Advanced' or 'A' level)—saw rising take-up of its science options and a new set of technical GCEs was introduced in the mid-1950s.[18] It made much more sense to LEAs to invest in labs and other technical facilities in existing grammar schools than to build expensive new schools that were unpopular with parents. Their most common response was to consider their grammar schools 'bilateral' schools, i.e. a combination of technical and grammar streams. Thus the 'tripartite' system became very quickly a 'bipartite' system, if it was any system at all.[19] This put more pressure still on selection at the 11+, with all allocation concentrated there on the basis of an IQ test.[20]

About a fifth of all LEAs in England and Wales wished to introduce an element of 'multilateral' education, which combined all three streams in common schools, now more often called 'comprehensive' schools, to downplay the element of allocation into streams. In total these plans would have provided about 12.5 per cent of all state secondary school places in common schools.[21] Mostly these were in the way of experiments. As few families had had any previous experience with secondary education, there was little evidence one way or the other about their needs and wishes that could be put beside the official tripartite orthodoxy—much more would come soon. But many of these LEAs—Anglesey, Caernarvon, Cardigan, Coventry, Glamorgan, London (the LCC), Manchester, Middlesex (which covered the northern and western suburbs of London), Oldham, Reading, Southend, Swansea, Westmorland, the West Riding of Yorkshire—had in mind a transition to a largely comprehensive system, either because there were not resources or enough concentrated demand for a bipartite system (mostly not Labour controlled authorities), or because as Manchester said they did not believe there were 'three distinguishable types of children' (mostly Labour controlled authorities).[22]

Very few of these plans were immediately realized, for multiple reasons. The reason usually cited is official pressure towards tripartism from both the Ministry and the SED.[23] The Ministry's Circular 73 recommended a target of 70–75 per cent in modern schools and 25–30 per cent in grammar and technical schools. The SED's Circular 206 was less specific but absolved Local Authorities from following the recommendations of the Scottish Advisory Council in 1947 that they move towards common schools. Though there were many more common or 'omnibus' schools in Scotland (at least to age 15) than in England or even Wales, SED policy was still to preserve a fairly strict distinction between three-year secondary courses, which led to no qualifications, and five-year courses which led to the Leaving Certificate and thereafter the possibility of progression to higher education.[24] And while the SED was more permissive of local option than the Ministry, in England and Wales it is true that many LEAs were bullied into scaling back their multilateral plans, especially in Wales.[25] The Middlesex plan was turned down on the grounds that there would be insufficient academic children to stock viable Sixth Forms—leading to A-levels and higher education—unless the comprehensives were very large indeed, and there was a powerful prejudice against large schools on the American model, impersonal and machine-like. That assumption would soon be falsified by the ever larger proportion of students demanding entry to the Sixth Form, but it would take some years of experience with universal secondary education for that demand to be felt; there was simply not in the immediate postwar years enough information about demand for secondary education to challenge bipartite assumptions.[26]

The LCC plan was impeded by other considerations. Its catchment included large numbers of voluntary grammar schools, which could not be converted into multilaterals against their will.[27] Furthermore, the LCC came up against a fundamental demographic fact that all reorganizing LEAs had to face. The crude birth rate had been falling throughout Britain since the beginning of the century. There was therefore considerable surplus capacity in existing grammar schools. Under tight resource constraints, it made more sense for reforming LEAs to expand the proportion of their population that they transferred to grammar schools than to close grammar schools and build new comprehensives, the same policy adopted by reforming LEAs before the war.[28] Because the British system was *not* particularly backward in European context—it had already a substantial stock of grammar schools, with established middle-class constituencies—it could not start from scratch and had to democratize its secondary system by stages. While Britain is often compared unfavourably to Sweden, in fact Sweden with a smaller existing stock of selective schools also only experimented with comprehensive education to 16 (not 18) in the 1950s.[29] This policy of expanding the grammar schools was thus adopted as a fallback position by many Welsh and Scottish authorities after the war, and in practice by many English authorities too.[30] The proportion of the age cohort transferring to grammar school nationally rose sharply after the war to 35–40 per cent—relieving potential pressure from parents in the short term, though storing up trouble for later (see Appendix, Figure 2.1).[31] In any case, the Ministry and SED were neither willing nor able to approve capital expenditure or ensure building materials for expensive new comprehensive schools. They insisted on filling up available grammar school places instead, and running up cheap, often prefab buildings on available sites for the remainder of the 11–15 age cohort who had not previously gone to secondary school at all. The funding formula rewarded LEAs for providing grammar-school places by allocating them 170 per cent of the per-capita funding for secondary-modern places.[32] In such conditions 'parity of esteem' was less likely still.[33]

Far from setting in stone a tripartite 'system', this concatenation of circumstances was highly unstable and not by any means consensual.[34] LEAs (and the Ministry) were benefiting temporarily from a demographic lull but they knew—because the raw birth rate had already begun to rise *during* the war—that they might be sitting on a ticking time-bomb. Furthermore, as neither Ministry nor LEAs nor parents themselves had had any experience of secondary education for most teenagers they had little idea of what to expect in terms of demand for different types of education. Again during the war there was some intimation—demand to take School Certificate exams surged—but there was little idea of whether that trend would continue, and it knocked up against conventional wisdom about the proportion of the population that could feasibly tackle academic examinations.[35] Above all, no-one could—or reasonably should—have estimated how the changing social and economic prospects of working-class families and their attitudes to social services arising from the birth of the modern welfare state would affect expectations of education. It is the complex combination of these three incalculables—the 'bulge', the 'trend' and the welfare state—which turned a putative triumph of meritocracy into its crisis.

The Bulge, the Trend, and the Welfare State

Many existing accounts of secondary school reorganization in the postwar decades allude to the 'bulge' and the 'trend'—what we now call the 'baby boom' after the Second World War, and the trend for more people to seek more education. But they tend to treat them as one piece of evidence for elites (both experts and political elites), which contributed to their policy-making, rather than as evidence for changes in the behaviour and attitudes of the mass of the people.[36] Thus it has been possible to acknowledge the existence of these upheavals while at the same time telling an almost entirely top-down story about how mass secondary education was provided. Here we will reverse the usual order of priorities, and take the bulge and the trend as the primary phenomena in their own right, driving educational change in what was increasingly a demand-led system. And we will add a further layer of analysis, considering attitudes to the welfare state, democracy and citizenship, which helps us interpret further the full meaning of the bulge and the trend.

As we've just seen, the demographic slump of the early twentieth century took pressure off LEAs to rethink their educational provision immediately, as growing demand for grammar schools could be mopped up with existing places. But when the war ended and fertility rates continued their wartime rise—very rapidly immediately after the war—the clock began to tick in earnest. Educational policy is uniquely sensitive to demography, in that planners knew for certain that the postwar 'bulge' would require a growing number of secondary places from 1956 precisely. LEAs knew therefore almost from the beginning, and with mounting urgency, that they would need to provide new places—that is, to build new schools—before the late 1950s: many new schools, as secondary education numbers trebled between 1945 and 1965.[37] If they were to hold to the bipartite model, that would mean building new secondary modern and grammar schools in close proximity, further dramatizing the cliff-edge of the 11+. Central government, less exposed to these immediate pressures, hardly noticed until later.[38] This imperative to build new schools caused even Conservative LEAs to rethink bipartism, from very early on. Rural counties like Norfolk and Wiltshire followed the Welsh example in querying the cost effectiveness of two separate school systems. Cambridgeshire, Devon, Somerset and Leicestershire began to dream up new approaches to schooling—'village colleges' that brought together not only all types of child but also children and adults; 'middle schools' that transferred children to secondary at 11 as the Butler Act required but educated them in common schools until as late as the school-leaving age, after which a minority could transfer to grammar school, as in Sweden.[39]

What was less obvious about the bulge, and which we can better judge in retrospect, was what direct testimony it gives about changing attitudes to children and education. The social theorists Richard and Kathleen Titmuss had argued during the war that the declining birth rate of the early twentieth century represented a 'parents' revolt' against the difficulties of acquiring secondary education for their children. From this point of view keeping family size down represented a rational strategy, 'while they jostled for the new careers and new jobs arising from an expanding clerical market in a world daily becoming more complex and "office-minded"'.[40] The rise of the birth rate after the war betokened a new era. The world was not becoming less complex and 'office-minded', but in an atmosphere of full employment, equal citizenship and declining deference, parents were evidently more confident about their ability to support their children, and more confident in the state's ability to support their children in the provision of family allowances, free health care, and free secondary education. This 'parents' revival' was strongly evident in much stronger and more open-ended expectations for children's future lives. Men and women who had grown up in the immediate postwar period remembered the war as a dramatic point of rupture, casting off fatalism about social-class assignment and deference to authority.[41] Opinion polls after the war showed a powerful belief that children were being educated better than their parents and that there was great scope for further improvement in future.[42]

Though children and parents did not always see eye-to-eye on their futures—the 1950s were after all also years of emergent youth sub-cultures, in more or less open revolt against the older generation—nevertheless it has been argued that postwar parents were highly solicitous of their children's education, job prospects and sense of freedom. Both parents and children showed signs of what Gambetta calls 'psychic mobility', which allows people to transcend their inherited class positions and to exercise more choice in how they live.[43] Whereas before the war, a minority had had to strategize to get their children into 'clean' jobs via education or the labour market, after the war the majority expected their children to live different lives from their own. Most parents did not now want their children to follow in their own line of work—they sought 'upward mobility', in the language of the sociologists.[44] These new expectations were strongest amongst the majority of less privileged families, who had both most incentive and most space to improve themselves.[45]

'Psychic mobility' was broadly vindicated by real forms of mobility that parents saw their children enjoying in the postwar decades. While in the first half of the twentieth century people moved home frequently, due to instability in the housing market and in ability to pay rent, after the war they moved less frequently but further—and increasingly from inner-city to suburban locations. This separated young families, especially mothers, from their kin, contributed further to psychic mobility and caused women to rely less on family networks for support—which in turn, as contemporary sociologists realized, loosened their inherited gender-role assumptions.[46] Trends in occupational mobility were even more striking. Men in the 1946 birth cohort were among the most likely of all twentieth-century generations to experience upward mobility, mostly from manual to non-manual jobs.[47] In general, people entering the labour market after the war were likely to find themselves upwardly mobile, whatever their level of education (see Appendix, Figure 3.1). Even in austerity, therefore, social security, full employment and upscaling labour markets encouraged parents to expect a better life for their children, and when affluence hit over the course of the 1950s those expectations seemed more reasonable still, and possibly more enduring.

Neither this interpretation of the bulge nor its application to hopes and expectations for education was so obvious to contemporaries, especially elite commentators who continued to believe that there was little working-class demand for education. But the 'trend' was harder to ignore, because it provided direct evidence of that demand. The 'trend' to seek more education was first evident in staying-on rates; that is, the tendency for those who did pass through the 11+ filter to remain in grammar schools beyond age 15, mostly to take O-levels at 16, and then possibly A-levels or other courses which led to jobs in teaching, nursing, clerical work, or business. Although staying on had faltered before the war, under severe economic stress, contemporaries were aware that it started to rise from the very first postwar 11+ cohort. A national study of grammar-school entrants in 1946 reported 'a clearly defined continuous tendency towards a longer school life since the war', though it may be characteristic that this was couched in terms of a decline in 'early leaving' rather than a rise in 'staying on'.[48] This trend only accelerated over the course of the 1950s, when there was a 5 per cent per annum growth in staying on after 15 and a 6 per cent per annum growth in those achieving the 2 A-levels usually regarded as the minimum requirement to proceed to higher education. Overall the proportion of 17-year-olds in full-time education rose from 4 per cent before the war to 15 per cent in 1962, with growth up to that point almost equally fast for boys and girls.[49]

But of course staying on was only really possible for those who had already passed through the 11+ filter. That filter was getting more severe: after the early postwar years, demography as well as policy dictated that the proportion of the age cohort going to grammar school had to adjust back to about 25 per cent at least in England (see again Appendix, Figure 2.1). So the 'trend' of demand for grammar school was even stronger than the proportion actually selected for it suggests, and correspondingly the significance of the 11+ loomed larger. Some modern schools began to allow students to stay on after 15 and to take O-levels (which could not be taken before 16), though that rather made a mockery of the 11+ which was supposed to have selected out all those capable of benefiting from such an academic course.[50] In Scotland a more radical step was taken from 1955 with the introduction of an 'Ordinary Grade' exam, eagerly taken up by the three-year secondaries, which required a fourth year to be tacked on to the three-year course, and naturally implied progression to higher qualifications and university even for the lower tier. The high levels of take-up of O-grade, coupled with the high levels of transfer to five-year secondaries in Scotland, provided ample evidence of the 'trend', and 'set a short fuse' under bipart-ism there.[51] But to assess the true extent of the 'trend' in England and Wales—towards greater demand for education, rather than greater take-up—we have to attempt to assess popular attitudes, and in particular working-class demand for grammar school amongst those who did *not* attain it.

Commentators at the time claimed that such evidence of this demand was 'meagre', but there was always more evidence than they admitted, and they often wilfully misinterpreted or even disbelieved the evidence they did admit, because it flew in the face of received meritocratic wisdom about both the desires and the abilities of most people.[52] With the benefit of hind-sight we can both take a fresh look at their evidence and generate more evidence of our own, such as has been done with extended tracking of the 1946 birth cohort. Long before that cohort (and the rest of the 'bulge') reached secondary school, indeed from right after the war, working-class parents showed a manifest preference for grammar-school education of their children, even though (or perhaps because) that implied later entry into the labour market, and even though (or perhaps because) they knew they were unlikely to get it.

A celebrated study by Floud, Halsey, and Martin in the early 1950s of parental attitudes in South-West Hertfordshire and Middlesbrough—respectively a middle-class and a working-class district—found that similar majorities of parents in both districts preferred grammar schools for their children. Because working-class parents were more likely not to get those places, they reported much higher levels of frustration with the results of the 11+—over half even of unskilled working-class parents, despite the fact that somewhat fewer of them expressed a desire for grammar school.[53] All of these figures were presented as percentages, suggesting that all classes were equally frustrated. But this disguises the fact that there were many, many more working-class than middle-class parents, making the vast majority of frustrated parents working-class, rather than the middle-class phenomenon as it was then (and has been since) often portrayed.[54] Even at this early date, before the postwar bulge approached secondary age, it was difficult to find more than a small minority content with relegation to secondary modern schools.[55]

A few years later, two surveys by Mark Abrams' Research Services Ltd derived similar results, though Abrams was very cynical about them. One sample of working-class parents in London in 1956–7, conducted by Abrams for an advertising agency, found them preferring grammar or technical schools to secondary moderns for their children by a margin of 3–1. Abrams concluded, 'A belief in the sovereign virtues of "education" is characteristic of our society', but he found it 'very difficult to take seriously the aspirations of parents', since so many would be frustrated by the 11+. While he noted the hostility of these parents to the 11+, he did not think they took their frustration as a 'major disaster', and simply resorted to criticism of the 11+ as a convenient 'scapegoat'.[56] To some degree this verdict was connected to the fact that the survey was aimed at assessing consumer spending on education, and Abrams did not wish his clients to think that working-class appetite for grammar school was ever likely to translate into fee-paying. It was the middle-class parent upon whom these schools should focus:

> The middle-class parent, generally speaking, expects to pay for the education of his children,[57] and to have a choice of schools corresponding to the amount of money he can afford. He expects to exercise considerable control, that is to say, over the kind of education which his children are to have. Against this, the working-class parent does not expect to have to pay, nor does he expect to exercise much control.[58]

But it also reflected Abrams' growing personal pessimism about the cultural tendencies of mass society.[59] A second survey in June 1957, a representative sample of parents of all classes, for the Labour party, found similarly that over half the population disapproved of the 11+. Of working-class respondents, Abrams summed up, one-third were fatalistic about the 11+, one third wanted their children to succeed at it and go to grammar school (and indeed if capable of it to university), and one third felt 'the dice are loaded against them', and wanted 'a fairer chance to win the social and educational prizes of a class society'. Yet he concluded again that far from seeking equal provision these working-class respondents were merely clamouring for grammar school, which he took to mean vainly seeking to ape the middle classes.[60]

A great deal more could be said about these surveys and Abrams' jaundiced interpretation of them. But for present purposes we must confine ourselves to the bottom line, which was the consistent evidence across the 1950s—in these and a number of other surveys[61]—of working-class preference for grammar schools and hostility to the 11+ which routinely frustrated their preference. What this amounted to was a demand for 'grammar schools for all'—a demand that simply made no sense to commentators like Abrams, for whom grammar schools were by definition *not* for all, and a demand that has since been almost as vehemently deplored by historians and educationists, seen as some kind of back-sliding from a true 'egalitarianism' and thus again a sad apeing of middle-class mores.[62] It was 'perhaps a contradiction in terms to the educationist', as one contemporary observer commented, 'but making sense to the ordinary man'.[63]

How can *we* make more sense of this demand? An obvious explanation turns to the labour market, and to the already established demand for 'clean' jobs—especially in the burgeoning retail and office sectors, and now also the public sector—that were widely seen as accessible only via grammar school. These sectors were indeed booming after the war. Although the overall share of services in the labour force remained relatively stable, what changed was the upgrading of many service jobs, away from domestic and personal services towards consumer, financial and public services.[64] As the Titmusses had noted during the war, society was becoming ever more 'office-minded'. The tendency of mothers especially to work to get their children into 'clean jobs', noted already for the interwar period by Todd, seems to have intensified, and their animus against the 11+ for blocking such progress could be particularly intense.[65] The Catholic Archbishop of Liverpool called the mounting fervour against the 11+ the 'revolt of the Mums'.[66] As industry scaled up its demands for high-quality labour, grammar school was even the gateway to good apprenticeships for boys in industry— engineering apprenticeships were the number one destination for male grammar-school leavers in 1948.[67] By 1965, the Youth Employment Service was noting, 'Employers in general were seeking the better type of boy or girl', which they measured simply by years of schooling—thus the advantage of grammar school, which did not assume (though it could not stop) early leaving.[68]

From this point of view, the demand for grammar school could be seen, in the economists' terms, as the prizing of education as an 'investment good'—a straightforward calculation of the payoff to education, in status as well as income. However, demand for grammar school went well beyond this kind of calculation. Though contemporaries were not so aware of this at the time, grammar school was *not* the sole gateway to 'clean' jobs—they were available in such profusion that as many went to secondary-modern leavers—but equally jobs were not the only thing on parents' and students' minds. When asked *why* they preferred grammar schools (on the rare occasions they were asked), parents were as likely to mention 'the better education, the higher level of qualifications and the greater opportunities for advanced education' as any specific occupational goals.[69] In other words, as the economists acknowledge, education was in this period as much a 'consumption good' as an investment—that is, 'one of the decencies of life', available to and demanded by more people as they become more affluent.[70]

In this period of social and economic change and extending mobility, parents seem to have had a growing appreciation of what was possible in education. They preferred not to criticize the schools their children attended, and certainly not to criticize their children for their lack of achievement.[71] But they wanted their children to have the opportunity to show what they could do. True 'equal opportunity' was not to be determined by others, based on some external assessment of fixed ability, but by the children themselves over the course of their lives. Thus parents could not see the sense in external authorities making decisions about their children's fate at 11. Similarly, though there was as yet little support for an extension of compulsory education to 16[72]—parents may have had in mind their own resentment at being held in primary schools to 14—there was strong support for children to have the chance (if they wished) to stay on past 15, to take O-levels and go further still if they wished, something again that was closed off by external judgements made when children were still young.[73] Parents of young children were particularly keen not to see any obstacles placed in the way of their children in the future.[74] As early as 1953, a survey of industrial workers showed a powerful awareness, long 'blocked and unsuspected', of the value of education 'less as a means to some definite end than as a master key to which many doors would open and the possession of which would give a sense of power and security'.[75] There was a much more developmental understanding of young people: instead of accepting a social position or a judgement of ability from birth, parents looked to a greater range of possibility in the future, and valued their children's education accordingly.[76]

Most parents therefore did not want the school 'best suited' to the abilities of their child, according to someone else's determination, along tripartite or meritocratic lines, but schools offering the widest opportunities for all. As Political Economic Planning reported after a survey of parents as consumers of public services, in 1957–8—a survey done for them by Mark Abrams— that while in educational policy circles '[t]he idea was that there should be a variety of schools, all equally attractive', '[t]he impression that is gained from talking to parents is a rather different one. It is that some schools are much more attractive than others. In such a situation the method of allocation to particular schools is bound to be very much in parents' minds.' They hadn't in fact asked about the 11+, but were bound to notice that many mothers raised it anyway.[77]

These findings about demand for education as both an investment and a consumption good may seem too individualistic or competitive for many people's tastes.[78] But there is no reason to consider investment or consumption as competitive. Parents seeking to advance their children's education as an investment in their future did not need to see it as a zero-sum game, given the buoyant labour market which made future prospects look rosy for most people. Equally the enjoyment of education as a consumption good in conditions of growing affluence need not be seen as 'positional'—the affluent prizing education that distances them from the less affluent—but rather it was obviously increasingly seen as 'one of the decencies of life rather than an extraordinary privilege reserved for people of high status or extraordinary ability'.[79] And there was an additional, more obviously egalitarian (or democratic) set of changing attitudes influencing educational preferences, conditioned by the emergent welfare state.

The ideal of social security had been one of the big winners of the Second World War. As we noted in the last chapter, the unfairness of unemployment was keenly felt in the long interwar Slump, and the 'means test' applied to unemployment benefits—and eligibility for free school places—equally keenly resented. Full employment was therefore one of the major social goals of postwar governments, largely achieved; on the whole, people preferred employment to benefits of any kind. But there was also an enormous and growing demand for certain kinds of free and universal benefits that were seen not as supplements or alternatives to labour-market earnings but as fundamentally infrastructural provisions that made possible equal citizenship and even 'equal opportunity' in life. Chief amongst these were free and universal secondary education and health care—the democratic demand for equal provision that we saw emerging long before the Butler Act.[80] Education and health were often twinned in this way in postwar public opinion. Both working-class families, who hated means tests and thought they had the most to gain from universal services, and middle-class families, who in health and education alone demanded the highest standards from the state, seemed to share this view.[81] Both education and health rose substantially up the political agenda over the course of the 1950s, as politicians of both parties belatedly woke up to this change in the public's priorities, and both took an ever larger share of government spending.[82] Public expenditure on both rose from around 3 per cent of GDP in the early 1950s to 5–6 per cent by the early 1970s.[83]

Of course it is possible to see these preferences too in more individualistic, investment-oriented terms, based on different classes' estimates of who was likely to benefit most from high standards of provision in education and health. Abrams' surveys, however, give us further evidence of what parents hoped to gain from equal provision, though he paid even less attention to this part of his findings. Two-thirds of his nationally representative sample said that it was best for society if children of all social classes were educated in the same schools—three-quarters of working-class but also just over half of middle-class respondents.[84] When asked further why they felt common schools were best, they specified that the 11+ made some children feel inferior (28 per cent), that common schools were good for society (15 per cent), that they mitigated class distinctions (10 per cent), and that they kept children together with their friends (7 per cent).[85] As Abrams' survey for PEP showed at about the same time, parents didn't want the best school 'for their child' as much as good schools for all children—thus 'grammar schools for all'.[86] No-one was suggesting that there should be good hospitals for some and average hospitals for others; why was this the choice offered to parents in secondary schooling? As one commentator belatedly appreciated, the promise of 'secondary education for all' had been interpreted by many parents from the beginning as 'grammar schools for all', the main type of secondary school they knew and valued; as soon as they realised this was not on offer, dissatisfaction was bound to result.[87] Parents were more dissatisfied with the education service than any other part of the welfare state, 'frustrated' working-class parents (who didn't get the 'best' schools for their children) most of all.[88] Even the Conservative Education Minister, David Eccles, recognized this at the time.

> The nation is no longer divided into rich and poor. We all have the vote at 21. But we are still divided by the two systems of education. Money can buy a better preparation for life than is provided out of public funds. The standards 'only the best is good enough' of the Health Service are not applied to education.

It was, he concluded, 'the most urgent of all social problems'. He was right.[89]

On the whole, however, this mounting tide of public opinion—evident in the bulge, the trend, and the new 'structure of feeling' engendered by the welfare state—was not well-recognized by national-level figures like

Eccles—and it has been scanted even by historians. Contemporaries tried to reduce resistance to the bipartite system to individual psychological problems. Anticipating selection induced '11+ strain'.[90] As Abrams had argued, people didn't really care about education but resorted to slagging off the 11+ as an easy 'scapegoat'. There was much contemporary anxiety about the isolation and maladjustment of the working-class 'scholarship boy (and girl)', who never quite felt they fit into the grammar school.[91] Historians have tended to regret the lack of overt enthusiasm or pressure for comprehensive schools; 'grammar schools for all' seemed a limp, unambitious demand, rather than a powerful cry for levelling up.[92] Few then or later recognized it for what it was, a massive social movement. Even the one educationist who did advert to the 'revolt of the Mums' oddly expressed a fear that the future historian 'studying the emotionally charged tirades against the 11+ examination in newspaper articles and editorials of the 1950s and 1960s' will 'exaggerate the width and depth of public feeling on the matter'. He preferred to focus on 'the most responsible and best-educated sections of the parents in England and Wales'—middle-class parents who organized pressure groups such as the Confederation for the Advancement of State Education and the Advisory Centre for Education—who could be credited with making the respectable case for common schools in the 1960s.[93] But by then the key decisions—the crucial registration of widespread public rejection of the 11+—had already been taken, not from the centre or the metropolis, but where we should expect them to have registered first—in local authorities, where much of the sensitivity, most of the authority, and all of the responsibility for delivering mass education lay.

4

The Transition to
Comprehensive Education

The transition from a largely bipartite to a largely comprehensive system of education has not been given a good press—or often even recognized, given how many histories of the transition begin much too late, with Circular 10/65 (the instruction to LEAs in early 1965 to prepare development plans ending selection at 11+).[1] It was seen to have started too late, and to have taken too long, perhaps in contrast with common schooling in the United States which arose earlier, or with the transition to comprehensive education in Sweden, which started at about the same time but is thought to have been shorter and sharper. It has been associated by its many critics from the left with a half-hearted or 'divided' Labourism and thus portrayed as a failed revolution, as well as from the right, with a catastrophic decline in 'standards'. If we start from the bottom rather than from the top, however, and from where most people were at rather than from an ideal-type 'comprehensive revolution', this transition looks rather different: pretty complete, no slower than Sweden's, faster than many countries (Germany, for example), and if more piecemeal and gradualist then perhaps better rooted in democratic sentiments, and harder to reverse. Certainly a consensus around a single system of 'neighbourhood' or 'community' schools has, despite other much more superficial reorganizations, prevailed ever since. To see this transition properly, we have to start not therefore from the top, with Circular 10/65, but from the bottom, with local government, and not in 1965 but back in the early 1950s when the bipartite system sputtered into existence.[2]

From Public Opinion to Local Policy

After the approval of initial development plans, the Ministry mostly fell silent on the form that secondary education for all should take, leaving both policy and practicalities to the LEAs. In conditions of austerity, little progress was made through the early '50s, one way or the other. As late as 1954, only one-third of the intake was accommodated in secondary-modern schools, the rest still in all-age schools or temporary accommodation. At this point there was actually more scope for LEAs to improvise, and to reflect their reading of local parent demand, than there had been in the conflictual process of setting out initial development plans.[3]

Among the early movers were, as we have seen, Conservative-controlled rural authorities. They had little incentive to construct a bipartite system and the same complaint registered against comprehensive schools—that unless enormous they would be too small to support a viable sixth form—also weighed against their very small grammar schools. Dorset determined to 'abolish' its grammar schools and by the end of the '50s had persuaded the government to accept a fully comprehensive system; by that point their example was already being followed by Cornwall, Gloucestershire, Westmorland and the East Riding of Yorkshire.[4]

Another model, which Dorset and Wiltshire later embraced, was developed by Leicestershire from 1957. There the LEA created a two-tier system of common 'junior' high schools from 11 to 14, and then offered transfer to 'senior' schools to parents who wished their children to stay on beyond the leaving age of 15. This model proved very popular, because it brought an end to the 11+—even at 13 or 14 selection could be avoided if all parents were offered transfer, amounting to 'grammar school for all' who wanted it—without requiring the 'destruction' of any grammar schools.[5] It was already being given an imprimatur by the Ministry as early as 1955, but another recommendation for the model is that it did not necessarily require government consent if it involved re-badging rather than closing or opening schools.[6] It attracted rural authorities seeking a smooth transition away from bipartism, mixed authorities like the West Riding, Fife and Renfrewshire which were finely balanced socially or politically, and urban authorities with strong middle-class lobbies and/or strong local pride in their historic grammar schools (such as Glasgow, Stoke, Sheffield, and Rochdale).[7] Another version, dubbed the 'Croydon model' after the outer London borough which first developed the idea in 1954, involved common schools to 16 (offering O-levels to all) and then transfer at 16 to 'junior colleges' for those who wished to proceed to A-levels and higher education. This model survives today in many places which (after raising of the school-leaving age in 1973) offer 11–16 comprehensives and (usually moderately selective) sixth form colleges or (less selective) 'tertiary' colleges. It must be seen as a central part of the transition to common schooling.[8]

Another strategy was to face the bulge, and population movements to new suburban estates or new towns, by building new comprehensives in these areas of growth without having to 'destroy' grammar schools where they already existed. This strategy too was adopted both by Conservative authorities, especially for suburban areas, and more divided Labour authorities, on new urban estates. These 'cautious counties' included West Sussex, Glamorgan, Shropshire, and Northumberland. West Sussex in particular faced intense population pressures in suburbanizing areas like Shoreham, Crawley and Three Bridges, and decided in the late '50s it could not justify building any new bipartite schools, in 1958 beginning to move to a comprehensive system.[9] With hindsight, the Conservative education minister Edward Boyle later reflected, 'I cannot from memory recall a single Conservative, with any interest in the subject, who really favoured building new grammar schools and secondary modern schools, side by side, in an expanding housing estate.'[10] Other LEAs took a similar view. Warwickshire proposed from 1957 to build only comprehensives on new estates while retaining most existing grammar schools elsewhere.[11] Nottingham, which had hitherto been preoccupied with closing technical schools and creating a bipartite system, planned a large comprehensive on a new estate from 1955 but was then paralysed by political division.[12] In Liverpool the opposite happened; it began to build a huge new estate at Kirkby in 1952 with tripartite schools, and then when political control shifted it junked them and built a comprehensive instead, which opened in 1955.[13] Bristol opened its first three comprehensives on new estates in 1954. These were said to be 'working-class communities with relatively few education-conscious parents', reflecting contemporary prejudices; given how few in those communities would have been selected for new grammar schools, it would be more correct to say these were communities least likely to be enthusiastic about new bipartite schools.[14] Politically divided Leeds, struggling with very poor secondary provision—it only closed its last all-age school in 1965—also chose to open four mixed-sex comprehensives in areas where new schools were required, starting in 1956.[15]

There remained of course powerful kernels of support for grammar schools as symbols of class or community pride, though Boyle perhaps exaggerated when he concluded that overall

> it was, paradoxically, in the most Conservative areas of the country that the bipartite system had come, by the end of the 1950s, to make little educational sense; it was much more often in a Labour-controlled city, or a coal-mining area, that one was most conscious of what the grammar school still meant to an able boy or girl from a modest home in a poor district.[16]

It is true that some of the most celebrated cases of grammar-school defence can be traced to Labour leaderships in older urban areas. The City of Leicester, famously, held on tightly to its grammars while its Tory-controlled neighbour the County was pioneering common high schools. But other Labour-controlled urban authorities were among the strongest crusaders for comprehensives—the LCC, Middlesex, Coventry—where grammar-school defence was organized not by the LEA but by powerful local lobbies of mostly middle-class grammar-school parents; the most densely populated urban areas were likely to have had *both* Labour LEAs *and* the largest concentrations of upper-middle-class parents.[17] Others flipped over the course of the 1950s, as a postwar generation, galvanized by the people's war and the welfare state, gradually succeeded the prewar generation indebted to a minority of free places in a selective system. Lincoln, for example, saw the advent in 1956 of a new kind of Labour group in power, 'of a new style, younger men and women educated in a climate of greater equality, the product of the war years', who promoted comprehensives over the resistance of an old-guard Chief Education Officer.[18]

Much of this story is known, not least from some excellent local case studies of comprehensive reorganization. But its significance tends to be underplayed—either because studies *have* focused on new comprehensives, rather than the wider variety of means deployed to end selection, or because ultimate credit is still given to changes in central-government policy after 1964. And local studies have almost always been fixated on *local* elites—political parties, Chief Education Officers, teachers and middle-class pressure groups—who are seen as the agents of change, while the immense changes in the 'structure of feeling' in local communities, evident in the bulge, the trend and the welfare state, are taken as their instruments rather than motive forces in their own right.[19] Very occasionally the great social movement that was popular hostility to the 11+ peeps out through the filter of committee minutes and development plans—the Archbishop's 'revolt of the mums', the mounting 'local feeling' against selection acknowledged by Lanarkshire's Director of Education, 'of which you were more generally conscious, as time passed', talk of a '"grass-roots" revolution', or the ways in which councillors acted to pre-empt 'anticipated reactions' of the electorate.[20] In 1960 the Chief Inspector of Schools, making a rare conspectus of LEA development plans, concluded that

> A system under which failure to win a place in a selective school at 11+ meant complete and irrevocable denial of the coveted opportunities associated with a grammar-school education could not hope to win the support of parents and could not survive the day when their wishes could gain a hearing.

But quite apart from his characteristic assumption that parents' wishes had hitherto been pretty irrelevant, even he credited internal experiments (such as the offer of O-levels) by secondary modern schools with pointing the way, rather than anything like 'external pressure', and consistent with government policy of the day he still did not see such experiments as fatal to bipartism.[21]

A similar late awakening about the same time by an upper-crust but left-wing barrister, later a Labour Lord Chancellor, provides a more vivid illustration of parents' wishes gaining a hearing. He had turned up for what he thought was a routine meeting to discuss boundary changes between Leicestershire and the City of Leicester, and was astonished to find a crowd of thousands:

> the vast majority were parents and they were hopping mad because in the city they had secondary and grammar schools whereas the county had comprehensive schools. Some of them had sold their homes in Leicester in order to get away from the city education system and the 11-plus and give their children the advantages of a comprehensive school education, and now they were being threatened with being put back into the city again... Of course, I had always known that the 11-plus was not very popular, but I had never known before to what extent it was both hated and feared.[22]

Such pressures, not necessarily for 'a comprehensive school education' but for something more like 'grammar schools for all', and against the lottery of the 11+, had been felt across the land for over a decade by that point. Driven by the bulge and the trend, they lay behind innumerable secondary-modern and LEA experiments with smudging the 11+ line; and by the early 1960s they had led to positive decisions to break with bipartism in the great majority of LEAs in England, and a break already realized in much of Wales and Scotland. By the end of 1963, no fewer than 92 of 129 English LEAs had initiated plans to end selection at 11.[23] While changes in the 'structure of feeling' amongst ordinary citizens do not leave direct traces in LEA archives, and may only belatedly register in metropolitan consciousness, only a 'silent social revolution' on this scale can account for the degree of commonality with which the great majority of local authorities came to roughly the same verdict.

None of the evidence above dates from 1964 or after—that is to say, it all pre-dates the election of a Labour government in 1964 and Circular 10/65 which enunciated government policy for comprehensive reorganization in 1965. Much of it originates in the mid- or even the early 1950s. In other words, central-government policy followed rather than led local government. Nevertheless, it did follow, and there was a (somewhat delayed) crisis of the meritocratic ideal in 'Establishment' circles—amongst experts, pundits, Labour and Conservative front-benchers—that echoed, yet was not the same as the crisis that registered in public opinion and the slow withdrawal from the 11+. At a time when it was still widely held that 'in the case of education, the gentleman in Whitehall really does know better what is good for people than the people know themselves', and when parents' wishes were only beginning to gain a hearing, it did still matter what the gentleman in Whitehall thought, even if his ability to control events in a mass society and an increasingly democratic polity were not quite as great as he imagined.[24]

From Public Opinion to National Policy

At the national level, amongst intellectuals, the commentariat, political leaders of both parties, meritocracy remained unchallenged for much longer. The Conservatives had come to embrace tripartism as their own, a support for the social order. Though grass-roots Labour was increasingly aligned with a comprehensive policy, enough Labour tradition was invested in the grammar school for working-class mobility—and in the very fact of free secondary education for all—not to disturb a consensus behind tripartism. The Labour front bench in particular put further school reorganization as a very low priority behind building the economy and broadly investing in the welfare state. A longstanding Fabian emphasis on elite education for 'national efficiency' was here reinforced by the predominance of producerism over consumerism in conditions of austerity. In the meantime, tripartism was the deal they had got. Surveying the 1953 party conference, front-bencher Richard Crossman smugly concluded, 'nearly all the delegates either were at grammar school or have their children at grammar school, and are not quite so susceptible to the romantic socialism of the 1920s'—one would have thought a very complacent response to a conference that voted that year to put comprehensive reorganization into the party programme.[25] But in those days the gentleman in Whitehall did still rule the roost.

Labour party leaders were used to ignoring or humouring the votes of the rank-and-file at conference. In this case the rank-and-file might have proved a reasonably sensitive barometer of public feeling. Teachers and local-government officers were very well represented.[26] On the other hand, it is true that the Labour rank-and-file was pulling away from (rather than towards) public opinion over the course of the 1950s, as that public elected three consecutive Conservative majorities. Much of the Labour left became very suspicious of public opinion, especially as measured by polls and sur-veys, and more stubbornly attached to their own ethical ideals—closer to 'romantic socialism' than Crossman was ready to acknowledge. Affluence and social change, it was supposed, were their enemies. It is surprising how rarely Labour's grass-roots support for comprehensive education was justified in terms of parental demands and aspirations, or hostility to the 11+, rather than socialist ideals. This in turn made the front bench more suspicious of their rank-and-file.[27]

Somewhat more influential on front-bench opinion was a new element in opinion-formation, the rise of social-science expertise. At first psychologists and sociologists focused on fine-tuning the tripartite system to optimize 'adjustment': how best to measure intelligence, how to ensure that selection captured 'measured intelligence' equally everywhere, how to nurture that intelligence wherever it was located and prevent 'early leaving', to minimize in other words the 'waste of talent'.[28] They were aware that family back-ground played a major role in educational success—something as we have seen that Conservatives were also aware of, and celebrated—but thought grammar schools could still mitigate this; David Glass, the LSE sociologist who led many of these early studies, thought it would take 40 years to see if the Butler Act was actually having the effect attributed to it of spreading equal opportunity regardless of social background.[29]

A breakthrough came with the study by Glass's students Floud, Halsey, and Martin published in 1956, though based on surveys undertaken from the late 1940s. They found that the 11+ actually captured 'measured intelligence' reasonably well. 'But', they went on to say, 'this does not dispose of the problem of equality of educational opportunity'. Unlike previous studies, theirs did not assume that 'measured intelligence' was randomly distributed. Drawing on the work of psychologist P. E. Vernon, they asserted that it was 'largely an acquired characteristic', developed over time both at home and at school. The 'pool of ability' or 'talent', they argued, was not fixed. It could be expanded with the proper mix of social and educational policies.

> The problem of equality of educational opportunity is now more complicated than when it took the simple form of the need to secure free access to grammar schools on equal intellectual terms...the need arises to understand the optimum conditions for the integration of school and home environment at all social levels in such a way as to minimize the educational disadvantages of both...

Furthermore, they had studied closely working-class attitudes to education and social mobility—theirs was the first to demonstrate the depths of working-class 'frustration' with the 11+—and they concluded unlike Abrams (and to some degree Glass) that there was substantial appetite for more education and more social mobility, which made proposals for social and educational change politically more viable.[30]

There was, of course, a political motive lying behind this new social science. Jean Floud was a grammar-school girl, daughter of a shoe salesman, and a sometime Communist; A. H. 'Chelly' Halsey was a grammar-school boy from Yorkshire, a lifelong ethical socialist.[31] Indeed the whole of postwar British sociology has been described as 'essentially an attempt to make intellectual sense of the political problems of the Labour Party'.[32] Their survey methods and scientific language added lustre to their underlying message.[33] Their work could now be deployed to demonstrate both popular and scientific objections to the 11+, removing some of the burden on socialist belief.[34] And crucially they also captured the attention of a rising Labour star, Anthony Crosland.

Crosland was a floating figure, not clearly attached either to the Bevanite left or the Gaitskellite right, though associated more with the latter, and his chief preoccupation in the 1950s was indeed to move Labour's thinking away from the Bevanite preoccupation as he saw it with public ownership of the means of production. Thus dubbed a 'revisionist', for casting doubt on the Marxist priority given to economics, Crosland felt the modern working class was more invested in leisure, culture, and education—'welfare', in short—than in work. He was also out of Parliament between 1955 and 1959 and so able to develop his thinking in full, notably in *The Future of Socialism*, first published in 1956. During a trip to America in 1954 he was exposed to academic sociology and subsequently he developed relations with a wide range of academic advisers, including Halsey and Floud.[35] In *The Future of Socialism* he was able to make arguments both on the basis of his revisionist understanding of socialism and on an improved understanding of the drift of public opinion. The tripartite system of education, he argued, was 'the most divisive, unjust, and wasteful of all the aspects of social inequality'. It was divisive because it literally divided the population into more and less favoured groups; as a result, he appreciated, the 11+ was 'bitterly disliked and resented', and 'there was quite sufficient truth in these intuitive fears to give them a genuine validity', an unusual admission of public opinion. It was unjust because, far from providing 'equal opportunity' as it promised, it over-rewarded groups already privileged in their private life with new badges of privilege in public life—grammar-school and university education—as Floud and Halsey had argued. And it was also wasteful because it concentrated too much of its resources on elite education, when what was called for in a modern society was 'a high level of general education' for all—a new argument for 'national efficiency' focused on the mass rather than the elite, which we will encounter again in the next chapter in the shape of 'human capital'.[36]

Close to Crosland at the time was another floating free-thinker, Michael Young, a sociologist but not an academic, a political player but not an MP. Young adumbrated his own critique of the tripartite system in another influential book, *The Rise of the Meritocracy* (1959), which introduced that term into public debate for the first time.[37] That Young's was a swingeing *critique* of meritocracy, rather than an endorsement, was very much a sign of the times in the late '50s, though the word came into general currency later, when it took on more favourable connotations.[38] Young like Crosland was a 'revisionist' who had wearied of Labour's obsession with public ownership during the period after the war when he worked for the party.[39] Subsequently he had teamed up with the sociologist Peter Willmott, founded the Institute of Community Studies, and authored a pioneering series of community studies in East London and the outer suburbs which were among those that revealed the extent of the dislike of the 11+ across all classes.[40] He was, therefore, rather more attuned to the 'revolt of the mums' than most. In *The Rise of the Meritocracy*, a dystopian satire set in 2033, rule by an academic elite—'the meritocracy'—was finally challenged by a women's revolt against a social hierarchy entirely defined by a male norm of measured intelligence.[41]

Young was not an egalitarian exactly in Crosland's mould; it was community, 'fraternity', that attracted him quite as much as equality, and especially the kind of mother-centred community he thought he had encountered in his explorations of Bethnal Green with Peter Willmott.[42] While he deplored the divisiveness of the 11+, he was almost as opposed to a common schooling that put traditional academic education at its centre. So he was not an advocate of 'grammar schools for all'—he shared the left-wing view that this was just a way to ape middle-class norms—and he suspected the comprehensive school as a means of smuggling a 'grammar stream' into common schools which ought to have a much more rounded curriculum, creating a more diverse and harmonious community.[43] Still, like Crosland's *Future of Socialism*, *The Rise of the Meritocracy* was clearly seen at the time—even if not so much later—as among the first intellectual challenges to a meritocratic understanding of 'equality of opportunity' as traditionally defined in the post-Butler Act era. Together Crosland and Young brought the crisis of the meritocracy into political visibility.[44]

But not much more than that. Neither Crosland, the temporarily retired politician, nor Young, the social investigator and satirist, were in a position to affect public policy much, or even as it turned out to affect Labour's front-bench policy either. In this crucial period of the late '50s Labour's front-bench spokesperson on education was Michael Stewart. Stewart was a reluctant advocate of comprehensive education and saw his task as finding a way to bridge rank-and-file sentiment for comprehensives with front-bench attachment to the grammar schools. Like Crosland, he was attached neither to Bevanites nor to Gaitskellites, and like Crosland he leant to the latter, though he worried that Crosland was too right-wing for party harmony. He shared some of the rank-and-file's suspicion of public opinion, certainly as measured by pollsters, and his dogged conclusion after Labour's third consecutive electoral defeat was that 'we must go on to seek to make Socialists'. He was not very well informed about local developments and unlike Crosland not at all connected to sociological expertise.[45] Still, as

Gary McCulloch has recently pointed out, Stewart did achieve his goal of converting a reluctant leadership to the abolition of the 11+.[46] Unfortunately, his means of doing so was by a study group on education that ran from mid-1957 to early 1958, and for which the only source of information on public opinion was the party's pollster Mark Abrams.[47]

The study group brought together interested Labour parliamentarians with educationists (including an ageing R. H. Tawney) and co-opted local-government representatives. It quickly agreed on a fifteen-year plan to phase out selection (which had been Labour party policy for some time), and spent more time fussing about other issues—whether to integrate the public schools into the state system or to leave them alone (resolution: leave them alone); how to expand higher education (resolution: appoint a Royal Commission). The resulting policy document, 'Learning to Live', was launched by the party leader Hugh Gaitskell in July 1958 and hammered out the party line of 'grammar schools for all'.[48] No doubt Gaitskell and his successor Harold Wilson, who were both ardent supporters of grammar schools, saw this as a fudge with which they could live. Politically it also defused the Tories' best line, which was opposition to the 'destruction' of grammar schools. But while it did align Labour's front bench with the common sense of the ordinary voter, and increasingly with LEA policy (which by this point was very widely to find ways to end selection without 'destroying' grammar schools), that is not the way the study group or the party leadership saw it.

To get a fix on public opinion, the study group commissioned a survey from Mark Abrams, who had already been exploring opinion on education privately for Gaitskell, and whose firm Research Services Ltd was also engaged in parallel surveys for other customers.[49] Abrams' presentation of his findings in December 1957 was deeply discouraging. He cherry-picked one headline finding: when asked about the present tripartite system, most parents expressed satisfaction, and of the minority who were dissatisfied, only half expressed hostility to social segregation (the other half gave other reasons to oppose the 11+). The conclusion he drew was that 'With the exception of a small minority, education for their children was of little consequence to working class parents and they were quite happy to leave things as they are.' They did not expect educational change to benefit their own children and the idea of comprehensive education had made little or no impact on them. An even balder assessment concluded, 'The survey reveals general satisfaction on the part of the majority of parents with the existing educational system and a lack of desire for change either in the LEA tripartite system or in the private sector...Most of the desires for improvement, with the one exception of larger maintenance grants, reflect middle class values, e.g. more grammar school or public school education.' In other words, Abrams' results pointed to 'a policy argued around conventional educational improvements' such as reducing class sizes rather than 'on manifestly doctrinal or egalitarian grounds', though it was conceded that if argued in 'conventional' terms a comprehensive policy might be 'reasonably popular' with working-class constituents.[50]

In drawing these conclusions, Abrams was skipping over not only the findings of other surveys of his own from the same period but also all the other questions in his Labour party survey. When asked directly a majority had expressed opposition to the 11+ (as in virtually all other surveys of the time), equally across classes. When comprehensive schools were briefly described, a majority favoured them too, especially working-class parents. When the arguments for and against comprehensives and tripartism were rehearsed in a studiedly balanced way, the same majority still favoured comprehensives, and the arguments for comprehensives were particularly approved by working-class parents. As we noted above, in fact two-thirds of parents 'agreed completely' that children should be educated in common schools for the social benefit, and three-quarters agreed at least in part, with working-class parents more strongly in agreement than the middle class. And in fact nearly a majority 'agreed completely' that grammar schools should be closed, a finding Abrams particularly disliked and tried to play down.[51]

No-one challenged Abrams' interpretation of his own findings, and historians have been largely content to repeat them as fact.[52] Importantly they coincided with prejudices rampant in the Labour party, even on the left, about working-class opinion, and encouraged the view that the campaign even for 'grammar schools for all' would be an uphill struggle, albeit a worthy one. In the next few years Stewart went around the country giving speeches at the opening of new comprehensive schools, more or less congratulating LEAs for their bravery in adopting his and his party's new policy, without really considering how long they had been in gestation and what might have been their real drivers. For him, and for much of the party, it was a political decision, taken at the highest levels, at best spearheaded by party true-believers in local government.[53]

More significant, probably, for the ability of LEAs to move towards comprehensive education in the late '50s and early '60s was the less well-known but decisive conversion of the Conservative government to the ordinary voter's 'common sense'. Here the key figures were David Eccles and Edward Boyle, who between the two of them held most of the relevant ministerial portfolios between 1954 and 1964. Eccles in particular was a party heavyweight who had few of the hang-ups about 'public opinion' held by his Labour peers, though his efforts to inform himself on it were rather scattershot. From early in his tenure he was well aware of the unpopularity of the 11+ in a more equal society and the inadequacy of elite selection to serve the needs of a modern economy, that is, democratic as well as technocratic reasons to question the tripartite model.[54] But he and his party were now wedded to the Butler Act, to a tripartite or at least bipartite system, and to some extent to middle-class interests which they saw as bound up with elite selection. The question was how to meet democratic and technocratic needs without superseding the 11+ or 'destroying' grammar schools.

Eccles was torn between expanding the secondary moderns by encouraging their development of O-level courses, but thereby infringing on grammar schools' province, and expanding the grammar schools by increasing transfer to them at 11+, but thereby widening the gap between the two types of education. He was tempted by two-tier schemes which seemed to achieve both, either the 'Leicestershire plan' which postponed transfer to 14 or the 'Croydon model' which postponed it to 16, and under his aegis the former though not the latter was sanctioned when initiatives came from LEAs.[55] But at this point the Ministry did not see it as its job to guide LEAs. It used its powers on a case-by-case basis to prohibit the closure of grammar schools and to block the opening of new comprehensives, but it did not attempt to set general principles for rates of transfer or types of school organization. It did not even know or care very much about what LEAs were thinking or doing, unless applications were made to it under its very specific central powers.[56]

Eccles tried to argue that such decisions about the organization of education *belonged* in the realm of party politics, where fundamental questions of social change and political direction were decided. 'A society which is not interested in its own future', he wrote in mid-1956 in very mid-1950s language, 'would become as unattractive as a woman who never thinks of her waistline...This is real politics and so much more interesting than finance and economics.'

It would be unreal to ask no more than how best to educate a child according to his ability and aptitudes. As politicians we have to consider the wishes of parents, the responsibilities of Local Government, the existing pattern of school buildings and supply of teachers, and the part which education plays in moulding the shape of society.[57]

While Eccles was successful at screwing more money out of the Treasury to upgrade school facilities, he was not so successful in getting his ministerial colleagues (or even his civil servants) to embrace a firm policy line; or perhaps it was simply that he could not decide which policy line to take, given the trade-offs involved. One alternative approach was to commission expert studies, which the Conservative governments did to impressive effect: first, an enquiry commissioned by Eccles in March 1956 into the expansion of post-compulsory education in light of the 'changing social and industrial needs of our society, and the needs of its individual citizens'; followed by an enquiry into the future of higher education, commissioned by the government in December 1960; then a study of the education of those not expected to stay on past school-leaving age, commissioned by Eccles in February 1961; and finally an enquiry into primary education, commissioned by Edward Boyle in July 1963. Only the first reported in time to make an impact on Conservative government policy—the Crowther Report of 1959.[58]

In the meantime, however, popular pressure on the 11+ had heated up enough to reach the highest levels. By late 1957 even the Prime Minister, Harold Macmillan, had noticed that the 11+ was 'very unpopular' and wanted to know what could be done about it. The then Education Minister, Geoffrey Lloyd, laid out the unpleasant alternatives involved in preserving the bipartite system, but having been offered extra money decided it would be well spent, politically, by shoring up the secondary modern schools just at the time the bulge had begun to hit them. This led to a White Paper, 'Secondary Education for All: A New Drive', and a commitment to pump £300 million into new school buildings and equipment. In the immediate post-Suez and post-Sputnik environment, when national competitiveness (in science and technology, and also investment in 'human capital') was at a premium, this would make, Lloyd wrote in a draft sadly not sent to

Macmillan, if 'serve[d] with a dash of Sputnik sauce ... an appetising—and nourishing—political dish!'[59]

Fortunately, the Crowther Report, which appeared just as this policy was rolling out, did not disrupt the party line too badly. While acknowledging 'increased public clamour against a competitive element in grammar school selection', they blamed this on the bulge more than the trend, and surprisingly played down the trend, still rather doubtful about actual levels of popular demand for post-compulsory education, though of course direct evidence for this was limited by the barrier posed by the 11+. In contrast, the Robbins Report on higher education a few years later not only based much of its recommendations for expanded post-18 opportunities on the established trend but also was bold enough to project it forward to the end of the century and beyond. Crowther, conveniently for the government, doubted that there was as yet sufficient demand for expanded opportunities after 15, and argued that any expansion would have to be gently engineered 'from the top downwards'. Instead the Report chimed in with the post-Suez drive for 'national investment' in modern schools and expanded opportunities on that arm of the bipartite system for technical and possibly academic education. Less conveniently, it did recognize—as Eccles had done—that such a continued reinforcement of academic education in the modern sector was likely to doom the bipartite system sooner rather than later.[60] Eccles, restored to the education portfolio, received Crowther warmly. He had half-expected Crowther to recommend a radical reorganization; gratifyingly, he had instead fallen into step with government's emphasis on investment.[61] That emphasis, Lloyd had crowed to Macmillan, had 'taken the sting out of the 11+ controversy' by highlighting 'national needs' rather than parental choice.[62] Even the Chief Inspector of Schools assured the government that its new policy, 'designed to preserve and develop the existing system', was relieving 'anxiety and sense of grievance' among parents and pupils by expanding opportunity inside secondary moderns without challenging the 11+ or destroying any grammar schools.[63]

That assurance could only be maintained, however, by ignorance or wilful disregard of the effects of public pressure on LEAs. Both were in operation. It is important to emphasize how little the Ministry knew about what LEAs were doing. They stumbled upon this knowledge almost by accident in the early 1960s. They had been aware in the late 1950s of a growing accumulation of applications from LEAs to open new comprehensives, and had been more liberal in their approvals; the number approved had ballooned from around 30 in 1956 to 120 in 1959. By then a wave of new applications was pending and civil servants were no longer sure what the ministerial line on them was. Nor was it even possible to say how many comprehensives were in the offing.[64] Secondary modern schools that had added an O-level stream were often doing much more than expanding 'opportunities' for their students, as the White Paper had imagined—they were comprehensives in waiting.[65] By 1960 civil servants were warning that there were many more comprehensive schemes than ministers might be aware of, converting schools in ways that did not require Ministry permission or even notification. The £300 million of new money released by the White Paper for improving schools was in reality likely to be used to reorganize them into a comprehensive system.[66] The 'really serious risk', wrote one, was the spread of Leicestershire-type two-tier schemes, motivated as the Chief Inspector Schools noted by 'external pressures'—by which he meant parental choice! This was indeed the point where he warned that the 11+ could not survive the day when parents' wishes gained a hearing.[67] But not even the Chief Inspector had much of a handle on the pattern across England and Wales. Proposals to survey educationists to determine the extent of re-organization were abandoned for fear of drawing attention to the Leicestershire plan and accelerating the pace of change.[68]

It took an urgent query from the Catholic Church at the end of 1963, concerned about the fate of their own grammar schools, for Eccles' successor, Edward Boyle, finally to authorize a systematic survey of LEA plans. The civil servants and school inspectors were shocked at what they found. The 'infection' had spread much further than they imagined. Almost three-quarters of LEAs in England had plans, some tentative, some already in train, for comprehensive reorganization. These were about equally split between 11–18 comprehensives, requiring merger of bipartite schools or new buildings, and Leicestershire or Croydon two-tier plans, rebadging grammar schools as senior high schools at 14, 15, or 16.[69] As Wilma Harte, a civil servant, explained to Boyle:

> The impetus to abandon the old-fashioned tri- or bipartite pattern comes from a number of sources. There seems to be a growing acceptance of the idea that selection at 11+ is just wrong - inefficient, unjust, wasteful, socially objectionable, out-of-date. There is also, though far from widespread, some growth of feeling among authorities that what parents want for their children in the way of education ought to affect what they get. There are a number of new Labour controlled authorities who are tired of waiting for a comprehensive

system, who see that at present rates of school building it will be a long time before their existing plant can be replaced with new purpose built comprehensive schools and so they are determined to do something to get rid of selection and all that entails with the buildings they have got. Hence many of the two-tier schemes whose forms are dictated by the availability of existing school buildings...[70]

That was the view from Whitehall. It certainly flattered the Ministry to think that there had only recently been a 'growth of feeling' against the 11+, which was as yet 'far from widespread'. Boyle himself later argued that it had only been around 1960 that parental opinion—which he considered to be mostly middle class (in part reflecting his natural focus on his own party's base)—had begun to tell against the 11+, and only in 1962 or 1963 that expert opinion had made it clear (at least to him) that the 'pool of ability' was not fixed.[71] In his introduction to the Newsom Report, released in 1963, he—a Conservative Minister—had embraced the principle of equal provision: 'The essential point is that all children should have an equal opportunity of acquiring intelligence, and of developing their talents and abilities to the full', that is not, the equal opportunity to demonstrate intelligence at 11 but the equal opportunity to cultivate intelligence through the school-leaving age.[72] As he later told it, only then was 'the nation's conscience' stirred to extend opportunity.[73] But by then it was practically too late, in two senses—most LEAs had already come to that conclusion themselves, and the Conservatives were out of office, finally ousted by 'public opinion' in the General Election of 1964.

From this point of view, it is the already well-established plans of LEAs rather than, in most cases, the Labour government's directives to plan for comprehensive reorganization that explain the spread of common schooling in the 1960s and '70s throughout the whole of the country. Michael Stewart took up the education portfolio in the new government; he was now Secretary of State for Education and Science, following the relabelling of the Ministry as the Department of Education and Science (DES) just before the election. His first inclination was to legislate but ultimately he and his Cabinet colleagues agreed not to compel LEAs but to direct them to do what most of them were doing already; by his estimate LEAs covering nearly two-thirds of secondary-age children were already on a path to comprehensive reorganization and only a quarter were as yet unplanned.[74] The main change was from ministers unwilling to endorse an end to the 11+, though willing to accept it, to ministers willing to do both.[75]

By an accident of fate, an emergency reshuffle of the Cabinet then dropped this task into the lap of Tony Crosland. There are still many people who believe that Crosland 'abolished' the grammar schools, or 'imposed' comprehensives.[76] He did nothing of the sort. Much of this mythology was generated by later controversies over school organization. Even his most famous line—'If it's the last thing I do, I'm going to destroy every fucking grammar school in England. And Wales. And Northern Ireland' (not Scotland because that was the province of the SED)—was not known until 1982, after his death, when this private observation to his wife was first reported in her memoir.[77]

In reality, Circular 10/65—issued in July 1965—simply asked LEAs to present development plans along the lines a majority had already prepared or were preparing. Either two-tier systems or 11–18 comprehensive systems were acceptable, so long as they secured comprehensive education to the school-leaving age. Circular 600, in Scotland, did something similar but it did appear to steer Scottish schools more towards the 11–18 model than its English and Welsh equivalent.[78] Replicating existing plans in this way meant for an initially smooth and rapid transition. Wales and Scotland naturally made easiest work of the task. In Wales, grammars had expanded to take in 34 per cent of the cohort, a further 12 per cent were already in comprehensives, and many moderns had long been comprehensives in waiting. Nine of the 13 Welsh counties and all 4 of its county boroughs had prepared comprehensive schemes by 1964. Nearly half the school population was in comprehensives by 1969.[79] Similarly Scotland had already 40 per cent of its population in exam certificate courses and nearly half in schools with comprehensive intakes at least to 14. By 1971 nearly two-thirds of students were in two-tier or all-through comprehensives and by 1974 85 per cent in all-through comprehensives.[80]

Yet even in England, within two years the great majority of LEAs had already submitted comprehensive development plans that were implemented or approved, though of course in many cases it took some years for purpose-built schools to be completed for full implementation of these schemes.[81] As Kerckhoff showed, they proceeded 'from the bottom up', starting with rebadging of the many secondary moderns in working-class neighbourhoods that had been comprehensives in waiting, already offering O-level courses anyway. More secondary moderns were 'abolished' in this first stage, unsurprisingly, than grammar schools.[82] As Stewart pointed out, 'Nobody has come forward to say, "Save the secondary modern schools."'[83]

Though there was a good deal of organized resistance by parent lobbies in grammar-school areas, this imbalance gradually evened out, especially in the early 1970s, when famously Margaret Thatcher 'abolished' more grammar schools in her tenure than any other education minister. The transition to comprehensive education was more or less complete by the end of the 1970s, when over 90 per cent of state school students were enrolled in comprehensives (see Appendix, Figure 4.1). This twenty-year transition is comparable to the same period in Sweden, though more reliant on drivers from the 'bottom up'. West Germany, in contrast, opened no comprehensives until 1968 and was educating fewer than 16 per cent of the age cohort in them by the end of the 1970s.[84]

In most places, comprehensive education proved popular. As Abrams had discovered in the late 1950s, the more people knew about, and especially the more they experienced comprehensive education, the more they liked it. In the 1960s, more people knew about it, more experienced it, and more approved of it. In a 1967 survey that Abrams did for *New Society* magazine, one-third of his sample lived in comprehensive areas, and of those nearly three-quarters favoured comprehensives, including 85 per cent of parents with children enrolled in them. In these areas, comprehensives were deemed the 'best schools' and had thus inherited the former status of the grammars. Of those who still lived in bipartite areas, opinion on the 11+ was evenly divided but three-quarters were against the abolition of grammar schools. 'Respondents were not voting against grammar education', was the analysis, 'they were voting—massively—against secondary modern education.'[85] Opinion polls of the period showed consistent majorities in favour of comprehensive reorganization.[86]

Another particularly revealing insight into public opinion can be gained from those LEAs that were divided over comprehensive reorganization and polled their voters in referenda to determine their views. Such referenda were only held in areas with strong middle-class traditions of grammar-school attendance—Eton, Slough and Amersham in Buckinghamshire; Gloucester; Cardiganshire; Leicester; Barnet in London. Where a straight question was asked about ending selection, very large majorities supported it: three-quarters in Barnet and Cardigan, two-thirds in Eton, Slough and Amersham. Gloucester's more complicated ballot gave a mixed verdict but most votes went to full comprehensivization or to the LEA's plan for some comprehensives and mostly bipartite schools. Even so, some LEAs ignored the vote.

Buckinghamshire retained the bipartite system for the entire county. Barnet became the site of a political tug-of-war that continues practically to this day.[87]

Despite these pretty ringing endorsements by parents and voters of the day, there lingers the impression that comprehensive reorganization was partial, contested, and, ultimately, disappointing. Much of this impression was formed later, around later controversies, which we will encounter in due course. But there were plenty of vocal opponents on both left and right to offer this critique at the time, and historians to endorse it subsequently. On the right, especially, the fight-back against the 'destruction' of grammar schools began almost immediately, and it was quickly forgotten how Conservative LEAs had led the charge to abolish the 11+. Boyle became the 'betrayer'.[88] Rearguard actions in a small number of LEAs through the 1970s and '80s were heroized and blown out of proportion, given the modest number of grammar schools (and secondary moderns) that survived the 1970s.[89] On the left, advocates of comprehensive reorganization saw the 'bottom-up' transition as a lost opportunity. No revolutionary new departure in secondary education had been struck; inequality had not been cut off at its roots. Two-tier systems retained selection at 15 or 16. Grammar-school ethos 11–18 comprehensives imported too much of the grammar school ethos, with their academic and non-academic streams recreating the bipartite system inside the school. A new 'second-class' exam, the Certificate of Secondary Education (CSE), planned for modern schools from the late 1950s, was now on offer in comprehensives alongside GCE O-level, perfectly bisecting the school on meritocratic lines. Comprehensives in reality were dismissed as ingenious new tools of social control by the professional middle classes, accelerating rather than impeding Young's 'rise of the meritocracy'.[90]

This is greatly to underestimate the significance of the transition to comprehensive education, and the way in which it successfully channelled public opinion in aligning the state school system much better with social changes already afoot and with the social and political expectations of the mass of the public.[91] Comprehensive schools borrowed from *both* secondary and grammar traditions and developed new styles of their own. They introduced new curricula—'social studies', for example, and more field and project work—and a new informality in relations between students and teachers. Some adopted grammar-school uniforms, prefects, 'house' organization; many others did not. Some recreated the tripartite system by 'streaming'; but over time many others experimented with mixed-ability teaching, especially to age 14, or 'setted' rather than 'streamed', allowing for different ability classifications for different subjects.[92] Comprehensives were much more likely than bipartite schools to offer mixed-sex education and to foster new opportunities for girls: just as abolishing the 11+ revealed pent-up demand for staying on, so co-education revealed pent-up demand for girls' education and careers.[93] Like the new hospitals also going up in the 1960s, their distinctive modern styles in glass and steel and concrete bespoke a new era of affluence and social security for all. For many they came to seem like other 'classless' commodities emerging in this period which had borrowed from both working-class and middle-class cultures and neither, and appealed to people of all backgrounds—football, jeans and dungarees, rock music, home improvements, indoor swimming and 'keep fit', foreign travel, TVs and transistor radios.[94] As 'community' or 'neighbourhood' institutions, they bolstered local identity formerly divided by selection, and in many places they also opened up more room for 'parent power', beginning a slow devolution downwards from LEAs.[95]

Above all, they had brought to an end the clearly undemocratic ordeal of a public examination at 11+ which then allocated children to 'better' or 'worse' schools, largely in line with their social background. Primary schools had always been neighbourhood schools, but they had also been fraught sites of academic and social selection; now they mostly became 'feeders' to neighbourhood secondary schools.[96] Those schools continued, of course, to be socially segregated on a residential basis.[97] Comprehensive reorganization did not create a classless society, but that was always an unreasonable expectation to heap upon schools, as the '50s sociologists who pointed out the significance of home as much as school to inequality had known all along.[98] When given a choice, most people preferred a neighbourhood school to larger catchments aimed at better social and ethnic integration.[99] Nevertheless, in general systems that allocate students according to residence tend to be *less* socially segregated than systems that allocate them according to academic ability, i.e. prior attainment. So Britain's comprehensive system ended up as unequal, and more unequal than Sweden's or Norway's, but less unequal in this respect than the selective systems—Germany's, for example—with which it is most often compared.[100] In that sense, neighbourhood schools satisfy democratic aspirations for equal provision imperfectly, but better than schools based on meritocratic selection, which tend only to reproduce social hierarchy.

Even if equality of outcome was not achieved, it mattered a lot to parents that the provision of schools was formally equal across all groups, at least for the period of compulsory schooling. The comprehensive school unleashed the world of choice that had been denied to most by the 11+: parents in comprehensives were much more likely, regardless of social class, to want their children to have the option of staying on after 15, to take exams, to aspire to further and higher education.[101] After school-leaving age—15 to 1972, 16 thereafter—there was still often selection for these qualifications on a 'meritocratic' basis. But even that post-compulsory selection was coming under searching democratic scrutiny.

5

The Robbins Principle

Unlike compulsory secondary education, higher education seems unassailably to be the province of meritocracy rather than democracy, of 'aptitude and ability' rather than equal provision or even popular demand. Before the Second World War no European country enrolled more than a few per cent of its age cohort in higher education—the measure is commonly referred to as Age Participation Rate (APR)—about 2–3 per cent in Britain, France, and Germany.[1] The United States, by far the world's pioneer in extending participation in higher education, reached 30 per cent APR on the back of the GI Bill in 1949.[2] Even in Korea today, with the highest APR in the world—73 per cent of 19-year-olds are enrolled in tertiary education—there is not only differentiation within but selection for higher education, with a substantial proportion of the population still dropping out of education altogether at that age.[3] Most such selection takes place on the basis of academic achievement in secondary school or public examinations at or after the school-leaving age or both. Across the twentieth century, then, judgements of merit have seemed to rule.

Needless to say, it's never been as simple as that. Before the war, when judgements of merit were largely based on assumptions of inherited capacity, there was thought to be a natural 'ceiling' on access to higher education, at somewhere around 5 per cent of the population (the proportion of Scottish students then completing the secondary course). After the war, when all of a sudden 'national needs' seemed to require a larger cadre of highly skilled technicians to boost economic growth, especially in light of intensified international competition, this natural ceiling magically lifted.[4] (The American example was not automatically persuasive to everyone—many felt US higher education didn't deserve the name, equivalent to the British sixth form or even lower.[5]) There ensued a national debate about how to balance 'ability and aptitude' against 'national needs'—in the language we've been using, meritocracy against technocracy. But democracy was not left out of the equation, even in that debate. There was a new belief that investment in workers' capacities—perhaps all workers' capacities—could contribute as much if not more as investment in technology: 'human' rather than 'fixed' capital. We have seen that belief already in the Conservative government's willingness to invest much more in secondary education in the late 1950s, though still only in education appropriate to different abilities and aptitudes.

Yet once the greater educability of all was acknowledged—and especially as the notion of a fixed 'pool of ability' was questioned in the late 1950s—then the door was open to much higher rates of progression beyond compulsory education, to O-levels, A-levels, what was called 'advanced further education', and higher education itself. At this point the 'bulge' and the 'trend' again came into play. More people evidently *could* qualify for further and higher education—more people evidently *wished* to. To what extent, then, should access to higher education be determined not merely by 'aptitude and ability', or even by national needs, but also by *demand*? The bulge hit higher education naturally some years later—in 1963, rather than 1956—and the idea of popular educability had moved on; not only the idea, but the practice, as O-level attainment rates were reaching 40 per cent and comprehensive education promised higher levels still. For these reasons, Britain found itself embracing in 1963 a demand-led higher education system practically at the same time as government was finally coming to accept the pressure of demand in secondary education. The difference between the Butler Act in 1944 and the Robbins Report in 1963 tells us a lot about the distance travelled. The Butler Act had pinned everything on 'aptitude and ability', and more or less assumed a fixed quota of about 25 per cent judged capable of post-compulsory education. In the Robbins Report government embraced what became known as the Robbins Principle—that higher education should be made 'available for *all* those who are qualified by ability and attainment to pursue them *and who wish to do so*' (emphasis added)—and assumed that the numbers qualified and willing would continue to grow for the foreseeable future.[6]

The Techno-State, the Bulge, and the Trend

Like most European systems, the British higher-education system at the end of the Second World War was small, compact, and very much oriented to elites. Oxford and Cambridge provided socialization and education mostly to established social elites—over half their students had attended fee-paying schools, the balance made up of state grammar-school students recruited on the roughly meritocratic basis of examination results. As usual, this meant gross under-representation of working-class students, who formed about 10 per cent of the Oxbridge student body after the war.[7] The proportion was higher, though still not high—25 per cent overall—in the 21 other universities scattered around the UK, older Scottish foundations and the English 'Redbrick' universities.[8] They mostly catered to a non-elite middle-class constituency, often seeking socialization in their own provincial milieux. As yet, there were few professions that required or even expected a university degree, medicine being the conspicuous exception. A very high proportion of non-Oxbridge university graduates became schoolteachers—a majority in some institutions—indicating that university graduates in this period were a rather unusually academic slice of the middle classes. A famous take on the English 'Redbrick' universities in 1943 called them 'a kind of preparatory school to the Department of Education'.[9] A minority of graduates went into technical and managerial posts in industry—jobs which mostly still did not require degrees, but for which the student experience sometimes provided networking as well as intellectual advantages.[10] All in all, universities remained on the margins of national life. Only one interwar Prime Minister, Stanley Baldwin, had gone to university. As John Carswell drily put it, 'The universities did not occupy a large place in the consciousness of the nation as a whole, for whom they came to the surface only in sporting events such as the Boat Race—and then it was only Oxford and Cambridge.'[11]

If that began to change after the war, the rising profile seems at first to have been driven not by the welfare state but by what we might call the techno-state,[12] the alter-ego of the welfare state. The idea that the state should take a growing role in boosting economic growth was embraced both by the left—which as we have seen was at first most focused on raising production levels, to provide full employment and rising living standards but also to pay for the welfare state—and by the right—which saw it as a potential ally for private enterprise. The higher-education sector would have grown after the war anyway, as a short-term 'bulge' of returning servicemen made up for lost time; to prepare for this, the Treasury allocation to the University Grants Committee (UGC) was doubled in 1945.[13] But the postwar Labour government was determined to give it a bigger boost as part of its productivity drive. The 1945 Percy Report on Higher Technological Education and the 1946 Barlow Report on Scientific Manpower recommended measures to increase the flow of scientists and technologists through higher education. The grant doubled again between 1945 and 1951.[14]

Labour saw higher education very much in terms of national economic planning. The UGC, which had begun after the First World War as a relatively simple machine to disburse modest sums of public monies to universities, now took on a planning function, 'in order to ensure that they are fully adequate to national needs', as the Treasury put it in 1946.[15] This was the point that the limit of 5 per cent APR imagined to mark the extent of 'aptitude' for higher education—only just set by Barlow in 1946—began magically to lift. The doubling of science and technology graduates recommended as a 10-year target by Barlow had already been achieved by 1947 and the UGC was in no doubt that higher targets had now to be set to meet 'national needs': 'If this country is to maintain its place in the world it cannot afford to fall behind in the pursuit and application of new knowledge.'[16]

The Conservatives when they came into power in 1951 were less enthusiastic about manpower planning but continued to believe that an increased flow of talent into scientific and technological education was necessary to keep up Britain's place in the world. A Committee on Scientific Manpower was established in 1951 to monitor the situation and in 1956 made its first attempt at a long-term forecast, projecting a 4 per cent per annum rate of economic growth and simply assuming that a 4 per cent per annum growth of scientific education was necessary to sustain it.[17] At first such forecasts required little planning to bring them about. There was sufficient demand to keep higher education expanding without government direction and there was a small 'swing to science' in subject choice among students across the 1950s. Attention was more congenially paid to the training of an elite within an elite. Eric James, the High Master of Manchester Grammar School, the most selective of direct grant schools, made a meritocratic appeal for special attention to the top 1 per cent, the future leaders of economy and society.[18] The Industrial Fund for the Advancement of Scientific Education in Schools set up in 1955 made grants only to direct-grant and independent schools. The Nuffield Foundation's programme to modernize science curricula in schools also focused on elite secondaries, the 'best minds', though state grammar schools were at least included.[19] As the Prime Minister, Anthony Eden, put it in 1956, 'The prizes will not go to the countries with the largest population. Those with the best systems of education will win. Science and technical skills give a dozen men the power to do as much as thousands did fifty years ago ... we shall need many more scientists, engineers and technicians.'[20]

The deeper we get into the 1950s, however, the wider this approach to investing in scientific and technological education gets. David Eccles was again a motivating force. The Percy Report had already recommended expansion and upgrading of those technical colleges run by LEAs that were providing 'advanced further education' (that is, post-A-level but sub-degree level), to encompass university-type courses—unfortunately using the dread word 'parity', and storing up trouble for the future.[21] In a White Paper on technological education in 1956, Eccles took this project in hand and created a new tier of Colleges of Advanced Technology (CATs), which duly became universities in the 1960s. In 1959 the government created the first-ever Minister for Science, Lord Hailsham, who proved a doughty ally to Eccles in screwing ever larger sums for education out of the Treasury; public expenditure on higher education alone expanded 50 per cent between 1959 and 1963. Whereas before the war the state covered less than half of universities' income, by 1963 it had reached 80 per cent.[22] Just before the 1964 election, the profitable connection that had been made between education and science was consecrated with the renaming of the Ministry of Education as the Department of Education and Science (DES), a label it retained until 1992.

One of the forces that impelled the Treasury to release its funds to education was the growing sense—panic, really—of international competition and the need to find ingenious new ways to keep up. As Germany and France recovered after the war, and especially as the global competition between the U.S. and the Soviet Union heated up—and most especially after 1957 when the Russians' launch of the Sputnik satellite triggered the 'space race'—Britain had a creeping dread of 'relative decline'.[23] Education, principally technological education (which was mostly higher education), was the beneficiary. It is at this point that international statistics began to be collected tracking various countries' performance in educating their populace, with a special interest in science and technology. The Organisation for Economic Co-Operation and Development (OECD), which had originated as a Marshall Plan advisory body after the war, was refounded in 1961 and became the source of regular benchmarks against which advanced economies measured themselves, as they still do today.[24] International comparisons were slung around with gay abandon, usually to advocate a policy based on Britain's alleged backwardness. Even the normally sober-sided A. H. Halsey was playing this game when he claimed in 1958 that 'England has probably less university students per thousand of the population than any other industrial country.' When the Robbins Report looked into this a few years later, it found that Britain's 5 per cent APR was higher than West Germany and the Netherlands, comparable to Australia, New Zealand, and Switzerland, and not far short of the USSR and Sweden, though lower than France and of course well behind the US and Canada.[25]

One line of reasoning for more investment in education that appealed strongly to the Treasury emerged at the end of the 1950s: the idea of 'human capital', more or less the economists' equivalent (in terms of original contribution to the educational debate) to the sociologists' ideas about the 'pool of ability'. Rooted in the free-market economics of Theodore Schultz and Gary Becker of the University of Chicago, human-capital theory posited that investments in workers' skills made as good a return in economic growth as investment in 'fixed' capital such as plant or technology. Schultz estimated that one-fifth of the American economy's growth between 1929 and 1957 came from schooling.[26] Becker thought that the returns on higher education had been rising since the 1940s and by the 1960s represented a rate of return as high as 11–13 per cent for white American men.[27]

These arguments were not entirely new, of course. We have seen them in embryo in the arguments for investment in education for 'national efficiency' dating back to the 1890s, and advanced most forcefully by Fabian socialists. A social-democratic version gained strength in the 1940s when 'positive eugenics', family-welfare advocates and architects of the social services like Richard Titmuss all argued for investments in health and education as just as crucial for economic growth as direct capital investments in nationalized industry.[28] Clement Attlee, not a Chicago economist, was the pioneer of the use of the term 'human capital', in this sense, in political discourse.[29] What made the new, Chicago-style understanding of 'human capital' more appealing to the Conservatives a decade later was not only that it justified investments in education—naturally attractive to the likes of Eccles and Hailsham—but also that it took some of the burden off the state. Schultz and Becker argued that much—perhaps half—of the return on investment in education was realized by the educated individuals, in the form of higher wages—the 'graduate premium', as it became known.[30] This 'private' as opposed to 'social' return ought to induce individuals to invest in their own higher education rather than to rely on the state. Suddenly economists were in much demand in government circles, to help balance the different considerations of private returns and social returns, as well as the prior concern with 'national needs' for scientific and technological manpower.[31]

Human-capital theory allowed Conservative politicians to advocate for the kind of ambitious educational expansion that we have already seen Eccles embracing in the late '50s. It lay at least in some measure behind the Crowther Report of 1959 and the White Paper of 1958 which authorized the release of considerable sums for school building. But the Treasury was happier about human-capital arguments applied to higher than to secondary education, for a number of reasons. First, the expense of the latter was much greater, and the idea that high rates of return might justify high rates of increase in the schools budget was daunting. Second, unlike schools universities lay within the Treasury's own remit. They had an established relationship with the UGC and a system of quinquennial grants which were not so vulnerable to sudden rushes of blood to the heads of politicians. Third, unlike schooling, which was compulsory to age 15 and free normally to age 18, universities had a more realistic prospect of drawing on private funding. Although fee-paying had been in decline since the war, when most LEAs had assumed responsibility for funding their students' university fees (with central grant), human-capital calculations argued that future funding formulae for higher education ought to apportion between private and social returns.[32]

The most important long-term effect of human-capital theory was to draw attention away from education as a consumption good—something people valued because it made for a better life, a more equal society, a fuller sense of citizenship—and fix it in politicians' minds at least as an investment good—something that made the economy grow. Schultz claimed he did not see it as a zero-sum game: 'The consumption benefits from schooling are not any the less valuable merely because it becomes known that there are also other benefits from schooling which increase future production and earnings.'[33] But that is not how it turned out. Economists have focused more and more on the relationship between education and economic growth, and politicians have moved with them, such that the 'public nature' of education has become progressively obscured over time. We will chart the progress of this shift amongst experts and policymakers, though not necessarily amongst voters, over time in the next chapters.[34]

In the 1950s and '60s, however, as yet human-capital theory—still less private returns—was not carrying all before it. Indeed, the techno-state was all along well aware that the calculations it was making about manpower needs and then educational investments were not even the most important drivers of educational expansion. Something else, for example, was responsible for the Barlow target of 1946 being met in 1947 rather than 1956. This something else was our old friends the bulge and the trend. Though less visible to historians than the techno-state—and so less likely to figure prominently in explanations for the expansion of higher education—they provided just as much as in secondary education the principal motor for growth in the postwar decades.[35]

Though higher-education numbers were naturally much lower than secondary numbers, the effects of the bulge were proportionately just as great and just as predictable: that is to say, the number of 18-year-olds would expand at the same rate as the number of 11-year-olds, just seven years later, and even without the trend would need to be accommodated in due proportion. As the bulge continued through the 1950s, planners knew that higher-education places would need to be expanded, almost doubled due to the bulge alone. So in addition to planning for new sub-university places, for example through the CATs, plans were already afoot in the late '50s to build new universities, resulting in the celebrated English 7 'plateglass' universities—Sussex, East Anglia, York, Lancaster, Essex, Kent, and Warwick—that opened between 1961 and 1965. In addition a number of older foundations had been already promoted to full university status, and, as William Whyte has pointed out, all of the older Redbrick universities expanded as well. Leeds and Manchester trebled in size in the postwar decades. Just as secondary modern schools were turned into comprehensives-in-waiting, 'Redbrick' universities turned into brick-and-plateglass ones. Sussex and East Anglia are famous for their modern university buildings, but so are Nottingham and Leicester.[36]

While the bulge was relatively predictable, and not thought to be endless, the trend was neither. Contemporaries at first paid less attention to the trend in higher education than in secondary education, because it seemed further away and more implausible, as access to higher education was still regulated by a quota on access to grammar school. Nevertheless, there were indications across the social spectrum of very high aspiration to higher education. Abrams' survey for the sociologist W. G. Runciman in 1962 found that more than 80 per cent of both working-class and middle-class parents wanted university for their children if qualified and so inclined. This confirmed his earlier finding, for the Labour party survey in 1957, about a hypothetical child aged 17–18 who was capable of higher education: half of all working-class parents said they wished they would go to university and only 10 per cent preferred immediate employment at that stage, because, they held, university offered a better chance in life, access to professional occupations, and, inevitably, because it was just 'the best sort of education'. Goldthorpe's 1962 study similarly found 'affluent' working-class parents eager to support their children's choice to go to university, if they qualified. Both Abrams and the 1946 birth-cohort study noticed a bellwether for the future: mothers of all classes who had had secondary education or white-collar jobs themselves were more likely to favour university education for their children. While Abrams thought this a middle-class 'infection', albeit one to be encouraged, it also pointed to the great transformation that universal secondary education was sooner rather than later to visit upon attitudes to higher education.[37]

The main difference, as Goldthorpe noted, between working-class and middle-class parents was not aspiration but attainment—the former were much less likely to attain the aspiration of higher education for their children. Their aspirations had already mostly been curtailed at 11+. Middle-class parents, whose children mostly passed the 11+, were more likely to have their aspirations curtailed at 16 or 18. Thus while the trend in secondary education put primarily working-class pressure on the educational supply, the trend in higher education applied primarily middle-class pressure. Although middle-class participation in higher education rose rapidly after the war—from 8.4 per cent of all non-manual offspring in 1940 to 18.5 per cent in 1950 and 26.7 per cent in 1960—there was still plenty of room for further growth, and as participation rates reached these higher levels they must have raised reasonable expectations of access to higher education still further.[38]

Unlike secondary education, there were few political or even expert voices to articulate (or to explain) the trend in higher education to policy-makers or to wider publics. There was no equivalent to Crosland or Young to challenge 'meritocracy' in the realm of higher education. The most articulate new voices, as we have seen, were economists serving the techno-state who zeroed in on the supply rather than the demand side, mostly to support manpower planning, on the principle that 'there "ought" to be a greater demand for technologists from industry'.[39] Human-capital theory, while it should have been more sensitive to demand (albeit on a very narrow and highly suppositious basis of predicted private return), was also still very much focused on the supply side: public investments to reap future GDP returns. Most public attention remained focused on the elite.

If there *was* a higher-education analogue to Crosland or Young, it was C. P. Snow's *The Two Cultures* (1959), and the ensuing debate with the literary critic F. R. Leavis. Snow's critique of contemporary education was that Oxbridge remained too focused on the arts.[40] 'Declinist' literature, such as Anthony Sampson's *The Anatomy of Britain*, voiced the same concern.[41] Snow (Cambridge) and Sampson (Oxford) were not wrong: Oxbridge *was* dominated by arts graduates. But neither they nor Leavis (Cambridge) showed much interest in most students at most universities, who were predominantly non-Oxbridge and taking science degrees, both sectors that were expanding in this period while relatively speaking Oxbridge and arts degrees were not.[42]

Another, rather more perverse defence of elite values—one of the best-known political responses to the growth of demand for higher education from this period—was one which paradoxically had least purchase at the time, the self-described 'lone voice' of a renegade socialist, Kingsley Amis. 'MORE will mean WORSE', Amis predicted in a short rhetorical blast in the magazine *Encounter* in July 1960, rejecting both the human-capital arguments and the sociological arguments for expansion. Like Snow and Leavis, he had protection of the upper reaches of the higher-education system firmly in mind, though he scorned both Snow's utilitarianism and Leavis's nostalgia. Expanding higher education just because more people wanted it was courting disaster. World-class universities would become like 'a rather less glamorous and authentic [teacher] training college'—a significantly feminized indictment. Unlike 'cars or tins of salmon', university students couldn't be indefinitely multiplied based on 'desire' rather than 'capacity'. Like 'poems or bottles of hock', 'you cannot *decide* to have more good ones'. But while Amis's words would resonate increasingly with Conservative dissidents from the national consensus from the 1960s to the 1980s (though not much beyond), they seemed puzzlingly—indeed, deliberately—counter-cyclical in 1960, an unfashionably frank embrace of meritocracy based on a fixed (and small) 'pool of ability'.[43]

A partial exception to the lack of serious discussion of mass higher education in this period was John Vaizey, Labour's principal expert on the economics of education. Vaizey was hardly immune to the lures of manpower planning and human-capital theory, and he spent most of his career in Oxbridge.[44] But he was also close to the sociologists Halsey and Floud, and to Crosland and Young, all of whom had a lively sensitivity to growing demand and to the social and cultural benefits that flowed from it. People wanted education, he argued, for those benefits and not only for economic advancement; it was a consumption as much as an investment good. And the more people who were given a broad general education, rather than a narrow technical one, the better for society, in terms of cohesion, equality, and well-being. 'In other words', Vaizey wrote in a 1959 report he co-authored with Halsey, 'we accept the phrase "equal opportunity" but interpret opportunity more generously than usual', as not just opportunity for personal advancement but for the making of 'an educative society' and 'a nation of individuals trained to do more than meet the demands of economics'. But Vaizey's was a pretty lonely voice, even in Labour circles. He failed to make much headway with Michael Stewart and manpower-planning considerations continued to dominate, especially when Harold Wilson took the leadership after Gaitskell's death.[45]

Even more than in the case of secondary education, then, demand for higher education outside the elite registered belatedly, as a practical problem which had suddenly to be tackled, rather than as an acknowledged political force that had to be accommodated all along the way. As with the 11+, the key was observed behaviour in the form of higher staying-on rates. Although the 11+ put a cap on staying-on, even so there was a sudden surge in staying-on when the bulge hit secondary school after 1956, when its annual rate of growth increased from 5 per cent to 7.5 per cent. Within the grammar-school population, as more middle-class students took O and A-levels, and as more moved on to higher education, employers who had previously recruited credentialed school-leavers at 16 or 18 began to have to recruit later, at 18 or 21, and the relevant credential was now more widely thought to be a degree and not just O and A-levels. A university degree no longer led inevitably to a teaching career; a much wider range of occupations, including local government, the law, and social services, could now be expected and a wider pool of potential applicants accordingly tempted.[46] As more secondary moderns started to offer O-levels, putting working-class teenagers too on this escalator, there was a danger that the 'infection' as Abrams called it might spread further. Comprehensive reorganization threatened to throw open the floodgates. Taking the bulge into account as well, numbers of O-level entrants rose 10 per cent per annum in 1955–8 but 15 per cent per annum in 1961–3.[47]

Panicky planners who had thought that the CATs, the English 7 and existing institutions would suffice to meet the bulge had to rethink.[48] There was also evidence that the forms of education dictated by the techno-state were not matching up well with the trend of demand. While university-type courses such as offered by the CATs were still in demand, sub-university courses aimed at building 'human capital' in technical skills were not. 'Further education' was not rated 'the best sort of education' in the way that higher education was. We have seen this tendency already in widespread scepticism about technical schools and colleges as alternatives to grammar school. Full-time further education in technical colleges grew only slowly after the war, though part-time further education flourished in the form of 'sandwich' courses with employers providing day release for part-time study. Teenagers were happy to go to 'the tech' as part of their job; but they were less happy to go to 'the tech' as a substitute for A-levels and university. Girls, in particular, a slowly growing proportion of stayers-on, were not at all attracted to the technical alternative, and to cater to them more general A-level courses were offered to prepare them for jobs in offices, as teachers, and in the health service. Far from representing some snobby 'academic drift' based on middle-class norms away from useful technical education, this instinct reflected continuing suspicion of second-class choices for working-class students, especially for girls, as well as awareness of a steadily diversifying labour market, where general academic qualifications were more valuable than narrowly defined 'vocational' ones.[49]

Thus the effects of the trend were felt politically, if belatedly, in higher just as much as in secondary education. The 'pinch', where supply failed to meet demand, came not only at 11+, but also at 18+. Participation rates (APR) in higher education had begun to accelerate in 1957, peaking at 8.3 per cent, but stalled in 1959, as the number of higher-education places available was not keeping up with the demand at 18.[50] There was evidence that qualified applicants were being turned away—bad for the economy, politicians thought, but also bad for them politically, representing more 'frustration' amongst the electorate. The refusal of a university place to a qualified applicant was quite as blatant and infuriating to parents as the refusal of an opportunity to progress to grammar school at 11+. As an ageing Chuter Ede put it in Parliament in 1961, 'the new row about 11-plus will be nothing to the row that will arise over 18-plus'.[51] Another participation rate—the 'Qualified Participation Rate' (QPR), or proportion of those qualified for higher education (defined as possessing two A-levels) who got places—loomed into view. A low QPR betokened rising frustration, and Britain's was falling fast—from 82 per cent to 60 per cent between 1954 and 1966 according to the OECD.[52] A full-scale row over falling QPR did indeed break out in Parliament in 1962.[53] As a result Labour set up another study group, this time to come forward with more concrete proposals for higher education, chaired by the medical researcher Lord Taylor, and including Crosland and Vaizey among their number. Spurred on by the eerie similarity between the 11+ and 18+ pinches, the Taylor Report argued for a 'rapid and continuing expansion' of higher education so that 'all who are capable of benefiting from higher education must have access to it', no longer as a 'privilege' but as a 'right'.[54]

By the time the row over the 18+ had blown up, however, the Conservative government had also already turned for solutions to Eccles' favourite policy expedient, an expert commission. The call for an expert commission on higher education had been part of Labour policy since the study group of 1957–8. Following the apparent success of the Crowther Report of 1959, in at least temporarily defusing the row over the 11+, the government thought it might make the same resort for higher education in 1960. Because jurisdiction over higher education crossed departments—the Ministry of Education for teacher-training and technical colleges under LEA control, and the Treasury which funded universities directly through the UGC—the commission came not from the Minister of Education but from the Prime Minister. The outcome was not at all what might have been expected from the predominantly technocratic discourse then prevailing in elite discussions of higher education. For this much credit must go to the unlikely figure of Lionel, Lord Robbins, the free-market economist who chaired the commission.

The Impact of Robbins

The Robbins Report has been dubbed democratic, technocratic, meritocratic—even aristocratic.[55] Lord Robbins was himself a complicated and not always predictable character: a free-market economist whose preparation for the task included reading John Henry Newman's *Idea of the University*, a classic Victorian statement of high-minded humanistic ideals, and who surrounded himself on the committee with socialist advisers.[56] His report—which unusually he drafted himself—certainly bore traces of all these influences. He was an outspoken advocate of a broad, liberal education, such as he identified with American liberal arts colleges (though which looked suspiciously to others like a gentlemanly Oxbridge model); he was among the first to broach seriously the notion of income-contingent student loans to capture some of the private return.[57] But if we stand back and consider the longer-term effects of his report—how its conclusions were actually embedded in the funding and planning of higher education—then the most striking outcome is undoubtedly the consensual acceptance of the demand-driven 'Robbins Principle': that higher education should be made 'available for all those who are qualified by ability and attainment to pursue them and who wish to do so'. The state should provide higher education to all qualified applicants who wanted it, Robbins firmly concluded, and it should assume that the pool of qualified applicants was not fixed but would grow steadily and apparently endlessly over time: a novel idea that as we have seen had appeared only recently, driven by the left-wing sociologists Halsey and Floud, and now in Robbins' circle reinforced by the statistical calculations of the LSE statisticians Claus Moser and Richard Layard. 'If there is to be talk of a pool of ability', Robbins wrote memorably, 'it must be of a pool which surpasses the widow's cruse in the Old Testament, in that when more is taken for higher education in one generation more will tend to be available in the next.'[58]

How was this conclusion reached? The Committee on Higher Education (as it was formally called) brought together a mixed bag of educators and public figures; amongst the most active were Sir Philip Morris, Vice-Chancellor of the University of Bristol, and H. C. Shearman, Chairman of the LCC. Most importantly, however, it called on an unprecedentedly wide range of information. It received over 400 memoranda from interested individuals and bodies—Michael Stewart, Michael Young, and John Vaizey were amongst those who contributed to the Fabian Society's submission—and called 121 of them for oral interrogation at some of its 111 meetings—Stewart and Vaizey were amongst those called for this purpose. Inevitably, it employed Mark Abrams—his Research Services Ltd did an opinion survey of 21-year-olds and gathered data from LEAs on A-level attainment and its outcomes—but despite his insistence that 'we did a lot of the research for the Robbins Report' most of the opinion research was done by the Government Social Survey department which canvassed undergraduates, postgraduates, teacher-training students and advanced further-education students; in all, 6 opinion surveys were undertaken.[59] Universities individually and the UGC, teacher-training colleges and further-education colleges also provided a mass of statistical information about admissions and the nature of the student body. The National Foundation for Educational Research compiled and analysed LEA data on entry to higher education. The Ministry of Education was induced to develop a special survey of school-leavers. David Glass at the LSE supplied data from his own survey of university entrants; the 1946 birth-cohort data was obtained from J. W. B. Douglas; Jean Floud and P. E. Vernon supplied their evidence on the 'pool of ability'; R. K. Kelsall who had done the main surveys of graduate employment advised on that subject. To draw international comparisons, including a check on the relatively gloomy OECD data, evidence was solicited from British Embassies around the world and the committee itself spent almost two months on visits abroad, to Switzerland, the Netherlands, France, Germany, Sweden, and, for extended periods, the US and the USSR.[60]

So Robbins was exceptionally well-informed on important topics such as the growth of staying-on rates, the growth of O- and A-level qualification, demand for further and higher education, the 'pinch' on admissions for qualified applicants, the social composition of the student body (at all levels of post-compulsory education), and the changing nature of subject choice (he was among the first to detect an end to the 'swing to science' of the 1950s). We have already encountered much of his evidence above in our discussions of changing attitudes to education at both secondary and tertiary levels. Most significant in marshalling and interpreting this evidence was Claus Moser, the LSE statistician. Moser's personal optimism and his statistical vision—not usually qualities we imagine go together—emboldened him to project recent growth in demand and qualification for higher education forward, not just a few years, not just a few decades, but a half century or more (see Appendix, Figure 5.1). As I write in 2019 we have still not yet reached the limits of the probe he sent into the future.[61]

Tracking backwards to Floud's data on entry to higher education earlier in the century, and then projecting forwards, Robbins and Moser saw that there had been a steady increase in the proportion of the population qualifying for entry to higher education. If one projected the rate of increase just over the past five years, then the APR would naturally increase to 10 per cent by 1970 and 14 per cent by 1980. Yet it was entirely possible that the growth of qualifiers would accelerate further. Robbins was particularly impressed by Floud's evidence of the social bias against university entrance that blocked working-class children even with high 'measured intelligence'. He also saw evidence that limits to grammar-school access in many areas were depressing the numbers of qualifiers further. More radically, he accepted that the elimination of the 11+ would extend much further the opportunities to 'acquire intelligence'. With social, geographical and selective barriers lowered, who knew what levels of participation were possible? And all of this could be achieved without affecting quality—'"more" need not mean "worse"' at all. The same level of qualification—A-levels—would apply. But the numbers qualifying would rise.[62]

Equally significant, and in some ways more surprising, Robbins swept aside the question of 'national needs'. Moser and his student Layard were sceptics about manpower planning, which made them unusual amongst left-leaning economists. They were much more confident about projecting forward demand for education amongst the populace than demand for particular skills amongst employers.[63] Robbins, the free-marketeer, had no disposition towards manpower planning at all. But he was very upbeat about demand. While acknowledging the provision of 'skills demanding special training' as one of the four aims of higher education, it was only one, and apparently the least, next to promoting 'the general powers of mind', 'the advancement of learning', and 'the transmission of a common culture and common standards of citizenship'. Above all, he felt, meeting the demand for education was not only a social but a political imperative—in the present democratic age, all citizens deserved to have their capacities fostered to the utmost. He later recalled Tawney's advice, 'You can never overestimate how much America has benefited from the fact that so many of her people have had at least the smell of a higher education.' In his Report he threw in an effective Cold War jab, 'We do not believe that the Soviet Union is the only country that can make full use of the brains of its people.'[64] The recent panic over the 'pinch' at 18+, following so quickly on from the revolt against the 11+, had revealed the strength of public feeling. If the qualified participation rate had been allowed to fall lately, it was certain—especially if unleashed by Robbins himself, and if the 'social esteem' showed to higher education in the US and Sweden were any indication of the future—to bounce back in the '60s and '70s. If, as he imagined, Britain was also on the cusp of a dramatic improvement in career expectations for women, then demand was likely to be stronger still—perhaps much stronger.[65]

Robbins had ideas about how to deliver 'what to many will seem a startling increase in numbers'.[66] Some but not all of these ideas have held up as well over the long term as his predictions of rising demand and the need for government to meet it. Robbins was particularly determined that universities, rather than other kinds of higher-education institution, would lead the expansion. For this he has been criticized as unrealistically elitist, strait-jacketing the British higher-education system in a Newmanesque ideal of small tutorial groups, residential campuses and 'academic' education for all.[67] Undoubtedly Robbins favoured small-group, residential and liberal education, on the model of the American liberal-arts college, but his concern to put the universities at the head of a unitary system had different motivations. He was more aware of the existing pluralism of British higher education than most contemporary commentators—thus the committee's commissioning of surveys of all school-leavers and of entrants to teacher training and technical colleges particularly—and aware too of the flows of the more marginal entrants into non-university institutions (see Appendix, Figure 5.2).

Britain already had an unusually high proportion of non-university higher-education students, accounting for over half of the APR of 8.5 per cent in 1962; that was where technology's strengths were greatest; that was where expansion, drawing from the ever-replenishing widow's cruse of new entrants, would have to start.[68] Teacher-training colleges, for example, already drew 40 per cent of their intake from working-class households and over 50 per cent were women, a strikingly higher rate in both cases than universities.[69] If Robbins wanted universities to take responsibility for these parts of the sector, it was not because he wanted to make them into universities—he was certainly aware that the American system was highly differentiated.[70] Rather he was rightly fighting shy of any binary system that would rely on 'parity of esteem', a point that had been forcibly driven home by Richard Hoggart in his written and oral testimony before the committee.[71] Anyone who thought non-university institutions 'can ever have parity of attraction with the university sector, either with the public or the student population', Robbins commented after the Report, was 'living in a fool's paradise'. Far better to put teacher training and technical colleges under universities' wing, and let them 'fatten up' on the universities' higher status and better funding—as eventually transpired, though not for many years.[72]

Along similar lines, his advocacy of tutorial teaching and a general, 'liberal' education was designed not to preserve an Oxbridge model but to open up higher education to a much wider range of applicants, on the American or Scottish models. A less specialist education would be accessible to a more diverse entry and could focus on cultivating common qualities of mind and social life. Testimony to the committee had also provided ample evidence of the widening range of occupations into which university graduates would be recruited in future. A liberal education, less specialised, flexible and cognitively rich, would have occupational value as well as civic value—as the Scots, and Tawney, had long argued.[73] Specialist training could best be pitched forward into the postgraduate years, as in America.[74]

Robbins did not in the end have it all his own way, but in all the important ways his Report had a decisive effect in building widening participation into the system. Governments of both parties eagerly embraced his conclusions in the immediate aftermath of the report in November 1963. The Conservatives, having been burned twice with the social movement against the 11+ and the panic in Parliament over the 'pinch' at 18+, now overtly accepted that the 'bulge' and the 'trend' must drive higher-education expansion at whatever pace they dictated; the idea of a fixed 'pool of ability' had been definitively trounced.[75] Alec Douglas-Home, the Prime Minister, sent out word to 'every father and mother in the country... that if they have in the family a child who wishes to pursue a course of higher education, there should be a place at technical college or university for that boy or girl to fill', 'one of the most exciting social prospects that we have faced in this country for a generation'.[76] It was decided immediately that the Robbins Principle would form the basis for future expansion and that as a first step, as Robbins had recommended, the CATs and some of the 15 'central institutions', where full-time advanced further education was offered in Scotland, would be promoted to university status.[77] Despite the assumption sometimes made that access to higher education remained in Britain more selective than elsewhere, the supremacy of the Robbins Principle—which pledged a place to all 'qualified leavers' (with two A-levels) who wanted one—was in fact pretty much equivalent to similar pledges in France and Germany to admit all who qualified via the *baccalauréat* or the *Abitur*.[78]

After the election, when Crosland took charge at the Department of Education and Science, it might have been expected that Labour would embrace a demand-driven system even more enthusiastically; Crosland, after all, had taken the lessons of Floud and Halsey not only on the theoretical 'pool of ability' but also on the pressure of popular demand well before Boyle. There was, however, a competing Labour tradition in favour of manpower planning, undoubtedly congenial to the new Prime Minister, Harold Wilson, the economist whose famous 1963 speech invoking the 'white heat' of the technological revolution had inveighed against the 11+ and the 18+, precisely on the basis that the nation needed to plan for more scientists and technologists.[79] Crosland mollified this tradition by speaking a new language of 'social demand', planning speak which nevertheless blurred the distinction between 'national needs' and popular demand.[80] In this his position was strengthened by left-leaning economists like Moser and Vaizey who doubted that true manpower planning was really feasible and doubted also that popular demand was politically resistible.[81] It helped that the Treasury was more comfortable with Moser's 'scientific' projections—they involved huge new spending commitments, but at least they seemed predictable, less subject to the whims of planning-mad ministers, and were compatible with new procedures for tracking public expenditure installed in the early '60s.[82] The DES liked it too: with university expansion now closely yoked to secondary expansion, responsibility for the former (in the form of the quinquennial grants to the UGC) was transferred to them from the Treasury, and they began to develop their own statistical apparatus to monitor and predict future demand after school-leaving age and at 18+. It was here, in the DES's Planning Unit and its Planning Papers, that regular, anxious brooding over measures such as APR and QPR began to be cultivated.[83] Student demand was clearly installed as the driver of higher-education planning for the foreseeable future. However, the temptation to overrule the Robbins Principle with instruments of manpower planning would recur, surprisingly amongst Thatcherite Conservatives more than socialist planners.

In one key respect Crosland deviated from Robbins' recommendations, in a way that has often been interpreted since as a socialist atavism back to manpower planning. To the surprise of his education advisers who had just watched him dismantle the bipartite system in secondary education[84], Crosland suddenly announced in a speech at Woolwich in April 1965 that future expansion would be secured through a 'binary' system of higher education, separating the universities from the 'public sector' of institutions still under LEA control. The 'English 7' already afoot, one new Scottish university planned to join them (Stirling), the CATs promoted, and expansion of all existing universities agreed, there would be for a while no further new universities created, although 40 bids from candidate localities—the likes of Scarborough, Perth, Inverness—had been received.[85] Elsewhere, the larger further-education colleges, especially the Scottish central institutions, were gearing up to join the CATs in promotion. But Crosland had decided instead to keep them out of the university sector. In a White Paper the following year, he proposed instead to group many of them into federated institutions called 'polytechnics'—the word had nothing to do with technical colleges, but simply referred to 'many arts', to indicate that often they were grouping together highly disparate institutions, art colleges, colleges of business or commerce, some teacher-training colleges, technical colleges. These polytechnics would remain under LEA control, as had been their constituent parts, but they and other 'public sector' institutions would over time be able to grant university degrees through a Council for National Academic Awards.[86]

Why did Crosland plump for a binary system? The explanation most often given is that his socialist instincts, and the ambitions of a minister, drove him to limit the universities' independent control over the higher education system and to retain a lever for 'social control' via the LEAs under DES oversight.[87] But this can't be quite right, because the policy was already being developed inside the DES before the election, before socialist planning was even on the agenda, well before Crosland. As early as March 1964 Edward Boyle had proposed it to Cabinet and moves were already under way to make it happen before the election. The truth is that for a variety of reasons no-one was as confident as Robbins about the ability or willingness of the universities to tackle such an ambitious expansion as was now contemplated. The Treasury was keen to hold down costs. The DES was, of course, anxious to retain some of its own control, in its traditional partnership with the LEAs, but it was also intensely concerned with the practicalities, especially regarding the very rapid expansion needed in teacher training dictated not only by higher participation rates but also by the continuing bulge and trend in schools. Toby Weaver, the civil servant responsible, knew enough to entice his masters with a whiff of 'social control', but this was not a particularly socialist policy, rather a language used by Boyle as much as Crosland. Crucially, the universities were also happy not to take up this burden. The UGC had a habit of jealously defending the elite qualities and the independence of the universities. While eager to take a manageable share of the expansion, and the enhanced revenues that went with it, they were quite content to leave to the 'public sector' the poorer new entrants with lower qualifications and allegedly more vocational goals, who might otherwise dilute the pure essence of liberal education—a UGC way of thinking about it, though not Robbins'.[88]

Was the binary system in higher education then just a re-creation of the bipartite system in secondary education, with universities standing in for grammar schools in slowing down the transition to a mass education system? Yes and no.

In many ways the universities did not, could not, may not have wanted to affect a 'classless' image as comprehensives did. They were, needless to say, much more 'middle class' institutions than the average comprehensive—as they would necessarily have been, until middle-class participation rates were so saturated that a more socially diverse intake was likely, which didn't happen until the much more ambitious expansion of the 1990s. Residential universities, the new ones on greenfield (even 'rural') sites with small-group teaching, did borrow from established elite models. Sussex was known as 'Balliol by the Sea', after the intellectual Oxford college. On the other hand, the image of the universities undoubtedly shifted substantially in the 1960s. The new universities, like the comprehensives, drew on both new and old models. Like the comprehensives, they were concrete even more than 'plateglass'; they offered new subjects, such as social studies; they offered more opportunities for co-education—Sussex began with an over 50 per cent female intake, double the old average. They were undoubtedly 'middle class', but they appealed to a 'new middle class' identity, modern, technical, 'strategically mobile', in some ways self-consciously going for a 'classless' style.[89]

A new idea of 'student life' was emerging that would contribute significantly to this 'new middle class' identity. Parallel to Robbins, not instigated by him, a national system of higher education was already emerging out of the patchwork of institutions dating back to the Middle Ages, with much greater homogeneity at least within the university sector, driven by the expansion of the system already under way in the late 1950s. A nationally guaranteed student grant, a national admissions system, less regional and more national catchment areas for universities were all coming into view before Robbins reported. On funding, Robbins' own preference for a mixed system of means-tested grants and loans had already been pre-empted by the Anderson Report, 'Grants for Students', which appeared in June 1960.[90] Its recommendation that all students accepted on degree courses or their equivalent should be given mandatory LEA grants for tuition fees and maintenance was accepted in the Education Act 1962. The disconnection between Anderson's willingness to spend generously on grants and Robbins' later, more ambitious projections for student numbers (and thus the costs of the grant) has made it appear to some commentators that Britain stumbled into its higher-participation regime almost by accident, storing up fiscal trouble for the future.[91] But Anderson was then more in the British (if not the European) mainstream on this issue than the economist Robbins. LEAs had been ramping up their grant provision in the late '50s anyway, consonant with the huge swell of government spending on education that had been building for some time. Over 90 per cent of applicants already had their tuition paid and some or all of their maintenance before Anderson: he was simply regularizing a system already then nearly complete.[92] Most European countries provided free tuition; what distinguished the British system was that it provided maintenance grants as well, though (against Anderson's recommendation) they remained means-tested, partly on the grounds that higher unlike secondary education was not a universal service.[93]

Similarly, it was probably not the availability of generous grants that encouraged all universities—including the new ones—to go for a national catchment area rather than local recruitment. Students were growing increasingly independent of their parents, parents as we have seen encouraged this trend, and physical mobility away from the family home for school-leavers and newlyweds as much as for students was rife. 'Student life' as a traineeship for middle-class adulthood, living with other students in residential halls or lodgings, was rapidly becoming the norm. But it is important to remember that this too was a 'new middle class' phenomenon, what the Crowther and Anderson Reports called the 'new family pattern'. Hardly any of the parents of these middle-class students would have gone to university. Those who did would mostly, apart from the small Oxbridge cohort, have stayed closer to home. 'Student life', like the comprehensive school, straddled the old world and the new.[94]

The public sector shared in some but not all of these developments. The new national admissions system set up in 1961 applied only to universities.[95] The teacher-training institutions had their own, much older Central Register and Clearing House. Other colleges and the new polytechnics retained control over their own admissions until much later, befitting their local orientation. Stylistically the polytechnics also set themselves apart, deliberately. They could not afford and did not want gleaming new plate-glass campuses on greenfield sites. They were supposed to be rooted in their urban communities, housed in repurposed inner-city buildings, and offering the full gamut of part-time, full-time, evening and day courses that could attract a much wider social catchment, cheaply and compatibly with work. There was, however, from the start much more overlap with the universities than the theory of the 'binary divide' allowed. Their intake, too, was predominantly middle class.[96] Some of them already had national catchments. Grants were available for their degree courses or equivalents on the same basis as universities. Their subject mix was never as differentiated from the universities as people imagined either, though it was always broader. Certainly 'polytechnics' were never only about technical education: 'many arts' included from the beginning art and design and social studies as well as technology. The goal of a more 'vocational' sector focused on applied science and technology was based on already outdated assumptions of a 'swing to science' and 'national needs', as we will consider in greater detail in Chapter 9. The real growth area in polytechnics, as in universities, and indeed in comprehensives, was 'social studies', appealing to new entrants on both vocational and non-vocational grounds, and to women as well as men. Though deplored as 'academic drift', the convergence between universities and the public sector—which was not ratified until 1991—was predictable from the outset; it also reflects the real, undifferentiated public hunger for higher education that was manifest across the 1960s.[97]

For although the binary divide might have put up some class barriers to university study, thus impeding democratization at the higher levels, it did nothing apparently to impede the remorseless operation of the trend towards higher-education participation predicted by Robbins. In an assessment of the 'the impact of Robbins' made by Richard Layard in 1968, higher education was described as the fastest growing industry in Britain after electronics and natural gas, student numbers having grown 76 per cent between 1961 and 1966.[98] Some of that was due to the bulge. But the trend was also operating more powerfully than Robbins had predicted, an international phenomenon—across the OECD the trend accounted for more than two-thirds of higher-education growth in the 1960s, the bulge less than one-third.[99] The participation rate in all forms of higher education surged from roughly 7 per cent to 14 per cent over the course of the decade—somewhat higher if we employ Moser and Layard's generous calculations (see Appendix, Figure 5.3).

The Robbins Report itself contributed to that surge: public awareness of the report at the time of its publication was remarkably high—67 per cent knew about the report and the same proportion approved of the higher spending necessary to implement it.[100] Growth ahead of Robbins' projections was also registered in teacher training and in further education, and there were signs that comprehensivization was continuing to generate growth from the bottom-up: in 1969 over 40 per cent of the cohort nationally was taking O-levels, a rate that only Scotland and parts of Wales had attained at the beginning of the decade. The qualified participation rate, which Robbins thought had fallen to about 60 per cent early in the decade, had bounced back up over 80 per cent by the end. The 'pinch', Layard thought, had not been fully relieved, but Britain was coming close to properly implementing the Robbins Principle that there was a place in higher education for everyone qualified who wanted one—and remarkably, almost everyone qualified wanted one. By the end of the decade, the Robbins escalator was well and truly rolling.[101]

And then it stopped.

6

What Has Happened
to the Students?

After two decades of acceleration, peaking at an unprecedented level in
the late 1960s, the trend stopped dead around 1970. 'Staying on'—the
trend to remaining in school for post-compulsory education after age 15—
was still growing at 5 per cent per annum for boys and 7 per cent per annum
for girls to 1969; growth then stopped nearly entirely for boys and slowed to
3 per cent per annum for girls.[1] At age 18 the trend of the trend dropped
more clearly and decisively. The participation rate for 18- and 19-year olds
in all forms of higher education (APR) peaked at 14.2 per cent in 1972 and
then stagnated at or below that level until the late 1980s (see Appendix,
Figure 6.1); by the DES's own figures, it actually dropped continuously
throughout the 1970s.[2] 'What has happened to the students?', wailed a gathering of higher-education policymakers at an emergency conference called
by North East London Polytechnic in November 1974.[3]

It is not easy to explain the check to widening participation in the
'long 1970s', a period in this respect unique in the history of the twentieth
century. Some even deny that it happened at all. Books aiming to cover the
'crisis' of the 1970s hardly mention education, though education was a
prominent feature of the 'moral panics' over national decline or degeneration
that besmirched the decade.[4] But it is more common to be overwhelmed by
the multiplicity of possible causes, for the long 1970s were highly eventful,
not just in the familiar terms of high politics but also in changing labour
markets, social attitudes, class structures and identities and particularly in
features of the education system. These multiple shocks confused contemporaries, too; it became harder to see their period as one of optimism and
general advance, and harder to see a democratic expansion of educational

opportunity as the key to their children's future or as a solution to present-day problems. In this environment, meritocracy enjoyed a breathing space and a chance for a comeback, as more people might be persuaded to enter a competition for a limited number of opportunities rather than insisting on the best for all.[5]

A list of the confusions confronting parents and teenagers would have to start with changing labour markets, which certainly played a role in questioning some well-established democratic assumptions about the benefits of education. Either because of educational over-expansion in the late 1960s or because of surging demand for manual labour—two quite different explanations—the 'rate of return' to education seemed to turn against staying on at the end of the '60s. Labour markets then fluctuated wildly over the next fifteen years, betokening a transition to a post-industrial and increasingly non-manual workforce. In the long run, this transition would be interpreted as a shift to a 'knowledge economy' in which education would become more, not less important in the labour market, yet in the midst of it that shift was not visible to parents and adolescents. To some degree, this was an international phenomenon; in the US, at least, there was a similar halt around 1970 to the otherwise remorseless rise in high-school and college graduation rates, and across the OECD a general deterioration of the labour-market prospects of graduates.[6]

But other factors too, not having to do with the economy, took the shine off higher education. The 'self-disciplined...restrained, quiet' student 'with an altruistic frame of mind, religiously inclined' whom Ferdynand Zweig had taken as typical when he studied elite universities in 1963 had been almost entirely eclipsed. In its place arose a distinct 'student estate', self-absorbed in its own idea of student life, and apparently driven by 'permissiveness' to set itself against established values and (evident in the rash of student unrest) against the university itself. Parents might have second thoughts about throwing their adolescents into this alien maelstrom (though again the adolescents might have had different ideas), especially in the peak period of student unrest from the late '60s to the late '70s. Politicians certainly had doubts about throwing more money into a higher-education system which seemed not to be delivering on economic growth but rather only throwing abuse back—not least when, as happened repeatedly during this period, education ministers met with a rough reception when they ventured onto campuses. This too was an international problem—the student unrest of 1968 and after had notoriously global reach, and in the United States in particular the resulting 'culture war' was said to have much reduced faith in education to address social problems or to fuel economic growth.[7]

At the same time, and for similar reasons, the integrity of the school system was cast in doubt. 'Permissiveness' seemed to pose a discipline problem in secondary schools quite as much as in higher education, though without the parental option to withdraw. In a rapidly pluralizing society, with more psychic, social and physical mobility among the young, growing racial diversity and diverging social attitudes, schools were on the frontline. As John Tomlinson put it, far from reproducing the old social order, schools became 'the cockpit in which the conflicts are first encountered by the young', to their parents' mystification or dismay.[8] 'Moral panics' about young people, often focused on indiscipline in schools, were so prevalent across the 1970s that that very neologism 'moral panic' coined by a sociologist in 1972 became the slogan of a decade. This was, inevitably, again an international problem, as the spread of informality and the decline of deference across the Western world made schools the theatres of culture clash. A Gallup poll in the United States in 1975 named 'lack of discipline' as the most important problem in schools: in the words of a 1984 White House report, there appeared to be 'chaos in the classroom'.[9]

More specifically in Britain, comprehensive reorganization was reaching its climax, with inevitable disruption as split sites were merged and mid-school transfers required, and this provided a ready whipping boy for the architects of such moral panics. The 1970s were also a period of growing ethnic diversity and fears about indiscipline often packed a racial charge. Borrowing from America, which was experiencing sharp conflicts at the same time over racial integration of schools, images of a feral inner-city adolescent horde were loaded with class and ethnic prejudice. And again politicians wondered what economic dividend they were reaping from investment in schools at a time when economic performance was rocky—though in reality there was probably little direct relationship between them. As if the British system hadn't enough change to absorb at the time, 1972 was the year chosen to finally implement the Butler Act's promise to raise the school-leaving age to 16, so that 1973–74 added an additional year of compulsory schooling for that troublesome cohort. In the same year, local-government reorganization redrew the boundaries of many LEAs.[10] Lying behind both permissiveness itself and its adversaries was a general decline in public confidence in state institutions, schools and universities not excepted, a crisis of confidence that was international and multi-dimensional. The state didn't help itself by falling into a fiscal crisis from around 1973 that constantly imperilled spending on schools and continued adhesion to the Robbins Principle.

As one pair of shrewd educationists commented at the end of this period, 'the basic problem in analysing social change—that everything is changing—is [now] particularly acute'.[11] We are not helped in disentangling this knot of causes and effects by its enhanced politicization not only by contemporary actors but also by subsequent commentators, the usual over-emphasis on the agency of politics being compounded by dramatically skewed diagnoses. Nor can we call so easily on the aid of the social sciences, as their fragmentation, each to their own source base and explanatory mechanism, leads again to remarkably divergent explanations—economists look to the labour market, sociologists to social structure, and historians mostly to their favoured political explanations, ideology and 'the cuts'. Usually they focus on the shorter time periods that suit their favoured explanations, rather than the 'long 1970s' as a whole. Putting the fragments back together is a hazardous and confusing operation. Fortunately we do have some unique assets, not least the nice coincidence of a second birth-cohort study after 1946—in 1958—which neatly comes of secondary-school age at the beginning of this period, is the first to experience the raising of the school-leaving age, makes for a natural experiment on the effects of comprehensive reorganization and higher-education stagnation, and enjoys the full roller-coaster ride of the 'long 1970s' labour market.

Crises of Confidence

Just because arguments for the crisis of the 'long 1970s' were highly politicised does not make them negligible. So we should begin with consideration of three of the most prevalent, yet very divergent (and highly politicised) explanations, all of which posit a major crisis of popular confidence in educational institutions.

The first was a fight-back for meritocracy, which we have seen already rear its head in Kingsley Amis's gloomy prognostication in 1960 that more would mean worse. It is notable that many of the born-again meritocrats of the 1960s and '70s had started out as Labour party members or at least 'moderate progressives'. They argued, against the dominant flow of public opinion, that selection of an elite on grounds of ability was necessary both to advance the economy and to protect civilized values, but was also egalitarian in its repudiation of inherited privilege; it represented true 'equality of opportunity'. Little knots of such people had been meeting in discussion groups throughout the '60s, but they surfaced into public visibility after 1969 with a series of 'Black Papers on Education', the moving force behind which were two 'moderate progressive' academics, Brian Cox and Tony Dyson.[12] Cox and Dyson, like Amis, were most concerned with what they saw as the degradation of elite education. They were moved to action, as Cox later said, by the wave of disorder unleashed by student protest in the universities—in other words, by permissiveness at the top. Their contacts with grammar-school teachers caused them naturally to extend this concern to the schools, especially elite selective schools such as the 'direct grants'— the rump of hybrid fee-paying and state-scholarship grammar schools that had survived into the 1970s but were finally squeezed out of the state sector by the Labour government from 1975. Schools of this type, like the top universities, were regarded by Cox and Dyson as guardians of 'the moral and cultural values of European civilization'.[13] If fed by more egalitarian modes of selection—Cox and Dyson did not support revival of the 11+, but proposed various alternatives—a renewal of genuinely competitive 'contest mobility' would not lead to a caste-like meritocracy of the kind decried by Michael Young, but to an open elite; it was at this point that the word 'meritocracy' began to be used more frequently in this positive sense.[14]

Mingling with the 'moderate progressives' in the Black Papers project, however, were some much harder voices. Right-wing Conservatives who had suffered indignantly under comprehensive reorganization came out of the woodwork in large numbers, especially after 1970 when the Conservatives returned to power and Boyle gradually withdrew from the fray.[15] Some of them were frank defenders of an hereditary elite.[16] Others were simply what Christopher Knight calls 'preservationists', fighting to preserve the remaining grammar schools and to keep the direct grants under the protection of the state, on meritocratic grounds. But whatever their reasoning they tended to be more explicitly and ideologically *anti*-egalitarian and ready for a fight.[17] At this point, appeals that might have had a wider purchase on a broad swathe of parents played only minor roles; the later Thatcherite emphases on 'parental choice' and 'standards' were not applied to all parents but mostly to those choosing grammar schools, and not to all schools but mostly those thought to represent the high standards of 'European civilization'.[18]

Especially after 1974 when the Conservatives lost power again, they sought to turn their party's influence actively in support of parents' groups campaigning for the retention or restoration of grammar schools. Tabloid newspapers and even the BBC fell on this newsworthy red meat. 'Moral panics' were concentrated in the mid-1970s, when the Black Paper series was also at its peak. The most dramatic actually focused on a primary school, William Tyndale in the London Borough of Islington, where in 1974 parents withdrew their children in protest at what they saw as a collapse of discipline in the name of 'progressive education'.[19] After a sequence of student protests at North London Polytechnic between 1971 and 1974, three Conservative academics there got a great deal of publicity for a book, published by the Black Papers' Rhodes Boyson, charging that a 'rape of reason' was taking place in Britain's new higher education institutions.[20] In 1976, when local elections were fought in Tameside in Greater Manchester in part over comprehensive reorganization, and a local Conservative bloc pledged to reverse it won, parents' groups took the Labour government to the High Court in order to restore their grammar-school places.[21] The BBC highlighted a London secondary school, Faraday, in a bleak fly-on-the-wall documentary 'Best Days' in 1977.[22] One or other of the Black Papers themes—student unrest, indiscipline, the abolition of grammar schools—was hardly out of the media at any time during these years.

Unleashed in opposition, the Conservative party did its best to make hay out of such flashpoints. Norman St John-Stevas, the Shadow Education Secretary, and his deputy Rhodes Boyson, elected as a Conservative MP in 1974, egged on seven LEAs including Tameside that were defying the Labour government on selection; the 'magnificent seven', St John-Stevas dubbed them.[23] These campaigns contributed to (but were not solely responsible for) an intensification of political polarization at local-government level. There were now fewer independents; boundaries had been gerrymandered in the 1972 reorganization for maximum political effect; the polarization of politics evident later nationally began here. Interest groups, especially if they had national backing—as parents' action groups did—loomed larger, perhaps at the expense of voter interest and engagement. The bipartisan consensus that had emerged in the late 1950s against selection was splintering.[24]

At the same time, perhaps oddly, a similar indictment of the educational system was being tendered on the left. As we've seen the old Labour left had always been ambivalent about education and its alleged effects on social mobility: they worried it would decapitate the working class or simply distract from more important issues of work and power. The running on comprehensive reorganization had been made, at least at the national level, by 'revisionists' of one kind or another who valued the ethical and social effects of common education for common citizenship—politicians like Crosland, critics like Young, sociologists like Halsey and Floud. In the 1970s, a new left emerged amongst radical sociologists who developed a critique of comprehensive education; it led to the view, now prevalent, that 'divided Labour' had failed to embrace true equality and only perpetuated social stratification under the guise of a comprehensive system. In this view, education had not only failed to combat inequality but was actively working to construct and consolidate it. Streaming, the CSE/O-level divide, selection at 16+ for A-levels and at 18+ for higher education, and the 'binary divide' in higher education were doing the job of the 11+, and the greater emphasis on 'certification'—taking and passing exams—had only consolidated the 'rise of the meritocracy', in Young's satirical sense.[25]

If the Black Papers targeted middle-class parents dissatisfied with comprehensives as their prime audience, the radical sociologists targeted working-class adolescents equally if not more dissatisfied with comprehensives. The indiscipline and protest which the Black Papers saw as the problem were reinterpreted as signs of healthy resistance on the part of the excluded majority. Led by Basil Bernstein, who in the early 1960s had developed a theory of working-class communication which emphasized its closed and exclusive nature, impervious to the 'elaborated' nature of polite speech, educational sociology of the 1970s embraced working-class adolescents' refusal of the educational ladder.[26] Bernstein had said already in 1965 that he wasn't interested in 'jacking up a child's I.Q. by half a dozen points or seeing the school as a launching pad for educational sputniks', but rather sought to serve the bottom 40 per cent who 'may as well have gone by submarine' and were being denied 'a fundamental educational right' by schools designed for others.[27] By the 1970s sociologists were less interested in securing educational rights and more interested in boarding the submarine. In *Learning to Labour* (1977), the most popular of these texts, Paul Willis practically celebrated 'the most aggressive aspects' of 'the male white working class counter-school culture' as the 'fun' that the non-academic majority claimed in compensation for its exclusion from middle-class forms of success. These displays of sexual prowess and sometimes even racial violence were congruent with 'shopfloor culture', the work life for which working-class youth yearned; no wonder they were so eager to leave school at 16! While of course as a socialist Willis was not endorsing sexual or racial violence, or for that matter the 'basically meaningless' work for which these young men were destined, he *was* delegitimating comprehensive schools (or probably any educational institution) as a vehicle for social change. 'No conceivable number of certificates amongst the working class will make for a classless society', he concluded; or, in Bernstein's formulation, 'education cannot compensate for society'.[28]

This turn away from the reorganization or extension of schooling on the part of 1970s sociology had implications not only for the current of opinion in those years but also for the evidentiary base left to historians. There were in these years few attempts to gauge the attitudes to education amongst either middle-class or working-class populations more generally of the type that David Glass's students like Halsey and Floud had pioneered in the 1950s. Even opinion polls tended to ask questions mostly about immedi-ately newsworthy issues such as indiscipline or examination standards.[29] This is partly an artefact of the end to the extended national debate over the 11+ and the culmination of comprehensive reorganization. But it also reflects an ethnographic turn amongst sociologists, who were now much more likely to spend their time in fieldwork in secondary schools, aiming at working-class youth, than in canvassing attitudes and opinion more widely.[30] There were still major social surveys undertaken in this period—the most important being Halsey and Goldthorpe's Oxford Mobility Study of 1972, discussed in Chapter 8. But Halsey and Goldthorpe felt themselves very much on the back foot in the face of radical critique. While Halsey acknow-ledged the inadequacy of social mobility alone to secure equality, he was not content to denounce it as 'a disguised legitimation of liberal capitalist soci-ety' and continued to work to equalize opportunities to achieve it through more equal provision of education.[31] Even the 1946 and 1958 birth cohort studies were finding it difficult to win continued public funding; the third study barely got off the ground in 1970; and the Conservative Education Secretary Keith Joseph flatly refused to countenance a fourth study in 1982. 'I'll start funding your research when you start telling me things I want to hear', he is alleged to have said.[32] As a result, though ingenious things can be done to glean information from later sweeps of the 1958 cohort, there is a decided lacuna in evidence about values and attitudes for the 1970s and '80s. The radical sociologists may not have done much to cultivate a political constituency for their views, but they did something to undermine the political constituency for educational reform in the mould of Halsey and

Floud. And in focusing on a shrinking working class, oddly and fatally for sociologists, they diverted attention from the forces of social and economic change diversifying communities and the workforce.

Between the Black Papers and radical ethnography, a third political course was steered by a moderate Labour government in the mid-1970s. From the left's standpoint, it was indistinguishable from—or, worse, a stalking horse for—the worst forms of Black Papers ideology and Thatcherism. But it is worth carefully distinguishing Labour's position, because it did try to retool democratic provision for a new age rather than to embrace older forms of meritocracy. James Callaghan who succeeded Harold Wilson as Prime Minister in 1976 was a culturally conservative figure of an older generation—born in 1912—who shared some of the wider concerns about permissiveness. He was not, however, in any way susceptible to the Black Papers' elitism. The Labour government had abolished the direct grant schools, resumed instructions to LEAs to complete comprehensive reorganization, taken Tameside to court over selection, and strove mightily to uphold the Robbins Principle. Callaghan's famous speech at Ruskin College in October 1976 should therefore be seen as an attempt to address supposed parental concerns about indiscipline without endorsing meritocratic policies with inegalitarian outcomes such as selection—the opposite as he said of 'a clarion call to Black Paper prejudices'.[33]

Callaghan chose as his text Tawney's dictum, 'What a wise parent would wish for their children, so the state must wish for all its children.' In tilting against 'the new informal methods of teaching' he sought to speak for all kinds of parents who wanted the best for their children. His prescriptions (such as they were—few and tentative) were aimed at the whole of society. One was technocratic; education, for girls as well as boys, seemed to be less focused than it ought to be on science and industry, a common complaint of politicians of both parties since the 1950s—and especially since the 'swing away from science' began in the early '60s.[34] The other was more democratic; all parents, not only those in grammar schools, were concerned about 'standards', and government ought to take stronger measures to guarantee them.[35] This latter shibboleth, because it was taken up by Thatcherite education reformers, has attracted most opprobrium.[36] For the left, 'standards' could only mean more subordination for the 'non-academic' working class, keeping them in their place at the bottom of an academic hierarchy. For some on the right, it did mean grammar schools. But Callaghan's adoption of 'standards' as a rallying cry had the effect of steering the right away from its more elitist appeals to grammar-school parents and couching its rhetoric in terms that could at least theoretically appeal to all. Indeed, some Conservative politicians—including Thatcher and St. John-Stevas—had already seen the sense of this, in distinction to the more explicitly elitist voices in the Black Papers crowd, such as Angus Maude.[37]

Not very much came of the Ruskin speech in the end. Callaghan called for a 'Great Debate' on education, but this amounted to a series of regional conferences organized by the DES in 1977 mostly for experts and educationists. The Great Debate passed Wales and Scotland by almost entirely.[38] It may have given some aid and comfort to grammar-school restorationists in the 'magnificent seven', but they were fighting against Callaghan's own government and mostly they lost their fights. Callaghan's speech probably did fix the idea of 'standards' more firmly in the public understanding of what was wrong with education and what might be made better.[39] But a new emphasis on standards, accountability and curriculum in state schools hardly amounts to a triumph of the New Right, as it is often portrayed; it sounds like something else entirely, something that had been growing since the 1950s, representing parents' greater attachment to state education, arguing against state paternalism (however benevolent the 'man in Whitehall' might be) and for the 'best' possible schools for all children, and a greater say for parents.

Was there really, then, as A. H. Halsey feared, a 'rotting of public confidence in public institutions' which lay behind the slump in participation rates?[40] Or was there something else going on, a crisis of confidence but also a search for a way forward that would improve life-chances for all? The political arguments may have stirred up even more anxiety, but they at least had the merit of addressing a wide range of constituencies—anxious middle-class parents, dissatisfied working-class students, 'ordinary' families concerned about accountability and standards. What all of these dissatisfactions had in common was a growing self-assertion on the part of disparate parts of the population against prescription and restriction from above. In some recent historical accounts, the 1970s saw a marked 'decline of deference' and a 'rise of popular individualism'. Trust in politicians began a dizzying collapse which crashed in the 1980s and has never yet recovered. While these phenomena are often associated with the New Right or with Thatcherism, resulting in dog-eat-dog competition and newly validated success mostly for the already privileged, they could also be associated with the welfare state and the sense of civic entitlement that welfare and democracy had spread among the less privileged.[41] The new confidence that led to the demographic bulge, the aspiration to a better life that led to the trend, and the belief in equal provision for all that drove comprehensive reorganization continued to manifest themselves in the 1970s, in new and enhanced ways; but evidently not yet to the benefit of widening participation in education. Why not?

To begin with, there seems little evidence of declining confidence in education per se, as opposed to specific educational institutions. As Peter Taylor-Gooby showed, public support for means-tested benefits—to help the low paid, the unemployed, lone parents and children—had always been shaky, both because of hostility to means testing and also due to older beliefs in self-reliance. These suspicions became better articulated in the 1970s but they did not amount to a repudiation of the welfare state or of democratic expectations of education. Support for universal entitlements to health and education remained as strong as ever. A more individualistic populace supported 'opt outs'—the right to buy private education or private health insurance—as a matter of choice, but they did not thereby support lower levels of public finance for education or health.[42] To the contrary, health and education expenditures as a share of national income remained stable, rising in per capita terms once the bulge finally tapered off in the 1970s and when the school-age population dropped rapidly in the 1980s.[43] Although advocates of private education talked up the 'growth' of their sector in this period of alleged public disillusionment with state education[44], there was very little deviation from the opt-out across the twentieth century of 6–7 per cent of the population. Most of the marginal growth that can be detected arose from the fluctuating fortunes of the small number of direct-grant schools: the transfer of some of these schools from the state (or semi-state) to the independent sector, the brief restoration of state scholarships under Thatcher's short-lived Assisted Places Scheme.[45]

If there was no 'exit' from state education, there was plenty of 'voice'. Parents had not falling but rising expectations of what the state could or should provide, and this caused them to criticize and clamour for more say.[46] The demand for more information about schools—at the very least prospectuses, perhaps inspection reports, later exam performance—and more participation in schools—in parent-teacher meetings, in PTAs, on governing bodies—to which both Thatcher and Callaghan sought to cater was surely evidence of commitment to and expectations of the neighbourhood school rather than the reverse. 'Parental choice', which could be code for selection, was more ambiguous, but most parents wanted voice not choice. Few of the noisy campaigns to retain selection succeeded. They were concentrated on areas with high middle-class populations and thus with high success rates at the 11+. Even the Tyndale affair, as John Davis has shown, resulted from an unusually sharp social and cultural conflict between pioneers in inner-city gentrification and a permissive policy maintained by radical young teachers.

These were atypical hotspots, where grammar-school constituencies were large or passionate. They did, however, contribute to greater uncertainty about what were really the 'best' schools. For a time polls asking people about selection showed them shifting back in favour, at exactly the time it began to feature less in their lives. While favouring selection in theory, however, people seemed reluctant to embrace it in practice for their own children. As we have seen, referenda in the early 1970s produced pretty unanimous verdicts against selection. After those failures, grammar-school preservationists relied on party-political manoeuvres rather than public opinion to secure their few victories. The pace of comprehensive reorganization continued unslackened through the '70s and '80s (see Appendix, Figure 4.1). The neighbourhood school became the norm and was embedded in most people's expectations and identities.[47] Support for selection began to fall again in the 1980s.[48] The LEA, which no longer directed pupils to separate schools, became less important than the school itself. In areas like Tameside where parents clamoured for the 'choice' of a grammar school, allocation to schools remained highly sensitive, but across the country most parents chose and got their neighbourhood school.[49] Even after 1979, when the return of a Conservative government emboldened some Tory LEAs to seek to restore selection after it had already been abandoned—Berkshire, Wiltshire, Solihull—it turned out, embarrassingly, that middle-class electors preferred to stick with neighbourhood schools.[50]

Combined with moral panics, voice could also translate into the language of standards. At a time when parents weren't told about inspection reports or examination results, and teachers actively resisted more parental involvement, who could blame them for wondering about the quality of education their children were receiving? Neither the man in Whitehall nor even the man in County Hall (that is, at the LEA) could be relied on any longer to know best. Gradually politicians responded. The Taylor Report of 1977 marked a turning-point, after which PTAs and parental representatives on governing bodies became the norm. Parents began to be invited into primary schools for the first time to help with language and reading; the practice became widespread in the 1980s.[51] Middle-class parents were always more likely to participate in such activities but all parents were taking more of an active interest in their children's schooling.[52] For the first time, after all, in this generation most *parents* had had experience of secondary schooling themselves, an experience which correlates both with parental involvement and with staying on. And, it cannot be said often enough, thanks to continued occupational change, many more parents were now 'middle class'.[53]

Nevertheless, if there was no general loss of confidence in education, only more exacting expectations of it, how do we then explain the stagnation of participation rates in further and higher education? Participation in compulsory education may have been a more positive experience than the moral panics suggested, but participation in post-compulsory education evidently was not. Secondary education had become a known quantity for most people, which they expected to be offered to all on the best possible terms. Higher education was still *terra incognita* for the majority, and in the unsettled cultural and economic circumstances of the '70s and '80s it looked like a wager with highly uncertain outcomes. Was an immediate wage or more education a better bet? How welcoming an environment would the new higher-education venues be, given their novelty, diversity and headline-grabbing outbreaks of "student unrest"? How could you plan for the future at all given the vicissitudes of a stop–go economy and a stop–go supply of places in education? Even bigger questions seem more obvious in retrospect, but intimations of them still troubled contemporaries. What was the future of industrial employment, now beginning a long decline? How important was education for a 'career'? The whole shape of a 'career' was now up for grabs in a way it had not been when young people were less socially and geographically mobile. What did people want from life?[54]

To see how they answered these questions, at least in the short term, we need to look more closely at the actual behaviours and choices that they made at the key transition points: attainment in schools to 16, 'staying on' for further education, participation in higher education at 18, and, as it turns out, new transition points thereafter.

16 to 18

By moving to a school-leaving age of 16 in 1972, Britain remained near the vanguard of European nations, requiring more years of schooling than any country except Belgium and the Netherlands, though still behind the

United States.[55] It also aligned the school-leaving age with its standard forms of certification—CSE and O-level in England and Wales, O-grade in Scotland—and this naturally boosted the proportion achieving certification. By 1977 70 per cent of 16-year-olds were sitting O-grade exams in Scotland (an exam originally planned for the 'top' 30 per cent).[56] Of those born in the 1960s in England and Wales (sitting exams between 1976 and 1985), 69 per cent achieved at least one O-level pass, with near-saturation levels for students from non-manual backgrounds, leading to some catch-up in working-class vs. middle-class attainment.[57] Although there was a lively, not to say vicious debate at the time over whether comprehensive reorganiza-tion had lowered standards, it is clear enough that the opposite was the case so far as minimum standards of attainment to 16 were concerned.[58]

The real concern was about progression after 16—'staying on'. This concern partly reflected the excessive focus of 1970s debate on the 'able' student—especially the able working-class student, who was supposed to have suffered from the 'abolition' of grammar schools—but it also reflected a genuine deficiency in British education, which is that its participation rates dropped off considerably after 16. Here the problem was specifically English, with staying on rates as low as 20 per cent compared to 40 per cent in Scotland and 48 per cent in Wales.[59] It's not at all clear that the English rate was lower than its international comparators, but the fact that it sputtered across the 1970s after such exuberant growth in the 1960s naturally raised a question, as well as fears about relative decline vis-à-vis competitors.[60]

This barrier at 16 lent some support to the radical sociologists' theory that comprehensive education was still modelled too narrowly upon the academic, middle-class student, against which working-class students were rebelling.[61] In one version, it was alleged that, at employers' behest, Callaghan's Ruskin speech was designed to *deepen* this divide by separating '16–19 client groups' to 're-vocationalise the last years of public schooling' for the majority and intensify academic training for the elite.[62] A more conventional version just deplored again the failure to *fully* vocationalize further education, depriving the non-academic of the 'parity of esteem' that was allegedly available in Germany's rigidly tracked system.[63] Both blamed policymakers. There was even a revival of the older idea that the British working class just didn't want or like education, and never would.[64] Economists however have offered quite a different diagnosis, which gives more agency to the 16-year-olds.

To the economists the issue was deceptively simple. Although they had conventionally accepted that education was a consumption good, demand for which rose with generally rising living standards, their own disciplinary trajectory—motored by human-capital considerations—and the global economic crisis of the mid-1970s caused them to seek investment-minded behaviour. Accordingly, they traced the slowing and then the reversal of staying-on behaviours to investment-minded decisions of 16-year-olds: either a decline in the longer-term economic advantages of staying on (e.g. a decline in the 'graduate premium', wage advantages to degree-holders) or a rise in the short-term advantage of leaving school and joining the labour market immediately. Whereas in the US, three influential papers by the future Nobel laureate Christopher Pissarides concluded in 1981–2, the former clearly applied, in the UK in contrast the latter was at work—sensible as relatively few 16-year-olds in Britain could as yet even contemplate higher education.[65] There was, he argued, 'unusually fast growth in juvenile earnings' (for boys, he meant) in the period 1969–74, just when staying on slackened.[66] Pissarides did not claim that consumption didn't matter. He admitted that it was a problem for his correlation that consumption continued to grow in the early 1970s and that staying on recovered for a few years before 1975. Indeed some economists began to complain that the British viewed education too much as a consumption good and were not regarding future economic prospects adequately, either for themselves or for the national interest.[67] The 'swing away from science' was a particular bugbear.[68] Still, Pissarides argued that the immediate attractions of the manual labour market in the early '70s were so strong as to overcome the usual effects of consumption, and that the slump in staying on then deepened when consumption did slacken in the mid-1970s economic crisis; in fact he argued that reduced consumption rather than enhanced labour-market prospects was most responsible for the continuation of the staying-on slump through 1978, the end of his study period.[69]

If we are interested in the motivations and behaviours of real people, as opposed to merely mechanical correlations, then it is hard to take too seriously Pissarides' model based on 16-year-olds sensitively assessing small shifts in wages, 'discounting' deferred wages from staying on, and switching back and forth between consumption and investment decisions. Clearly education remained a consumption good throughout, which most people sought more of as national income grew. But equally clearly something did happen around 1970 to deter 16-year-olds, especially boys, from staying on.

'Student unrest' probably mattered little, as 16-year-olds weren't thinking much about university; even Pissarides rejects the idea that their calculations were affected by conditions in higher education.[70] Neither did the academic barriers at 16 nor the counter-school culture suddenly loom up in 1970. But the mood did shift, and the Indian Summer of manual employment experienced by Britain in the first half of the '70s surely influenced decision-making. Then, when the economic slump hit, the worry about deferring wages undoubtedly deepened. The uncertainty of immediate prospects under these successive, unpredictable shifts encouraged a 'safety first' approach to foregoing further education, given more urgency by the raising of the school-leaving age in 1972—undoubtedly increasing impatience with schooling in the short term—and the gathering drumbeat of moral panics over the value of schooling. And boys were more directly affected by all of these factors than girls.[71]

Furthermore, staying on rates began to rise again almost immediately after Pissarides' study period ended, despite rising youth unemployment and continuing uncertainty both in labour markets and in graduate prospects. Between the 1958 and 1970 birth cohorts—that is, between 1974 and 1986—staying-on rose especially among lower-ability students, though erratically. Some of this reflects a hitherto unknown phenomenon—'parking'—whereby teenagers stay on in education just to avoid the dole queue, or the dead-end training schemes that came into vogue under Thatcher. But as we will see even parking led eventually to higher attainment rates from the late 1980s. By the 1980s it was also clearer that the future of the labour market lay in non-manual jobs and that more education could only help further down the road.[72] It looks like Pissarides' investment-focused model only worked for a short time in the 1970s when successive shocks cast doubt on the immediate value of further education—and only ever worked well for boys, at a time when the participation of girls was rising in both education and the labour market. After that short period teenagers resumed the pursuit of further education either as a longer-term investment or as a consumption good or both. The long-term trend between 1960 and 1990 followed a generally upward course, more or less impervious to educational politics.[73]

As staying on rates recovered, what did students stay on for? The fact that APR continued to flat-line through the 1980s suggests that they did not get as far as higher education, and so another chokepoint had arisen between 16 and 18 (see Appendix, Figure 6.2). What were they doing instead?

The big growth areas were in so-called 'tertiary colleges', either sixth-form colleges offering A-levels or, more often, further-education colleges offering A-levels as well as other advanced qualifications. Since the 1944 Act guaranteed access to further education, there were no formal barriers or limits on places; there was also becoming evident a growing wage premium for those who had further education at least to 17 and especially to 18; furthermore, part-time education and apprenticeships (which fell short of full-time further education) were declining in appeal, as long-established fears about 'second-class' qualifications were intensified by growing awareness of the greater flexibility in a changing labour market offered by more academic qualifications.[74]

On the whole, this period of continued stagnating APR for higher education through the late 1980s did then seem to handicap lower-achieving students, who stayed on but did not attain the two A-level qualification for higher education.[75] It may have been that the jump from CSE or even O-levels to A-levels was too steep, lending support to the argument that Britain's was still a bipartite system with a significant barrier to widening participation after 16.[76] There is some doubt as to whether the qualified leaver rate—that is, the proportion of 18-year-olds attaining the two A-level threshold—was in fact stagnating as Pissarides and others have concluded from the statistics or was 'buoyant' as the DES thought at the time.[77] In Scotland, for example, the equivalent attainment rate was clearly rising, and the DES thought the same factors were applying in England and Wales: 'the stabilising and increasing spread of comprehensive secondary education', 'increased participation in full-time education amongst 16–19 year olds' and 'the lessons of the employment market i.e. the message that higher qualifications in general mean better chances of employment'.[78]

There did seem to be more of a barrier than in Germany or France, where attainment rates for the *Abitur* and the *baccalauréat* were surging.[79] In Britain, it appeared, there was suppressed demand.[80] There were, however, increasing signs that this suppressed demand was finding ways to express itself that the formal accounting did not recognize. It was becoming more common for teenagers to pause their education in their late teens, reconnoitre the confusing trade-offs between education and employment, and then return to full-time education a bit later.[81] Importantly, 'Access' courses providing non-traditional students a path to higher education began to be offered in tertiary colleges from 1978, notably by the Inner London Education Authority.[82]

More importantly still, this period saw an unprecedented return to full-time education by a very large reservoir of mature entrants—married women. Many of these mature women had had high levels of qualification already when they left education or careers to start families; as we have seen, they had been expressing mounting dissatisfaction since at least the late 1950s with the cultural norms and the formal barriers that excluded them from higher education.[83] Now they broke out. Unlike men, who were deserting part-time education in droves, they were now enrolling in a wide range of part-time courses compatible with child-care responsibilities and part-time employment: Access courses, other tertiary qualifications, part-time degree courses almost entirely at colleges and polytechnics, the Open University (which allowed you to study part-time at home). Within a few years they were also piling into full-time courses and their share in full-time higher education began to climb rapidly, no longer so overwhelmingly concentrated in teacher training.[84] None of these mature entrants appeared at all in estimations of QLR and APR, which were based only on full-time entrants at 18 or 19. Demand was mounting both below and above the radar.

If we turn to participation in higher education itself—explaining the very long halt in the growth of APR, right through the late '80s—we need to bring into play another explanation beyond school performance and trade-offs between education and employment, that is, aspiration for (rather than attainment of) higher education, the demand-side factors that we have been emphasizing all along in explaining the rise of mass education. For at this juncture—entry to higher education, and the crisis of the long 1970s in particular—supply surely does matter as well as demand. The 1944 Act guaranteed access to secondary and further education for all who desired it, but it was only the pious declaration of the Robbins Principle that guaranteed higher education on the same basis. Let us give the politicians their due. They did agonize about maintaining the Robbins Principle through one of the greatest crises of public finance in modern times, and also through a demographic bulge that continued in higher education into the early 1980s. But *did* they maintain it?

'Tunnelling through the Hump'

Government took a while to waken to the crisis in higher education. They did not track the slowdown in staying on rates from 1969 and as late as

December 1972 Margaret Thatcher's White Paper as Education Secretary, tellingly titled 'Education: A Framework for Expansion', was still aiming for a much higher APR in 1980 than Robbins had predicted.[85] However, within a year grim fiscal news was already causing the DES to doubt whether it could meet this level of demand; shortly thereafter a new tranche of leavers' statistics caused DES to doubt also that those levels of demand would be sustained.[86] Thus at the same time government was faced with declining demand and at least the prospect of declining supply. This conjuncture posed a tense political dilemma by encouraging government to reduce supply *because* of reduced demand, thereby deepening the slump by depressing demand further. In a period of demographic growth which required more expenditure even at constant levels of participation, the temptation was to try 'tunnelling through the hump'—in the vivid words of a 1977 government memo—by holding down participation rates until the demographic 'hump' turned down too.[87] But would this really be maintaining the Robbins Principle?

Both demand and supply slumped further as Labour came into office in early 1974. Another set of leavers' statistics in mid-1974 made the end of the trend look like a trend in itself. Policymakers felt they could no longer rely on Robbins' gay predictions of a continuous upward progress, and entertained new thinking—and commissioned new research—about what might be depressing demand.[88] Some of their new considerations will look familiar— the costs and benefits of education vs. employment, the counter-school culture ('increasing dissatisfaction with formal education'), the raising of the school-leaving age—but others now seem bizarre—renewed doubts about whether a sufficient 'pool of ability' did exist after all, and a brief eugenic fashion for deploring the low birth rates of middle-class professionals. DES had been reluctant to air its suspicions for fear of further depressing demand, but the second set of leavers' statistics in 1974 confirmed the end of the trend.[89]

The emergency conference called for November 1974, 'What Has Happened to the Students?', brought these arguments out into the open. Both the government minister sent along to launch the conference, Lord Crowther-Hunt, and the DES civil servant responsible for student-number forecasts—the felicitously named K. G. Forecast—argued that government was still deeply committed to serving the Robbins Principle and was only responding to a slump in demand.[90] They now used human-capital theory as a shield, passing responsibility off from educational policy to labour markets and young people's economic calculations.[91] But participants, mostly from the colleges and polytechnics, were sceptical. And they had some reason to be, for checks on supply independent of demand were already in evidence.[92]

The most blatant effect of supply constraints on participation rates had already been prepared before Labour came to power. Anticipating the passing of the bulge through the school system (and into higher education), the 1972 White Paper had announced a reduction in teacher-training numbers, though in its otherwise optimistic way had hoped that the excess capacity would be re-used for other higher-education purposes. As that optimism faded in 1973, government began twisting LEAs' arms to cut back or even close many of their training colleges altogether. Although Crowther-Hunt tried to reverse this policy in 1974, the demographic and economic currents were flowing too strongly against him, and a huge reorganization of teacher training ensued, reducing the number of training colleges by a third and merging most of the remainder into polytechnics and colleges of higher education, so that the total number of training institutions was cut almost in half by 1977. Although teacher training was shrinking anyway as a share of all higher education, cuts to this sector disproportionately affected lower-achieving new entrants, as the participants at 'What Has Happened to the Students', mostly from public-sector institutions, knew all too well. Widening participation thus got off to a bad start in 1974.[93]

For the rest of its time in office, Labour relied on 'tunnelling through the hump'—that is, it accepted the fact of lower demand and reduced its targets accordingly, hoping they weren't depressing demand further. Higher education numbers projected for 1981 were reduced from 750,000, the White Paper projection in 1972, to below 600,000 by 1977, despite the fact that the cohort of 18-year-olds continued to grow into the early 1980s.[94] There was much agonizing about whether these reduced targets were likely to be self-perpetuating. In addition to the headline participation rate, APR, the DES now tracked closely the qualified leaver rate, QLR (a measure of demand for higher education), and also QPR, the proportion of qualified leavers participating in higher education (a measure of how well supply was meeting demand).[95] Fortunately, a statistical study concluded that five-sixths of the drop in participation was due to declining demand (i.e. QLR) and only one-sixth due to declining opportunity, or supply of places (i.e. QPR). Further study amongst 16-to-18-year-olds commissioned for 1975 persuaded them that declining demand had little to do with declining opportunity, but was rather rooted in the more profound social and economic transformations we have already discussed, which had caused staying on to begin to fall well before any cuts in supply.[96]

These conclusions were sufficiently reassuring to relieve the pressure on government, though as Crowther-Hunt argued they dodged the bigger question of whether government was doing enough to *increase* participation, which it ought to be doing on democratic grounds.[97] In the mid-1970s survival was enough. For a time government consoled itself (and the public) with predictions that staying on would gradually recover of its own accord.[98] However, as the cuts to teacher training bit hard after 1975, and QPR dropped sharply, indicating real violations of the Robbins Principle, doubts crept back in and discussion of the relationship between supply and demand resumed in 1978.[99] The DES now spoke of QPR as an 'opportunity/willingness' measure, recognizing that the willingness to participate in higher education did depend on the opportunity to do so actually offered by the availability of places.[100] Although there were some sharp disagreements within the civil service as to whether 'free demand' for higher education should always be met—with suggestions now that the Robbins Principle might be abandoned—government decided to reaffirm the Robbins Principle and even to promote demand by announcing new targets involving minuscule but serial increases in APR to 13.8 per cent in 1982, still below its 1970 levels, by which point they would be coming out the other side of the hump and fiscal pressures should relax (see Appendix, Figure 6.3).[101] Before it had to renounce even this rather miserable policy, the Labour government fell in the spring of 1979.[102]

What difference did Labour's policy struggles make? As we have seen, government told itself that the running was mostly made by private decisions about staying on, beyond its control. The staying on record was indeed gloomy through 1979. It is possible—though hard to demonstrate—that uncertainty about a sufficiency of higher-education places might have depressed staying on, too, though there were many other uncertainties to reckon with, some much more obvious to 16-year-olds than the projected future supply of HE places. The sudden cuts in teacher training must undoubtedly have changed many teenagers' plans, especially among young women, triggering a sudden drop in their qualified participation rates.[103] While this helps to explain the drop in women's full-time participation rates, it does not address the longer-term stagnation for both men and women. Much of that must have been due to the stagnation in staying on, aggravated by uncertainty; there was in addition probably some additional deterrence factor inhibiting entry to higher but not further education due to the very bad public image of higher education in the mid-1970s.[104]

A more significant effect on student behaviour in the 1970s was delivered not by the *amount* but by the *type* of higher education on offer. From the beginning of the binary policy, Labour had determined to pursue widening participation more through the polyechnic sector than through the university sector. In the 1970s the incentive to do so increased. Polytechnic places were a good deal cheaper than university places.[105] The UGC remained happy to accept less than its fair share of places in order to maintain its per capita funding levels and its elite status.[106] When times were tough, the public sector was equally determined to show its commitment to the social mission of higher education by expanding opportunities and actively courting underserved groups, thus their role in posing the question, 'What Has Happened to the Students?' As a result, at a time when university numbers were experiencing slow or no growth in absolute terms, numbers in polytechnics and colleges grew, sometimes very rapidly. By 1991 the polytechnics and colleges were educating almost twice as many higher-education students as universities were.[107]

To an extent the polytechnics were therefore taking on functions and students formerly the province of the universities. This 'academic drift' was deplored by some of the original architects of the polytechnic experiment, who had envisaged a distinctive role, catering to a working-class constituency, closer to employers, more technological, above all less 'academic' and more 'practical'.[108] The diversion of qualified leavers from universities to polytechnics was seen to imperil this distinctive vision, forcing the latter to behave more like the former to cater to their intrusive new constituency. But that vision as we have already noted reflected a misunderstanding of the public sector's natural constituency, based more on what socialists and employers wanted than what new entrants wanted. First, most new entrants to both universities and polytechnics were middle-class, and the fastest rate of growth was amongst white-collar workers.[109] That was where demand was highest, but—again, it cannot be repeated too often, because it is so often forgotten[110]—it was also where the general population was growing.[111] Second, the subject mix of polytechnics was not that different from universities. What differences there were arose not because of their closer links to employers but because of their greater openness to new entrants, whose interests and abilities differed from those of traditional entrants.[112] Third, the greater openness of polytechnics to unorthodox entrants (which did benefit some disadvantaged groups, especially ethnic minorities in London) was of most immediate use in the long 1970s to relatively well-educated women, who wanted to re-enter as mature students and often part-time.[113] Thus the shift of balance to the polytechnics during the long 1970s, even if triggered by financial and supply constraints, had the desirable effects of making higher education more directly responsive to the new demand there *was* in the system, whatever policymakers wanted.[114] Curiously, in this respect the Black Papers school was half-right about the polytechnics. They welcomed 'academic drift', because they held up a high ideal of the university, and wanted polytechnics to become just as aloof from immediate social needs as the universities were; in fact, 'academic drift' was precisely the agency by which polytechnics responded to the demands of new entrants to the higher-education system who would otherwise have been denied a place in it at all.[115]

If widening participation was in a bad way in the 1970s, though facilitated by a shift to the public sector, then the 1980s opened with even worse news: the advent of a government which did not share Labour's scruples about the Robbins Principle, which was uninterested in pretending to foster minute increases in the participation rate, which was bold enough to renounce Robbins altogether, even in public. This was a government eager to take public uncertainty about higher education as a sign that meritocracy was back in fashion, not as a complement to but as an alternative to democratic participation. At the same time, as we have seen, the early '80s saw a renewal of growth in staying on and even at last in the qualified leaver rate, as 'suppressed demand' began to build up. Something would have to give. We close the long 1970s with an important glimpse at this explosive situation in the early '80s.

Retreating from Robbins?

The mood music changed almost immediately upon the advent of Margaret Thatcher's new government in May 1979. Thatcher's determination to cut back public expenditure swept away pious hopes of minor annual improvements in APR and 'tunnelling through the hump'. Immediate caps on higher-education expenditure ('cash limits') were imposed, regardless of the state of the hump, and in March 1981 a cut of over 8 per cent by 1983 was announced. Universities and polytechnics were given the choice between

cuts in student numbers—which the universities preferred, swallowing a
3 per cent cut—or a reduction in unit costs—which the polytechnics preferred, leaving open the possibility of further expansion albeit at reduced
per capita funding levels.[116] This split proved convenient for the government, as it allowed it to pretend that it was still observing the Robbins
Principle, though privately it poured scorn on it as incompatible with fiscal
responsibility and sound national investment strategies.[117]

The real breach came with the advent of Keith Joseph as Secretary of
State in September 1981, with Rhodes Boyson as his understrapper.[118] Joseph
was a complex, highly intellectual person who spewed out a blizzard of
policies that are sometimes difficult to reconcile. As we will see in the next
chapter, these policies did not run solely in the direction of restricting access
to education, as they have been characterized by his ideological enemies.
However, in the field of higher education, he and Boyson certainly worried
that 'more is worse'. So in addition to market-based policies aimed at
driving up standards and attainment for all, he became a frank advocate of a
highly directive central-government policy of restricting access to higher
education—Robbins be damned. Fiscal restraint would be a good market
discipline for higher education, making it more cost-conscious and efficient.
But it was also good in itself—spurning demand that came in forms of
empty 'consumption' rather than targeted investment, and driving up standards by force majeure especially in the universities. In short, the best for
some, a meritocratic principle, would trump the best for more.[119]

Accordingly in the next fiscal year the previously announced cuts were
extended to 10 per cent by 1985, with planned reductions in teaching staff of
1/6th, in what was now explicitly called a 'rundown' of higher education.[120]
To ensure that the government would be able to engineer the rundown
across the binary line, it began to prise the colleges and polytechnics out of
local-authority control, erecting a UGC-type structure called the National
Advisory Body (NAB), and then agreed with both UGC and NAB a redefinition of the Robbins Principle. Government would now only endeavour
to fund places for all those 'willing and able to benefit' from higher education. Joseph saw this as an improvement upon 'willing and qualified',
because it no longer pledged him to regard mere numerical projections of
qualified applicant numbers, but introduced an element of judgement as to
'ability to benefit'. In this he was probably reflecting New Right thinking
about the limits to the 'pool of ability' that takes us back to the meritocratic
1950s, mixed with technocratic criteria based on cost-benefit analysis and

human-capital calculations.[121] Joseph was also encouraged to think that the whole landscape had been altered permanently by economic insecurity and that people of all classes had become more cautious about attempting higher education.[122] But it would prove a costly mistake, both politically and empirically, as few people in the 1980s any more than in the 1950s liked to consider themselves by definition excluded from such a pool, and more importantly many more people would be able in future to show that they were qualified.[123] Nevertheless, in the short run Joseph was confident that he would be able to achieve reductions on *both* sides of the binary line. He had hoped that the UGC would not reduce their student numbers but would accept as the NAB did the reduction in unit costs, but again they chose to stick to the higher funding levels and accept the hit in cuts to staff and students.[124] Either way, he looked to make a substantial contribution to the government's overall spending reduction plans.[125]

In this too he proved mistaken. Two factors escaped his notice or his control. One was the willingness of colleges and polytechnics to admit more students even at lower unit costs, with knock-on effects on public expenditure. The other was the returning willingness in the 1980s of formerly hesitant students to come forward for higher education. As we have seen, staying on rates were enjoying a period of recovery. Some of this was 'parking', as youth unemployment rates soared in the early '80s, and the labour market looked deeply unattractive. But nevertheless the qualified leaver rate was rising too and the DES now expected it to continue rising.[126] And so finally was the participation rate, APR, which Joseph had counted on to drop. Applications to higher education increased by 4 per cent in 1981 and by a further 4 per cent in 1982. Though university numbers were capped—and the university participation rate was falling—colleges and polytechnics were welcoming these new entrants with open arms and their participation rate was rising. This triggered a second unexpected factor. So long as they were accepted to a college or polytechnic, every new entrant was entitled to a mandatory LEA maintenance grant, with resulting higher costs to the Treasury.[127] To Joseph's horror, far from the planned 10 per cent expenditure cut making a contribution to the government's programme, the growth in APR was undermining it. APR was supposed to drop to 12.9 per cent in 1981–2 and then to as low as 11 per cent by 1984–5, something like a 10 per cent decline in participation rates to go with the 10 per cent expenditure cut.[128] In reality, DES knew already by March 1983 that APR was in fact rising to 13.5 per cent, as Joseph had disconsolately to report to Thatcher.[129]

And of course APR alone didn't even account for the full cost to the Treasury: think of all those mature women piling into the polytechnics, who didn't figure in APR at all.

While Labour had already made some play in Parliament with what they saw as the threat to the Robbins Principle in the proposed cuts and planned drop in APR,[130] it was the rise in APR that proved more threatening to the government—and, in the end, fatal to Joseph. Far from those 'willing and qualified' or even 'willing and able to benefit' being turned away, the qualified participation rate was now rising again, from 83 per cent to 88 per cent between 1979 and 1982, reaching levels that had been hopefully established as a healthy norm in the early '70s.[131] The DES's own projections now recognized, in stark contrast to the static ideas of society still prevalent in the 1970s, that absolute social mobility into non-manual classes was growing rapidly and that demand for higher education was likely to accelerate too, right up to the end of the century. By 1984 a whiff of Robbins' optimism had returned, at least among the social scientists employed by the DES.[132]

But not among Keith Joseph and his circle. He remained determined to keep down participation. Whereas for Labour, the hump was a regrettable demographic phenomenon, the passing through of the bulge, after which the trend might comfortably resume, for the Conservatives the end of the hump marked an opportunity to reverse direction. They substituted for Robbins' ever-rising curve of participation a new phase of falling participation, the reversal not only of the bulge but also of the trend. This was an ideological shift made conceivable by the long period of stagnation in higher-education growth, which lifted democratic pressure for more provision. Instead of setting a minimum standard and admitting all who passed it, on the assumption that more and more would pass it, government policy was henceforward to ration higher education, subject to meritocratic competition for a number of places set by governmental assessment of national needs.

This new policy was highly vulnerable to the resumption of democratic pressure, which was already building up under the radar in Joseph's period of office.[133] Still, as late as 1985, in his Green Paper, *The Development of Higher Education into the 1990s,* Joseph was grimly pursuing the rundown on both fiscal and social grounds. The Green Paper promised to bear down heavily on the requirement of 'ability to benefit': high standards must be maintained and *public* benefit must be considered as well and weighed against costs. Future estimates of demand could no longer be measured by numbers of qualified leavers, but must take into account this stringent definition of 'ability', including 'the intellectual competence, motivation and maturity' of leavers, as well as positives such as rising standards in schools and higher participation rates among women and negatives such as possible reductions in levels of grant, the greater attractiveness of the labour market, the need for further efficiency gains—oh yes, and manpower planning, back from the dead since the 1960s but crucial to boost the production of scientists, engineers, technologists, and technicians. Taking all these factors into account, the Green Paper grudgingly accepted a very slow rise in APR to 15.2 per cent by 1999, happily coinciding with the end of the bulge and thus producing a decline in student numbers from about 680,000 to 620,000 by the end of the century.[134]

Joseph's Green Paper was probably the most widely scorned government document on education policy of the twentieth century,[135] but even before its issue he had met his Waterloo. Determined to cut costs despite his failure to cut numbers, he had floated Rhodes Boyson's proposals for a partial replacement of the mandatory grant by loans a few years earlier, and though rebuffed even by Thatcher he returned to the fray in late 1984 with a new proposal for shifting the balance from grants to loans.[136] The reaction on the Tory backbenches was indescribable. Even worse than violating the Robbins Principle, by denying their constituents' children places, was charging them for it. 250 MPs attended an open meeting of the Education Committee on 4 December, the largest gathering of MPs since the Falklands War, and cheered on a backbencher who told Joseph bluntly to scrap the plan. The plan was scrapped.[137] A few months later Joseph tried again. Thatcher's advisers were divided but in the end the Cabinet decided definitively to preclude a loan scheme. Even Joseph's backer Oliver Letwin concluded, 'The best policy is for Keith Joseph to remain silent on this issue.'[138] Joseph limped on for nearly another year until Thatcher put him out of his misery in May 1986. In replacing him with a technocrat, Kenneth Baker, she signalled not only a change of personnel but an almost complete reversal of policy. From leading a government devoted to a 'rundown' of higher education, Thatcher became the prime minister who provided over its greatest-ever expansion, in truth its expansion into a mass higher-education system. It was an historic change of course, but what lay behind it was, as so often, the irrepressible and politically unstoppable force of demand for more and more education.

7

The Transition to Mass Education

To appreciate how dramatic were the changes of scale and ambition that began in the late 1980s—leading to the true culmination of Britain's transition to mass education that had begun in the 1940s—we need first to recall how low were expectations and ambitions just a few years before. Fifteen years of stagnation in educational participation had led to widespread despondency, even amongst the most ardent educationists. What would very soon seem to be wild theories about the British allergy to education were widely prevalent. There was 'a latent anti-intellectualism' in British society. The 'working class' had lost interest in education, or perhaps, as Orwell had observed, never had it, and 'there is little to suggest that a rejection of education does not remain a cultural phenomenon forty or more years later'.[1] The 'middle classes', education's natural constituency, were failing to reproduce.[2] This line of thinking was fuelled by the peaking of 'declinism', which since the late 1950s had been arguing that Britain was on the wrong path, held back by its semi-feudal, anti-industrial attitudes; after a brief period of resurgent optimism in the white heat of the 1960s 'technological revolution', the gloomier 1970s had brought declinism back with a vengeance, on both left and right. Britain needed a revolution, either of the workers or of the capitalists, to modernize itself. Education on its own was unlikely to achieve either. To the contrary, education had become the 'scapegoat', the 'whipping boy' for British economic failure, seen as the problem rather than the solution.[3]

The twin beliefs that both the people and the politicians had lost confidence in education fed on each other. On the one hand, the evidence that demand for education had slumped in the early 1970s allowed politicians to depress supply in order to 'tunnel through the hump' and avoid fully funding education at its demographic peak. The best that could be achieved in these circumstances, it was held, was scraping together enough non-traditional entrants—mature and part-time students—to start 'bridging the valley' when the demographic downturn arrived, and prevent a catastrophic shrinkage of the higher-education sector.[4] On the other hand, Labour's attempt to 'tunnel through the hump' in the late 1970s gave Keith Joseph confidence that he could suppress demand deliberately and for the longer-term without any serious political consequences, despite repeated warnings to the contrary from the DES.[5] No 'bridging the valley' for him. These two mutually supportive brands of pessimism permitted most pundits to ignore contrary (though still contradictory) evidence—rising attainment to 16, still stuttering staying-on rates, growing evidence of unsatisfied demand pressure for higher education—right through the mid-1980s. Demand for education had been building up for some years before the supply tap was turned on, and there is good reason to think that the power and irrepressibility of that demand was itself responsible for the restoration of supply.

Once again, however, the predominant political narrative has credited heroic politicians—in this case, principally Joseph's successor Kenneth Baker—with the reversal; and once the supply tap is turned back on, the resulting resurgence of demand, a true torrent this time, is simply taken for granted.[6] In charting the Conservatives' dramatic reversal of policy in the late 1980s, we will not take demand for granted; neither will we take at face value the arguments that Conservative politicians made for the new policy, mostly technocratic and meritocratic. We will as ever seek to embed the achievement of mass education in a wider context of changing class structure, changing occupational structure, expectations of the state and of education in particular. Britain was undergoing a massive set of social changes in the closing years of the twentieth century, which still embroil it today. It is not necessarily a criticism of gloomy contemporaries of the early '80s that they failed to see it; it is hard to find anyone who did. No-one really saw coming deindustrialization, the shrinking of the working class, multiculturalism, the rise of the 'learning society' and the 'knowledge economy'.[7] No-one foresaw the most extraordinary expansion of educational demand and provision in modern British history. That's the value of history: hindsight by no means gives 20:20 vision, but it sure helps.

Returning to Robbins

Explanations for the Conservatives' shift to rapid expansion of the higher-education do not of course solely focus on the personality of Ken Baker; they are multiple and often confused, to suit a complicated juncture, much like the stagnation of the 1970s. To many well-informed commentators it seemed almost an accident—'a fit of absent-mindedness', in a verdict of the educationist Peter Scott, or '[a] typical British muddle', not by will but by inertia.[8] Certainly much seemed to turn on Thatcher's reluctant decision to ditch Joseph and 'more is worse' and to embrace Baker's cheerful, even populist optimism. Both world-views, it should be said, lay at the heart of Thatcherism, which wove together strands of 'neo-conservatism'—hostility to the permissive society, the exaltation of 'standards', a focus on elite leadership, a degree of reverence for tradition—and 'neo-liberalism'—a belief in the liberating power of markets, an appeal to 'ordinary' people and their desire to better themselves and their families, a scepticism about traditional elites and an excitement about entrepreneurship, innovation, and change.[9] In educational terms, therefore, Thatcherism could encompass both a narrow, ladder-like understanding of meritocracy—the 'sponsored mobility' of the grammar school and the elite university, evident in Joseph's thinking—and the 'more generous' understanding of meritocracy formerly associated with the left—not just 'contest mobility' where all could contend for prizes, but more provision so that more people could succeed, evident in the thinking of Baker and also of his junior minister Robert Jackson who came on board in 1987.[10]

Why, then, did government policy shift from the one foot to the other?[11] The immediate impetus, as we've seen, came from the backbench revolt against Joseph's schemes to replace grants with loans. But the moment was propitious in other ways. After two successive electoral victories, and another one in the offing, the Thatcher governments were relaxing into office; more significantly, the economy was recovering from the depths of its deindustrializing depression in the early 1980s, and the lineaments of a new economic settlement were taking shape. Economic recovery also relieved the pressure for fiscal austerity. It was possible, as Baker and Jackson argued, to see the rigours through which Carlisle and Joseph had put higher education as simply a preliminary exercise to improve efficiency and drive down unit costs, after which expansion could be safely and more cheaply attempted; the 'rolling revolution', Jackson called it. That was the way the authors of the new policy tended to interpret it in retrospect, thus conveniently disposing of Joseph's contractionist policy and his 'more is worse' thinking. 'More' could now be better, so long as it was more efficient. By the late 1980s, faced with the horrors not only of the rundown but of the deepening demographic slump, the universities had come to share this view, at length accepting the formula long exploited by the polytechnics of taking more students at lower unit costs. They had little choice; after the Croham Report of 1987, the UGC was disbanded and replaced by a funding council, much more frankly an 'agency of Government'. While the new funding councils were touted as exposing higher education to 'market forces', it was not intended to give more, but rather less weight to the market force of student demand; instead, what government had in mind was 'cost-effectiveness and the employment market for graduates'. In this they would be half-satisfied; lower unit costs would certainly become the order of the day, but so would the market force of demand, and only indirectly the employment market for graduates.[12]

Driving down unit costs was of course a pretty uncontroversial goal in the Thatcher world, including amongst the likes of Keith Joseph. Much depended on how far growth in participation would then be expected or desired. Baker was initially cautious about this. His first major statement, the April 1987 White Paper *Higher Education: Meeting the Challenge*, offered a choice between a return to Labour's incremental growth in APR (from the current 14.2 per cent to 15.8 per cent by 2000) and a more optimistic projection dependent on widening participation to 18.5 per cent. Still, even modest optimism in 1987 made a refreshing contrast to Joseph's determination as late as 1985 to keep APR down. In this White Paper, Baker offered two reasons for thinking participation might grow: one was the awareness of social change that the DES had been voicing since 1984, pointing minimally to the positive effect of more educated parents on their children's choices; the other, exemplifying Baker's characteristic bumptiousness but also tickling Thatcher's tummy, was 'to reflect the success of the Government's policies for schools and non-advanced further education' by raising standards for all. This more expansive and populist version of Thatcherism wanted to remind voters that, far from seeking to keep them in their place, the government shared in their aspirations to a better life.[13]

Baker's own motivations, and very often his public rhetoric, were straightforwardly technocratic—'a very un-Conservative approach', as he admitted, at least in Thatcher's world.[14] He did believe, in a way reminiscent of the 1960s, that investments in human capital would pay off in economic growth, so long as (in the words of the White Paper) that investment 'serve[d] the economy more effectively' and 'promote[d] enterprise', based on 'closer links with industry and commerce' and consideration of 'the needs of the economy so as to achieve the right number and balance of graduates' and to achieve 'the necessary shift towards science, engineering and vocational courses'.[15] The new funding councils were initially intended to do just that. Baker's most telling argument was that, while the qualified workforce was likely to shrink during the demographic trough, employers' need for qualified labour would not; certainly not if economic growth was to continue. Therefore the proper response was to 'bridge the valley' with higher participation rates—though the argument could be extended to ever higher levels of participation so long as the returns on investment remained high.[16] It wasn't at all neo-conservative and not even very neo-liberal. Though Baker certainly believed that markets could help break up vested interests, he was also a great believer in direct government investment for growth, including the funding of more higher-education places, especially if firmly directed to technical education and the support of manufacturing industry, where he had worked before entering politics.[17] Thus growth in participation ought to parallel economic growth, two things which in Baker's mind were closely connected.

There were more purposively expansive voices in the mix as well. Interestingly one of them was an industry lobby, the Council for Industry and Higher Education, founded by technocrats in 1986 and funded by a galaxy of the biggest British-based multinational companies. These funders included a fair share of manufacturing giants—food processors, oil companies like Royal Dutch Shell for whom Baker had worked, engineering firms— who could be relied upon to promote a technocratic policy of 'employer needs'. But they also included heavy hitters in the newly expanding service sector—accountancy, information technology, management consultancy.[18] They were less concerned about training engineers and more about training managers. They were even more concerned with raising the general level of education in the whole population. As they put it in a characteristic statement in 1988:

> We must change our higher education system from one geared to a small minority to a more open system which brings many more people to a generally higher level of education than they attain now. Broadening access and increasing

the numbers and variety of students in higher education is seen by companies as the most important and the most urgent [priority]. They see this to be not only a matter of their narrower self-interest, but as critical for the nation's economic and social future. The Government's present unambitious plans for expanding the number of highly educated people are at odds with industry's hopes for growth and its perceptions of what the UK needs to develop its position in world markets.[19]

This was industry striking a new and perhaps unexpected note, critical of a Conservative government and boosting an educational programme aimed not at regenerating manufacturing industry but at feeding the 'knowledge economy', a neologism then gaining currency.[20] The main employers' organization the CBI chimed in similarly; puzzlingly to some ministers they seemed more interested in general education than in connecting universities directly to industry. 'The size and nature of higher education should be largely determined by the demands of the customers', that is, the students as much as the employers, they told Baker in 1986.[21]

With industry taking this view, there was wind in the sails of those Conservatives who favoured a general expansion of educational opportunity, of course in tandem with continuing attention to 'standards', without the same close attention to direct impacts on the economy. The most vocal and influential of these was not Baker but his junior minister, Robert Jackson. Jackson was a keen advocate of markets to break up vested interests; he defected to the Labour party in 2005 in protest at the Tories' failure to support Labour's introduction of higher tuition fees.[22] But he was also a self-consciously cultivated man who wanted very much to spread 'the higher values of our civilization' as well as 'the allocation of its material rewards' to as many people as possible, as he said in a 1988 speech extolling the virtues of expanding higher education. This combination of views made him a doughty advocate for a more generous meritocracy, using both markets *and* government provision to expand what he called the 'opportunity society', at the same time acting as a useful check on Baker's narrower technocratic tendencies.[23] And in fact Jackson served as an inspiration to Baker: he wrote the famous Lancaster speech of 1989 (not as famous as it should be) in which Baker put forward an ambitious vision of widening participation more than just 'bridging the valley'.

At the time of the Lancaster speech the government's public and private targets for participation had been steadily creeping up from Joseph's low points for a few years, but no major breach with the recent past had been bruited. By January 1989 the target had risen to 16 per cent APR by 1991–2 and 18.6 per cent by 2000, mostly because resurgent demand had already breached the incremental targets set in the previous few years, but still on a trend more modest than Robbins' and not much above the levels of the 1987 White Paper. The goal was simply to bridge the valley and then to see if a further demographic upturn in the 1990s might restabilize the sector's numbers.[24] The speech that Jackson wrote and Baker delivered at Lancaster University in January 1989 represented a step-change in tone and numbers. Unusually, the civil servants reported, the ministers had taken it out of their hands and plotted it themselves. In many respects it resumed the language of long-term expansion pioneered by Robbins but long in abeyance. Across the developed world, Baker argued, 'a more affluent society' and 'wider aspirations' were powering a dramatic expansion of higher education. Europe was reaching American levels of affluence and should aspire to similar levels of educational participation. Not just an incremental growth, but a possible doubling of participation levels ought to be anticipated. Current expectations of a rise to 20 per cent APR—even that figure higher than the one the government had publicly committed to—would be exceeded and 30 per cent or higher could reasonably be accommodated if Britain also emulated the Americans in adopting a more diversified, market-led model of provision. More would not mean worse—or at least the ideas about 'quality' suited to 3 per cent were irrelevant to 'mass higher education' roping in 30 per cent.[25]

This was language and these were numbers far exceeding even Robbins' wildest expectations. Almost as interesting as the dramatic change of tone from ministers was the lagging expectations of everyone else in the world of education, still immersed in the stagnant gloom of the 'rundown' and disinclined to believe Tory promises. The *Times Higher Education Supplement* ran a special spread on the speech, but all of its commentators were highly sceptical. Where would the students come from? Would the Treasury fund it? Do we really want to become more like America? A year later, by which time Baker had been replaced, Alison Utley, the weekly's universities correspondent, was still dubious that the bodies could even be found: surely there would never be enough qualified leavers to reach a 30 per cent participation rate for the whole cohort of 18 and 19-year-olds?[26]

Yet the bodies had been presenting themselves in ever increasing numbers—in truth, since the late 1970s, albeit squelched by a declining supply of places; and certainly since the mid-1980s. Within a few years even the most committed sceptic could hardly deny it. A further government White Paper, *Higher Education: A New Framework*, was rushed out in May 1991 because the 1987 targets had already been so comprehensively exceeded. The 2000 target for APR had been reached—in 1991!—and a new target in line with the Lancaster speech of nearly a third of all 18- and 19-year-olds in higher education by 2000 had to be set. Even that line underestimated the growth in the system as it turned out that more mature students as well as young entrants were pouring in; taking into account renewed demographic growth from 1996 as well, something like a 50 per cent growth in numbers was expected by 2000. The White Paper admitted that growth was almost entirely driven by demand, though of course it gave itself a pat on the back by crediting this to the government's school reforms. But it had to admit that Baker's quid pro quo—more students would have to study science and technology to justify the investment—had been abandoned. A lower proportion was studying science and technology; but never mind—the Robbins escalator was rolling again, and the overriding goal, as the new Prime Minister John Major said in his foreword, was simply to ensure that 'even more of our young people . . . go on to higher education'.[27]

This ambitious target was also quickly overtaken. 28 per cent APR was reached not in 1995 as projected but in the very next academic year. The valley had not only been bridged but had been filled to overflowing. This extraordinarily rapid growth continued for a few more years and then slowed somewhat, though it had still met the one-third target hypothesized for some time after 2000 in 1997 (see Appendix, Figure 6.1). Nothing like it had ever been seen before or has been seen since, not only in British history, but practically in the history of any other country in so short a time, except Korea in recent years; and yet it has been systematically short-changed, explained away, under-appreciated or unexamined.[28] Not only did it betoken a reservoir of demand on a scale completely unimagined, but the force of demand in breaking open the system also changed the rhetoric and the direction of government policy, so that expansion of higher-education provision essentially for its own sake became the explicit goal of both main parties, as John Major's foreword suggested.

One curious feature of this extraordinary boom, which suggests further how much it took even the best-informed by surprise, is the slowness of the Treasury to wake up to its fiscal implications. Normally the Treasury, especially under Conservative governments, acted as an effective brake on escalating public-expenditure commitments. In this case, they seemed as overtaken by events as anyone. Some complacency had set in after a sharp downturn in public expenditure in the early '80s had produced balanced budgets, and public expenditure was generally allowed to rise for some years though revenues did not.[29] The Treasury was further appeased by Baker's promise in the Lancaster speech that higher-education growth would not outpace economic growth to the year 2000.[30] In the short term, too, it was widely believed that incremental growth could be paid for by an incremental reduction in the teaching grant paid on a per capita basis to institutions, the policy pursued with the polytechnics earlier. That could only go so far, as the teaching grant was not infinitely shrinkable (it shrank by a third per capita between 1989 and 1997); and, as the Treasury had discovered, the costs of mandatory maintenance grants had clawed back most of the savings achieved earlier in the decade. In fact the government had made a rod for its own back by eliminating intermediary bodies like the UGC with whom it could have negotiated limits on student numbers; the new funding councils were simpler structures with funding formulae rather than bargaining agents. Since '[o]nly a government with an electoral death-wish' could abandon the Robbins Principle now, as the last UGC chairman Peter Swinnerton-Dyer observed in 1991, it was left with only the limited and clumsy tool of the per capita grant to staunch the outflow of public funds.[31] And that tool proved *very* ineffective—the growth of student numbers greatly outpaced the decline in the per capita teaching grant, so that public expenditure on higher education grew 50 per cent in real terms between 1985 and 1995 (see Appendix, Figure 7.1) and nearly as much as a percentage of GDP.

As a credible counterweight, however, the government showed a renewed appetite for higher-education fees and loans to offset public expenditure, feeling perhaps that these bitter pills were more easily swallowed in Baker's period of rapid expansion than in Joseph's of grim contraction. Maintenance grants, already means-tested, were frozen in autumn 1990 and topped up with loans; in return for this concession, the Treasury agreed to fix the per capita grant at a level that would cover the cost of an unlimited number of new entrants.[32] As costs continued to mount with soaring participation, Robert Jackson was working hard to extend the idea of loans for the first time to tuition.[33] But after Joseph's debacle such proposals would take a long time to mature, and by the early '90s the Treasury had finally woken up to the great peril which student demand posed. In 1994 a new formula to control total student numbers was finally imposed which did not end expansion but slowed and channelled it.[34] By then, the barn-door, having been opened wide, would prove impossible to close. Even with a plummeting per capita grant, and demographic shrinkage, public expenditure on higher education grew more rapidly in the period 1986–97 than virtually any other category. Politically, too, once unleashed the force of demand was hard even to impede, much less to halt. Limits to student numbers, if not quite an 'electoral death-wish', certainly provided another nail in the coffin of Major's deepening unpopularity on educational grounds with the electorate that led finally to the Labour landslide of 1997.[35]

Where Did All the Students Come From?

Despite (or perhaps because of) the fact that student demand on this scale came as such a surprise, not much attempt was made at the time to try to understand it; there was no equivalent to the 1974 conference that asked 'what has happened to the students?' to ask 'where did all the students come from?'. In part because it came so unpalatably on a Conservative watch, not much further attempt has been made since by historians of education, except to explain the Conservatives' own motives;[36] the motives of the students remain relatively unplumbed. We can begin by asking who they were.

One obvious, immediate source of demand was that which had been temporarily suppressed by constricted supply, at least since the late 1970s. The DES had calculated in 1983 that something like one-sixth of demand was being frustrated by the 'rundown', and when released this would obviously provide a ready source of new entrants; however, that backlog would presumably be exhausted within a few years and in any case it was still predicated on lower APR than actually materialized in the 1990s.[37] Clearly more novel sources of demand were being drawn on. Much of this derived from groups that had been staying on at school after 16 but (because they were lower attainers) were supposed to be 'parking'—that is, waiting out a period of youth unemployment, avoiding the unpleasant, dead-end youth training schemes of the Thatcher era, bound to return to the labour market when it turned up.[38] But they didn't. Staying on rates began to rise sharply in the mid-'80s, even as high unemployment eased off, reaching saturation rates for the well-off (86 per cent of the top quintile by the late '90s) and topping 60 per cent even for the bottom quintile.[39] If this was 'parking', it was parking with a purpose, including among lower-attaining groups. From 1984 many were studying at further-education colleges for qualifications from the Business and Technical Education Council (BTEC), designed to provide more vocational alternatives to O- and A-levels. The polytechnics however had come to accept them as qualifiers for higher education and gradually they provided access to almost as wide a range of degrees as did conventional academic qualifications, in England and Wales for about 10 per cent of higher-education entrants.[40] The Access courses opened from the late 1970s, also mostly at FE colleges, provided a different route for another 10 per cent, more likely to be mature students;[41] the Open University's foundation courses yet another.[42] What in the early '80s had seemed desperate hiding places from the labour market became an unparalleled platform for mass further and higher education. All in all, Britain had more non-traditional routes to higher education than most other European countries.[43]

Even more striking, however, from the low point of expectations in the early 1980s, most of the new entrants—and indeed a growing proportion of them—came via traditional academic qualifications, A-levels in England and Wales, Highers in Scotland. In Scotland, especially, FE colleges provided school-leavers with Highers and then actually started them out on higher education with sub-degree courses, so that over half of all HE entrants in Scotland by 1999 had started in an FE college.[44] In England and Wales, about a third of 18 year olds now had A-levels, although despite this massive growth that level was still being taken as a ceiling. They provided half of all polytechnic and nearly all university entrants.[45] All sorts of people who had not previously been considered likely to qualify for higher education, certainly not via A-levels, were doing so in growing numbers: ethnic minorities (now over-represented in HE), women (similarly, in the 1990s now a majority of HE entrants), working-class offspring (whose participation rates were growing at pretty much the same levels as everyone else).[46]

One final and crucial factor which kept the surge going long after suppressed demand had been cleared was Britain's ultimate ability to lower the barrier its divided school system had previously erected at 16. Here the unexpected architect—or at least facilitator—was Keith Joseph. It was on his watch that the entrenched divide between lower achievers at school, taking no qualifications at 16 or only CSE, and higher achievers, taking GCE O-levels and A-levels, was finally bridged. A new qualification, gradually extended to nearly all students, the General Certification of Secondary

Education (GCSE), had already been approved when Baker took the reins; it was first examined in 1988.

For present purposes we shouldn't linger over the question of *why* Joseph let this longstanding demand of the left and of teachers' unions slip through. It was certainly consistent with Conservative rhetoric from the mid-1970s, arguing that driving up 'standards' for all would benefit the less advantaged most, even if it didn't fit neatly into either neo-conservative or neo-liberal boxes.[47] Joseph was more enthusiastic about it than Thatcher, whose own neo-conservative side worried about diluting standards for the elite and whose neo-liberal side worried about an academic drift away from 'practical skills'. Joseph endeavoured to persuade her that GCSE was both *more* differentiating—it would mark out the elite from the mass—and *more* practical.[48] Whatever their motives, the tide of opinion was running strongly in favour. Scotland already had in preparation the S-grade, introduced in 1984, with much the same character.[49] Growing awareness of the attainment gap at 16 in England and Wales, combined with Joseph's conviction that higher education was going to contract, may have made GCSE seem to him like a vocational programme—much like BTEC—aimed not at the high flyers who would go on to A-levels and university but at the lower achievers who needed to be dragged up to improve British competitiveness.

Whatever Joseph's and Thatcher's motives, the consensus is that GCSE was the single most important supplier of new entrants to higher education during the long boom.[50] GCSE provided a bridge that took larger and larger tranches of the 16–18 cohort into post-compulsory and ultimately into higher education. Of course O-level qualification rates and staying-on rates would probably have risen steadily anyway, but GCSE gave easier access to the non-traditional, quasi-vocational routes to higher education such as BTEC and, in conjunction with a later reform, dividing the A-level into two steps (AS and A-level), helped narrow the gaps between each year of attainment from 14 to 18. Pedagogically it combined subjects and techniques from both CSE and GCE, thus integrating the mix of secondary-modern and grammar-school traditions that comprehensives had always embodied.[51] Ever since GCSE takers emerged onto the higher education scene in the 1990s, they have kept the demand tank full, as the proportion of those with 'good' GCSEs eligible to progress to A-levels continued to rise even when other considerations might have been checking progression.[52] Because the principal effect of GCSE and S-grade was to give more opportunities to lower attainers who had had less success with O-level and O-grade, these

Thatcher-era examination reforms have a claim to be among the few government policies clearly not only to raise overall attainment levels but also to narrow the attainment gap between social classes.[53]

The Knowledge Economy and the Learning Society

So the new students came from all classes, both genders, all ethnicities; they came via Access courses and the Open University and FE colleges, and most of all from schools. But why did they come? Government policy may have invited them in, but supply (despite Say's Law which pretends otherwise[54]) could not at least in this area literally create demand: it couldn't raise attainment levels or staying-on rates to ensure the flow of qualified leavers and it couldn't on its own coax previously reluctant qualified leavers into higher education. Clearly the gloomy prognostications about the limits to educability and the crisis of confidence in education had been falsified; but what had changed between the 1970s and the 1990s to drive so many people to staying on so much longer in post-compulsory education?

Insofar as anyone has even sought to answer this question, the conventional answer has been an economic one: it was a better investment to study than it had been.[55] While once economists might have havered between seeing education as an investment or a consumption good, they now tilt strongly to the former, and many others without the same intellectual rationale have followed their lead. In general terms, it has become conventional since the late 1980s increasingly to consider our economy as a 'knowledge economy', where education (an investment in human capital, rather than in plant or technology) plays a larger role in most jobs. In more specific terms, economists have described a process of 'skill-biased technological change' (SBTC) whereby the new technologies driving economic growth have tended to require a more skilled workforce.[56] The strongest evidence for this process is often taken directly from Britain's educational experience—the fact that despite the huge, sudden growth of British higher education the 'graduate premium', the extra amount that employers are willing to pay graduates over those with only A-levels, has remained stable for 25 years, at around 50 per cent. Surely only a mounting demand for the particular skills evidenced by higher education could explain this extraordinary phenomenon?[57]

Answering this question proves much more complicated than it appears, and whole books could be (and have been) written in the attempt.[58] Economists have tended to consider it simple. Increasingly they have reduced changes in educational participation (among many other things) to matters of rational investment choice. Every cost—foregone income, fees for education—must have its commensurate benefit. If more people participate in higher education, it must be on the basis of a preternaturally accurate estimate of future earnings, 'discounted' for the interval which it takes to realize them—so a 50 per cent premium sounds about right to explain expansion, expansion will continue as long as that premium holds up, and that premium will hold up as long as there is some bias in the labour market towards the skills that graduates have (such as the aforementioned SBTC).[59]

It was not always thus. Recall that the progenitors of human-capital theory around 1960, Theodore Schwartz and Gary Becker, were happy to acknowledge that 'consumption benefits' (without income payoffs) and 'social returns' to education were available alongside private returns. As late as the early 1980s Christopher Pissarides' model to explain staying-on rates alternated between periods when education was paying off and periods when it wasn't—that is, between considering education as an investment *and* a consumption good. But economists since have veered away from this more complex understanding.[60] Better datasets—the birth-cohort studies, labour-force surveys, household surveys and the like—and more sophisticated statistical manipulations have allowed them to tailor quantitative models based on investment that fit at least some periods of recent history; when the models no longer fit, they move on, as Pissarides did. Policymakers like investment models because they justify educational expansion (which voters favour) in technocratic terms that appeal to the Treasury. And economists, sociologists, historians, and others drift further apart as they become more specialized and less interested in each other's findings.

So economists usually content themselves, in explaining the great expansion since the late 1980s, with models that show a sizable and stable graduate premium sucking more and more students into higher education, and they hypothesize SBTC to explain this phenomenon. Even on their own terms there are problems with this model. As we saw at the outset, over the longer-term there is no clear correlation between educational growth and economic growth or between participation rates and economic incentives. Even the prime movers of SBTC, Goldin and Katz, in describing the 'race between education and technology' in the US seem to accept that education came first; perhaps supply created its own demand (reshaping the labour market around educated workers and thus triggering SBTC), but leaving in question what created supply.[61] Something similar has been said about the British experience more recently—a sudden surge in graduates has enabled a late exploitation of SBTC.[62] But in other places there appears to be little connection between high productivity and a high graduate premium; Denmark, for example, has had high productivity, high living standards, and a low graduate premium.[63] Indeed, if you make international comparisons, the statistical correlations tend to vary wildly—16-year-old boys in England but 18-year-old boys in Germany appear to treat education more as an investment good while their Dutch and Swedish counterparts treat it as more as a consumption good, at least for the initial period of widening participation.[64]

Furthermore, if you decompose the overall graduate premium to see *who* benefits from it and when, as sociologists prefer to do, you can discover many other factors determining graduate premia other than high productivity earned from more education. For example, women's graduate premium has in the recent period consistently exceeded men's—perhaps because they were traditionally underpaid as graduate workers, or because they are still underpaid as non-graduate workers. Since women make up an increasing share of the graduate workforce, their improving position may help to account for the overall graduate premium, not necessarily skill-related.[65] Or it may be that the real changes are taking place at the lower end of the labour market, with a proliferation of poorly paid, low-skill jobs, boosting the graduate premium from the other end—'routine-based' rather than 'skill-based' technological change. Though mounting demand for these jobs (for example, in caring and catering) ought to produce wage gains, conventional and status distinctions prevail over market considerations, driving 'routine' and 'skilled' occupations further apart.[66] Both routine and skill-biased changes may be occurring at the same time, in what is termed a 'hollowing out' or 'polarization' of the labour market, driving graduates and non-graduates further apart. The routinization of many jobs seems to bring with it a need for more managerial skill to superintend them.[67]

Most significantly, it may just be that as more people are entering the graduate labour market more employers need to go there to find their necessary labour, whether or not more skill is entailed. People had encountered this phenomenon before, in the earlier phase of expansion in the 1960s, when employers who had formerly taken on workers at 16 or 18 found themselves having to wait until 21 and thus willy-nilly becoming graduate employers; thus law and accountancy became graduate professions alongside teaching. The premium attaching to these good jobs was won at 21 rather than 18, and became a graduate premium—the earnings were reaped with the acquisition of a degree, not A-levels.[68] Something similar happened in the post-1980s expansion. A huge swathe of jobs necessarily became graduate jobs, notably jobs traditionally held by women, such as ancillary medical jobs—nursing, ophthalmics, nutrition, physiotherapy—and in hospitality and tourism, but also jobs traditionally held by men—most recently, for example, public relations and estate agency.[69]

In such cases, employers would not seem to be requiring higher education to meet their need for new technological skills, such as data processing or higher analytical skills, but as a 'screening' mechanism to find the right kind of employee, defined by the same criteria they had always applied— 'soft skills' or behavioural characteristics associated with the upper social classes predominant in higher education ('looking good and sounding right'[70]), trainability (since employment-specific skills are still mostly acquired on the job rather than in education[71]), or at best generic skills characteristic of higher-achieving students at whatever level they end up.[72] The larger and more diverse the graduate workforce, the more employers need simple screening mechanisms to make sense of it. It is striking that in the UK most job advertisements don't specify educational qualifications—the skills they require are generic, and they will be trained on the job—but employers still use those qualifications to screen for the 'best' candidates.[73]

Although in theory economists admit education might work in this 'allocative' way, not so much buying skill as sorting the workforce, in practice they prefer all decisions involving cost to have a more direct benefit.[74] They argue that it's skill-generating education that is driving higher productivity and thus higher incomes in the modern world. If not, they say, drawing larger and larger tranches of the workforce into the graduate labour market must eventually dilute it and lower the graduate premium at the bottom end, leading not only to inefficiency—why pay for the education if it doesn't pay off?—and also to 'under-employment' and frustration. But this is exactly what has happened. As we are all now uneasily aware, the 'dispersal' of wages within the graduate labour market is getting greater and greater; 'within-group inequality' is higher. If the graduate premium remains stable, this may be not because graduates are still paid well but because *some* graduates are paid *a lot* more. Graduate doctors and lawyers and bankers are pulling away from graduate estate agents and baristas, and keeping the overall premium high. One model shows exactly this—a growing graduate premium for the top quintile of graduates, stagnation or decline for the rest. (That may mean that polarization is not only dividing graduates from non-graduates, but also some graduates from others, as SBTC or some other driver of income inequality benefits only a relatively small group.)[75] This should in theory slow or reverse educational expansion even if the overall graduate premium remains stable—unless, that is, people have other reasons for seeking higher education.[76]

What might those other reasons be? As we noted at the outset, while education may well be a driver of economic growth (that is, a human-capital investment that raises productivity[77]), people have many other reasons to seek it apart from 'private returns'. In the pioneer case of the United States, the 'high school movement' may have driven the nation's rapid economic growth in the twentieth century, but it preceded it, driven itself by other, social, civic, and democratic motivations. By the 1960s, governments in many developed countries had awakened to the potential of educational investment to promote growth—thus the novel popularity of human capital theory in policy circles—but as we saw in Chapters 3–5 their technocratic arguments for investment were just as often a rationale for responding to demand as the principal stimulus for educational expansion. In Britain, disillusionment with the payoffs to these human-capital investments had led to a slump in state support for education in the 1970s, which was then again overwhelmed by demand pressures in the 1980s.

It was of course possible (and probably true to some extent) that parents and adolescents saw the way the wind was blowing better than politicians, and demanded education in order to benefit from the emerging 'knowledge economy'. But many other factors are as likely to affect people's educational preferences as the 'hyper-rationality' imputed by economists' models of rational, discounted expectations of future returns on investment, as if teenagers and their parents were econometricians.[78] As entrants get more numerous and diverse, you might expect in fact their motivations to be rather different and more various. Educational demand depends on the past as much as the future. The best predictor of educational trajectory is 'prior attainment', and thanks to accumulating improvements in educational attainment in the 1970s and '80s—higher staying-on rates, higher O-level and O-grade attainment, the extra boost given by GCSE and S-grade, the multiple paths now available from S-grade and GCSE to higher education—there was plenty of fuel in the tank to power expansion well into the future.

Whatever constraints on supply had been imposed by government from the mid-'70s to the mid-'80s had now been removed. Whatever uncertainties about education felt by parents and children in the early-to-mid-'70s now seemed to have been overcome. The Robbins escalator was well and truly moving again. What is more, as Gambetta points out, educational decisions are much less constrained than labour-market decisions—that is to say, the former rely primarily on motivations among parents and children alone, while the latter require matching between their motivations and those of employers.[79] In looking forward, parents and children can bring to bear a much wider set of motivations and hopes for the future than just econometric ones. We can characterize this cluster of motivations impelling the tide of widening participation with another neologism that came into currency in the late 1980s, rather more popular than 'knowledge economy'; the 'learning society'.[80]

While a great deal of attention has been paid to the alleged loss of confidence in education that set in during the 1970s, very little has been accorded the evident resurgence of confidence in the 1990s and after.[81] Education had always been second only to health in people's stated preferences for public expenditure; now support for more education spending rose from a half in 1983 to two-thirds in 2002, with support for higher education growing most rapidly. The pollsters who monitor these results have tended to assume along with everyone else that young people were almost sullenly being herded into higher educational levels by the demands of the labour market—'the entry fee for young people into adult society . . . had simply gone up'—but their own results show greater optimism at all levels. Support for selection which had peaked in the early '80s dropped. People were much more confident that secondary schools were instilling the basics 'quite' or 'very well'. They favoured more investment in teachers and buildings and put better job preparation and training low down their list of priorities. Their concerns about job security dropped and the emphasis they placed on 'interesting work' in the first job grew. Over the course of the 1990s, education became one of the government's public-opinion black spots because they were seen to be under-investing.[82] Once again education joined health as a centre of voters' concerns; once again 'local schools and hospitals' were twinned as welfare-state commitments which inspired intense attachment.[83] After all the hesitations of the long 1970s, many of the assumptions about education familiar from the 1960s had returned: that education was a core entitlement of citizenship, that everyone deserved the best schools, that a general advance for all and not only a contest for relative advantage was possible. John Major's appeal to apparent public support for selection, promising to restore a grammar school to every town, fell flat as a pancake; one Conservative educationist called selection 'like unilateral disarmament for Labour; it appeals only to activists'.[84] Sure enough New Labour's 1997 landslide came on the back of Tony Blair's commitment that his government's three main priorities would be 'education, education, and education'.[85]

Some aspects of the 'learning society' of course drew on the 'knowledge economy'. As economic growth resumed in the 1990s, and the economic switchbacks of the preceding two decades receded into memory, people undoubtedly grew more optimistic about the economic potential of education. You didn't need an accurate estimate of the wage returns to education to see in the 1980s and '90s that the number of manual jobs was shrinking rapidly, that opportunities for less-skilled youth employment and apprenticeship were collapsing, that more people were being employed in the 'knowledge economy' of offices and services, and that education was (as always, but now for many more people) the best route into these jobs. As we will see in the next chapter, the same applied to the unusually rapid decline in industrial jobs, including non-manual ones, relieving any pressure students might have felt to study 'technical' subjects.[86] Apprenticeships were in decline along with the industrial (especially engineering) jobs for which they had conventionally been designed.[87] In the same way, new vocational qualifications like those offered by BTEC from 1984 proved more useful as routes to higher education equivalent to A-levels than as stand-alone vocational qualifications. Even 'modern' apprenticeships introduced in 1994, aimed at those who still leave school at 16, are now mostly taken up at advanced or higher levels which either give access to or are accepted as higher-education qualifications.[88] The traditional popular suspicion of vocational courses as second-class—far from '[snobbery] about the horny-handed' (a characterization by academics revealing their own inverted snobbery)—encouraged most to seek A-levels and higher education as the 'best' route to the widest range of jobs, while at the same time avowing the importance of 'good practical skills'.[89]

But occupational change was only part of a bigger picture. As prior attainment built up, education simply became a more normal part of most people's lives. Instead of most people leaving school at 16, most people stayed on as a matter of course.[90] Given the apprehensions caused by the raising of the school-leaving age to 15 and 16 in 1947 and 1972, it is striking how the raising to 17 and 18 (enacted in 2008 and implemented in 2013 and 2015) attracted hardly any notice.[91] 'Going to uni'—the demotic Australianism was significant—also became ordinary. Of course progression through these phases still remained formally meritocratic, and thus sharply stratified by class, but the common democratic experience of secondary schooling was now extended very largely to A-levels and even to university. 'Student life' was no longer seen as a strange indulgence of mostly privileged young people; forms and practices of 'ordinary' student life from America and Australia seeped into British society.[92] 'Student life' now provides the transition from childhood to adulthood for more adolescents formerly provided only for young men by apprenticeship.[93]

As the trailblazer of studies in America's transition from elite to mass higher education, Martin Trow, has put it, higher education has become 'one of the decencies of life rather than an extraordinary privilege reserved for people of high status or extraordinary ability', not only in America and Britain but across the developed world. It is widely recognized as a consumption right of citizenship in a way that secondary education had come to be recognized after the war.[94] This normalization of educational attainment has its self-perpetuating elements. Economists speak of 'role model effects', in which people look around them and emulate those whom they think they resemble or, notably, whom they would like to resemble.[95] Groups that were formerly under-represented in post-compulsory education—women, ethnic minorities—are now over-represented. Aspiration to the highest levels of education, always higher in Britain than elites imagined, has become nearly universal. In the latest birth-cohort study—commissioned by New Labour for 2000 after Joseph had nixed one in the 1980s—96 per cent of mothers with the *lowest* educational qualifications themselves wanted their 7-year-olds to go to university. Whereas high aspirations in the 1950s and '60s were shadowed by awareness of the unlikelihood for many of achieving them, leading to sharply reduced expectations for older children, the mothers of the millennium cohort are much more likely to see their early optimism redeemed.[96]

When asked what they sought from education, 18-year-olds entering higher education and 21-year-olds leaving it continued to cite a wide variety of motivations, without betraying the singular obsession with wage returns attributed to them by economists. One representative study of final-year undergraduates in 1996 explained their choices variously in terms 'hedonistic' (pure enjoyment of the course), 'fatalistic' (other people's advice or lack of options, often determined by prior attainment) and 'pragmatic' (the labour-market considerations favoured by economists).[97] Enjoyment was the most commonly cited factor on most courses, including humanities, social sciences, and natural sciences, suggesting once again that education is almost always both a consumption and an investment good. Economists are inclined to mistrust such surveys, preferring the hard data of 'observed' to 'reported' behaviour, but as two leading economists of education observed in this period, after all, 'people want to go to university because they enjoy the education process, irrespective of the financial return to a degree'.[98] Britain's true transition to mass education from the late 1980s, finally bulldozing through the bifurcation at 16 so that staying on had become nearly universal by the 2000s and higher-education participation rates had trebled even from their mid-1980s levels, surely partook as much of the learning society as the knowledge economy.

From State to Market?

With the advent of GCSE and the end of the most rigid forms of streaming in secondary schools (that is, between CSE and O-level), the adoption of a core curriculum to standardize the educational 'offer' across geographical and social divides, the huge growth in staying on, the restoration of the Robbins Principle guaranteeing places in higher education to those able and willing to take them up, you would have thought that the democratic approach to education had scored decisive victories over the meritocratic and even the technocratic in the period since the late 1980s. Yet it has rarely been recognized as such. Instead, historians of education have characterized it in quite different terms: 'the death of the comprehensive school', the abandonment of a national education system, even 'the death of secondary education for all'.[99] A leading sociologist of education asked in 2001, 'why has British education become so miserable?'; we might ask rather why are its historians and sociologists so miserable?[100]

One obvious answer might be that they, like most people, mistake the history of educational policy for the history of education. They fixate on the blizzard of legislation and regulation that has beset education since the late 1980s and not the actual experiences, attitudes and behaviours of those who are allegedly suffering under it. The fact that Conservative governments are held to have set these changes afoot—then continued by New Labour governments apeing them—has not helped amongst a largely left-leaning community of educationists. Suddenly left-wing critics of the 'distinctly backward', 'unintegrated' British education system, resistant to 'standardization or rationalization' (as opposed to its supposedly superior European counterparts),[101] became its rather small-c conservative defenders, faced with something they imagined as worse. LEAs, which were supposed to have been obstacles to comprehensive education, became its line of last defence. Policies that democratic critics had long advocated—an end to a bipartite examination system, a 'common' or 'core' curriculum that equalized the educational 'offer' to all children and built a common citizenship, in short, 'standardization' and 'rationalization'—were now suspected, as coming from the wrong hands.[102] But above all, left-wing critics have fixated too much on the *means* apparently used to bring about mass education, which are said to have substituted the reassuring comforts of the welfare state with the harsh rigours of the capitalist marketplace, and have extrapolated from these means too easily to assume a palpably less fair set of outcomes. Before we turn from the causes of mass education to some of its consequences, we should therefore ask whether the undoubted enthusiasm of policymakers for market mechanisms since the late 1980s has in fact undone mass education at the very moment when it appeared to be attained.

Of that enthusiasm there can be little doubt. It was evident in policy relating both to secondary and to higher education. Taking the former first, alongside his expansionist policy Kenneth Baker also set about creating more of a secondary-education market. Picking up the 1970s discourse of parental choice, he sought both to empower parents and to create a more diverse menu of schools from which they might choose. In the 1988 Education Reform Act schools were enabled to opt out of local-authority control—to be maintained instead by central-government grant, much like the old direct-grant schools, though without selection—and to change their character by introducing a 'specialism'. At first, true to Baker's technocratic instincts, the only allowable specialism was technology; later the designation was extended to languages, arts and sport, and to schools under LEA control. 'Local management of schools' was at the same time applied to schools under LEA control, giving them financial independence and requiring LEAs to fund them on a strict formula basis determined mostly by student numbers. All schools were henceforth required to offer 'open enrolment' to any parents who might choose them, the reward being higher funding for those able and willing to expand.

Free choice and a diversity of schools to choose from: the very model of a market. It has often been remarked that this market approach seems to be at odds with Baker's other, more centralizing moves—for the first time, a national curriculum for children below the age of 14; centralized testing at ages 7, 11, and 14; a new national exam at 16, the GCSE.[103] Although there was undoubtedly a tension here (between 'neo-liberal' policy preferences for 'choice' and 'neo-conservative' policy preferences for standards), they did also fit together: in default of a price mechanism, a market for schools could only exist if there was some fixed standard, comparable exam results, by which schools could be measured. The assumption was that choice was not only good in itself—returning to people more responsibility for their own lives[104]—but that it would also drive up standards, by rewarding the 'best' (most popular) schools and inducing competition amongst them all to be the best they could be.[105]

Each element of this programme drew objections from the left, though mostly not from New Labour. The introduction of diversity is part of what is meant by the 'dismantling' of a 'national education system'.[106] But Britain had always had an unusually decentralized system, long defended on the grounds of liberalism and local democracy. The piecemeal demolition of the LEAs—more or less completed in England in the early twenty-first century when most schools removed themselves or were removed from local-authority control, now no longer as 'grant-maintained schools' but as 'academies'—only took this a step further, devolving control to individual schools. With the advent of the 'neighbourhood school' after comprehensive reorganization, the school rather than the local authority did seem a more natural locus of control. There is little evidence of popular attachment to local authorities, especially after the boundary changes of the 1970s. While LEAs had been reasonably efficient instruments in channelling public opinion against the 11+, a policy which they had been nominally responsible for implementing, once neighbourhood schools were established in most places LEAs were not either the best or the most obvious agents for addressing further parental and public concerns about the nature, quality or equality of educational provision. A very few LEAs, such as the Inner London Education Authority, could claim to be innovators in pedagogy.[107] Some LEAs had already devolved financial management to schools and extended parental choice and representation on governing bodies. Most had lost touch with the curricula actually being taught in their schools.[108] Often, again, a brittle defensiveness had been the left's response to proposals for more devolution of power to parents and communities. When the Labour government had toyed with legislating to extend parental choice in 1977, Tony Benn from the Labour left warned against raising 'parental expectations' which 'would certainly lead to a terrific pressure on the local education authorities, on the ministers and, of course, MPs as well'—not a great vote of confidence in grass-roots democracy.[109] Advocates of the LEA system have found it difficult to explain why sporadic voting for local councillors was more 'democratic' than participation on school governing bodies or other identifications with a neighbourhood school.[110]

There were technical functions that still needed to be performed on a larger scale than the individual school, and new institutions have had to be devised to fulfil them—thus academies have formed 'multi-academy' chains to provide central services; there are now shadowy Regional Schools Commissioners operating at a higher level; and local authorities still perform a residual function in overseeing open enrolment.[111] But most affairs that concern parents are located in the individual school, and, with open enrolment, admissions (which is probably their greatest concern) only requires oversight for schools that are over-subscribed. While parents do not seem overly concerned either way who runs their school, they have not obviously felt disenfranchised by decentralization; to the contrary, as one study has put it, 'governing schools has become an important arena for the exercise of citizenship'.[112] And in the 'marketplace of ideas' that operates among a more mobile and affluent electorate today it is hard to make the case that parental choice is a *bad* thing.[113]

The strongest objection to choice and diversity is actually a rather abstruse sociological one, and a contested one too—it is that choice and diversity is likely to re-stratify the nation on a class basis; this is what is meant by claims of the 'death' of the comprehensive school or, more strongly, a return to the tripartite system.[114] First, it is argued that diversity is only a stalking horse for selection, that is, something like the 11+, which had indeed had the effect of stratifying educational opportunity by class. Many confident predictions were made after the 1988 Act that it would lead inexorably to a restoration of selection[115] (and even, sometimes, fee-paying and privatization of schools[116]). It is true that the Tories liked to tease Labour with this possibility. The Education Secretary John Patten contributed a piece to the left-wing weekly *New Statesman* entitled 'Who's afraid of the "S" word?', which it transpired was about specialism not selection. In fact, the article held up the national curriculum with its testing and auditing apparatus as an equalizing policy that would raise standards for all rather than reintroducing the divisions of the tripartite system. And Patten's 1992 White Paper praised specialization as a form of selection that is 'always parent-driven', never imposed from above.[117] There were undoubtedly some Tories who would have liked to embrace selection outright, and some who still see devolution to individual schools as preliminary to privatization.[118] Even New Labour permitted specialist schools to select 10 per cent of their intake with regard to aptitude in their specialist subjects.

But in fact the confident predictions have—so far, thirty years later—not come to pass. Specialization did not lead to selection, which remains the third-rail of educational policy; the provision that specialist schools could select 10 per cent of their intake was not widely employed.[119] The only step in this direction has been the recent authorization for a few existing grammar schools to expand. No new selective school has entered the state system.[120] It is of course possible that support for selection will surge again as it did in the 1970s, now with the added advantage that most people have little experience with a selective system. 'Grammar schools for all' might still have a potent appeal if grammar schools are considered the 'best' schools. Whether that appeal could long survive awareness of selection's inegalitarian and even anti-democratic implications, as the majority of children are denied access to those 'best' schools, is another matter.[121]

However, the claim that choice and diversity led only to greater stratification does not rest primarily on the return of selection. Rather, it is argued that, more insidiously, choice and diversity leads naturally to more stratification by empowering the powerful.[122] Continuing their ethnographic turn of the 1970s and '80s, sociologists have made close study of working-class and middle-class parents' different attitudes to and strategies for schooling, showing the latter to be better 'choosers' more likely to get the 'best' schools for their children.[123] This continuing emphasis on working-class parents— defined as parents in manual occupations—shows an enduring concern for the least privileged, but it also of course focuses attention on a smaller and smaller proportion of the population, a fact rarely acknowledged and some- times even denied.[124]

However, quantitative studies do not support the argument that more parental choice has led to more educational inequality. There are several different grounds for this counter-argument. One is that most parents of all backgrounds just choose their neighbourhood school, either for lack of any practical alternative (in more thinly-populated areas) or by preference. Outside of England, especially, parental choice has never been very popular and since education became a devolved question there has been much less governmental effort to stimulate choice. Even in England, more privileged parents benefit from residential segregation, as they had done since comprehensive reorganization, but they don't benefit more from school choice, and still benefit less from both than under the bipartite system.[125] Another is that school choice may even have initially benefited disadvantaged parents more, as they alone were able to improve their position by choosing schools outside their residentially segregated areas, but that this was a one-off change limited again by the limits to feasible choice in all but the most densely populated areas.[126] A third is that while the market reforms of the 1988 Act had a potential to aggravate disadvantage, subsequent reforms by New Labour after 1997 closed loopholes to minimize gaming of the system by the privileged and reduced school segregation after 2002.[127] A final, more recent and dramatic finding is that working-class parents do not in fact make 'worse' choosers; they are just as likely to choose better schools for their children as middle-class parents, and just as likely to get the school they choose. In this respect, choice actually narrows the gap between aspiration and attainment that habitually held back working-class parents.[128]

In any case, educational inequality has not grown since the late 1980s.[129] Income inequality grew dramatically in the 1980s, but principally at the top end, where most of the families were opting out of the state system anyway; outside the top 10 per cent, there was very little change in the income gaps between the bottom 10 per cent, the median and the second 10 per cent.[130] Residential segregation appears not to have been exacerbated and school choice, to the extent that it has disrupted the neighbourhood catchment (which is disputed), appears not to have exacerbated educational inequality either. The major change of this period has not been in greater or lesser educational inequality, but in higher minimum common standards based on more equal provision—a common curriculum, a national examination at 16, higher staying-on rates, widening participation in higher education. Most parents continue to choose a school near their home, on the basis of proximity, 'feeder' schools (that is, the primary their children and their friends attended), or their children's desires, without any greater disparity based on social class than previously.[131] Though politicians of course talk up their legislation, and claim to have fundamentally reshaped the educational equation, parents' actual attitudes and behaviours tend not to respond to that noise. They do now pay more attention to their schools' attainment records and local reputations, being better informed and more experienced with secondary schooling. In this way they seem to be seeking both 'community' in the neighbourhood school and a degree of self-determination in the form of choice.[132]

Something of the same sort can be said about higher education. Here a more marketized system also began in 1988 when the UGC was dissolved, the polytechnics were detached from local-authority control, and new funding councils were established that replaced the old planning bodies with funding formulae. The 1992 Further and Higher Education Act also detached the FE colleges (including sixth-form colleges) from the local authorities, subjected them to their own funding council, and erased the binary line between universities and polytechnics, consigning them to a single higher-education funding council.[133] Until the Treasury slapped on tighter student-number controls, higher-education institutions were more or less free to compete for as many students as they could manage with the reduced per capita grant.

A more significant element of market competition was then imposed with the innovation of tuition fees, principally in England; as the advent of tuition fees coincided with the further devolution of power to the four nations of the United Kingdom, England and the other nations began to diverge. England has gone for the highest levels of fees; Wales and Northern Ireland have moderated this approach; Scotland has stuck to free tuition for young entrants. At first tuition fees took the form of 'top-up fees', a flat fee paid by the student that merely supplemented the government's per capita tuition grant to universities. That innovation was cooked up in a cross-party deal just before the 1997 general election, seen to be necessary to induce the Treasury to permit the resumption of student-number growth and preserve the Robbins Principle. An independent committee of enquiry chaired by Sir Ron Dearing, with a small staff and only a year to report, was tasked with finding a quick technical solution to the funding problem that would not staunch growth or widening participation.[134] The obvious solution was to try to capture more of the 'private return' to higher education through a fee system that hit the better off hardest. The first top-up fee was a relatively small £1000 p.a. fee dependent on a means test. But Dearing himself hoped that fees would do more: that they would sharpen students' awareness of wage returns, discourage excessive demand for higher education, and induce price competition between universities.[135]

A major step towards these goals came in 2004 when the fee was raised to £3000, the means test removed and a 'graduate contribution' element put in its place, such that the level of the fee would not depend on students' parental income but on their own post-degree income, forging a clear link between the cost of the education and its supposed payoff. At the same time universities were now permitted to vary the fee to compete on price. The new system reached its apotheosis, after an even briefer and more exiguous independent enquiry, the Browne Report, again the result of a cross-party agreement before an election.[136] Browne recommended a much higher fee—up to £9000 p.a.—although with the student-contribution element engineered to ensure that most students didn't end up paying more than about two-thirds of the total debt. Even with this proviso, very large debts would be incurred at the outset, not only by the £9,000 maximum annual tuition fee but also by loans for maintenance and high interest rates over a 30-year term. Suddenly English higher education had become among the most expensive to students in the world; this was meant to concentrate the mind.[137]

It was clearly now intended that the decision to enter higher education should be attended with much greater calculation about future returns— essentially, spelled-out messages of what the economists said students should already have been doing for themselves. Universities were expected to compete on price at the institutional and even, it was hoped, on the subject level; a huge data project was compiled to show exactly what were supposed to be the returns to studying a particular subject at a particular university; students, it was hoped, would enter more cautiously and choose more wisely as a result.[138] Governments had rejected means-tested top-up fees and a much simpler graduate tax largely because they wouldn't embed this essential market mechanism, which was intended to steer students only to courses that would pay off both to themselves and to the government alike by ensuring higher incomes and full repayment of the loan.[139] Education was to become the investment good par excellence, even if (or perhaps because) in the past parents and students had not generally viewed it as such, and despite the lip-service paid to its many other values and purposes.[140]

Critics of marketization levelled the same charges against its application to higher education that they had to schools—it would exacerbate inequality by privileging choice. Because in higher education unlike schooling a price mechanism was introduced, marketization would exacerbate inequality further by deterring new entrants from under-served groups. Again neither has come about. Existing inequalities in higher education have not been aggravated.[141] Interestingly, universities have chosen not to compete on price—all charge virtually the same, maximum fee. Undoubtedly no university wants to be seen as second-class by charging less, and they don't see the high fee as a deterrent to widening participation; the result has been to retain a more unified system than policymakers had hoped for, keeping 'going to uni' more standardized. Most strikingly, the high fee has *not* served as a deterrent to widening participation. Participation rates which had levelled off in the mid-'90s under Treasury discipline resumed their upward progress at precisely the moment that fees were first introduced. While nominal student-number control remained in place, the New Labour governments were firmly committed to the Robbins Principle and the fee revenue ensured that participation rates could rise *without* further reductions in the per capita grant (which levelled off after 1997 and then returned to 1960s levels with the higher fees after 2004, as shown in Figure 7.2; see Appendix).

At the same time as the per capita grant began to recover, so did participation rates resume their upward trend. APR which had levelled off in the mid-1990s began to climb again slowly in 1998. Longitudinal comparisons are difficult because the education statisticians abandoned APR around this time and (rightly) introduced a new measure, Higher Education Initial Participation Rate (HEIPR), which counted not only young entrants aged 18–19 but also mature entrants to age 30; they then also changed their 'methodology' in 2006. But in 1999 Tony Blair set a new target for HEIPR to reach 50 per cent participation and by 2017 this had been virtually achieved (see Appendix, Figure 7.3).

An interesting feature of this trend is its even, incremental, sustained growth over a decade, about the same level of growth as in the 1960s. The introduction of the new high-fee regime had the disturbing effect of causing a rush of applications to beat it the year before it was introduced and a resultant slump the year afterwards. But ignoring those two anomalous years the trend appears quite even; that is, the high-fee regime had no effect at all.[142] People continued to enter higher education in growing numbers despite the prospect of much greater personal costs over most of their working lives—not at all what you'd expect if they were making the all-seeing rational calculations imputed to them.[143] Growth in participation has actually been stronger in England since 2012 than in Scotland, Wales, and Northern Ireland where there were lower or no fees.[144]

Participation also seems to have been undisturbed either way by the nominal lifting of student-number controls, another policy innovation of this period, linked to the high-fee regime. The argument went that, in conditions of austerity supposedly necessitated by the post-2008 financial crisis, higher education would inevitably have been subjected to another rundown—and another retreat from the Robbins Principle—unless large tranches of public funding could be replaced by the graduate contribution. Only then could the Robbins Principle be guaranteed for the future and expansion continued. Accordingly having implemented the higher fees the government proudly lifted student-number controls in 2015. The universities minister David Willetts hailed this as one of his government's greatest social reforms.[145] But there is no evidence that these controls had much effect on access to higher education (see Appendix, Figure 7.3). And over the longer term, as Willetts elsewhere grants, governments of all stripes have managed 'perhaps more by accident than design'—in fact, by accepting and implementing the Robbins Principle—to keep the supply of places roughly in step with demand.[146] They suffer politically if they do not. This matching of supply and demand could be and was achieved by means of negotiation with the old planning bodies, or by no controls as briefly in the late '80s and early '90s, or by student number controls as applied in the later '90s, or by the 'lifting' of student-number controls in the last few years.[147] Of course governments differed in the fiscal and planning mechanisms they used to achieve steadily widening participation; the point is simply that no government could deviate much from the Robbins Principle, and therefore sufficient places were generally provided to satisfy demand, whatever the mechanisms.

The lifting of student-number controls and marketization more generally may have one effect—it may be intensifying competition between institutions for students, without affecting the total number of students in the system. Whether this competition lifts standards, or, as some would say, triggers a 'race to the bottom', is hard to determine; but it may well have the effect of driving some institutions into bankruptcy. This *is* part of the marketization programme. Its Conservative advocates wish to inspire new entrants into the higher-education market: so far a few small corporate entities trying to cherry-pick demand for expensive specialist courses in law and business, and not yet the pile-'em-high distance-learning programmes like the notorious University of Phoenix in the United States. But they also foresee that the expansion of successful universities will lead to 'market exit'—the collapse of 'unsuccessful' ones. This hasn't happened to schools; the attachment to the neighbourhood catchment and the limited flexibility that individual schools have to expand have constrained the amount of market churn, either new schools or growing ones or collapsing ones.[148] Universities are larger and more flexible. They can grow, and they can, theoretically, shrink to nothing. It would be a great loss of historic investment if government was to let this happen, but it could. That might be the single greatest legacy of the lifting of student-number controls—not widening participation.

As always, to understand widening participation we need to look at demand. Demand for higher education remained buoyant before and after the 2008 crisis, before and after the new fee regime inaugurated in 2012, before and after student-number controls were lifted in 2015. The reasons we have already laid out. Most important has been the much improved supply of qualified leavers made possible first by GCSE—after 2004 there was an acceleration of growth in good GCSE passes, a decline of one-third in the numbers with no GCSE passes—then by higher staying-on rates, higher A-level attainment, more routes to higher education, and the funding of more higher-education places to satisfy the Robbins Principle.[149] It may be that students were continuing to progress to higher education despite the greater cost because of their far-sighted awareness of the long-term value of higher education in the 'knowledge economy'; or it may be that they were just embracing the valuesof the 'learning society' where education to 16 and beyond was taken as a basic qualification for citizenship and a route to well-being. But either way their levels of demand were not much affected by marketization or by the alleged barriers it throws up to widening participation.

All in all, the course of education under governments of all stripes since the late 1980s has run smooth—unbelievably so in light of the apparent loss of confidence in it during the 1970s. If electors were unhappy with the Tories' record on education in the 1990s, it was now because they expected a lot from it rather than a little. The system of neighbourhood schools was little challenged, and perhaps much enhanced, by the provision of more information, more opportunities for participation and, to a lesser extent, by some more choice for those in urban areas who had a choice of local schools. A common minimum standard at 16 was achieved by means of a national curriculum and a national examination which for the first time gave the vast majority of the population academic qualifications. As attainment levels rose, participation in further and higher education greatly increased. Even apprenticeships recovered from their low point in the early 1990s, re-fashioned for a post-industrial economy and dovetailed with academic qualifications so that they looked less like a second-class vocational track. Perhaps most tellingly, politicians responded to the demands placed upon them, and public investment in education—which had risen continuously to the mid-1970s, and then fell steeply through the 1990s—returned to its all-time high of well over 5 per cent of GDP before the 2008 financial crisis.[150]

The marketization of secondary and higher education, such as it was, did not therefore destroy a national service, and it did not even seem to blunt much the democratic drive for more equal provision. The thirty years after the 1988 Education Act have seen some equalization of attainment in secondary school thanks to GCSE, vastly expanded access to higher education, the maintenance of the Robbins Principle despite efforts to tinker with its wording or dilute it. From this point of view the trajectory of educational provision followed the upward path that began in the late 1950s, taking up in the late '80s where it had left off in 1970, when the long pause intervened. Public support for state education—as evident in surveys, levels of public expenditure, abstention from fee-paying—remained strong, its fortunes still closely linked to health as a civic good. Local schools and hospitals have been of more interest to voters on the doorstep than national issues, whatever manifestos and electoral propaganda have suggested.[151] As we will see in the following two chapters, on subjects studied and the effects (or non-effects) of education on social mobility, the period from the late 1950s into the 2000s can be seen as a single arc of massifying educational provision with parents and students firmly in the driver's seat, choosing which subjects to study and associating improved access to education with upward social mobility, on the whole empowering experiences. But these democratizing effects have been severely tested since the 2008 crash, tests which have not yet resolved themselves, and to which we will return in an epilogue.

8

The Swing Away from Science

The drive for more education for more people did not only change who studied; it also changed what they studied, to an unusual degree in Britain. England and Wales developed an early-specialization system which left adolescents as early as age 13 free to choose what subjects they studied. Neither England and Wales, nor Scotland despite its later specialization, had a national curriculum until the late 1980s and even then it still applied only *until* age 13 or 14.[1] After the war, when the earlier system of School and Higher School Certificates was replaced by O- and A-levels, choice extended further as certification came not for a package of subjects but for individual subjects which could be cherry-picked according to students' interests and aptitudes. This freedom of choice led to what was seen as an unusually British (or at least English) degree of 'subject-mindedness' at school.[2] And as we've seen, choice, for self-development, became more not less important over the postwar decades.

'Choice' at these early ages is obviously a problematic concept. To some extent subject choice reflects family background and for this reason some sociologists deride it as a myth, yet another way in which education only reproduces social stratification.[3] But in many ways subject choice is a sensitive barometer of wider changes in society, economy and culture. As new entrants push themselves into the upper echelons of the education system—O- and A-level, then degree level—they bring with them a quite different set of expectations, interests and motivations than the more elite groups which monopolized these levels in the first years of universal secondary education. All groups are also influenced by changing expectations and opportunities in the wider world. Even economists—who as we have seen have increasingly tended to view the decision to pursue further education as a calculation of future wage returns (an investment good)—have not until recently ventured to suggest that 13-year-olds (or even 18-year-olds) are making subject-choice decisions on an investment basis. What makes a subject interesting, or what makes a student good at it, is partly again a function of their prior attainment (and thus family background) but also prone to influence by a host of social and cultural factors.

The most obvious illustration of this truth, to which we will pay closest attention, is the impact of changing gender roles. Girls' ideas about what was interesting and why changed dramatically as old stereotypes melted away and new opportunities opened up. This did not mean their choices simply became more like boys', though within limits they did. It also meant that older gender stereotypes of 'woman's mission' and 'service' could be reformulated for the modern world of the welfare state and social services. Boys, too, were influenced by changing values and opportunities. New entrants who lacked academic backgrounds were more likely to be attracted to new subjects that emerged to reflect novel aspects of modernity, such as the large and ultimately dominant group of subjects lumped together as 'social studies'. Given all these influences, covert and overt, it is not surprising that widening participation from the late 1950s led to a long-term shift in the choice of subjects studied at school and university—what may be more surprising, perhaps, is the direction of that shift: away from science.

The Dainton Swing

If there is any popular stereotype about the subject bias of the British educational system after the war, it is surely the one formed by C. P. Snow's instigation of the 'two cultures controversy' in 1959, which argued that arts subjects were far too dominant in British education and culture. Snow's intervention formed part of a broader declinist critique (mostly from the left) of Britain's gentlemanly culture which was held responsible for its alleged economic decline, and which could only be addressed with a stupendous state investment in science and technology such as Harold Wilson promised with the 'white heat' of a technological revolution. Not even Snow's principal adversary, the Cambridge literary critic F. R. Leavis, argued against Snow's contention on factual grounds—how could he, when in the years just after the war 71 per cent of his own university's undergraduates were pursuing arts degrees, and a whopping 86 per cent at Oxford?[4]

Under the noses of these Oxbridge-obsessed pundits, Britain's school and university system was in reality dominated by the sciences. In the year of Snow's 'two cultures' intervention, the sciences' share of A-level passes reached its all-time peak at 55 per cent. This superiority was then entrenched at degree level, largely due to gender effects. The majority of boys (57 per cent) did only science A-levels and two-thirds of them then progressed to study science at university. 'Subject-mindedness' grabbed boys early, directed them to science, and then pushed them on to higher education.[5] The majority of girls (66 per cent) did only arts A-levels but more of them stopped short of university, likelier instead to progress to teacher training. Nationally, therefore, not a minority but a majority of undergraduates were studying science—56 per cent at the time of Robbins' enquiry in 1963.[6] Oxbridge, as ever, proves a poor barometer of the educational system as a whole.

Together, selection, gender and subject-mindedness explain a lot about the dominance of the sciences in grammar and independent schools (where nearly all exam-takers were educated) in the 1950s. Public exams were for an elite of serious and hard-working boys and girls, with most at stake for the boys who were more likely to apply their school subjects to careers. Physics, usually deemed the most difficult subject, enjoyed its golden age under this regime: already in 1948 there were more takers for Physics at Higher School Certificate than for English or History and that edge widened in the transition to A-levels when it became the fastest-growing subject.[7] Indeed, given that boys with only science A-levels were the most likely to proceed to university and boys with only arts A-levels the least likely, the position of the arts in higher education would have been perilous were it not for the schoolteaching profession.[8] Not only girls who went into teacher training but also girls who went to university were very likely to end up as teachers. Almost two-thirds of women graduates in 1960, and a third of men graduates, went into teaching.[9] Most of them were arts graduates.[10]

Despite the rhetoric of the declinists, Britain in fact had one of the highest science and technology uptakes in further and higher education in the developed world in the 1950s, though studies and statistics did not yet exist to say so.[11] Many European systems gave access to higher education only through elite secondary schools that favoured a classical education; they had science streams, but those students were the least likely to go to university, whereas in England and Wales they were the most likely.[12] Nor was the British situation worse at sub-degree level, where declinists had identified a distinctively British failure to develop vocational tracks. Enrolments in full-time and part-time 'sandwich' courses in technical colleges grew steadily across this period and into the '70s.[13] A great deal of government time, attention, and money was poured into upgrading them, as we saw in the development of the Colleges of Advanced Technology and the polytechnics. They were most successful when not competing with the grammar schools, which parents favoured, but when seen as supplementary, especially after age 16. Much of this work was of very high quality—half of the 1st-class degrees in Physics awarded by the University of London went to technical college students taking external degrees.[14] Later the OECD would show that Britain had 'the greatest concentration on science and technology in higher education and the biggest proportion of qualified scientists and technologists (graduates, diplomates and certificate holders) in relation to population and labour force' in Europe.[15]

Across the 1950s there was a mild swing *to* science. Despite Snow's end-of-the-decade philippic, governments of both parties had been determined to steer more students to science and technology to meet 'national needs': this code-phrase meant their contribution to economic growth, specifically industry, most specifically engineering. As we noted in earlier chapters, this technocratic understanding of education was the main political challenger to a narrow view of meritocracy, which had assumed that only a fixed and small proportion of the population was usefully educable at all after 15. Especially after Sputnik and Cold War competition for international economic competitiveness heated up, it produced a raft of initiatives in further and higher education to boost the supply of 'qualified manpower', 'particularly in the pure and applied sciences'.[16] 'Manpower planning' was briefly fashionable and the UGC was encouraged to create more places for scientists to meet the needs of government and industry. But even manpower planners realized that the pipeline began amongst adolescents and they had few tools to adjust supply at that early stage.[17] Other factors may lie behind what was a relatively modest swing. The failure of most LEAs to develop technical schools meant that more technically minded boys were likely to have been selected for grammar schools and channelled into science O-levels instead of technical qualifications. Employers were perfectly happy to hire technologists with these academic qualifications, especially as a system less rigid than most European rivals allowed grammar-school leavers to acquire additional qualifications at technical college.[18] Independent schools also saw that their traditional employment fields in the home and imperial civil service elites were likely to shrink and began to re-tool to service the needs of commerce and industry.[19]

When the bulge and the trend hit the exam-taking years at the beginning of the 1960s, however, all this changed.[20] Robbins was as so often the canary in the coal mine, detecting already in 1963 'a marked swing towards the arts', even more marked among the failed applicants who had suffered from the insufficiency of places.[21] Nevertheless he predicted a steady state 45 per cent arts / 55 per cent science split across higher education for the foreseeable future.[22] In the next few years, the swing away from science continued; in January 1965 the universities reported 'a shortage of pure scientists at the university level', that is, a shortage relative to the number of places they had provided. A full-scale panic built up in government. The early '60s were peak years of belief not only in science education as a motor of economic growth but also in manpower planning, the belief that government could and should steer students to serve 'national needs', held as firmly by the former Tory science minister Lord Hailsham as by leading figures in the new Labour government. While abjuring what he called 'the techniques of the Party Chairman' in directing scientific research, which he associated with Labour interventionism, Hailsham saw himself as an 'enlightened patron' of a whole raft of efforts to boost the teaching of science and technology to elite students in grammar and independent schools.[23] One argument behind Crosland's binary policy was to provide government with new tools of manpower planning via colleges and polytechnics that did not have the autonomy the universities enjoyed.[24] Accordingly the new Labour government set up an enquiry in February 1965 to address 'the flow of candidates in science and technology into higher education', chaired by the chemist and academic leader Fred Dainton.

Dainton's research over the next three years and his 1968 report documented the continuing swing—sadly, it didn't slacken but actually accelerated during the period of his work, and became known as the 'Dainton swing'. Dainton also stimulated amongst social scientists an intense period of study of the driving forces behind subject choice in an expanding educational system that for the first time drew close attention to the young people themselves.[25] Going well beyond Dainton's work into the mid-1970s, the accumulating body of research did for the questions of what students wanted to study what the earlier work of Floud and Halsey had done for the question of why people wanted to study in the first place. Dainton equipped himself with Claus Moser, the statistical wizard behind the Robbins Report, and Moser happened to have a student, Celia Phillips, who was just starting to undertake basic research on subject choice in Britain and elsewhere in Europe.[26] Her findings formed the basis of the Dainton Report and also suggested its recommendations, which were issued in February 1968.

Thanks to Phillips' work, Dainton knew that Britain had more science specialists at university than its European rivals and that the swing away from science was manifesting itself internationally as well. He was not inclined therefore to indulge in 'two cultures' rhetoric or a brand of declinism that singled Britain out as uniquely disadvantaged. Nevertheless, as a scientist himself and conscious that government had asked him to investigate 'a future supply of qualified manpower which in consequence might possibly prove inadequate to the nation's needs', he felt obliged to identify ways to raise the profile of science in the educational system. Noting that England and Wales were unusual in allowing students to drop science and mathematics altogether as early as 15, he proposed delaying specialization later so as to give students a wider range of options at least up to university entrance. The admired comparator here was France, where *baccalauréat* students combined arts and science subjects and where a highly *dirigiste* government therefore had greater control over the subject balance at university to which students could and would adjust themselves. However, Dainton also concluded that Britain was not France. 'The tradition of respect for the choice of the individual is rightly embedded in our educational as well as our political institutions', the report concluded. 'We esteem that tradition and would not wish to see it altered.' The Robbins Principle had re-asserted the priority of student demand. The liberal Zeitgeist of the '60s was hostile to state direction of young people's life choices. Over the span of their three years, the committee had altered its course in tune with that Zeitgeist. Whereas it had set out initially 'to correct the swing away from science', it had ended up embracing 'the wider objective of meeting the needs of the individual pupil' by keeping their options open as long as possible. If that meant that the swing continued, so be it: now more than ever, 'the individual's choice and the factors which bear upon it have become critically important'.[27]

In thus aligning himself with the Zeitgeist, Dainton was following in the footsteps of politicians and policymakers. After the Robbins Report, as we saw in Chapter 5, Labour shifted away from manpower planning and began to speak the language of 'social demand', implying a planning ambition but in reality conceding to student demand. Although the UGC had been eager to show itself cognizant of 'national needs', when that strategy had resulted in a wasteful surplus of lab facilities and scientific teaching staff it happily readjusted to the levels dictated directly by student applications.[28] The poly-technic sector may have been intended to give Crosland a lever on subject balance, but 'academic drift' almost immediately set in as student demand in their sector as well swung away from science and technology. The rising discipline of sociology took an interest in student demand and built on Phillips' work to provide a more rounded understanding of the swing away from science.

It quickly became clear, for example, that early specialization wasn't itself a *cause* of the swing; even Dainton in the end advocated later specialization to expand student choice, not to stop the swing. The young sociologist Andrew McPherson pointed out that Scotland, with its later specialization system, experienced the same swing as England and Wales.[29] More systematic OECD data began now to filter in about the situation in other countries, showing conclusively not only that Britain had a relatively high proportion of qualified scientists but that swings against science, medicine or technology were being experienced by all kinds of systems, centralized and decentralized, early and late specialization, 'old' and 'new' countries, even now in France.[30] So what *was* the cause of the swing? McPherson was unusual in drawing attention to cohort effects. New tranches of students were bringing with them new priorities. But those priorities were also changing because British society, culture and economy were changing. Overall, McPherson argued, 'what we need is an explanation of subject choice which places it in the context of an individual's total social behaviour in the idiosyncratic educa-tional system of an idiosyncratic society.'[31]

As a comprehensive study of the swing by Derek Duckworth pointed out in 1978, probably the most important factor was the cohort effect caused by widening participation: the rapid expansion of sixth forms and universities had brought in groups of lower-achieving students who lacked the back-ground and ability to tackle science. It was partly but not only about perceived or actual 'difficulty' of subjects. Cumulative subjects like the sciences, though also languages, which benefited from an early start and continuous study over longer periods of time, were for obvious reasons less accessible to students whose decision to stay on came later.[32] The swing was accentuated at A-level by a gender effect, as girls surged into sixth forms in the late 1960s, but it only hit higher education later; the proportion of women in universities in 1968 had hardly budged from 1930 levels. That came too in the 1970s, especially among mature women. After a pause in the swing between 1968 and 1972, except in Physics which continued to suffer, it resumed with a vengeance in 1972–6, hitting Maths, Physics and Chemistry badly but benefiting Biology, the science subject overwhelmingly favoured by women. In absolute numbers, as opposed to share, Biology had caught up with Chemistry by 1976 and for the next fifteen years would closely track the 'hard' sciences, after which it took off, never to look back (see Appendix, Figure 8.1).[33]

Contemporaries worried that beyond cohort effects there was also a deeper anti-science trend in the culture that was affecting the decisions of teenagers; that concern was one of Dainton's principal motivations in recommending delayed specialization. There's a hard version of this argument and a softer one. The hard version considers overt anti-science feeling evident in the rise of environmentalism, a democratic wariness about the growing dominance of technology (and technologists) in everyday life, and perhaps distrust in expertise of all kinds, a phenomenon quite as much of the 1960s and '70s as of the 2010s.[34] Dainton was concerned that these 'ethical and moral' objections might have developed 'real repugnance in the minds of many young people to the harder and more materialistic manifestations of science and technology'.[35] The softer version posited a turn towards humanistic concerns and social consciousness. The social psychologist G. N. Carstairs put it rather pejoratively as a shift

> away from doing and towards feeling. The young seem less interested in science, factual knowledge and cognitive mastery in general – the very skills which underlie technical efficiency. Instead they seem to express a mood of irrationality; they delight in fantasy... the exaltation of inner freedom, of the exploration of subjective experiences, the fullest possible realisation of one's personality. Self-discovery and self-fulfilment are seen as the supreme good and anything which cramps these endeavours is deplored.[36]

'Self-discovery' was certainly an increasingly important theme in young people's self-presentation in the 1960s.[37] More positively, teachers detected a growing 'concern for people rather than things' linked to but not confined to gender. An A-level General Studies exam question of the period— 'General Studies' was itself an innovation aimed at softening the scientific bias of boys in technical colleges—asked students 'to account for the fact that the number of students wishing to study arts and social sciences is increasing more rapidly than the numbers wishing to study the natural sciences'. Difficulty, lack of opportunity for self-expression and boredom

were the predominating replies, but girls especially referred to 'their desire
to help the community directly through social action' to justify their choice
of arts courses.[38]

So far none of these considerations can be seen to be very vocational.
Indeed these early studies of subject choice were among the first to reveal
that 'enjoyment of a subject' was nearly always the prime ostensible motivation
lying behind subject choice, though enjoyment was socially conditioned by
class, gender and culture.[39] This realization offered a healthy check to the
emerging view from human–capital economics that educational decisions
were investment decisions. The older assumption that education was a
consumption good was therefore reinforced by empirical findings.[40] But
of course careers remained in the equation as part of wider process of
identity formation—'self-discovery' and 'self-fulfilment'—equally influenced by social and cultural change. Career aspirations lay behind much of
the extraordinary surge of demand for 'social studies' in the 1960s and '70s.[41]
The social sciences benefited from new levels of social consciousness, the
desire to understand not only self but society, in both genders; they also
catered to girls' 'desire to help the community' in more career-oriented
ways than traditionally feminine subjects such as the domestic sciences
usually afforded.[42]

New subjects, taken up for the first time at A-level or undergraduate
level, were also more open to new entrants than longer-established and
more cumulative subjects. General Studies, an omnibus social studies course,
originated as an A-level in 1959 and became very popular in the '60s and
'70s, especially in FE colleges. In 1975 there were as many A-levels awarded
in General Studies as in French, and not far behind Physics.[43] Sociology
and Psychology took longer to root themselves in schools but took off in
higher education, especially in the polytechnics.[44] Sociology had long been
seen as a vocationally oriented subject for relatively small numbers of
women training for social work, but in the '60s it became more attractive to
both women and men aiming for a wide range of careers in the burgeoning
welfare state.[45] By the end of the 1970s 55 per cent of Sociology graduates
and 40 per cent of Psychology graduates were finding work in the public
sector.[46] The greater opportunities in the public sector, especially for career-
minded women, may help to explain why the subject choices of women
did not converge with men's as greatly as they did at the same time in the
United States.[47]

But there was in this period a weakening link between subject choice and vocation that was also a result of widening participation. As we have already noted, as aspiration for more equal attainment drew more people into post-compulsory education, the labour market adjusted to them rather than vice-versa. Employers seeking accountants, lawyers, social workers and teachers, to name just a few, found that their usual candidate pool was no longer available at 15 or 16 but had to be recruited at 18 or even 21. Whereas previously only medicine and (partially) teaching had been viewed as 'graduate professions', now a wider range acquired that status almost serendipitously. These older and better educated jobseekers now had more academic specialisms—O-levels and A-levels and single-honours degrees— but there was no reason for most employers to care much about them beyond the extra maturity and intellectual ability that educational credentials signalled.[48] New or growing professions such as advertising, consultancy, and public relations also had little experience of what kinds of candidates were most suitable, and even less connection to specific academic subjects, and so were even happier to take higher qualifications of any kind.[49]

This 'screening hypothesis'—that employers were using educational credentials to screen for the 'best' candidates in a 'single job queue' rather than in a segmented market for specific skills—was naturally strengthened by the sudden influx of new graduates with whom employers had little experience; but it was also a consequence of the emerging 'knowledge economy' of jobs requiring flexibility and trainability rather than technical skills.[50] Already it was being discovered that half of all 'graduate jobs' did not require a specific degree subject, said to be distinctive to Britain. British employers were more interested in certification itself than in the subjects the certificates nominally denoted.[51] Science graduates often started in science jobs but then fanned out to better-paying jobs in management. Arts graduates of course fed into a very wide range of jobs in public-sector, commercial, financial and even industrial jobs; British arts graduates were more likely to find employment in industry than elsewhere in Europe.[52] Both because of this weakening link between subject and job, and because of the greater tendency of new entrants in the '60s and '70s to choose their subjects at school with enjoyment and ability rather than career in mind, it was found that while at university most students were still not yet focused on career.[53] It was not even clear that allegedly more 'vocational' polytechnic students or students from a working-class background were focused on career, at least not in their subject choices.[54]

Given how much concern there was after 1970 about the stagnation in widening participation, blamed by many on the declining rate of return to staying on or higher education, it is surprising how little attention this drew to subject choice. The swing away from science continued across the 1970s, as science's share of degrees dropped below 50 per cent. The OECD was now able to show that expansion was leading to a similar and indeed more pronounced swing almost everywhere, as new entrants overwhelmingly chose arts and social science subjects across Europe.[55] In Britain (as elsewhere), women's widening participation, especially mature women in part-time degrees not counted in stagnating APR, formed a good deal of the explanation. The DES thought that teacher-training cuts had also shifted younger women into arts and social science degrees at university.[56] But it was the stagnating APR and the danger that supply cuts (such as in teacher training) would endanger the Robbins Principle that fixed most attention. There was a conviction in some quarters that even with the swing the '60s expansion had led to an over-supply of scientists and thus a declining rate of return that put off new entrants. From that point of view, it could be held that the swing represented a canny judgement by young people and that a reallocation of resources to the arts was warranted.[57] In times of economic stringency, there was even more cause for the universities not to over-provide expensive laboratory facilities and student places in science and technology subjects that were out of fashion. As late as 1977 the UGC was still planning for a steady state, though it could not bring itself to predict a continuing swing. For its part, the DES was happy to accept the swing as a fait accompli.[58] That 'complacency', as it has been called,[59] or responsiveness to demand as we might otherwise see it, could not long survive the advent of the Conservatives in 1979. They would prove determined to reverse the swing and even to revive a version of manpower planning that had been formerly associated with socialism, in the good cause of economic growth. But would they be any more successful than Labour had been in the 1960s?

Thatcherite Social Engineering

Almost immediately upon taking office, the Conservatives signalled that they were determined to get maximum value for money out of the education system. That meant backing off from the Robbins Principle—'free demand for places would be constrained', as the DES noted in October

1979—but it also imposed a duty 'to attempt to influence the availability of places in particular subjects in the interests of the national economy'.[60] How that might be achieved, however, was not easy to determine. There was a neo-liberal argument that, if there was indeed a shortage of scientists and technologists, there would be a high market premium on those jobs, a high rate of return on those subjects at A-level and degree level, and consequently market signals to students to swing back to science in their subject choices. There was however as yet little evidence about rates of return to individual subjects; there was also an awareness that subject choices had not apparently been made on such a narrow investment basis in the past, and also that subject choices did not translate smoothly into employment outcomes.[61] Against this, there was a more *dirigiste* argument that if students had not in the past made decisions based on rates of return they could or should still be encouraged to do so, and even that if rates of return were for whatever reason not high students should still be steered into science and technology in the national interest.[62] 'Declinism' was back in fashion, in both left-wing and right-wing versions, once again asserting Britain's congenital backwardness in science and technology education.[63]

Upon his arrival on the scene, Keith Joseph adopted an aggressive policy. He believed much of higher education's output to be 'economically valueless' and 'damaging to the spirit of enterprise'.[64] His interpretation of market forces shifted the definition of the market in question from student choice to employer need. 'Demand' began to be redefined as the economy's demands for high-skill workers rather than student demand for places.[65] At just the same time, 'social demand', the codeword for student demand, began to give way to 'social return', referring narrowly to the productivity gains from education that did not accrue to individuals (that is, whatever contribution 'externalities' made to economic growth on top of individual return).[66] 'Can you trust 18 year old students to make sensible choices?', was one question asked by the Central Policy Review Staff in an enquiry into higher education's responsiveness to industry commissioned by Thatcher in the autumn of 1982. At the very least they needed more skin in the game, a 'personal financial commitment' through fees and loans. It was not even clear to the CPRS that you could trust employers to make sensible choices; they may 'misread the worth of general, flexible, degree courses'. Unlike the Departments of Employment and Education, the New Right thinkers in the CPRS believed in manpower planning and encouraged Joseph to use his levers on the UGC and the public sector to boost science and technology.

Although they recognized that 'the national interest may indicate more
market-oriented solutions to many problems, in some areas we may conclude
that the Government and other public bodies should take a more interven-
tionist stance'.[67]

Joseph certainly hoped to use the rundown to shrink capacity in the arts
and social sciences and to build up science and technology. He had a particular animus against the polytechnics, which he thought combined low
standards with 'academic drift' towards particularly worthless degrees, and
against the social sciences, which he saw as propaganda for socialism.[68] DES
Circular 5/82 forbade public sector institutions to introduce any new HE
courses except where 'of value to industry or otherwise essential in meeting
employment demand'.[69] Joseph had less leverage over the more autonomous
universities. In a notorious episode in 1982 he tried to kill off the Social
Science Research Council but was foiled when the Rothschild Report he
had commissioned for the purpose recommended against it; all he got was
a change of name to Economic and Social Research Council.[70] As we have
seen, he was more successful in thwarting the funding of a new birth cohort
study due in the early 1980s. But it was harder to bully the UGC and even
harder still to devise policies that might improve the flow early enough in
the pipeline to stock a larger share of science and technology places. As the
UGC pointed out in September 1980, previous attempts to steer students at
university had only resulted in diluting the 'feedstock' for science and
technology. They pressed their newly-discovered principle that 'the skills
required by the economy change rapidly' and that in this new economy
what employers needed was not 'narrow professional training' but 'a foundation of knowledge and skills related in a general way to employment as well
as to personal development'.[71] Joseph was having none of it. He insisted that
steering subject provision 'towards the natural sciences and technology' was
an essential part of the rundown. In response the UGC warned that Joseph's
threats represented 'a significant change in its relationship with Government'
which threatened the whole principle of university autonomy.[72]

For a few years Joseph was buoyed up by signs that the swing had halted,
perhaps even gone into reverse.[73] In the late 1970s, when the demographic
bulge had been at its peak, the absolute numbers of science A-levels had
grown robustly (see Appendix, Figure 8.1). Though they levelled off in the
early '80s, keeping a share of just above 40%, this improved supply fed
through briefly into higher education at just the right moment for Joseph.
The science share of all degrees edged up close to 50%, where it had been

in 1975, though still well below the 1960s peaks. Some economists were
saying that the roller-coaster labour market had 'scarred' young people and
they had become 'very responsive to changes in relative earnings and
employment opportunities when deciding...which subjects to study'.[74]
More realistically, as the DES suggested, the end of teacher-training cuts had
halted the growth of young women's participation in universities with positive knock-on effects for science share. Broadly, the lid kept on APR
excluded young entrants who were more likely to be women; women's
participation in higher education which had been gaining on men's lagged
briefly in the late '70s and early '80s.[75] In any case, a retreat from expansion
was always likely to reverse the cohort effects that lay behind the swing:
fewer students meant a higher proportion of young men studying science, the
policy Joseph hailed as 'high *standards* for the universities via low *numbers*'.[76]

By the same token, the resumption of expansion was always likely to
mean a resumption of the swing. Joseph's failure to staunch expansion in the
mid-'80s, and then Baker's eager embrace of it in the late '80s, had an
immediate effect on the share of science degrees, which had its short-term
peak in 1984 and began a steeper, longer, twenty-five year decline in 1985
(see Appendix, Figure 8.2).[77] The arts and humanities' share remained more
stable; the beneficiaries of the sciences' decline were mostly that collection
of subjects loosely labelled as 'social studies'—social sciences, but also business, law, communications.

As we have seen, Baker sought at first to maintain the position that
expansion should *also* entail a swing back to science, on technocratic
grounds,[78] but that position became increasingly untenable; by the time of
the Lancaster speech in 1989 he had more or less ditched it. In the 1991
White Paper it was openly acknowledged that student demand was once
again driving the trend in a direction opposite to the one which 'the
Government would have wished'.[79] A swing much greater and more
extended than the Dainton swing had commenced.

The Swing Continues

If the Dainton swing provoked considerable anxiety in political circles
(albeit relatively little interest amongst historians), the resumed swing since
the mid-1980s attracted very little comment from contemporaries (and virtually none from historians). For a long time, expansion itself garnered all

the attention and its effect on subject choice seemed marginal or uninteresting. To some extent the more optimistic readings of the 'learning society' and the 'knowledge economy' had triumphed, as the general upskilling of the workforce through widening participation in higher education was celebrated. Any degree was better than none. Thatcherism's 'neo-conservative' impulse to steer students to the desired outcomes gave way to purer 'neo-liberal' policies across the OECD, where 'product control'—the output of graduates—was given up in favour of 'process control'—where governments contented themselves with reducing costs and ramping up accountability.[80] It was deemed safer to assume that consumers—students and employers— knew what they were doing without help, or at least would suffer the consequences. The apparent survival of the graduate premium (across all subjects) during even the most rapid expansion seemed to demonstrate that sufficiently.[81] With the eclipse of the UGC and its replacement by funding councils with per capita formulae, it would have been difficult for government to steer subject choice even if it wanted to, especially if the price mechanism is not used (which it hasn't yet been).[82] More interesting than the subject balance, for example to the Dearing enquiry, have been the effects of widening participation on under-represented ethnic and working-class groups, which we will examine in the next chapter.[83]

Meanwhile the cohort effects already witnessed during the Dainton swing set in with a vengeance. Women's share of higher education grew rapidly from 38 per cent in 1980 to 50 per cent in 1996 and continues to climb to this day. Although the participation gaps between the classes remained similar, as the overall participation rate extended to 50 per cent the undergraduate body was composed of more students with lower academic attainment, and many now from FE colleges with BTEC or similar (less academic) qualifications.[84] Many of these non-traditional students were enrolled in former polytechnics, whose degree numbers were after 1992 included in the university statistics. As we have noted repeatedly, this alone made little impact on the share of science, since the general subject composition of the polytechnics and the universities had been converging for years already; once the statisticians worked out how to categorize the ex-polytechnic courses, the overall share of science continued to decline at the same rate after polytechnics were included as they had before (see Appendix, Figure 8.2). What the former polytechnics contributed was not more (or fewer) science students, but a wider range of students and a wider range of subject choices.

The share of science degrees dropped from about 50 per cent in 1984 to 38 per cent in 2012, therefore, and the beneficiaries represented a much wider range of new subjects than had been the case during the more limited Dainton swing. One important group of new subjects—'subjects allied to medicine' such as Nursing, Physiotherapy, Nutrition, Ophthalmics, Pharmacy—did bolster the sciences with new recruits; after Education these subjects were the most disproportionately female and also most disproportionately low-income, their entrants holding Biology rather than Physics or Chemistry A-levels.[85] Another important group of new subjects—the 'creative arts', including Fine Art, Drama, Dance, and Music—bolstered the arts and humanities, such that their share did not decline between 1984 and 2008, remaining stable at around 22 per cent.

In between a much wider variety of subjects proliferated, mostly still lumped together as 'social studies'. The established social sciences were notable successes; between them, Psychology and Sociology grew to around 10 per cent of all degrees, from under 4 per cent in the mid-1980s. The success of Psychology indeed tends to exaggerate the science share, because it gets counted by the statisticians as a biological science degree rather than, as it has increasingly become in reality, a social science degree. Surveys of Psychology students show that their motivations to study the subject stem from the same impulses that drove the growth of social studies during the Dainton swing—a feeling for 'people over things', a desire for social service—fortified now with a heftier dose of self-discovery.[86]

A new set of social studies subjects, also concentrated in former polytechnics, experienced the most rapid growth—business and communications, today accounting for about 18 per cent of all degrees. These comprise a range of subjects, mostly also not taught (or less commonly taught) in schools or even colleges. They too had mostly been gestating inside polytechnics. By the end of the polytechnic era, business had become their largest subject area, with relatively high proportions of men and of ethnic minorities, and one of the prime recruiters for those progressing to higher education from a BTEC qualification.[87] Despite the widely held view that business degrees were not properly vocational—at least the 'soft' business degrees, the miscellany of 'social and administrative studies' outside 'business, accountancy and law'[88]—they were increasingly seen as 'generalist' degrees giving a good grounding in modern life and suited to a wide variety of jobs. As it turns out, they also provided a healthy income premium for people from less advantaged backgrounds, 'soft' or not.[89]

Was this influx of new students more 'vocational'? On the one hand, you might expect them to be, as they largely came from families without other 'non-utilitarian' associations with higher education and from FE colleges and polytechnics which were *supposed* to be more vocational. Awareness of the 'knowledge economy' was now firmly established and university degrees of all sorts seen as tickets to a much wider array of jobs. The rise of social studies (especially as now augmented by the business subjects) was clearly to some extent motored by expanding career opportunities, first in the public sector and latterly in the private sector.[90] On the other hand, the ever-widening array of subject choices gives a much more mixed picture. The creative arts are usually seen as not vocational enough (though of course they carry their own sense of vocation, albeit not one well measured by income premia or even by employment). The same applies to communications and, as we have seen, the 'softer' business subjects.[91]

The very fact that most jobs required no particular subject background—a recent estimate found this to be true of no less than 75 per cent of advertised graduate jobs—loosened further the connection between subject choice at school and university and occupational outcome.[92] Surveys continued to find that most adolescents chose subject specialisms on the basis of enjoyment and ability as much as on their career prospects; less advantaged new entrants were not very different from established middle-class students, women not much different from men, though women seemed to put a higher premium on 'non-pecuniary' motives than men. Both genders and all classes still felt strongly that higher education was valuable in its own right and for the opportunities it gave for personal growth and independence, as much as representing a good investment for the future; even that investment tended to be posed in terms of personal development, that is, giving the opportunity to clarify career desires and options. Few—less than a fifth—had clear career expectations at the outset of their course.[93] This does not mean, of course, that their choices didn't still stratify along lines of class, gender, and ethnicity—they did, because background, prior attainment, and school type to some degree constrained their choices—but it does mean that consumerism and vocationalism had not become much more significant in young people's subject choices as a result of the transition to mass education.[94]

For quite a while this promiscuity in subject choice, and the consumption as much as investment-minded thinking that seemed to lie behind it, was not too worrisome for economists or even policymakers. The abortive

Thatcherite experiment in social engineering had put them off manpower planning or less *dirigiste* efforts to steer students to science, and the overwhelming demand for more access to higher education trumped all lesser considerations. There was considerable evidence that the swing away from science was not impairing economic development—that there was no 'STEM skills shortage' to adopt the newly fashionable abbreviation for Science, Technology, Engineering, and Mathematics.[95] The high and stable graduate premium for all subjects, masking some major differences between subjects, reassured most commentators that there was not yet a problem of 'over-education'. Employers seemed happy with 'graduateness'—the maturity and educability conveyed by any higher education—and were not overly concerned about subject choice.[96] Although there was a flurry of hostility on 'more means worse' grounds to Blair's adoption of the 50 per cent participation target, it didn't last long.[97]

There *was* repeated concern expressed that so many people had been sucked into higher education that the higher levels of further education were being neglected. That concern formed a principal theme of both the Dearing Report in 1998 and the Augar Report in 2019. Both advocated more 'sub-degree' education, especially (of course!) in 'technical' subjects.[98] Concern about advanced further education could be seen as a happy upgrading of the old argument that too many young people left school at 16 without any qualifications; now that 84 per cent had attained good qualifications at 16 and 58 per cent further qualifications at 18, it was found that too few young people progressed any further *unless* they went into higher education.[99] But there was something increasingly perverse about this argument. As more and more 18 year olds went on to higher education, the relative paucity of 18–21 year olds in further education might be seen as a positive rather than a negative outcome. To view it as negative it was necessary to find another skills shortage, not at the highest but at intermediate technical levels—'skilled trades' such as plumbers and electricians, for example. And while it is true that there are shortages at these intermediate technical levels, in absolute numbers they play a relatively small part in the labour force. There are far more vacancies in retail, office, health and social care, leisure and hospitality roles, which don't require technical training and/or thrive on generic skills gained at school or even in higher education.[100] As we have seen, employers seem generally happy to use academic qualifications (including most subjects) to screen for flexible, trainable employees and then to train them to specific work roles on the job.[101]

As Dearing's and Augar's concerns suggest, there has remained all along a powerful voice in policy circles arguing in conventional, technocratic terms—often amplified by engineering and other interested employers— for a greater focus on STEM. Although the strength of this voice may have dulled (or been muted) for periods—in the 1970s, in the 1990s—it was consistently amplified by politicians' preference for a quick fix for both educational and economic problems.[102] It is easy to point to exemplars in the period of rapid expansion: for example, the Roberts Report of 2002, 'SET for Success' (using a different acronym for STEM), which granted that Britain had a 'relatively large' share of scientists compared to other countries but still claimed to have detected a STEM skills shortage.[103] A politically important decision was made in 2006 to detach higher educa- tion from the Education department and to move it closer to business.[104] But with one exception which we will note shortly there was for an extended period no stomach for direct interventions to steer students' subject choice, and no change in the general direction of the swing either, away from science and towards social studies. Both of these conditions changed after the 2008 financial crisis, at which point the long swing finally came to an end.

The Swing Ends

As Figure 8.2 shows (see Appendix), the sciences' share of university degrees which had been dropping since the mid-'60s finally bottomed out in 2012 at 38 per cent; since then it has been rising, and not slowly, reaching 42 per cent in 2018. Behind it lies a surge in A-level candidacies in Mathematics and Science as well. Maths' share of A-level candidacies rose from 7 per cent to 12 per cent in the decade after 2004. Even Physics which had attracted only 23,000 candidates in 2005–7, its lowest levels since the early '60s, enjoyed a relative resurgence to 33,000 in 2018, late '70s levels.[105] A partial explanation can be found in one effective policy intervention by New Labour launched in 2006 which took effect in 2008, ensuring that all students had a chance if they wished to take 'triple science'—that is, Physics, Chemistry, and Biology as separate subjects—at GCSE. Triple science was widely seen as the passport to A-level and degree-level science, and the reform has progressively made triple science more common at least for high achiev- ers, with greater gender parity than previously. For once the pipeline problem had been addressed and the supply of scientists at the highest levels potentially augmented.[106]

More sweepingly, the very much altered political, economic and even cultural environment brought on by the financial crisis of 2008 and the extended period of low productivity, low income, and public-expenditure cuts that followed must have played its part. Certainly on the political level the mood changed markedly. The technocratic temptation had never gone away; the Roberts Report was an indication of that, and 'triple science' was also motivated by the evergreen ambition 'to get more students to do more science, with the long term aim of increasing the supply of scientists, engineers and technologists in the workforce'.[107] But around the developed world the 2008 crisis and its aftermath led to a renewed panic about international competitiveness, once again focused (however misguidedly) on STEM subjects. As one book published in 2015 put it, characterizing the present moment as 'the age of STEM', the myth of a STEM skills shortage seemed to have triumphed over reality, triggering 'somewhat hysterical' reactions in the English-speaking countries at least; another book, published in 2014, connected the current panic to a series of booms and busts that had beset the STEM employment market at least since Sputnik.[108]

There was no new evidence of an actual STEM skills shortage in the UK. To the contrary, though Britain's share of science graduates had slipped next to some of its European comparators (though not the US),[109] it remained the case that most science graduates went into non-scientific jobs and that only a relatively small elite was needed for research and innovation.[110] One study found that if there was a 'skills shortage' at all as evidenced by wage premia, it was in Law, Economics, and Business and not STEM. Given the expansion in these social-studies subjects, the implication might have been taken that it wasn't 'shortage' at all that was producing wage premia, but embedded status distinctions or other criteria for which employers used these subjects to screen for good all-round employees.[111] Apart from the economic slump, however, there were new factors that seemed nevertheless to put STEM in a more positive light. Rising Asian economies—China, Korea, Hong Kong, Singapore—had higher proportions of STEM graduates (especially engineers) than any European countries; though it was pointed out that comparisons with city-states like Hong Kong or Singapore (or even Shanghai, which got its own 'national' ranking in the PISA measure of literacy and numeracy skills) were of limited usefulness.[112] The 'tech boom' centred on the United States brought Computer Science, hitherto a relatively unnoticed, backwater subject, into the limelight.[113] None of these comparisons was truly relevant to Britain's large and diverse labour market with its greatest strengths in services. But they whipped up an international rivalry for STEM education very similar to the post-Sputnik rivalry of half a century earlier, except that the OECD, which acted then to dampen down such comparisons, was now talking them up.[114]

Policymakers had long reached desperately to science education for solutions to economic problems. The Coalition and Conservative governments that took over in the wake of the 2008 crisis resumed this strategy with a vengeance. On the part of the universities minister, David Willetts, there may have been a tactical element—touting the contribution of science education to economic growth was a way to shield higher education from the worst consequences of austerity—but in other quarters the enthusiasm seemed genuine.[115] In a widely reported speech in 2014 the Education Secretary Nicky Morgan announced the new tack in no uncertain terms:

> Even a decade ago, young people were told that maths and the sciences were simply the subjects you took if you wanted to go into a mathematical or scientific career, if you wanted to be a doctor, or a pharmacist, or an engineer. But if you wanted to do something different, or even if you didn't know what you wanted to do, and let's be honest – it takes a pretty confident 16-year-old to have their whole life mapped out ahead of them – then the arts and humanities were what you chose. Because they were useful for all kinds of jobs. Of course now we know that couldn't be further from the truth, that the subjects that keep young people's options open and unlock doors to all sorts of careers are the STEM subjects: science, technology, engineering and maths.[116]

It would be difficult to find anyone (certainly in political circles) who had advised young people in the past to study the arts and humanities; but it was pretty clear now that once again policymakers were advising them to study STEM, despite the acknowledged difficulties of getting 16-year-olds to think about their 'whole life mapped out ahead of them'. It was essential, as the Augar Report put it in 2019, that students' choices not stand 'at odds with the government's Industrial Strategy and with taxpayers' interests'.[117]

If this rhetoric was an old story, redolent of the 1960s and the 1980s, what was new was that governments were arming themselves with more effective tools to add muscle to their rhetoric, tools that eschewed the *dirigisme* of manpower planning in favour of student demand, but better 'informed' student demand to ensure that teenagers made decisions better aligned with employer demand and thus with 'national needs'. The contradictions between student demand and employer demand that had so vexed Keith Joseph could thus in theory be resolved. The pioneer here was the Australian government which had reintroduced fees as early as the late 1980s and thereafter worked hard to use the market mechanism to align student demand with national needs. Initiatives were floated to use differential subsidies, differential fees, and improved 'market signals' to induce more students to study STEM, though with limited impact, as Australia was experiencing the same swing away from science as Britain, and for much the same reasons.[118]

The Australian experience was used as a model when Britain began to design its own new fee regime. Its income-contingent loan scheme aimed to give students the skin in the game that Thatcher had sought, in deciding whether to undertake expensive higher education rather than cheaper apprenticeships or further education. But there was also now the possibility of making students more sensitive to the putative wage returns of particular subject choices. Willetts claimed that in doing so he was only responding to students' own keener vocationalism, but he and his colleagues were determined to ensure that students *did* choose more vocationally in order to maximize their payback on student loans as well as supposedly to boost economic growth.[119] The whole higher-education system could be re-engineered into a wage-premium machine, with universities as well as students held responsible for maximizing the income growth (and loan repayment) of graduates. As the Business department put it, it was hoped to 'create an incentive and reward structure at universities by distinguishing the universities that are delivering the strongest enterprise ethos and labour market outcomes to their students'.[120] At the same time, public opinion could be steered towards a more exclusive definition of education as an investment good, its value determined by the private rate of return.[121]

To this end, ambitious new research projects were launched by the Business department to develop data on which subject choices led to the highest wage premia.[122] The principal end-product was the Longitudinal Educational Outcomes (LEO) database which allowed researchers to connect data about students' background to their educational choices and their wages as graduates. Of course background and other exogenous factors, once controlled for, tended to reduce the direct effect of educational choices on wages, but there remained residual effects, though as it happens choice of institution mattered more than choice of subject. Even after controls, medicine and business still produce higher returns, and creative arts lower returns; but for most subjects variation lay in the band of plus or minus

10 per cent only. In theory, these effects pointed to the 'value added' of certain subjects and certain institutions which if students followed these cues would lift the general level of skill in the workforce.[123] In reality, as even the economists working for the government granted, these wage premia might represent only the screening that had always operated in the labour market—employers using subjects and institutions as rough proxies for the best all-round employees, without necessarily testifying to the quality or value of skills gained through education.[124] Drawing more students into these subjects and institutions might in this case only have the effect of reducing their screening value; it might also reduce their economic value if students studied subjects they didn't like and weren't good at.[125] And of course graduate earnings are only revealed over time so that the data is always telling us about the past, not the present, still less the future: the first full study published in 2018 was based on graduates in 2008–12, a particularly bad moment for labour markets of all kinds, as Willetts himself pointed out (from retirement).[126]

As yet, government has confined itself to providing more information to guide student choice, confident that information about wage returns will align student demand with employer demand and 'national needs'. The message has been, as the 2011 White Paper announcing the high-fee regime put it, that student choice was 'at the heart of the system'. Higher education was to be a market and students were to be the consumers.[127] Accordingly government has resisted the temptation to adopt more *dirigiste* methods which appear to put employer demand or 'national needs' ahead of student choice. The high-fee regime which eliminated most government payments to universities for teaching retained an element of subsidy for STEM courses, but only on the grounds that these courses cost more to provide; as Willetts explained, the aim was to provide 'a continuing level playing field for STEM'.[128] Nevertheless, the capacity and the appetite for using fees to steer student choice persists.

There remains, for example, the possibility of differential fees. Differential fees between institutions had always been part of the new fee regime, though as we saw in Chapter 7 institutions themselves resisted them and more or less settled on a uniform fee at the maximum level. Might it not still be possible to engineer differential fees by subject? Initially government considered an indirect route to this end, introducing in 2016 an exercise called the Teaching Excellence Framework (TEF) aimed at assessing universities' performance on a variety of metrics, none of which really assessed teaching excellence at all. One of the most important metrics was in fact a measure of graduate wage premia,[129] which could then be linked to maximum allowable tuition fees, ensuring that only those universities whose graduates paid back more of their loans could charge higher fees. It was intended that a *subject-level* TEF would soon follow, raising the possibility of differential fees at subject as well as institutional level. However, political opposition to these highly instrumental reforms proved too great—especially after 2017 when the government lost its majority—and at the time of writing it has backed off from linking fees to TEF and possibly from subject-level TEF altogether. Again, from retirement, Willetts decried attempts to connect fees to wage returns, because so many other factors had a bearing on those returns.[130] Still, the idea of variable fees by subject will not go away as long as the both the fee regime and prevailing orthodoxy of a STEM skills shortage appear to demand it. The Augar Report of 2019 gave it serious consideration. In the end, it too backed off from the idea, unsure how to charge higher fees for higher-earning subjects without at the same time dis-couraging the swing back to STEM. It is difficult to promote a subject by charging students more for it now with the undeliverable promise that they will earn more from it later.[131]

In the spirit of this chapter, and the argument of this book, however, we should end not with government attempts to engineer the swing but rather with our own attempts to explain it, in terms that give due regard to students' own attitudes and behaviours. Despite Willetts' conviction that students had become more vocational during the transition to mass higher education, it is notable that the swing did not halt or even slow until the 2008 crisis hit. A similar pattern has been noted in the US.[132] For whatever reason, until that point more students meant proportionately less STEM, not more. Sustained wage stagnation since 2008, the effects of the high-fee regime, and possibly the renewed exhortations of government have changed students' choices markedly, in a STEM direction but not uniformly in a vocational direction. The fastest growing subjects are all scientific ones, but social studies and creative arts continue to grow at higher than average rates, while business and computer science lag behind. Languages, literatures and education, and to a lesser extent history, have declined.[133] The most striking decline is in part-time students across all subjects, to some extent due to rising full-time rates (because there are fewer mature students who missed out on higher education earlier), to some extent due to the fee regime, perhaps also to precarity in the labour market.[134]

Such evidence as we have suggests that neither student nor broader public opinion is persuaded by the overwhelming emphasis on private return. One problem is that public-opinion research also embraces the focus on private return so that questions are often framed to exclude other kinds of value. Still, surveys continue to find support for both education and health as public goods, worth more public investment, and in the case of education meriting further expansion.[135] The only piece of research commissioned by the Browne Review found that students and parents believed that government should pay at least half the cost of higher education, but this research was not published in the Report—which argued that private benefits exceeded public benefits—and was only revealed later after a Freedom of Information request. In the event, since all institutions opted for the maximum fee, the total private contribution was even higher than Browne had imagined, at around two-thirds to three-quarters of the fee.[136] The high-fee regime remains highly controversial. In backing off from differential fees by subject, and the more *dirigiste* attempts to steer students to STEM, government has shown it respects the public's sensitivity on this subject. For the time being, student demand is aligning better with government's estimate of employer demand and national needs without further duress. It will be interesting to see whether that alignment survives the end, if there is one, of the now decade-long stagnation in wages.

9

Effectively Maintained Inequality

It may seem perverse, in a book titled 'The Crisis of the Meritocracy', to leave social mobility for last. Today's political discourse, which is still (or perhaps once again) profoundly meritocratic, holds that social mobility is the prime function of education; education gives 'equal opportunity' to rise in the social scale, regardless of your social origins. In the middle of the twentieth century, too, many politicians and social scientists looked to education to make society more meritocratic. It was the great claim of the bipartite system of universal secondary education, in its heyday (though also in its crisis) in the 1950s, that it had substituted merit, as determined by the 11+, for heredity in determining who went to grammar school and university and therefore who ended up in the top jobs. Of course, not all politicians were meritocrats then. Many felt more frankly than they do today that heredity, or in its friendlier form 'family', was a perfectly acceptable and functional way to select an elite. But the idea of 'equal opportunity' to rise in the social scale was something like an official ideology that lay behind the Butler Act and was widely accepted across the leaderships of the political parties.

The focus on the 11+ and the selection of an elite aimed at university—perhaps only 5 per cent of the population—indicates, however, how narrow an idea that postwar notion of equal opportunity was in practice. It was not really about social mobility at all, but about elite selection—an interesting and important subject, but not one that was necessarily very relevant to most people. Revisionist socialists like Michael Young and Tony Crosland objected that it only substituted one form of inequality and rule by the few for another. Whether or not they shared the revisionists' egalitarianism, most citizens were untouched and unmoved by these processes of elite selection. They had not previously had much experience even with secondary education, much less with higher education. They did not aspire to be judges or doctors or bankers. They prided themselves on their 'ordinariness', and viewed those in elite social positions as Others—sometimes with hostility, sometimes with benevolent neutrality, but rarely as objects of envy. What they did want and expect (and got), increasingly after the war, was a better life for their children. The bulge and the trend represented that optimism and aspiration. Their idea of equal opportunity, as represented by the welfare state especially in health and education, was that 'the best' services would be provided by the state for all equally. They opposed the 11+ because it seemed to limit artificially the number of people who could attain that better life by means of education; they opposed grammar schools for some, however meritocratic their selection was, and favoured grammar schools for all. Their interests, therefore, lay less in meritocratic selection for an elite and more in better chances for all.

In this chapter, I will have more to say about politicians and especially about social scientists than about public opinion—because it was mostly politicians and social scientists who expected meritocracy to lead to social mobility and puzzled over why it didn't. Over the course of the 1950s and 1960s, it came to be better understood that the 11+ had not made elite selection more meritocratic. As we saw in Chapters 3 and 4, that understanding contributed to, though it did not drive the transition to, comprehensive education. As comprehensive education rolled out, social scientists also came to realize that this more equal provision of secondary education had not made elite selection more meritocratic either. Other factors, often linked to family background, continued to play the same role that they had always done in reproducing the social order—in 'effectively' maintaining inequality, as some sociologists put it.[1]

Those realizations didn't affect public opinion much; it's hard to see how they would have done, since they pointed to no clear educational solutions to social inequality. Politicians of all parties generally ignored the implications. They valued educational policy as one of the key policy options in their armoury to address a wide range of social problems, including inequality when that reared its head. At the end of the twentieth century, they tried to revive the link between education and social mobility to deal with growing income inequality. But public opinion was, at least until the end of the twentieth century, not much troubled. It held education to be a consumption good as much as an investment good—it was one of the 'decencies of life', and not only an avenue to social mobility. It was also a consumption right of citizenship. Since the state decreed compulsory education to 15 or 16 or 18, it had an obligation to offer high-quality provision to all. 'Standards' became important. Most of all, however, public opinion was untroubled by the impact of educational change on social mobility because, whatever forms of education they experienced, most people enjoyed unprecedented upwards social mobility. The period from the 1950s to the 1980s, at least, was a 'golden age' of social mobility. But it may have had relatively little to do with education.

Testing Meritocracy

Social mobility as a concept was almost the sole preserve of sociologists from the 1920s, when they coined the term, until the 1990s, when it began to enter political and to some extent public discourse. In that period people had other terms to represent roughly the same idea—dominantly, 'equal opportunity' or, more bluntly, fairness—but for sociologists the technical term signalled their unique ability to measure and assess whether education in particular was making opportunity to rise in the social scale more equal; in other words, to test meritocracy. To make these measurements and assessments required a firm analytical structure. People had to be classified rigorously into different social groups to determine their social origins; their life experiences had to be monitored closely in order to track their movement over time; new tools had to be devised to weigh up which experiences counted for most in that movement from social origins to social destinations. It also took a long time, as sociologists were keenly aware. Social mobility is by definition inter-generational: it is measured by the difference between one generation's class status and the next. The effects of universal and bipartite secondary education on social mobility would not be knowable until at least a generation after 1944.[2] The later effects of comprehensivization would again not be knowable until the 1990s at the earliest.[3]

Classification was relatively simple. Although there were (and are) multiple models available, from the earliest social-mobility studies a seven-class scale has been most commonly used to sort people into higher (Class I) and lower (II) professional and managerial jobs, white-collar (III) and self-employed (IV), and manual workers at variously levels of skill (V–VII). More simply, these groups can be clustered into three 'big classes'—the salariat (I–II), the intermediate classes, a highly varied group (III–IV and some V), and the working classes (some V, VI–VII). Since the 1990s, a version of this seven-class scale has become the standard classification used by the Office of National Statistics (National Statistics Socio-Economic Classification, or NS-SEC). The same scale retains its utility over time because jobs are continuously re-classified, to reflect changes in the labour market. For example, 'routine' occupations in Class VII which used to be mostly male-dominated unskilled occupations such as labourer or production-line worker now include many female-dominated occupations such as cleaner or carer.[4]

Tracing people's movements from one class to another is more difficult. First of all, it requires data. Initially social scientists had to generate their own data. David Glass's pioneering enquiry at the LSE in 1949 was based on a representative sample of 10,000 men, where respondents were asked about their father's occupation as well as their own.[5] The next major survey of this self-generated kind would be the Oxford Mobility Survey of 1972, led by A. H. Halsey.[6] Similar use could be made of other surveys where respondents' origins and present status were both observed: election surveys, for example (where voters were asked about both), or official government surveys such as the General Household Survey and its successors (from 1971), the Labour Force Survey (from 1973), and the British Household Panel Survey (from 1991).[7] The birth-cohort studies, which began in 1946 initially as child health and development studies, were taken over by sociologists in their later stages and became the most useful data sources for social-mobility research because they measured so many different aspects of people's lives continuously over their whole lives, and thus allowed for a much more complex understanding of what did or did not affect social mobility.[8]

As the cohort studies in particular revealed, assessing social mobility involves so much more than determining's people's origins and their destinations. For a long time sociologists were much less interested in how many people were mobile, how they moved and where, than in what factors determined their movement—and in particular what role education played. Even more specifically, they were fascinated by the composition of the top classes. Social-mobility research was of interest to them, and eventually to politicians, principally because it *was* a test of meritocracy. They assumed that the top classes should be composed of the most 'able' or 'intelligent', that 'ability' and 'intelligence' were randomly distributed at birth, and therefore that it was the job of the educational system to ensure that ability and intelligence wherever found would be promoted into the top classes. Merit, not birth, would be the determinant of your ultimate social class.

This relationship was captured analytically in what became known as the OED triangle (see Appendix, Figure 9.1).

This schematic represents the relationship between social origins (O) and social destinations (D) over time. In a meritocratic society, the relationship between origin and destination should weaken—your social status should not depend on birth. Instead, it should depend on education. For that to happen, the relationship between social origins (O) and educational level attained (E) also had to weaken—your ability to achieve educationally should not depend on birth—and at the same time the relationship between educational attainment (E) and social destination (D) had to strengthen—educational attainment alone should determine where you ended up. As the sociologists gradually discovered, this particular alignment—weakening OE relationship, strengthening ED relationship, and overall weakening OD relationship—proved a great deal more difficult to attain than anyone had imagined.[9]

As we saw in Chapters 3 and 4, the early studies of social mobility by Glass and his students, notably Jean Floud and A. H. Halsey, tested meritocracy and found it wanting. Their principal interest lay in how far increasing access to grammar school was facilitating social mobility. Mostly they assumed a strong ED association—on the grounds that nearly all higher-status jobs must have required at least a grammar-school education—and focused therefore on the OE association, which they hoped to find weakening. Merely extending access to grammar school, as before the war, did not necessarily accomplish this. But extending free places did, and, it was expected, 100 per cent free places as was achieved after the Butler Act would do more.[10] That would leave only a residue of non-meritocratic places in fee-paying schools.[11]

However, as we have seen, doubts about meritocracy arose and deepened as the 1950s drew on. Initially these doubts were as much political as socio-logical. Floud and Halsey's finding that intelligence, at least as measured in IQ tests or the 11+, was *not* randomly distributed but suspiciously concen-trated in more privileged groups suggested that it might be impossible to weaken the OE relationship, unless selection was abandoned at 11+; instead, more people needed to be given the opportunity to *acquire* intelligence by keeping them longer in academic programmes.[12] Glass and his students were also increasingly open to the revisionist-socialist argument that the good society was not necessarily one that replaced an elite determined by birth with another determined by education, even if the latter were more 'meritocratic'.[13] Nevertheless, it is striking that they continued to focus their attention on testing meritocracy by delving deeper into the ways in which education did or did not reproduce social privilege.

That was still the main purpose of Halsey's 1972 Oxford Mobility Study, based on another representative sample of 10,000 men—women were not yet deemed occupationally reliable enough to include.[14] It showed that as education extended in the postwar period the service class or salariat— Classes I and II—continued to be the prime beneficiaries. For those born just after the war, their access to grammar schools had reached saturation levels—79 per cent of them went to grammar or independent schools—and that proportion only shrank thereafter because grammar schools began to give way to comprehensives. At that point, the dominance of the salariat began to extend further at higher levels. Whereas the salariat who formed only 10–15 per cent of the general population made up 27 per cent of all selective secondary school students, they represented 36 per cent of all those attaining O-levels, 49 per cent of those attaining A-levels and 52 per cent of those entering university. Because overall levels of attainment were rising, working-class participation rates were also rising: as the proportion of the salariat attending selective schools increased from 70 per cent to 79 per cent, so the proportion of the working class attending grammar schools increased from 20 per cent to 27 per cent through the 1950s. Working-class attainment at O-level upwards increased (from a low base) at the 'fastest rates of growth'. But the salariat were enjoying the 'greatest absolute incre-ments of opportunity'.[15] That is to say, the attainment gap (to use a later turn of phrase) between the top and the bottom was not shrinking—the OE relationship was not weakening—'relative mobility' was not improving. Meritocracy was therefore not working. Halsey had discovered what soci-ologists would later call 'effectively maintained inequality'—the tendency of privileged groups to make better use of educational expansion than less privileged groups and thereby to maintain their relative advantage.[16]

Much more research was done later on these same cohorts, as they reached occupational maturity—even the earliest beneficiaries of the Butler Act were only just reaching that point in 1972—and much the same find-ings resulted, though with more data and an ever more elaborate statistical apparatus behind them. There was not much evidence that education was becoming more meritocratic as access expanded.[17] As mobility research spread from the US and UK to other countries, it became clear that this was an international phenomenon—'persistent inequality' in educational attain-ment, as one influential formulation put it. In that analysis, only Sweden and the Netherlands showed any strong signs of weakening OE associations in the postwar decades.[18]

These international comparisons pointed up some of Britain's distinctive features. The Swedish and Dutch welfare states were doing more to equalize life chances, not through reform of the educational system but by reducing class distinctions in everyday life.[19] Effectively maintained inequality applied to education, but not to other forms of inequality, which could be effectively eroded, for example, by high-quality public services and income redistribution. In Britain, it remained easier for privileged groups to use their cultural capital to get ahead educationally.[20] However, in other respects Britain's social and educational structures were less rigid and permitted greater equality. Germany's very rigid educational tracking, which sharply distinguished vocational and academic tracks at an early age, meant that its educational system provided very limited opportunities for social mobility (whatever 'declinist' British public opinion might think).[21] In Britain, by contrast, not only was the bipartite system being dismantled, but a much more flexible educational structure allowed people to acquire a wider range of qualifications and at many stages of the life course. As we have seen, for example, A-levels and degrees could be and were being increasingly acquired as mature students, especially by women; higher vocational qualifications could be and were being acquired by men already established in the workforce, and not only as youths.[22]

Britain's flexible educational system may have permitted more routes to social mobility, but its relatively high levels of inequality tended to moderate that effect. Social scientists came to understand this better when they looked *beyond* the role of education—something they found it difficult to do, so fixated were they on testing meritocracy. But gradually it came to be understood that education was not the only, or the strongest, or an increasing factor in determining social mobility. In other words, the ED association, which should have been strengthening, may not have been; more seriously, direct OD associations, even controlling for education, remained powerful. In determining your social destination, where you came from remained significant regardless of how much education you had. This position is particularly associated with John Goldthorpe, Halsey's associate on the 1972 Oxford Mobility Study. Starting with that study, and pursuing the question through the birth-cohort studies, Goldthorpe argued with growing insistence (and later alongside his collaborator Erzsébet Bukodi) that education was not becoming more important over time in determining people's destinations. Of course, as educational access widened, more top jobs required more education. In other words, education *mediated* social mobility—it was the vehicle by which people attained top jobs. But that didn't mean that more education meant more meritocratic mobility. The beneficiaries of more education were (due to the strong OE association) generally already privileged. Furthermore, over the life course other factors apart from education continued to weigh heavily in determining people's destinations. Education may matter most for the first job, when employers use qualifications to screen for the 'best' applicants; thereafter, other factors which loosen the ED association count for more. In the meritocratic equation, OE associations had to weaken and ED associations had to strengthen—Goldthorpe didn't think that the first had happened much, and the second not at all.[23]

But the killer punch to meritocracy in Goldthorpe's equation was that those other factors (other than education, that is) remained as strong as ever, and many of them derived directly from social origins. The *direct* OD connection, controlling for education, failed to weaken across all three of the main birth cohorts—1946, 1958, 1970—that is, for those entering the workforce from the late 1960s onwards.[24] Goldthorpe illustrated this connection with some startling statistics. In the 1970s, for example, he showed that people from both working-class and salariat backgrounds who had attained degree-level qualifications were practically guaranteed to be found in the salariat—about 90 per cent of them in both cases; but whereas only 8 per cent of those from working-class backgrounds with the lowest level of qualifications had made their way into the salariat, 20 per cent of those from salariat backgrounds with the same low level of qualifications had done so. By the 1990s, this bias had *increased*. Still only 10 per cent of those from working-class backgrounds with the lowest level of qualifications could be found in the salariat; but 35 per cent—over one third—of those from salariat backgrounds with the lowest qualifications had ended up in the same top jobs.[25] A more recent finding makes the same point: children of upper-salariat backgrounds who get a poor degree at a top university (a 2.2 at a Russell Group university) are considerably more likely to enter the salariat than children of working-class backgrounds with a good degree (a 1st) from the same kind of university.[26] As Bukodi and Goldthorpe argue, it doesn't even take 'opportunity hoarding'—special favours like internships or family networks—to achieve this result; employers will ensure it happens themselves by over-rewarding the cultural capital of privileged applicants.[27]

From this point of view, the greater flexibility of Britain's labour market, and not just its educational system, allowed for *less* meritocratic outcomes because educational qualifications mattered less; that is, the ED association was weaker. Goldthorpe thought that employers did use educational qualifications to screen for the 'best' employees, but thereafter there was more opportunity for other traits (associated with class origins) to determine employment outcomes over the life course. The whole system, he suggested, was 'self-maintaining', his version of 'effectively maintained equality': not only were advantaged people always and everywhere able to use their advantages to maintain their advantage however rapidly society might be changing, but less advantaged people tended to be 'conservative' in both their aspirations and their behaviours.[28] International comparisons, however, cast doubt on whether these 'self-maintaining' features were as rigid as they seemed. Educational tracking systems, as in Germany and Britain during the bipartite regime, undoubtedly limited the upward mobility of the less advantaged. Political culture and ethos, as in Sweden and the Netherlands, did seem able to limit the purchase of cultural capital; so, naturally, did greater social equality. And as Diego Gambetta argued, mobility was affected by a 'dense combination of mechanisms' which were not always self-maintaining: in Britain, as we have seen, the bulge, the trend, and the welfare state reflected and affected people's aspirations and expectations for a better life. Britain was becoming a more equal society even if its educational institutions weren't mostly responsible.[29]

Nevertheless, Goldthorpe's findings contributed to the growing disillusionment with educational reform as a vehicle for social mobility among social scientists. For radical sociologists of the 1970s and 1980s, they were only confirming what they had thought all along, which was that meritocracy was impossible in capitalist society. As Basil Bernstein had put it, 'education cannot compensate for society'. It would soon become clear that, if grammar schools hadn't done much for social mobility, neither had comprehensive schools—the OE and OD associations remained strong under both systems, as privileged children got better results in school *and* better jobs regardless of school.[30] But what nearly everyone had missed until surprisingly late was that while education wasn't changing society, society was changing, rapidly and dramatically, all the same.

The Golden Age of Social Mobility

Between the 1950s and the 1980s, education was not making society more meritocratic, but nevertheless many more people from less privileged origins were rising into higher-status occupations. It is startling how even the sociologists who were monitoring social structure very closely either didn't notice this change or didn't accord it much importance. As late as the 1972 Oxford Mobility Study, on which Halsey was reporting in 1980, their emphasis remained determinedly on meritocracy—the extent to which education had equalized chances between the classes, or 'relative mobility'.[31] It was Goldthorpe, reporting on the same study in the same year, who began to shift attention to 'absolute mobility'—the proportions of men moving into different (at this point, mostly higher) classes than their fathers, regardless of their origins. Of the majority who had started at birth in working-class positions, fewer than half had ended up in working-class positions by 1972: 17 per cent had risen as far as the salariat and 34 per cent into the intermediate classes. This degree of upward mobility had been steadily rising even before the war, and continued to rise after.[32] The postwar decades of the bulge, the trend and the welfare state turned out to be a 'golden age of social mobility' after all.[33]

This high level of upward mobility didn't mean that the working class had been cut in half; there were of course others, mostly from the intermediate classes, who were downwardly mobile into it.[34] But the rate of upward mobility consistently and increasingly exceeded the rate of downward mobility, for the simple reason that the class structure of Britain was changing—there were many more professional, managerial, and especially white-collar jobs and many fewer manual working-class ones. Goldthorpe called this phenomenon 'room at the top', tellingly playing on the title of a late 1950s novel and film about the moral perils of upward mobility; as we'll see, elite concerns about upward mobility were noticeably more agonized than the experiences of the upwardly mobile.[35] The growth of the salariat continued inexorably after 1972, as others using later survey material discovered. It had grown from around 18 per cent of men who had reached occupational maturity born in around 1900 to 32 per cent of men born in the 1930s, the youngest cohort available to Goldthorpe, and continued to grow to 42 per cent of men born in the 1950s. The proportions of men in all classes who were upwardly mobile had risen (also to 42 per cent) though by the 1950s birth cohort growth was levelling off; the proportions of men who were downwardly mobile continued to drop to 13 per cent.[36] At least before the 1970 birth cohort and possibly after it, more men were upwardly mobile than downwardly mobile, as measured by occupation. When economically active women began finally to be assessed—and this could be done retrospectively—the same was found to be true for them, though less markedly; more women were formally downwardly mobile because they took part-time jobs on returning to work after childbirth, but more significantly the occupational distribution of women's employment was less favourable than men's, though improving over time.[37]

These high levels of absolute mobility were consistent with no improvements in relative mobility because, just as less-advantaged people were moving up, more-advantaged people were avoiding moving down. Nevertheless, occupationally Britain was becoming less polarized between a small salariat and a large working class. The salariat was growing and becoming more various; the working class was shrinking and becoming more homogeneous. Yet because the social scientists continued to focus on relative rather than absolute mobility (with the partial exception of Goldthorpe, who observed both) we have relatively little to go on in assessing the very widespread experience of upward mobility. As we've noted, observers of widening participation in higher education remained fixated on the proportion of students who came from working-class backgrounds, which you would expect to be in decline as the proportion of people from working-class backgrounds was in decline, even while more and more people were participating.[38] This concern for the working-class share was, of course, motivated by considerations of social justice; but it also betokened an attachment, even by some on the left, to a stable society where upward mobility was seen as in many ways problematic and often ignored. In considering future demand for higher education, for example, right up until the early 1980s the DES paid more attention to relative birth rates in social classes than to mobility between social classes; only in 1984 did it realize its mistake and begin to prioritize changes in social structure over changes in fertility, recognizing that nearly half of those 18-year-olds found in Class II in 1981 had actually started out in a different (usually lower) class at birth in 1963.[39] The persistence of assumptions about a static social order meant that even social scientists interviewing representative samples during the 'golden age' tended to put words to that effect into their respondents' mouths, systematically recording a more fixed language of class than their respondents supplied, and portraying mobility as a problem, even when their respondents extolled it.[40]

Nevertheless, thanks to the richness of the birth cohort studies and to historians' re-reading of the social scientists' field notes, we're now in a position to say a good deal more about the trajectories that people actually followed in the 'golden age' and even something about how they felt about them. As we've seen, upward mobility was common. Before the Second World War, more men were immobile than upwardly mobile; after the war, the reverse. Downward mobility was also in decline from that point. Economically active women followed a similar pattern, though their upward mobility started later, in the 1960s and '70s.[41] Upward mobility, now the most common of the three experiences, was also very diverse. In the 1972 Oxford Mobility Survey, Goldthorpe found that while 24 per cent of men from working-class backgrounds entered a higher occupational class at first employment, another 28 per cent were found in higher occupational classes at the time of the survey. While only 4 per cent of these men went straight to the salariat at first employment, another 14 per cent ended up there. More commonly, 20 per cent went straight into the intermediate classes, to be joined later by another 20 per cent.[42] So both rapid and staged mobility were important, and although over time there was more rapid mobility, staged mobility remained most significant. Later studies of the 1958 cohort—which was only reaching occupational maturity in the early 1990s—found that their trajectories were rather more erratic; no wonder, since they entered the labour market in the highly volatile circumstances of the '70s and '80s. But while their upward mobility was 'scarred' by this experience, which meant they started out at lower levels, staged mobility meant that they recovered much of their position in later life.[43] These later studies using the birth cohort results allowed social scientists finally to extend their findings to women. They found that for men upward staged mobility remained common until the end of the century, while for women it increased up to age 30 and also continued later in life.[44] Another study of the 1958 cohort found a similar diversity of mostly upward trajectories, and that a third continued to be mobile (up or down) well past supposed occupational maturity in their mid-30s.[45]

Short-range mobility was much more common than long-range mobility: the 'rags to riches' trajectory specified in studies of elite formation was rare, even when upward mobility was very common. 70 per cent of fathers in the bottom class (VII) had sons who ended up in the bottom three classes

(V–VII): mobility, but only so far. Women were much less likely than men to rise high—Class I was pretty much closed to them, Class II more open (thanks especially to teaching and nursing), Class III (with its rich opportunities in white-collar work) very open—but they were also more likely than men to leave the working classes, largely via Class III. Very strikingly, the economically active daughters of *all* fathers, of every social class, were more likely to end up in Class III than in any other class. There was 'less room at the top for women . . . [b]ut there has been much more room in the middle'.[46]

Importantly, this staged, short-range mobility meant that—contrary to the picture of mobility given by the exclusive focus on the scholarship boy or girl—upward mobility was not experienced by many people as a wrenching, one-time passage across the working class/middle-class divide, and not as an impressionable teenager either. Rather, it was often experienced as a gradual, accumulating set of life-changes as people worked themselves up or down the occupational ladder. It was, partly for that reason, met with general satisfaction, rather than the psychic disorientation attributed to the scholarship boy or girl. In a follow-up to the Oxford Mobility Study that Goldthorpe did in 1974, specifically asking his respondents about their experiences of mobility, he concluded that 'they had not for the most part experienced their mobility as socially stressful', but valued it for 'improved living standards', 'greater security' and often 'the economic and psychological rewards directly associated with the work'.[47] In the words of Geoff Payne, the sociologist who has emphasized most the significance of 'room at the top', occupational mobility widely distributed across the population generated 'a sense of class well-being that lasted into the mid-1990s'.[48]

The experience of upward mobility had relatively little to do with the educational level previously attained by the mobile. As we noted in Chapter 3, upward mobility was likely to be experienced by all cohorts in the 'golden age' whatever level of education they had (see Appendix, Figure 3.1). White-collar employment was expanding much more rapidly than were educational qualifications; all groups benefited. Of course educational qualifications *were* expanding rapidly, and therefore they mediated a growing number of upwardly mobile transitions, especially to the very top, in Class I; thus accountancy and law became graduate jobs, for example. But as the market for higher-status occupations was growing even more rapidly, employers as we have seen had to take more people without educational qualifications and train them on the job, as they were used to doing.[49] That is why the ED association didn't strengthen.

Britain's flexible educational system and labour market permitted all sorts of upward-mobility trajectories. You could leave school and get a job, then acquire educational qualifications while on the job more easily than in most other countries.[50] Or you could leave school and get a job and climb the occupational ladder regardless of your educational qualifications. These things were harder in systems that divided people between vocational and academic qualifications earlier, or that tied jobs more closely to vocational qualifications, as in Germany. In Germany, vocational qualifications upgraded the industrial workforce and contributed to the strength of the manufacturing sector: there were more skilled workers and closer ties between them and manufacturing employers. But vocational education made it a good deal harder for workers to rise much above the lower end of the intermediate classes. In contrast, Britain's more flexible educational system permitted more longer-range mobility into the salariat.[51] This kind of longer-range mobility was also easier in systems where social inequalities were less, and where aspirants had less opportunity to use the social and cultural capital that came with privilege, as in Sweden. In the postwar years, social inequality was reducing in most places, including in Britain, thanks to the redistributive functions of the welfare state and also to the upgrading of the occupational structure, with fewer people at the bottom and more in the middle as well as the top.[52]

What implications might these patterns of mobility have had for popular attitudes to education and its connection (or lack of connection) to social mobility? As we saw in Chapter 3, there had been a longstanding connection in people's minds between better education and better jobs, but before the Second World War that connection had limited purchase and limited utility, given how little secondary education of any kind was available. With the advent of universal secondary education after the Butler Act, the connection became clearer and potentially more useful to more people. But precisely because the aspiration for better jobs was so widespread, it overflowed the bounds of meritocratic selection for grammar school. By the late 1950s, most people considered themselves able to benefit from grammar school and the opportunities it offered; thus the demand for 'grammar schools for all'. At the same time, the supply of better jobs also overflowed the bounds of grammar school. Students who went to secondary moderns were as likely to be upwardly mobile as those who went to grammars; that followed not only from the over-supply of good jobs, but from the fact that grammar-school students were already nearer the top in terms of family background and so had less opportunity for upward mobility (see Appendix, Figure 3.1).[53]

Contemporaries were not aware of this lack of correlation between education and social mobility. Their attachment to the 'best' schools for all did not weaken. But neither did they notice that comprehensive schools made little difference to relative social mobility. They remained content with both education and absolute social mobility because so much of the latter was available under all educational regimes. In John Goldthorpe's study of 'affluent workers' in 1962, which launched his career, he had found that most of his respondents wanted both grammar school and white-collar jobs for their children. Although parents in white-collar jobs were more successful in achieving their aspiration for both—as he would put it later, the OE and OD associations remained strong—parents in blue-collar jobs were more successful in achieving the good jobs than the good education. As he would discover later, that success would carry on past first employment as staged mobility brought increasing rewards to children of very different backgrounds over their life course. In the meantime, blue-collar parents did not feel 'relative deprivation': their optimism about the future, albeit of a different kind to that of white-collar parents, was redeemed.[54] International comparisons show that this phenomenon was general—expanding opportunities at the bottom compensated for persistent inequalities across society.[55]

As educational opportunities expanded at the bottom, for more people education did mediate their mobility. Without comprehensive reorganization and, later, GCSE (and S-grade in Scotland) and later still the rapid expansion of higher education, just as many people might have been upwardly mobile but they would not have been upwardly mobile because of their education. As we have seen, this may also have affected the *kind* of mobility they enjoyed, improving access to higher occupations which vocational tracks, less flexible structures, or other forms of rationing of higher qualifications impeded. As Goldthorpe pointed out, the fact that many people with Class I backgrounds remained in Class I regardless of their education did not negate the fact that nearly all people with higher education entered Class I, including nearly all of those who came from working-class backgrounds.

Neither did most people feel in an environment of widening opportunities that social mobility was a zero-sum game. Experts' anxiety about social mobility had fixated on the disorientation of the mobile and on the loss of community that mobility seemed to entail. But that does not seem to have been the feelings of the mobile themselves. Staged mobility meant that movement was not as sudden or disorienting as the scholarship boy or girl phenomenon implied. Most people continued to feel loyal to their social origins; thus the persistent finding of sociologists that people continue to describe themselves as 'working class' long after they have technically left it. In any case, 'working class' was used to differentiate the great mass of 'ordinary' people from a small elite of non-workers rather than to demarcate a clear divide between the working class and the middle class.[56]

As the historian Jon Lawrence has argued, as well, immobile and mobile people alike feel a tension between the integrity of the individual or family and the appeal of community. This tension has to be navigated whether people are socially and geographically immobile or whether, as increasingly was the case, they were in both senses mobile. Mobile people formed 'elective' rather than inherited communities, through social networks or when settling into new neighbourhoods; the inevitable communitarianism of child-rearing and neighbourhood schools forms an important part of 'community' in socially mobile Britain.[57] The desire for better schools and jobs was seen as a unifying force in modern life, making people 'allies in a general advance', not combatants in a war of all against all. Lawrence's re-analysis of social-survey transcripts from the 1960s to the 1990s showed that people were very aware of the American scramble to 'keep up with the Joneses', but they tended to deny that that was what they were doing. Everyone wanted a better life and more people were getting one.[58]

But what would happen when the 'golden age' came to an end? What if there was no more room at the top, and not everyone could reasonably aspire to a better life? Would education then become re-embroiled in a contest for relative position? We now tend to think that that was exactly what happened at some relatively recent point, when the 'golden age' came to an end, and concerns about 'social mobility' came explicitly to the surface.

After the Golden Age?

Sure enough, rates of upward mobility began to slow towards the end of the century. There was still room at the top, but less of it. Between 1991 and 2011 the proportion of economically active men in the salariat only grew from 35 per cent to 42 per cent, a slower rate of growth than between 1971 and

1991, and for women only from 27 per cent to 30 per cent. The shrinkage of the working class also slowed for men and came to an end for women.[59] One more precise estimate found the growth of salariat almost halted after 1997, especially for men. Women were more likely to continue to find their way up to Class II and after 2000 even to Class I, as they learned to 'lean in' to male-dominated power structures, in the famous diagnosis of a 2013 book by a female tech entrepreneur.[60] If there has been 'skill-biased techno-logical change', as discussed in Chapter 7, it hasn't shifted employment towards the salariat very much.[61] Perhaps due to Britain's flagging economic performance vis-à-vis the global market, its service and financial sectors ceased to grow very rapidly, and though educational attainment had con-tinued to rise it alone could not create more high-skill jobs—that would take, presumably, more investment in the workforce, more innovation and entrepreneurship, more global competitiveness. These effects were particularly strong in Wales and Scotland, where industrial employment shrank very rapidly and opportunities for non-manual employment did not grow as fast as in England; migration to England was one result.[62] The same effects applied within England, leading to migration out of former industrial districts. And due to post-2008 austerity, in England at least the welfare state ceased to grow as well, further sapping the supply of good jobs in the public sector, including those most accessible to people from less advantaged backgrounds.[63]

Just as importantly, because more people started out nearer the top in the 1990s, there was less overall opportunity for upward mobility than there had been when most people started out at the bottom. This is what the social scientists call a 'compositional effect'—the effect has to do not just with changes in the environment (such as the creation of more jobs in the salariat) but also with the initial composition of the population. There will tend to be more chances of upward mobility if more people start at the bottom, as they did in the 1950s and '60s, than if they start at the middle or the top, as they did in the 1980s and '90s. The apparently declining proportion of working-class students in higher education was a compositional effect, due to the declining proportions of working-class people in the population; so was the declining proportion of upwardly mobile men from the 1990s, due to the higher proportion of men in higher groups in the population.[64] Worse still, the slowing growth of 'room at the top' and compositional effects have combined in a particular way to limit upward mobility still further. Those who start from top class positions already may be getting better at *retaining* their position in those top classes—especially those at the very top, in Class I.[65] In this case there would be even less room at the top for those seeking to move upwards. Skill-biased technological change would thus have an additional burden on it to expand top jobs even more rapidly just to keep a stable level of opportunities for upward mobility.

The declining chances of upward mobility should eventually have had some effect on public attitudes to the social order, and to education too. But attitudes would depend on one's diagnosis of why upward mobility was in decline. Was the evident slowdown in upward mobility due to the failure of new job creation, or to compositional effects, or to insufficient downward mobility from the top, or due to something else entirely (for example, education)? Between the first three options, the sociologists could adjudicate, and even suggest a solution. They couldn't help with the compositional effect, but they could (and did) advocate for more 'room at the top', economic and labour-market policies that helped create more high-quality jobs. They could also argue for more downward mobility from the top, though that was a tough call for politicians. Faced with intractable compositional effects, and the unpalatable need for downward mobility, politicians turned to the fourth option. If compositional effects were at fault, it made sense to ask whether the occupational measures sociologists had traditionally employed to assess social mobility were the right ones. It should be possible to measure social mobility in ways that were not frustrated by compositional effects, and perhaps suggest another way out. Enter the economists.

The economists had of course entered already in the 1990s. They had been making human-capital arguments about the effects of educational investment for decades, but as we saw in Chapter 7 in the 1990s their econometric data and tools proved useful specifically in measuring the effect of educational expansion on the graduate premium—showing that it had held up rather well. Now they offered their services to the cause of social mobility as well. If you measured social mobility not by occupation but by income, dividing the population into four or five equal parts (quartiles or quintiles), you could say something about changes in mobility over time that were not affected by composition. Assessing people's likelihood of moving from one income quartile or quintile to another would provide a measure of relative mobility, much like assessing their likelihood of moving from one occupational group to another, but unaffected by changes over time in the size of the occupational groups. Measuring mobility in terms of income offered other advantages. It might for example prove easier to accommodate data about

women as well as men. It might also factor in better those non-educational
effects that the sociologists themselves had acknowledged, but had no easy
way to measure, by which people used their social, cultural, and economic
capital to secure better jobs for their children, regardless of their educational
levels.[66]

The first systematic attempt to assess changes in social mobility over time
with reference to education came in work sponsored by the Sutton Trust,
an education and social mobility charity, and led by economists Jo Blanden
and Stephen Machin. Starting with a relatively straightforward comparison
of the 1958 and 1970 cohorts, the latter of which had by the mid-2000s
begun to reach maturity, they found that social mobility as measured by
income had slowed. Of the 1958 cohort, only 31 per cent who started from
backgrounds in the bottom quartile ended up there, and 17 per cent made
it into the top quartile. Of the 1970 cohort, 37 per cent starting in the
bottom quartile were still there, and 16 per cent had made it to the top.
There was still upward mobility, but it was in decline. An equivalent study
of the US showed that there had been no such decline over the same period.
Worse still, on international comparisons, intergenerational income mobility in Britain was low in the developed world, not as low as the US but
substantially lower than Germany as well as the Nordic countries.[67]

Why had this happened, according to the economists? Perhaps income
inequality was itself responsible for low rates of income mobility; if the
rungs of the ladder were farther apart, then it would be harder to clamber
up them. And there was indeed a sharp increase in income inequality, at least
at the top, in the 1980s. Blanden and Machin shared that view,[68] but they
also had another explanation, one amenable to the Sutton Trust, which put
education back in the spotlight. They found that the expansion of higher
education had mostly benefited wealthier groups, and that this benefit then
paid off in terms of future income. The attainment gap, in other words,
measured by income quartiles rather than occupational groups, had not
remained stable as the sociologists claimed but had widened. It was educational inequality that had exacerbated income inequality rather than vice-
versa. In other words, education *did* matter more than the sociologists had
claimed, at least in terms of relative mobility; the OE association was very
strong in income-unequal Britain, and this had significant and increasing
effects on OD association.[69]

The sociologists fought back. They defended the use of occupation as a
better measure of social position than income and made many technical
criticisms of the economists' income data.[70] They disagreed with the finding

that Britain had exceptionally low mobility, and in fact some economists soon reported discrepant results, showing British income mobility to be closer to Scandinavia's than America's, including both mobility out of the bottom and 'rags-to-riches' mobility from bottom to top.[71] Goldthorpe in particular stuck to his 'self-maintaining' analysis which insisted that relative mobility rates were unlikely to change much over time or to differ much between societies.[72] But what particularly incensed him and also other sociologists was that, though they had struggled for so long to show that education was *not* the most important factor in social mobility, the economists seemed to be dragging it back into the spotlight. Rather than focusing attention where it belonged, on the failure of the economy to provide more good jobs, the economists had reopened the can of worms that was the disputed relationship of education to social mobility.[73]

It's not easy to referee between the economists and the sociologists. To some extent there has been a moderating of their positions in the last ten years. In a follow-up to their initial study, Blanden and Machin reported that the decline in income mobility between the 1958 and 1970 cohorts did not seem to be continuing in post-1970 birth cohorts that could be constructed from other data, and the effects of educational inequality that they had identified for the 1980s did not extend beyond the early 1990s. 'It seems', they concluded, 'that the oft-cited finding of a fall in intergenerational mobility between the 1958 and 1970 cohorts appears to have been an episode caused by the particular circumstances of the time.'[74] A few years later Blanden also revised her estimate of Britain's place in the international mobility tables, putting it closer to the middle of a wider array of comparators, and offering a peace pipe to the sociologists on the issue of occupation vs. income: 'the two have different, but arguably equally valid, conceptual bases'.[75] Machin in a later book with former Sutton Trust CEO Lee Elliot Major granted that no educational reforms 'consistently reduce attainment gaps, and life prospects', but provided only at best 'a counter-balance' to income inequality.[76] For their part, some sociologists seemed more willing to accept that income inequality, particularly at the top end, *was* partly responsible for deteriorating relative mobility: there might be still plenty of churn between the bottom and the middle parts of the distribution, but at the top very high incomes were surely improving high-earners' ability to pass their income on to their children.[77]

In short, there remained some more room at the top, mainly for women, but downward mobility became more common especially for men, both because occupational change had slowed and because income inequality was being used by the privileged to maintain their privilege at the very top. Educational change apparently had little to do with it, one way or the other. While GCSE had undoubtedly had some short-term effect in providing more educational opportunities for the disadvantaged, the expansion of higher-education that followed was exploited rather better by the more advantaged, cancelling out the relative-mobility effects.[78] The attainment gap between the classes (or income quintiles) remained pretty stable, even as overall attainment rose: more effectively maintained inequality. Education mediated more people's mobility but it did not improve their relative or perhaps even their absolute chances of upward mobility. What was needed was either reduced inequality, to improve relative mobility, or investment in better jobs, to improve absolute mobility, or both.[79]

However we choose to adjudicate between the sociologists and economists, what is undeniable is that concerns about social mobility grew dramatically among the political classes after 2000 and among the wider public after the financial crisis of 2008. In both cases, too, hopes for education as a solution to declining social mobility were on the rise, whatever the social scientists counselled. The term 'social mobility' had already begun to trickle into political discourse in the 1990s, when John Major began to use it to describe his own trajectory—from grammar-school boy to Prime Minister, without university education—and to endorse his rather feeble attempts to resurrect public interest in grammar schools in the 1997 general election.[80] Here Major tried to associate social mobility with his own individual effort and enterprise in a meritocratic spirit, portraying Labour as the enemy of self-improvement. But the time was clearly not yet ripe. It was only after Labour returned to power in 1997 that social mobility entered the political mainstream of all major parties.

Why did this happen? One argument is that politicians found it impossible (or undesirable) to tackle the surge in income inequality that had occurred in the 1980s, and New Labour in particular, concerned about inequality, looked for new, more feasible and electorally amenable solutions.[81] Given the popular enthusiasm for education, education as a vehicle for social mobility was an attractive option.[82] There remained the problem that more equal opportunity would require downward as well as upward mobility. A Cabinet Office review in 2001 emphasized the need for more downward mobility—not so easy to sell to an electorate that now comprised more people from higher occupational groups. Accordingly, it recommended that government focus on creating more room at the top.[83] In the meantime, government could (and did) focus on the attainment gap between less and more advantaged groups, in the hopes that more equality in educational attainment might still at least provide some moderate counter-balance to income inequality.[84]

The publication of the Sutton Trust report in April 2005, warning about declining social mobility and pointing to education as one of the culprits, thus fell on fertile ground; but it had an independent effect too.[85] All parties pounced on it as an opportunity to advance their favoured educational nostrums. On the right, this meant making much of the fact that the alleged decline had taken place between the 1958 and 1970 birth cohorts, that is between the 1970s and the 1980s, suggesting in these quarters an indictment of comprehensive education as the enemy of social mobility. Grammar schools, it was claimed, had been the true engines of social mobility during the golden age, though the Sutton Trust report had cited higher education and not secondary education as the only likely educational factor.[86] On the centre and left, emphasis on narrowing attainment gaps—principally now in higher education—redoubled. It was strongly argued that narrowing attainment gaps, even at the higher levels, was the best contribution government could make to improving social mobility.[87]

This mounting enthusiasm for education as a motor of social mobility—perhaps as a distraction from inequality—was then crowned by the 2008 financial crisis and its after-effects. Huge popular anxiety, especially among the young, about the future of employment dissolved what was left of optimism about the likelihood of upward mobility—or even stability—that had been eroding since the 1990s. Politicians rushed to address it with the now familiar educational nostrums of widening participation (which might at least upgrade the whole workforce) and tackling the attainment gap (which might improve fairness). As shown by one crude measure—references to social mobility in The Times newspaper—sensitivity to social mobility which had surged in 2005 soared after 2007 to new heights; by the election year 2010, readers of The Times might expect to encounter social mobility every day in their newspaper (see Appendix, Figure 9.2). New Labour's last major statement, a White Paper in 2009 entitled New Opportunities: Fair Chances for the Future, hailed social mobility as 'the modern definition of social justice', citing a wealth of social-science literature in its support, and pledged itself to improving both relative and absolute mobility, even claiming that the one inevitably fed the other, though there was no evidence that 'room at the top' led to more equal life chances.[88]

Ever closer attention was being paid to gaps opening after 16—not 'staying on' any longer, but attainment particularly of A-levels, access to higher education, and degree attainment. Short-term movements in these gaps were seized upon as evidence of progress or regress, shorn of the broader context which would determine whether they would in fact make any difference to social mobility.[89] In England, Scotland, and Wales alike, as education had been a devolved responsibility since 1998, attainment gaps became a matter of absorbing and pressing attention, though with little difference in outcomes between the three nations.[90] In contrast to New Labour, which had at least attempted a joined-up policy to tackle attainment gaps at all levels from early years upwards, the Coalition Government after 2010 focused its attention more narrowly on higher education.[91] David Willetts, for example, poured scorn on evidence that attainment gaps were already present at birth and widened throughout the early years. For him, the fact that the attainment gap *didn't* widen much further at university was a sign that higher-education interventions could be crucial to social mobility.[92] But of course if the attainment gap was already sufficiently wide at 16 or 18, such interventions might have little effect; and they could in any case only affect the OE relationship at that higher level, they couldn't strengthen the ED relationship or mitigate all the direct OD relationships that were evident even controlling for education.[93] Studies by economists, for example, found that the attainment gap at higher education counted for little or none of the gap between income quintiles, except possibly for the gap between the top and second quintiles. They recommended more focus on reducing inequalities in the early years.[94]

If government attempts to tackle short-range attainment gaps made little contribution to social mobility, especially in conditions of continuing widening inequality, the new attention being paid to education and social mobility might still be having an effect in altering popular perceptions. Education and social mobility were already closely linked in people's minds. But did the darkening economic environment wipe out the optimistic belief in the possibility of 'general advance' still prevalent in the 1990s? It had been easy for people to assume that everyone would benefit from the 'best' education when most people were still enjoying upward mobility. When upward mobility slackened, might people not begin to see educational more as a positional good—a zero-sum game, where you had to scramble to get the advantages you needed to retain your place on the upward escalator?

Although nostalgia is a constant temptation in all periods, there's no doubt that young people today think that they live in a more turbulent and competitive world than their parents did. The growing threat of downward mobility and, especially since 2008, the precariousness even of good jobs dog many people's lives. The evidence on subject choice presented in Chapter 8 suggested at the very least greater calculation on the part of students. For some on the right, there is cause to celebrate this greater sense of competitiveness: it incentivizes striving and enterprise, and contributes to overall economic growth. The problem is not poverty but poverty of aspiration. In these quarters, meritocracy came back in fashion.[95] New Labour was not immune to it, either.[96] More emphasis was placed on breeding 'winners', who were fully deserving of whatever advantages they achieved; the belief that educational attainment was all-important and represented intrinsic merit seemed to absolve the new meritocracy from the democratic criticism to which older elites had been exposed, just as Michael Young feared. Indeed, late in life Young upbraided Blair for falling for the myth of meritocracy, to which as he had argued in 1958 the Fabian left was just as susceptible as the right.[97]

In practice, however, as we have seen, governments found it difficult or impossible to make too frank an embrace of pure meritocracy.[98] Democratic pressure against it was too strong. Both Labour and Conservatives preferred policies that emphasized a general upgrading of the school system— 'standards' rather than 'choice'—and a general upgrading of the labour force, rather than a too unseemly scramble for top position. The Conservatives made one more pitch for choice in the 2005 election, but 'the party's research showed that choice did not resonate at all with target voters'.[99] Nevertheless, social scientists detect a more pronounced embrace of meritocratic thinking among the citizenry. Working-class people are thought to blame themselves for their failure to rise, in what has been called 'disidentification' with their own class position.[100] People are thought to be essentially consumerist and individualist, rather than welfare-oriented and civic, in their personal and family orientations. 'Aspiration', another of Tony Blair's favourite words, is rife and in conditions of greater inequality delusional.[101]

Aspiration, however, is nothing new. Most people aspired to a better life for themselves and their children in the golden age of social mobility, too.[102] They were mocked for it then, not least by pundits (including those on the left like Abrams) who thought their aspirations were deeply unrealistic. But in fact they turned out to be more realistic than contemporary experts imagined. They may not have achieved levels of grammar-school or university education to which they aspired, but they were likely to become better off and reach higher occupational classes all the same. They didn't see this as a zero-sum game and didn't on the whole see themselves as competitive with their neighbours.[103] They thought government ought to facilitate a 'general advance' by providing high-quality health and educational services to everyone, after which there remained plenty of room for meritocratic determination at the higher levels.

What is different now is that optimism about 'general advance' has understandably dimmed. In the absence of widespread upward mobility, people may well feel that they have to fight each other to bag what few top jobs there are. But it's not clear that people are in fact targeting each other in this way. After all, the political rhetoric about social mobility intensifying since 2000 said that social mobility wasn't a zero-sum game, that more education (and more STEM skills) would upgrade the whole workforce and give everyone better jobs. If blame for immobility is cast anywhere, it's on a small elite at the top. The fact that inequality is much worse at the top of the scale than elsewhere—the growth of income inequality is concentrated not only in the top 10 per cent but in the top 1 per cent, and income inequality within the three middle quintiles has hardly shifted at all—has caused many people to identify the '1 per cent' as the major problem.[104] Although that can't literally be true—declines in upward mobility are only minimally affected by the greater ability of the top 1 per cent or even the top 5 per cent to keep their position[105]—this concern with the 1 per cent has manifested itself not in greater competitiveness but in calls for greater fairness, in education but also in the job market and in everyday life. Private schooling, differential access to top universities (the attainment gap), the use of social capital to secure labour-market advantages through personal connections and unpaid internships, and other social advantages that persist throughout the life course have all come under scrutiny.[106]

Regardless of how competitive people may feel with each other, in matters of education as in health the state is still expected to provide the best for all. Just because the labour market appears to be a zero-sum game, that's no reason to make education work that way as well. 'Disidentifying' working-class respondents, who think social background is crucial to help you get ahead, expect equal provision in compulsory education: as much of a level-playing field as they can get.[107] The same applies to the majority of people who are some steps higher up the occupational ladder, but have not much more ability to access private education or even social connections: high-quality state education remains top of their list of assets in securing themselves against downward mobility. This may explain the relatively weak support that grammar schools yet enjoy at a time when unchecked merit-ocracy is said to be rampant. When asked about grammar schools in polls, people sometimes express very high levels of approval, presumably feeling that grammar schools remain 'the best' schools.[108] But are they eager to expose themselves to the lottery of selection at 11+, knowing their chances of being winners are limited and that the consequence of losing is relega-tion to a school not 'the best'? A Sutton Trust survey in July 2017 asked not about grammars in isolation but specifically about education and social mobility. A majority expected their children would have a worse life than they did themselves, a pessimism that had grown substantially since 2008. But when asked what was the best educational solution to the problem of social mobility, only 8 per cent chose grammar schools. 23 per cent proposed lower tuition fees at university and 47 per cent 'high quality teaching in comprehensives'.[109] Similarly, although the resurgence of 'modern' appren-ticeships has charted an alternative path to higher education, better suited to women, tied to growing rather than declining industries, and not so clearly demarcated from academic qualifications, nevertheless participation rates in higher education continue to rise. Young people may be less certain about the costs and benefits of university, but their demand for it has not yet slackened, despite the obstacles and alternative temptations thrown in their path.[110] 'The best for all' remains a potent formula in a democracy that feels vulnerable but seeks security.

Epilogue
More and More Education

I have argued in this book that the postwar meritocratic settlement—supposedly embedded in the Butler Act, and in some people's views persisting today—was challenged by a demand for (and a take-up of) more and more education from the 1950s to the present. Where did this demand come from? The dominant view, insofar as anyone has any ideas at all on the subject, has become an economists' view that there has been a 'race between education and technology' driven by the technological needs of the most developed economies. This view puts employers' demand for educated labour in the driver's seat. It also gives a role to technocratic politicians who are sensitive to employers' needs and supply more education, or sometimes only what they consider to be the right kind of education, to suit. It gives a further role to parents and students, who come to see education as an 'investment good' and take up the opportunities provided by politicians in order to reap the benefits provided by employers ('pecuniary returns') in the form of wage premia for more educated workers.[1] In economic theory, all of these roles match up neatly and there is really no need to prioritize them (or even to explore very far how they might work in practice or to explain the pace and extent of expansion over time). No increment of education would be provided *or* taken up if it didn't pay off. Others, not so ready to rely on economic theory, fall back on other explanations.[2] Historians tend to emphasize politicians and their ideological predispositions to provide more or less education. Sociologists, with their keen eye on social distinctions, see a 'self-maintaining' system whereby advantaged people consume more education in order to protect their advantage and everyone else has to scramble to keep up. One well-informed participant-observer, the former universities minister David Willetts, concludes with a shrug that 'successive governments, perhaps more by accident than design, have delivered an increase in graduates that roughly matches the increase in demand for them'.[3]

In this book I have tried to shift attention to demand from parents and students. This demand was, to some degree, economic. From early in the twentieth century, growing numbers of parents sought grammar-school education for their children because in part they thought this the best route to better jobs and a better life. In the early 1970s, there came a moment when they doubted that proposition and demand slackened for a time, at least as far as 18-year-olds entering higher education went. In the 1980s, growing awareness of the needs of a 'knowledge economy' helped to restore confidence in the economic value of education. But student demand could not be very highly sensitive to employer demand: new entrants especially, and young people making important decisions from their early teens, were hardly in a position to play the role of 'econometricians', as John Goldthorpe has put it.[4] Furthermore, with rare exceptions, demand seems to have been growing more or less constantly over the whole of the last century. To understand the sources of demand, we have to be more curious about what Diego Gambetta called the 'dense combination of mechanisms' operating on young people making educational choices, and not just brute economic calculations.[5] This requires a broader understanding of changing norms and expectations in postwar British society which caused people to see education as not only an investment good but also a consumption good, 'one of the decencies of life', and, even more, a right of citizenship.[6]

Democracy, I have tried to show, was the essential context in which those changing norms and expectations took shape. Formal political democracy only came to Britain early in the twentieth century; the expectation that the state would serve the interests of the whole of the people, and could enhance their quality of life in everyday matters, only crystallized around the time of the Second World War. After the war, these democratic expectations came to be applied to education, which had before the Butler Act only affected most people lightly and relatively briefly. Not only did the state now engage to provide universal secondary education—though on its own terms, meritocratically sorting the sheep from the goats at 11—but in post-war conditions of social security and economic growth most citizens were increasingly concerned about and committed to a better future for their children. These heightened expectations were manifested in the bulge, the trend and support for the welfare state. And they were not generally expressed in terms of individual expectations and advantages, but rather in democratic norms of what all citizens should expect—what McPherson and Raab have called the 'consumption right of citizenship'.[7]

In this sense, education was not a positional or a status good, where individuals strove for advantages over others, but a collective good where all could be expected to benefit. 'The best for all' was applied, not to all features of the welfare state, but distinctively to health and education which were seen as crucial infrastructures of citizenship, rather than limited goods that should be confined to the deserving. Thus the demand for an end to the 11+ and the provision of 'grammar school for all'; thus the suspicion of vocational tracks as second-best and the preference established early on in Wales and Scotland for a 'liberal' education for all, and increasingly in England too; thus the growing expectation that more and more people should be educated to a level where they could benefit from and therefore expect access to higher education. Seen in this light, the 'self-maintaining' tendency of educational inequality was driven not so much by individual rational action, but rather by a 'race between education and democracy'. Each time equal provision was secured—by the abolition of the 11+ or by the adoption of the Robbins Principle—advantaged people would rush to take maximum advantage of the higher levels of provision and disparities would open up. But democratic expectations provided a counter-balancing effect. Demands for equal provision at the higher levels would result: a common examination at 16 giving equal access to post-compulsory education, or a dramatic expansion of higher education to benefit the less advantaged as well. Democracy, and not just technology, had a ratchet effect in eliciting more and more education from the state, and not just in its early stages, but right up to the present.

In this race between education and democracy, democracy had further essential aids deriving from postwar social changes. I have placed emphasis on two factors in particular, often overlooked by contemporaries and by subsequent commentators. First, more educated parents tend to demand more education for their children, providing an escalator effect noted by Robbins and embedded in its projections, but then temporarily forgotten during the slump of the 1970s, so that nearly everyone was surprised when the escalator jerked back into action in the 1980s. Second, widespread upward mobility not only raised people's expectations of that better future for their children but it also widened their horizons so that they were less burdened by inherited expectations than previous generations. These social changes wove themselves virtuously into the fabric of democracy, connecting optimism about the future with the more equal provision of education (as of health) provided by the postwar welfare state.

What did more and more education achieve? As we saw in Chapter 9, it did not on its own achieve greater social and economic equality, as educational inequality was effectively maintained, even while at the same time higher levels of attainment were achieved for all. Undoubtedly it made a contribution to economic growth. That contribution may not be easily measured by income premia; education may be only one source of skill that increases productivity, even possibly a diminishing source; investments in human capital in any case only form part of investments in growth. But it would be absurd to deny the investment value of education. One recent estimate puts the contribution of higher education to Britain's productivity growth between the 1980s and the 2000s at 14–20 per cent, about average for developed countries.[8] Though income premia for specific qualifications may represent employers' efforts to screen for the best employees rather than to reward specific skills, it would be hard to deny that in the process they are showing they consider better-educated people to be better employees. When higher education expanded in the 1960s, employers like lawyers and accountants who used to take new workers with A-levels now took the same new workers with degrees. They were still the best-educated, but now the best-educated had higher qualifications. They may also have become more productive as a result, but employers couldn't know that until long after the fact; they were responding to greater provision, rather than causing it, while at the same time benefiting from it. Similarly, when higher education expanded rapidly in the 1990s, employers used subject and institution to screen for the best employees; whether those subjects and institutions provided better education and more useful skills is as yet hard to determine, but employers were certainly using these signals to find flexible and trainable employees who might more easily acquire productive skills on the job.

At some basic level, education has become more and more necessary to function as a productive citizen (in all senses of the phrase) in modern society. Socialization—learning how to get along with others, learning the ropes of an increasingly complex world, learning how to navigate a world where formal knowledge is increasingly implicated in more and more aspects of daily life—that used to take place in the family, the neighbourhood or the church is now assigned to schooling in all developed countries. As James Flynn has shown, in what is known as the 'Flynn effect', since the early twentieth century daily life has become much more cognitively demanding, evident in steadily rising average IQ scores. Analytical and symbolic forms of thinking are required in both work and leisure; analogies, abstractions, and logical puzzles abound. Wider vocabularies and faster thinking are called for. Some of these skills can be honed just by doing cognitively demanding things (much as skill can be acquired on the job as well as in education). But again formal education is tasked with key aspects like literacy and numeracy and, in higher education, proliferating cultural capital.[9]

Many other benefits have been attributed to education, though high-wire statistical manipulations are required to show that education is causing rather than mediating these things, much as we saw in the case of social mobility. Social mobility is of course one of the most touted benefits; and it's closely linked to another, greater individual income, as a meritocratic allocation of more income via education, on the basis not of origin but of 'ability', is the alleged basis of social mobility. As we have seen, economists have laboured mightily to demonstrate the pecuniary advantages to individuals, and sometimes to society as a whole, not only of more education in general but of education in specific subjects and specific institutions. Partly in response to these economic calculations, non-economists have been intensifying in recent years their efforts to demonstrate the non-pecuniary benefits, both to individuals and society. Often these arguments have been firmly cast in a non-quantifiable form—moral and cultural—which has the advantage of making them incommensurable with the economists' calculations, therefore unassailable by them, though also it is hoped more easily grasped by lay people.[10] Stefan Collini, for example, has isolated 'the extension and deepening of human understanding' as the central function of higher education, in some ways essentially and always in tension with a policy discourse which seeks to reduce the meaning of life to specific social and economic goals, and seeks to reduce education to a vehicle for those goals, while higher education itself stands for 'a sense of the "more" to human life'. Public opinion, he argues, recognises this special function of the university as 'a partly-protected space in which the search for deeper and wider understanding takes precedence over all more immediate goals'; and this attachment to higher education as a place of 'disinterested enquiry and the transmission of a cultural and intellectual inheritance' ought therefore to be juxtaposed with or incorporated into our understanding of higher education as a democratic or civic good.[11] Parallel arguments have been advanced from many quarters for the particular moral and cultural value of the humanities, first when economic arguments seemed to be drawing too much attention to the sciences, then more recently after 2008 when a 'crisis of the humanities' threatened.[12]

Probably to Collini's distress, more arguments have been made which seek to quantify the *non*-pecuniary benefits of more and more education in ways that *are* commensurable with the economists' findings. One of the more celebrated arguments comes from a figure who should be familiar to readers of this book, if their memories can stretch as far back as Chapter 5: Richard Layard, Claus Moser's deputy in the statistical team that worked on the Robbins Report. In the 1960s Layard had helped to put 'social demand'—that is, demand from students, whatever their motivations—at the heart of government planning for educational expansion, rather than attempts at manpower planning or narrow human-capital investments. Almost fifty years later, as Lord Layard, he made the case for considering 'happiness' as a better measure of 'welfare' than the economists' preferred measures such as income or labour mobility; indeed, Layard said, the contest for more income or relative social position could actually reduce welfare by contributing to unhappiness. Happiness, he thought, could be taught, and therefore 'education of the spirit is a public good', unconnected to GDP or social mobility. On the whole, though, Layard felt that the direct effects of education on happiness were limited.[13]

Others took up the challenge to find non-pecuniary effects of education that were stronger and more quantifiable. Using the same comparison of the 1958 and 1970 cohorts that the economists used to address the effects of education on income and social mobility, another team sought to show that more education was correlated with feelings of well-being, bodily health, the development of 'social capital' which connected people into networks and communities, civic participation, racial tolerance, the decline of deference, less cynicism about politics, and the inculcation of skills useful in life outside the workplace. On the whole, they found, these measures had a tendency to deteriorate between the two cohorts but that higher education especially—which was just taking off among the 1970 cohort—inoculated you against this decline.[14] These findings were useful to New Labour in touting the benefits of its efforts to narrow the attainment gap—which would by this reasoning not only improve social mobility but would also spread contentment and liberal values to less advantaged groups[15]—and similar correlations were popularized in the 2009 bestseller by the social epidemiologists Richard Wilkinson and Kate Pickett, *The Spirit Level*.[16]

Perhaps the most ambitious of these arguments was made by the American economist Walter McMahon in the same year when he deployed economists' accounting measures to measure all of the pecuniary and non-pecuniary benefits of higher education that had previously been thought to be *not* quantifiable. Thus in addition to the graduate wage premium for individuals, McMahon found enormous economic benefits for society as a whole from the provision of more education and also non-pecuniary benefits as various as longer life, lower fertility, more individualism, more civic consciousness, more happiness, all for individuals, and also non-pecuniary benefits for society as a whole including more human rights, more political stability, lower crime rates and a better environment. All in all, he calculated, non-pecuniary benefits to the individual and to society were each worth almost as much as the pecuniary benefits. McMahon hoped that this full accounting would persuade the public and policymakers to invest more in higher education, well beyond what seemed to be justified by the graduate premium.[17]

These calculations were aimed at appealing to policymakers because they were comparable to and added to the purely economic benefits claimed for investment in human capital via education. Not only New Labour, but its successor the Coalition government paid at least some attention to them; the Business department in 2013 issued a long bibliography of attempts to parcel out benefits of education between four 'quadrants' (pecuniary and non-pecuniary benefits to individuals and to society), and David Willetts talked up the quadrants in his retrospective book. Still, it is doubtful whether all of these economist-friendly calculations have really penetrated very far. Willetts devoted about four pages to the non-economic and twelve pages to the economic benefits.[18] McMahon's accounting, more evenhanded, hasn't made much difference. It's the individual economic benefits that government is seeking to measure with its databases and to reward with its funding schemes, as repayment of student loans is the highest good, and only individual graduate premia pay off student loans, not happier or thinner or more tolerant graduates.

While it is relatively easy to gauge government's priorities, it is harder to say if any of these widely touted benefits of more education have influenced parents and students in their choices and behaviours. Just as we shouldn't expect them to be skilled econometricians, calculating accurately the pecuniary costs and benefits of staying on, neither should we expect them to weigh up the non-pecuniary benefits with any degree of specificity or accuracy (still less to convert them into a common currency allowing economic valuation, as McMahon does). However, many of these benefits in terms of health and wisdom and civic participation surely do figure in people's ideas about the better life that they hope to bequeath to the next generation, just as the pecuniary benefits of education also figure. They are integral if hardly calculable parts of an idea of democracy that doesn't pit all against all but respects everyone's desires for steady improvement and equal treatment by the state—desires that proved powerful and sustainable throughout the optimistic postwar decades, surviving the slump of the 1970s, and resuming their hegemony in the late 1980s and 1990s.

How powerful and sustainable are these ideas now, after the 2008 crisis, when optimism seems in much shorter supply and steady improvement out of reach for so many? In the last three chapters, we have ended with some hints, which tug in different directions. On the one hand, participation levels after compulsory training or education to 18 have continued to rise, despite the obstacles of cost and bureaucracy put in their way. Politicians still feel under pressure to maintain high standards for all in secondary education, to tackle the attainment gap, and to defend the Robbins Principle that offers a place in higher education for anyone who qualifies for it. Hints recently that the student funding regime might be rejigged to discourage those with the lowest passing A-level grades (on the grounds that their education was unlikely to serve either the government's industrial strategy or 'taxpayers' interests') were met with furious objections. How dare politicians rather than parents and students seek to determine who should and who shouldn't go to university? The Augar Report of 2019 commissioned to propose reforms of the funding regime drew back sharply from the suggestion—'an example of social engineering—and breach of concepts of fairness—that do not fit comfortably within a meritocratic education system'—notably annexing the label of meritocracy to concepts of fairness that owe more to democracy; rather, meritocratic ideas of selection for an elite reminiscent of Keith Joseph lay behind the 'social engineering' that was proposed rather than the concepts of fairness with which Augar rejected it. Nevertheless, Augar floated the possibility of reviving the idea if universities continued to produce graduates unable to pay back a larger share of their student loans: a proposition that is certain to be resisted violently in future by those who don't think short-term individual pecuniary benefits are the goal or even the most important outcome of higher education, not to mention those who will be debarred from higher education as a result. Keith Joseph's example ought to stand as a warning to politicians who want to rein in rather than extend widening participation.[19]

On the other hand, optimism about a happy end to the educational journey has sagged. As we saw at the end of Chapter 9, the experience of upward social mobility began to fail even before the 2008 crisis, and has intensified as the labour market becomes more precarious as well as failing to provide more room at the top. Those born after the 1970s expect not to end up better but worse off than their parents.[20]

In a recent survey by the Sutton Trust of secondary school pupils, over three-quarters expressed their determination to proceed to higher education—indicating that there is plenty more scope for continuing the trend to higher participation levels—while at the same time only two-thirds thought that higher education was important (down from 86 per cent in 2013). The least affluent were those likely to be most discouraged. (Note, however, that attitudes to learning and studying were much more likely to be cited by discouraged respondents than financial reasons.)[21] As we saw at the end of Chapter 8, those who do proceed to higher education, still in growing numbers, are shifting their subject choices away from arts, humanities and social studies towards STEM, perhaps with an eye on the difficult labour market ahead. Furthermore, it's notable that under the austerity policies of the post-2008 governments education spending has dropped substantially as a proportion of GNP, back to the level around 4 per cent characteristic of the Thatcher years (see Appendix, Figure 10.1).

The contrast with the peaks of the 1960s and 2000s is striking. In the 1990s Conservative governments were punished for this neglect of education (and New Labour correspondingly rewarded for embracing 'education, education, education'). There isn't much evidence yet of a sharp turn against austerity on educational grounds at the end of the 2010s, certainly nothing on the scale of Labour's landslide victory in 1997. This may be because everything else has been obscured by the constitutional issues surrounding Brexit and the four nations of the United Kingdom and the deep divisions they have revealed. Or it may be a token of declining public certainty about education as the high road to a better tomorrow.

It would be a mistake for me to conclude with any long-term predictions based on a supposed turning-point in the recent past. The evidence of the post-2008 period is still profoundly mixed. One of the advantages of the longer-term perspective I have adopted in this book is that it turns away from the instant cultural punditry that is so often applied to education. As such a crucial feature of the modern world, and the democratic state, education offers too convenient a mirror on where we are just now—thus the temptation to argue, for example, that History and Politics may be on the verge of a renaissance as subjects because of our contemporary excitements over Brexit, even though we should know that subject choices are formed over a much longer period, and respond better to much more profound social changes such as changing gender roles or the growing attention paid to self-identity and self-discovery. Instead, I have focused on those more profound social changes and the ways in which they have manifested themselves in the drive for more and more education in the postwar decades. While the bulge may have tapered off, as family size shrank to accommodate women's education and careers, the trend has worked a far greater transformation than even Robbins anticipated, despite significant setbacks between the late '60s and the mid-'80s. And education like health has continued to loom large in most people's understandings of their equal rights as citizens in a democracy even while other features of the welfare state have been reconfigured out of recognition.

In its Christmas number for 1963, the *Times Educational Supplement* published a spoof entitled 'The Whythitt Report on Comprehensive Universities'. Coming a few weeks after the Robbins Report, and coinciding with the mounting pace of comprehensive reorganization, the 'Whythitt Report' mocked the contemporary 'ambition fever' which was driving up the proportion of parents 'likely to detect promise in their children' to unforeseen heights. After interviewers had explained 'in full detail to the 27 per cent of negative responders the benefits that higher education would bring to their children', ambitions for higher education extended to as many as 95 per cent of the population—much as Mark Abrams found what he took to be unbelievably high aspirations for qualifications after he had explained in his surveys what might be the benefits that comprehensive education could bring.[22] Even while observing this rising tide of aspiration, neither Abrams nor the *TES* could truly credit it—or at least they felt obliged to make fun of it. Yet as we have observed 96 per cent of the *least* advantaged mothers in the Millennium Cohort Study expressed a desire for their 7 year olds (in 2007) to go to university. No-one has ever yet lost any money in betting on widening participation, and a continued upgrading of educational qualifications, far into the future. On the other hand, I am not advising you to bet on it either. After all, history is full of surprises.

Appendix

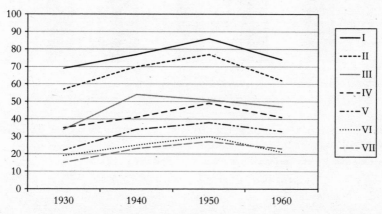

Figure 2.1 Percentage of males in each class age-cohort attending selective secondary schools.

Source: Adapted from Smith, 'Schools', 198. The first two data points (represented here as static points at 1930 and 1940) represent men born in 1910–19 and 1920–29 respectively, all of whom would have entered secondary school by 1940. The data comes from the Oxford Mobility Study (1972), based on retrospective queries of men of all ages. Earlier awareness of the relationship between social class and educational selection was dim—for an early study, see Lindsay, *Social Progress*—and still tended to focus on the obstacle of fee-paying. For the development of sociological interest in this subject after the war, see pp. 56-7; and for the I-VII class scale—ranging from upper professional and managerial (I) to unskilled working classes (VII)—see pp. 182-3.

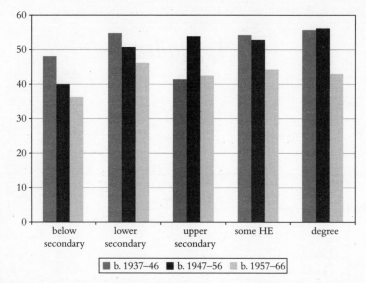

Figure 3.1 Proportions of birth cohorts who were upwardly mobile (by level of educational attainment): entry into labour market 1952–82.

Source: Data from Paterson and Iannelli, 'Patterns of Social Mobility', Table 8.

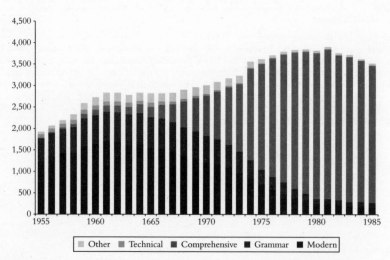

Figure 4.1 Pupils at state secondary schools, by type, England and Wales.

Source: Bolton, 'Education: Historical Statistics'.

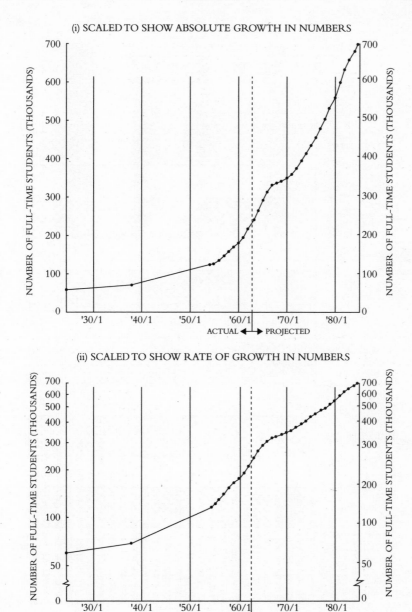

Figure 5.1 Projections of higher-education growth to 1986.

Source: Robbins Report, I, 68.

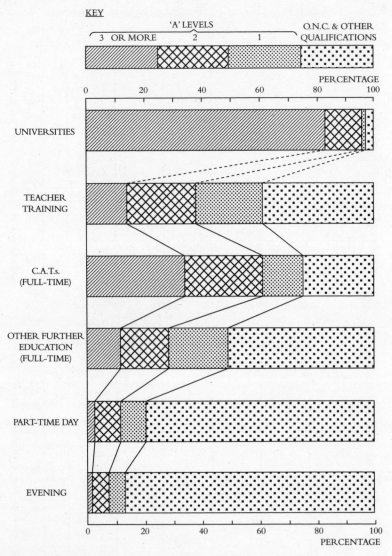

Figure 5.2 The flow of entrants to higher and further education.

Source: Robbins Report, I, 19.

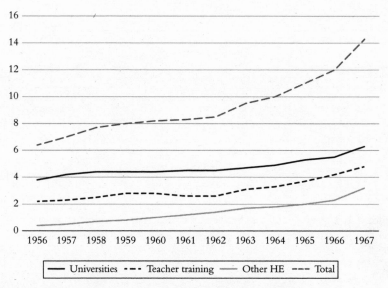

Figure 5.3 Age participation rate (APR), England and Wales.

Source: Data from Layard, King, and Moser, *Impact of Robbins*, 24. Note that the definitions of 'higher education' adopted here are slightly different (and somewhat more generous) than those accepted by the DES later, reported in Chapter 6, this volume, though the trends are identical.

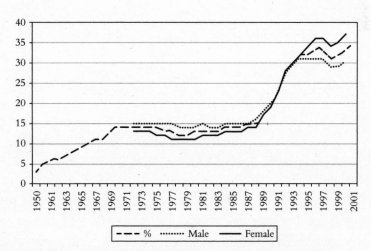

Figure 6.1 Age participation rate for all higher education, 1950–2001.

Source and note: Whitty et al., 'Who You Know', 29. Note that the basis for calculation of APR varied somewhat in the 1960s—see p. 264, n. 101—but roughly comparable measures are used here.

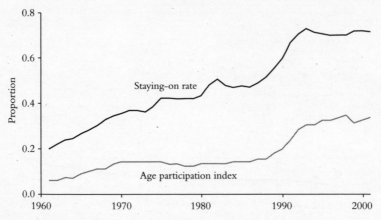

Figure 6.2 The widening gap between staying on at 16 and APR at 18–19.

Source: Machin and Vignoles, 'Educational Inequality', 110; data from the Department for Education and Skills.

Age participation rate, willingness rate and qualified leaver rate

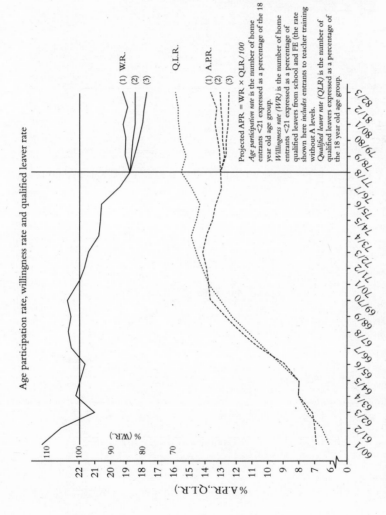

Figure 6.3 DES projections for APR, QLR, and 'willingness' (QPR) from 1978.

Source: DES, *Future Trends*, 7.

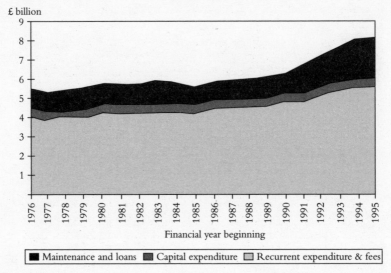

Figure 7.1 Public expenditure on higher education in the UK (1995–96 prices).
Source: Dearing Report, 44.

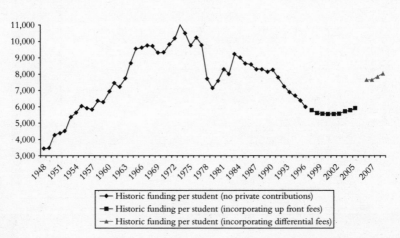

Figure 7.2 University funding per full-time student in the UK (2006–7 constant prices).
Source: BIS, *Review of Student Support Arrangements*, p. 10.

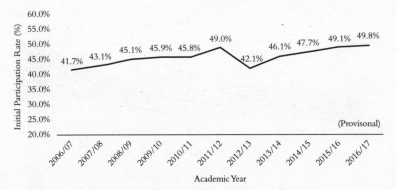

Figure 7.3 Higher Education Initial Participation Rate (HEIPR).

Source: Department for Education, *Participation Rates in Higher Education*, 27 Sep. 2018: https://assets. publishing.service.gov.uk/government/uploads/system/uploads/attachment_data/file/744087/Main_ text_participation_rates_in_higher_education_2006_to_2017_.pdf.

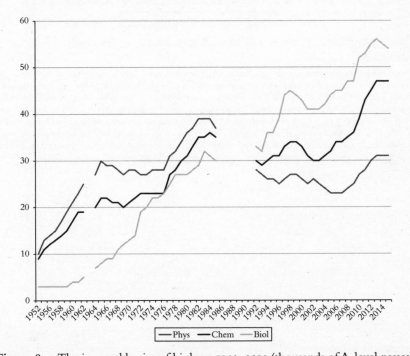

Figure 8.1 The inexorable rise of biology, 1952–2015 (thousands of A-level passes).

Source: DES, *Statistics of Education*, vol. 2 (1961–79); *Statistics of School-Leavers CSE and GCE* (1980–5); *Statistics of Education, Public Examinations GCSE and GCE* (1992–2000); GCE/Applied GCE A/AS and Equivalent Examination Results in England, 2009/10 (Revised) (2000–10): http://webarchive. nationalarchives.gov.uk/20110907100731/http://education.gov.uk/rsgateway/DB/SFR/s000986/ index.shtml, retrieved 7.9.16; Subject Time Series Tables (2011–15): https://www.gov.uk/government/ statistics/a-level-and-other-level-3-results-2014-to-2015-revised, retrieved 7.9.16. Statistics are for England. No comparable data series is available for 1986–95.

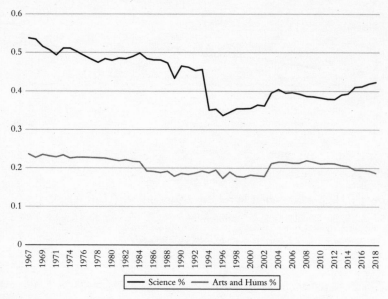

Figure 8.2 Shares of science and arts and humanities degrees in universities, 1967–2018.

Source: DES, *Education Statistics for the United Kingdom* (1967–78); *Statistics of Education*, vol. 6 (1979); Universities' Statistical Record, *University Statistics*, vol. 1 (1980–92); Higher Education Statistics Agency, *Higher Education Statistics for the United Kingdom* (1993–97); HESA Online: https://www.hesa.ac.uk/data-and-analysis/releases (1997–2018). Great Britain only 1980–92. Data for 1993–2003 is anomalous as a result of the ending of the binary divide; it took some time for statisticians to reconcile the two bodies of data, but the overall trend is clear enough. The figure only tracks science vs. arts and humanities degrees; the residue, almost entirely the group of subjects known as 'social studies', followed an upward trajectory until levelling off around 2000, by which time it had equalled the science share.

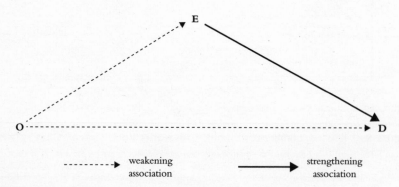

Figure 9.1 The OED triangle: origins, education, destinations.

Source: Bukodi and Goldthorpe, *Social Mobility and Education*, 91.

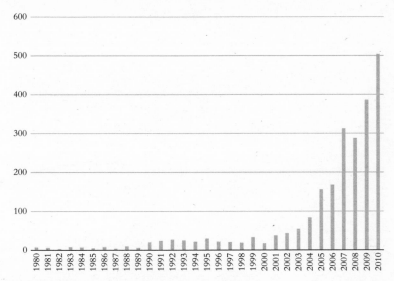

Figure 9.2 'Social Mobility' in *The Times*, 1980–2010.

Source: Calculated from digital editions of *The Times*; cf. similar pattern but with very different values, based on different databases, in Payne, 'A New Social Mobility?', 58, and different again in Payne, *New Social Mobility*, 41–3.

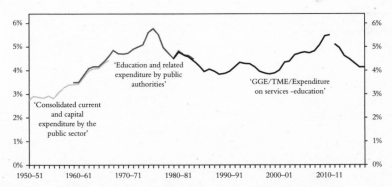

Figure 10.1 Public expenditure on education as percentage of GDP.

Source: Paul Bolton, 'Education Spending in the UK', 3, 13, 20–2. As Bolton points out, these figures need to be viewed in the light of demographics and economic growth. As far as the former goes, the chief distortions are the bulge until the early '70s followed by the trough in '80s, but with little variation since. With these corrections, the 2000s still represent a remarkable period of growth and the years since 2010 a remarkable period of decline.

Notes

CHAPTER I

1. That is, fewer than 14% of state-educated children progressed to secondary school, to which one must add a further proportion of the age cohort, perhaps 5%+, who were privately educated at primary level.
2. 14.5% of boys and 13.1% of girls left public elementary schools to pursue secondary education. These represent about 93% of the age cohort, the remainder being enrolled in private elementary and secondary schools. *Education in 1938*, 98; Sanderson, *Educational Opportunity*, 34.
3. 3.1% in Scotland and 1.5% of the population in England and Wales, but most of these would have been graduates not of state schools but of private schools; see Dyhouse, 'Going to University Between the Wars'.
4. A 'declinist' literature has until recently aggressively asserted otherwise. Andy Green's contention that education in Britain has been 'distinctly backward by comparison with other leading western states' has been highly influential but pretty much unexamined: Green, *Education and State Formation*, vii; and see Fenwick, *Comprehensive School*, 23; Sanderson, *Educational Opportunity*, 120–34; Lowe, *Education in the Post-War Years*, 200; Aldcroft, *Education, Training and Economic Performance*, 7–8; McCulloch, *Educational Reconstruction*, 14–15, 21; Wooldridge, 'English State', 231; Benn and Chitty, *Thirty Years On*, 6–7; and, strikingly, still Reay, *Miseducation*, 30, 32, as recently as 2017. The 'declinist' diagnosis originated from politically-charged arguments in the late '50s and early '60s for reform; see e.g. Jackson and Marsden, *Education and the Working Class*, 236.
5. Ramirez and Boli, 'Political Institutionalization of Compulsory Schooling'; Brockliss and Sheldon (eds), *Mass Schooling*, 1–2.
6. Murtin and Viarengo, 'Compulsory Schooling in Western Europe', 507–8; Viarengo, 'Expansion of Compulsory Schooling', 30.
7. Berg, 'Mass Education in the United States', 192.
8. Meyer, Ramirez and Soysal, 'World Expansion of Mass Education', 142–3.
9. An influential recent formulation of this argument is Goldin and Katz, *Race Between Education and Technology*, but notice the gap between the overall argument for a 'race between education and technology' and specific arguments for why mass education took off so early in the US: cf. 7 ('grass-roots movement'), 29 ('general training'), 164 ('substantial pecuniary returns'), 194 ('community support'), 197 ('other factors'), 208 ('a standard model of human capital investment' but also 'community support' again), 217 ('several factors'), etc.

10. I am indebted for these arguments to Boli, Ramirez, and Meyer, 'Explaining the Origins of Mass Education'; and see also Wolf, *Does Education Matter?*, 42–5; cf. Ansell, *From the Ballot*, a quantitative argument favouring both democratization and, to a lesser extent, openness to the global economy.

11. Turner, 'Sponsored and Contest Mobility'; on the operation of 'sponsored mobility' in England, see Sutherland, *Ability, Merit and Measurement*, 100–6.

12. We can find even a Conservative MP using the term approvingly in Parliament as early as 1902: Sir Albert Rollit in *Hansard*, 4th ser., 105 (1902), 914–15 [25 Mar. 1902].

13. H. Paterson, 'Secondary Education', 137–9. Wales had an even smaller elite but a much more recent tradition of radical Protestantism and very little control over its educational provision. It thus started from a very low base but grew rapidly, reaching a low target of 1% in secondary education by 1915 and still lagging behind England up to the Second World War. Davies, *County Intermediate Schools*, 35, 55; Evans, Smith, and Jones, *Secondary Schools of Wales*, 69–71.

14. Speech by David Eccles to the National Union of Teachers Conference, 13 Apr. 1955: TNA, ED147/209.

15. Cuin, 'Durkheim et la mobilité sociale'; Besnard (ed.), *Sociological Domain*, 91–3.

16. In fact Marshall was equivocal on whether social citizenship would in fact realize political equality or only give citizens 'the equal right to be recognised as unequal': Marshall, 'Citizenship and Social Class', esp. 63–8, 72. See further p. 239 n. 14 and Moses, 'Social Citizenship and Social Rights', esp. 16–18. On the 'consumption right of citizenship', see McPherson and Raab, *Governing Education*, 14–15, discussing the educational sociology of the 1950s.

17. On the virtues of pluralism, see McPherson and Raab, *Governing Education*, x–xii, 10–21, 24 (on Scotland but surveying the literature on Britain more broadly), and Kogan, *Politics of Educational Change*, 23–51.

18. E.g. Wooldridge, 'English State and Educational Theory', 231–5, which calls English education 'a shambles rather than a system', and pines for the centralized control allegedly typical of 'advanced European states' like France and Prussia.

19. Hobsbawm, *Age of Extremes*, part 2, and see also Mazower, *Dark Continent*, ch. 9.

20. These two approaches to 'equal opportunity' are roughly equivalent to those adopted by the economist John Roemer: what he calls 'nondiscrimination' on the one hand and 'pervasive social provision' (he also uses the 'level playing field' analogy) on the other (*Equality of Opportunity*, 1–3). Mine are not ideal types, however, but attempts to describe a range of attitudes that manifest and develop historically.

21. See, for example, Jones, *Working Class in Mid-Twentieth Century England*, where education hardly features even in the discussion of social mobility, 54–8, 63–5; Davis, *Modern Motherhood*, which has much to say about antenatal care, child guidance and child-rearing advice, but virtually nothing about education; Abrams and Brown (eds), *History of Everyday Life*, covers almost every aspect of everyday life (work, health, home, consumption, leisure) except for schooling, with mentions in other contexts (nutrition, work) only at 138–9, 142, 246–7,

and see Brown on higher education at 24, 27–8. For some recent exceptions, see Todd, *The People*, 217–34, and Sutcliffe-Braithwaite, *Class, Politics and the Decline of Deference, passim*.

22. Banks, *Parity and Prestige*, 8–10, 239–45.

23. Among the interesting explanations for this (from an historian of education) is a longer, more defensive tradition of methodological conservatism exacerbated from the 1970s by educationists' greater exposure to political regulation: Richardson, 'Historians and Educationists', esp. 114–15, 127–8, 135–7.

24. CCCS, *Unpopular Education*, esp. 205–10, 262–5, showing hostility to all purported expressions of public opinion on education and no substantive ideas about how it might be acceptably expressed or mobilized; Reay, *Miseducation*, 47, 193–5, deploring the indifference of the public to educational stratification and the ideal of common schooling, and almost equally despairing of any substantive alternative. Her misreading of her principal piece of evidence—a 1957 poll—is discussed on pp. 43–5, 60–1. Even the Marxist historian of education Brian Simon bemoaned this tendency, as noted by Richardson, 'Historians and Educationists', 123.

25. Barker, *Education and Politics*; Simon, *Politics of Educational Reform*; Parkinson, *Labour and Secondary Education*; Jefferys, 'R.A. Butler'; Bailey, 'James Chuter Ede'; Barber, *Making of the 1944 Education Act*; Francis, 'Socialist Policy for Education'; Francis, *Ideas and Policies*; Lawton, *Education and Labour Party Ideologies*; Simon, *Education and the Social Order*; Lowe, *Education in the Post-War Years*; Lowe, *Schooling and Social Change*; Lowe (ed.), *Changing Secondary School*; Lawson and Silver, *Social History of Education* (despite the title largely built around legislation, committees and experts); Jones, *Education in Britain* (promising a 'broader perspective' but then offering a 'Westminster chronology'); McCulloch, *Educational Reconstruction*; McCulloch, *Failing the Ordinary Child* (despite its subtitle, 'theory and practice', almost entirely about policy); McCulloch, 'British Labour Party Education Policy'; Ellison, 'Labour Party, Equality and Social Policy'; Rao, 'Labour and Education'; a sequence of policy histories by David Dean organized by ministry (see bibliography); Aldcroft, *Education and Economic Performance* (despite its title almost entirely about political failure); Glennerster, 'Education: Reaping the Harvest'; Crook, 'Edward Boyle'; Exley and Ball, 'Conservative Education Policy'; Knight, *Making of Tory Education Policy*; Wooldridge, 'Education: From Boyle to Baker'; Wooldridge, 'English State and Educational Theory'; Salter and Tapper, 'Politics of Secondary Education'; Morris and Griggs (ed.), *Education: The Wasted Years?*; Callaghan, *Conservative Party Education Policies*; Tomlinson, 'The Schools'; Ball, *Education Debate*; Chitty, *Towards a New Education System*; Chitty, *New Labour and Secondary Education*; Salter and Tapper, *State and Higher Education*; Shattock, *Making Policy in British Higher Education*; Stevens, *University to Uni*; Taylor and Steele, *British Labour and Higher Education*; Brown, *Everything for Sale?*; Willetts, *University Education* (which claims to almost entirely abjure reference to 'individual politicians', 9, but which is still, understandably, almost

entirely organized around his own policies and achievements). Timmins, *Five Giants*, the standard history of the welfare state now in its 3rd edition, is entirely organized around a sequence of governments and their legislative programmes. Not all of these histories are 'declinist' in the way I describe above, though most are. My point here is not that these are poor political histories—some of them are excellent, as my use of them in ensuing footnotes should indicate—but only that even where they purport to incorporate 'social change' (or similar) they rarely stray far from a top-down policy and political narrative, in which the principal actors are politicians, civil servants, educationists, and teachers, rarely parents and students, not even very often LEAs.

26. Lowe, *Schooling and Social Change* (which subordinates 'the deep-seated changes taking place in wider society' to 'the relative inflexibility of school systems'), 1–2; and see further Lowe, *Education in the Post-War Years*; CCCS, *Unpopular Education* (which privileges politicians and educationists as 'the most active political agencies' in the construction of the educational settlement), 65; Bloodworth, *Myth of Meritocracy*, which dwells on New Labour educational policy and says nothing about working-class kids and working-class jobs, despite its subtitle ('Why Working-Class Kids Get Working-Class Jobs'); Jones, *Education in Britain*, claims to seek a 'broader perspective' located in 'educational space', then populates that space almost exclusively with experts and politicians, 1–2, 5 and *passim*; McKenzie, *Changing Education*, begins every chapter with a brief overview of 'socio-economic change' but then dives into her real subject, politics and regulation, often with little connection to the sociological prelude.

27. Franklin and McCulloch (eds), *Death of the Comprehensive School?*; Pring, *Life and Death of Secondary Education*.

28. Quoted by Simon, *Education and the Social Order*, 17–18.

29. The classic case is the attempt to assess social mobility with regard to occupation (the sociologists) and income (the economists) discussed in Chapter 9.

30. See on these developments Jackson, *Equality and the British Left*, 163–76, McCulloch, 'Parity and Prestige', and Delamont, 'Olive Banks'; also further pp. 56–7. But cf. the more radical sociology of education which tended to depreciate educational changes of any kind, or considered them merely to be mechanisms of social control, consonant with the fatalism of the educationists discussed above.

31. Though there are some recent signs of a return to longitudinal and mixed-methods approaches, for example in the enduringly interdisciplinary work of Mike Savage and Andrew Miles, or in revisionist work on class and social mobility by Geoff Payne, Sam Friedman, and Daniel Laurison, a development that I survey in Mandler, 'Social Mobility and the Historians'.

32. Blaug, 'Empirical Status of Human Capital Theory', 829–30.

33. Meyer, Ramirez, and Soysal, 'World Expansion of Mass Education', 130, 143, and see fn. 9 re the struggles of Goldin and Katz, *Race Between Education and Technology*, and further struggles in Carpentier, 'Public Expenditure on Education and

Economic Growth in the UK', 10–13, 'Public Expenditure on Education and Economic Growth in the USA', 684–5, 688–93, 705.

34. Vaizey and Debeauvais, 'Economic Aspects of Educational Development', 40–3; Vaizey, *Economics of Education*, 45–7, 66–7; Schultz, *Economic Value of Education*, 8, 20, 50–1; Blaug, 'Rate of Return', 228–30, 242–5; Machin and Vignoles (eds), *What's the Good of Education?*, 3–4; Peston, 'Higher Education Policy', 127–8; Gambetta, *Were They Pushed?*, 78–80, 173–7; Dolton and Vignoles, 'Overeducation', cf. 118–20 with 120–1; Marginson, *Education and Public Policy*, 20–1, 38–40, 52–3.

35. E.g., most explicitly, Lupton et al., 'Education: New Labour's Top Priority'; Heath et al., 'Education under New Labour'; Whitty and Anders, 'How Did New Labour Narrow?'; Lupton and Thomson, 'Schooling under Coalition Government'.

36. Pissarides, 'Overview of the Demand for Post-Compulsory Education'; Pissarides, 'From School to University'; Pissarides, 'Staying-on at School'; Gambetta, *Were they Pushed?*, 78–80; Whitfield and Wilson, 'Staying-on in Full-Time Education'. As far as I can tell, Pissarides never responded to the latter critique; nor did he answer my later email query about it. The issues are discussed further in Chapters 6 and 7.

37. See, further, Mandler, 'Educating the Nation II. Universities', 11–15, and esp. Mandler, 'Educating the Nation IV. Subject Choice', 2–3.

38. I have been particularly influenced in this respect by Savage, *Identities and Social Change*; Todd and Young, 'Baby-Boomers to "Beanstalkers"'; Lawrence, 'Class, "Affluence" and the Study of Everyday Life'; Robinson et al., 'Telling Stories about Post-War Britain'; Sutcliffe-Braithwaite, *Class, Politics, and the Decline of Deference*.

39. Gambetta, *Were they Pushed?*, 167–9.

40. Kerckhoff et al., *Going Comprehensive*, 4–5, 9, 160–1, 167–9; Byrne, *Planning and Educational Inequality*, 19, 26–8, 304–7; James, *Reorganization of Secondary Education*, also marshals a mass of unpublished MA and PhD research, and Boaden, *Urban Policy-Making*, offers some helpful statistical insights into the forces bearing on LEAs. Sharp, *Creation of the Local Authority Sector* is supposed to be about local government but nevertheless announces itself (1) as 'a survey of educational policy-making in England at the national level'.

41. McPherson and Raab, *Governing Education*, 24; Gray, McPherson and Raffe, *Reconstructions of Secondary Education*, 5–7, 15.

42. Another body of work, a companion to this present book, is being undertaken on the experience of universal secondary education, in the form of the Secondary Education and Social Change (SESC) project in which I am engaged with Drs Laura Carter and Chris Jeppesen, funded by the Economic and Social Research Council (ESRC). See the website sesc.hist.cam.ac.uk to track the progress of this project.

43. Smith, *Schools*, 187.

44. Northern Ireland is included in the SESC project.

45. For example, in Lowndes, *Silent Social Revolution*, originally published in 1937, with the Whiggish message preserved in the later edition, published in 1969, and still in Sanderson, *Educational Opportunity and Social Change* (1987), though here with gloomy touches of declinism, and Wooldridge, *Measuring the Mind* (1994).

CHAPTER 2

1. Various loopholes were exploited instead—'whisky money' and central grants from the Department of Science and Art to support technical education for the over-14s. Daglish, *Education Policy-Making 1895–1911*, 13–15; Davies, *County Intermediate Schools*, 11–13, 44–7. Scottish school boards were not permitted to make grants to secondary schools either until 1892, but in rural areas parish schools provided enough secondary education to make a narrow bridge to higher education. Finn, 'Progressivism and Secondary Education in Scotland', 176–7, 180.

2. H. Paterson, 'Secondary Education', 137–8; H. Paterson, 'Development of Secondary Schooling', 200.

3. McPherson, 'An Angle on the Geist'; H. Paterson, 'Development of Secondary Schooling'.

4. Searle, *A New England?*, 8.

5. Tonooka, 'Cult of Japanese Efficiency', esp. 102 on Wells's Samurai.

6. Barker, *Education and Politics*, 15–17, 38–9; Sanderson, *Educational Opportunity*, 75–7; Wooldridge, *Measuring the Mind*, 185; Sherington, *English Education 1911–20*, 10–12.

7. Wooldridge, *Measuring the Mind*, 185.

8. See, for example, its use by the future Liberal Prime Minister H.H. Asquith in 1902, at a prize-giving at St Olave's Grammar School, Southwark, reported in *Manchester Guardian*, 1 Aug. 1902. No use of the term in this sense can be found in Parliamentary proceedings until after the First World War.

9. The 'ladder' metaphor was popularized by the Liberal scientist T. H. Huxley, as early as 1871. Its proximity to the 1867 Reform Act and the 1870 Forster Act for state elementary education indicates Huxley's desire not only for civil rights but also some assurance that 'our new masters' would be taught to behave themselves. See Sutherland, *Ability, Merit and Measurement*, 100–7.

10. Gordon and White, *Philosophers as Educational Reformers*, 80–2, 135; Griggs, *Trade Union Congress and Education*, 51.

11. Even by the chief Liberal advocates of state secondary education, James Bryce and H. A. L. Fisher: see *Hansard*, 4th ser., 105 (1902), 932–2 [24 Mar. 1902]; *Hansard*, 5th ser., 104 (1918), 390–1 [13 Mar. 1918].

12. See the powerful revisionist case made by Rose, *Intellectual Life of the British Working Classes*, esp. ch. 5, adopting a 'demand-side' approach against the accounts based almost entirely on 'official sources', 146.

13. Notably Barker, *Education and Politics 1900–51*, 19; Sherington, *English Education 1911–20*, 113–14; Daglish, *Education Policy-Making 1895–1911*, 433–4; and even in Griggs, *Trade Union Congress and Education*, e.g. 60–1. Barker argued strongly that trade unionists were always tailing behind Liberal intellectuals on education in this period, because they had no experience of secondary education and relatively little interest in citizenship, though his own evidence often strongly suggests otherwise. Fidler, '"Secondary Education for All" in Liverpool', 89, says more or less the opposite.

14. Griggs, *Trade Union Congress and Education*, 23–4, 51, 164–5.

15. Barker, *Education and Politics 1900–51*, 17–18; Sherington, *English Education 1911–20*, 9–10.

16. F. D. Acland, *Hansard*, 5th ser., 104 (1918), 342 [13 Mar. 1918]. Acland was A. H. D. Acland's son. Hobson referred in 1909 to a 'broad, easy stair' and not 'a narrow ladder': cited by Sherington, *English Education 1911–20*, 9–10.

17. McDermid, 'Education and Society'; Davies, *County Intermediate Schools*, 44–52; Gordon and White, *Philosophers as Educational Reformers*, 135–8.

18. For claims about these early origins and lasting effects of 'tripartism', see Gordon and White, *Philosophers as Educational Reformers*, 162–3, 212–15; Green, *Education and State Formation*, 306–7, 314–15; McCulloch, *Failing the Ordinary Child?*, 7, 12–13.

19. Daglish, *Education Policy-Making*, 445.

20. Sutherland, *Ability, Merit and Measurement*, 166–7; McCulloch, *Failing the Ordinary Child?*, 30–1; Sherington, *English Education 1911–20*, 26–8.

21. Quoted by Sutherland, *Ability, Merit and Measurement*, 111.

22. McPherson and Raab, *Governing Education*, 41–6; Finn, 'Secondary Education in Scotland', 187, 190–2; H. Paterson, 'Incubus and Ideology', 198–205.

23. Quoted by Susannah Wright, 'Citizenship, Moral Education and the English Elementary School', in Brockliss and Sheldon (eds), *Mass Education and the Limits of State-Building*, 35.

24. Sherington, *English Education 1911–20*, 62–5; Davies, *County Intermediate Schools*, 231; Banks, *Parity and Prestige*, 125–8; Fidler, '"Secondary Education for All" in Liverpool', 100–3; Simon, *Politics of Educational Reform*, 15.

25. *Hansard*, 5th ser., 104 (1918), 749–50 [18 Mar. 1918].

26. Percy, *Some Memories*, 94.

27. Tawney, 'Experiment in Democratic Education' (1914), 76–8.

28. *Secondary Education for All*, 60–1, 64–7.

29. This latter point is well made by CCCS, *Unpopular Education*, 43, and see also Jackson, *Equality and the British Left*, 30, 32; Rogan, *Moral Economists*, ch. 1; cf. Tawney, *Economics of Public Education*, 36–8, for his growing consciousness of the links between education and social mobility (or immobility). Benn, 'Comprehensive School Reform', 201, suggests that towards the end of his life Tawney broke with the tripartite system in practice when he became a Vice-President of NALT.

30. Gordon and White, *Philosophers as Educational Reformers*, 162–3; Sutherland, *Ability, Merit and Measurement*, 174; McCulloch, *Failing the Ordinary Child?*, 56; Barker, *Education and Politics 1900–51*, 43–4, 47, 54, 57, 139–40; Wooldridge, *Measuring the Mind*, 199–200; Simon, *Politics of Educational Reform*, 126–8, 231–2; Goldman, *Life of R.H. Tawney*, 204–5, 208–11; Renwick, 'Eugenics and Social Mobility', 864–5.

31. Sherington, *English Education 1911–20*, 82–90, 106–7, 116–18; Dean, 'Fisher at the Board of Education', 59–62, though oddly this article is mostly about other, non-educational aspects of Fisher's career.

32. A parallel Act for Scotland retained independently-elected Educational Authorities, though also put them more firmly under the central direction of the SED. For contrasting verdicts on the effects of this reform on common schooling in Scotland, cf. H. Paterson, 'Secondary Schooling, 1900–1939', 203–14, and L. Paterson, 'Secondary Schooling, 1900–1930'.

33. My analysis of the divisions recorded in *Hansard*, 5th ser., 104 (1918), 2029–31 [13 May 1918], 106 (1918), 875, 920 [29 May 1918].

34. e.g. Percy Alden, Noel Buxton, Edward John, Joseph King, Richard Lambert, R. L. Outhwaite, Arthur Ponsonby, and Josiah Wedgwood.

35. Notably J. H. Whitehouse: *Hansard*, 5th ser., 104 (1918), 402–3 [13 May 1918]. Joseph King also led the charge for democratically elected school boards (as in the U.S. and Scotland) against the 'Prussian' central control of the Board of Education. Ibid., 104 (1918), 773, 776–7 [18 Mar. 1918], and see further the exchanges between King, Whitehouse, Fisher, and Sir Henry Craik, ibid., 105 (1918), 2004–9, 2022 [7 May 1918].

36. Daglish, *Education Policy-Making 1895–1911*, 114. Not quite true after 1918, as the amendment to the Fisher Bill permitting LEAs to set a school-leaving age at higher than 14 was defeated.

37. Floud, Halsey, and Martin, *Social Class and Educational Opportunity*, 12–14.

38. Jones, *Which Nation's Schools*, 27.

39. Lindsay, *Social Progress and Educational Waste*, 11, 149–58, 180–6.

40. Jones, *Which Nation's Schools*, 33–8, 107.

41. Simon, *Politics of Educational Reform*, 27–62, 182–6.

42. Bradford achieved for a time and other LEAs aimed at 100% free places in their own grammar schools: ibid., 82–3.

43. Sutherland, *Ability, Measurement, and Merit*, 293–4. By contrast, by the 1930s a third of the age cohort started 5-year secondary courses in Scotland, though only 5% completed them. L. Paterson, 'Secondary Schooling 1900–1930', 100.

44. Beers, *Red Ellen*, 19, 27, 440–2. Chuter Ede, the wartime Parliamentary Secretary to the Board of Education who led Labour's contribution to the making of the Butler Act, was also a scholarship boy, a shopkeeper's son who won an LEA scholarship to secondary school and then another scholarship to Cambridge. Bailey, 'Ede and the 1944 Education Act', 210. Alice Bacon, in contrast, was a scholarship girl, a miner's daughter, who became a Labour MP in 1945 and was a lifelong proponent of comprehensive schools—in large part because she had

taught at a secondary modern school and rued its lack of opportunities. Reeves, *Alice in Westminster*, 23–6.

45. Lowndes, *Silent Social Revolution*, 93–6; Simon, *Politics of Educational Reform*, 75–7, 114, 117–18.

46. Board of Education, *Education of the Adolescent*, xix–xxiv, 79, 101.

47. Barrow LEA, just after the Second World War, quoted by McCulloch, 'Local Education Authorities', 240.

48. E.g. Woolf, 'Equality', 41–5.

49. Banks, *Parity and Prestige*, 69, 123–8.

50. Barron, 'Parents, Teachers and Children's Well-being'.

51. Todd, *Young Women, Work, and Family*, 24–5, 68–71, 102–4, 134–42; Baines and Johnson, 'Social Mobility in Interwar London', 700–8; Vincent, 'Mobility, Bureaucracy and Careers', 224.

52. Sanderson, 'Education and the Labour Market', 273–5.

53. Banks, *Parity and Prestige*, 80–2, 92–6, 112–14. Percy, *Some Memories*, 94–5, made similar observations.

54. For the development of thinking about multilateral schools amongst Labour teachers, see Simon, *Politics of Educational Reform*, 131, 140–5, 258–9; Barker, *Education and Politics 1900–51*, 66–79.

55. 'A Critical Moment in Education' [leader], *Manchester Guardian*, 16 Oct. 1928, attributed to Tawney by Simon, *Politics of Educational Reform*, 140–1. Even Barker, *Education and Politics 1900–51*, 76–7 and cf. n4, notes Tawney's uneasiness about bipartism.

56. L. Paterson, 'Secondary Schooling, 1900–1930', 100, 112–15; Maclure, *One Hundred Years of London Education*, 125. Still, the SED was very keen on differentiating 'junior' (three-year) from 'senior' (five-year) secondary courses.

57. See further Vincent, 'Mobility, Bureaucracy and Careers', 223–4, on the 'shadows' cast by frustrated aspirations amongst parents of this period.

CHAPTER 3

1. The mild misnomer '11+' arises from the idea that selection was to take place at or around the 11th birthday, though in fact it was normally conducted between 10 and a half and 11 and a half years, so '10+' would be more accurate. Vernon (ed.), *Secondary School Selection*, 27–8. For the explicit recommendation of the tripartite system in 1943, see *Norwood Report*, 4, 15.

2. For characteristic examples of academic literature embracing this model from very different political standpoints, see e.g. Lowndes, *Silent Social Revolution*, 264–8; CCCS, *Unpopular Education*, 47–64; Sanderson, *Educational Opportunity and Social Change*, 37–8, 45–6; Wooldridge, *Measuring the Mind*, 253–9; McCulloch, *Educational Reconstruction*, 14–15, 46–7, 68, 79.

3. On 'the primacy of the religious question' in Butler's parliamentary strategy, see Green, *Passing of Protestant England*, 230ff. As Hillman points out, 'Public Schools and the Fleming Report', 240–3, apart from the question of fee-paying

in state secondaries, the Butler Act debates did not impinge much on the independent fee-paying sector, which was separately being considered by the Fleming Committee. This left in suspense the question of integrating independent schools into the state sector, a prospect that gradually faded away as independent schools retained (though did not extend) their market share in the '50s and '60s.

4. As a snapshot: in 1963, of 1295 state grammar schools, 965 (or three-quarters) were LEA or 'county' schools, 174 voluntary-controlled, and 156 voluntary-aided; there were in addition 179 quasi-independent direct-grant schools. M. L. J., 'Re-organisation of Secondary Education', 17 Nov. 1964: TNA, T227/1604. On the whole voluntary schools were smaller so educated a smaller proportion of the cohort than their numbers suggest. There was a similar small cohort of schools in Scotland that continued to charge fees for some students into the 1960s: McPherson, 'Angle on the Geist', 241n90.

5. In contrast, state-educated Labour candidates outnumbered by almost 5-to-1, including a third who had no secondary education at all: Haxey, *Tory MP*, 180; Nicholas, *General Election of 1950*, 45; Fenwick, *Comprehensive School*, 16.

6. Green, *Passing of Protestant England*, 213–14.

7. Eliot, *Notes toward the Definition of Culture*, 103–7; James, *Education and Leadership*, 104–11, a more ambivalent view from a Fabian increasingly disillusioned with Labour's educational doctrine; Goldman, 'Opportunity in Education', 78–9; Bantock, 'Education in an Industrial Society', 208–11, 214. A lot of attention has been paid to Labour's growing interest in family background but relatively little to this theme in Conservative thought.

8. *Hansard*, 5th ser., 491 (1950–51), 226 [24 July 1951].

9. 'Leadership' was another commonly-used defence, as was 'national efficiency', but these tended to be more purely meritocratic arguments than they had been previously. On the former, see James, *Education and Leadership*; on the latter, see pp. 18–33.

10. Education Act 1944, 7 & 8 Geo. 6, c. 31, s. 8(1). Similar reference was made to 'age, ability and aptitude' in the Education (Scotland) Act 1945, 8 & 9 Geo. 6, c. 37, s. 1(3).

11. Bailey, 'Ede and the Education Act', 216–18. Party conference, where CLPs and trade unions were dominant, regularly passed resolutions in favour of multilateralism; the Parliamentary Labour Party was more attached to grammar schools. Cf. Francis, 'Socialist Policy for Education?', which places more emphasis on the latter, and Rubinstein, 'Ellen Wilkinson', and Benn, 'Comprehensive School Reform', which place more emphasis on the former.

12. Famously evident in the late Fabian defence of 'an aristocracy of brains' in 'Labour and Secondary Education' (1951), and in Eric James, 'The Challenge to the Grammar Schools', *TES*, 1 Feb. 1947, 63, and his *Education and Leadership* (1951). These were already controversial views in the Labour party at this point.

13. Rubinstein, 'Ellen Wilkinson', 167; Wooldridge, *Measuring the Mind*, 256; Fenwick, *Comprehensive School*, 53–7; Barker, *Education and Politics*, 84–91.

14. Banks, *Parity and Prestige*, 141–3; Francis, 'Socialist Policy for Education?', 330; Francis, *Ideas and Policies*, 156; McCulloch, *Failing the Ordinary Child*, 62–8. See also the official Ministry line under Wilkinson, *New Secondary Education*, 30. Even T. H. Marshall floated an idea of 'equality' based on 'parity of esteem' 'in which every man was content with the station of life to which it had pleased citizenship to call him', an extraordinary circumlocution which was immediately belied by real people: 'Citizenship and Social Class', 76. More surprisingly, Michael Young also assumed that for the majority 'unfortunately' destined for 'routine and semi-routine occupations' education could only offer enhancements of domestic life and leisure. Young, *Labour's Plan for Plenty*, 117.

15. E.g. Green, *Education and State Formation*, 237–8, 314–15; Wooldridge, *Measuring the Mind*, 195–8, 259–61; Timmins, *Five Giants*, ch. 5; but cf. McCulloch, 'Local Education Authorities', esp. 238–9.

16. Banks, *Parity and Prestige*, 79–82, 92–6; Todd, *Young Women, Work, and Family*, 102–4; and see pp. 45–6. Toby Weaver, 'Secondary Technical Schools', 14 Jan. 1955; A. G. Gooch, 'Secondary Technical Education', 28 Dec. 1954: TNA, ED147/207.

17. McPherson and Raab, *Governing Education*, 360–1.

18. A. A. Part to R. N. Heaton, 17 Jan. 1955: TNA, ED147/207; on the swing *to* science in the early postwar period, see pp. 156–8.

19. This was already evident by 1952, when LEAs were planning to provide about 60% of their places in modern schools, 20% in grammar schools, 12.5% in comprehensives and 7.5% in technical schools; as technical schools declined further, bipartism was seen as the 'orthodox' pattern: Thompson, *Secondary Education Survey*, 6–8, 14–15; W. R. Elliott (Chief Inspector of Schools), 'Notes on Various Forms of Secondary School Organisation', 10 Dec. 1960: TNA, ED147/641.

20. As noted for Scotland by McPherson and Raab, *Governing Education*, 367. Admission to technical schools had taken some pressure off the 11+, as it normally occurred at around 13.

21. Thompson, *Secondary Education Survey*, 6–8; Simon's differing calculations, *Education and the Social Order*, 129–30, are based on an earlier survey, which covered only a third of LEA plans, whereas this update covers almost three-quarters.

22. Thompson, *Secondary Education Survey*, 16–20; Jones, *Which Nation's Schools?*, 58–65, 77–86, 106–7, 135–42, 147–50.

23. Simon, *Education and the Social Order*, 106–10; Lowe, *Education in the Post-War Years*, 6–8, 17, 39; Gray et al., *Reconstructions of Secondary Education*, 31–5.

24. Humes, 'Governance of Scottish Education', 95; Raab and McPherson, *Governing Education*, 350–1.

25. Jones, *Which Nation's Schools*, gives a more detailed account of the negotiations between the Ministry and the LEAs in Wales over their initial development plans than we have for any other part of Britain, but see also Byrne, *Planning and Educational Inequality*, and McCulloch, 'Local Education Authorities', for England; Fenwick, *Comprehensive School*, and Kerckhoff et al., *Going Comprehensive*, consider development plans but their main focus is on comprehensives alone.

26. It is significant, for example, that the 1946 and even the 1958 birth cohort studies—as well as regional studies such as the Newcastle Thousand Families study of the 1947 birth cohort—began in this period as studies of infant and child health. Only later could they, and did they, transmute into studies of the effects of education on longer-term development. Pearson, *Life Project*, 63–4, 71–2, 74–80, discusses this in relation to the 1958 cohort.

27. Bentwich, 'Two Views', 140; Thompson, *Secondary Education Survey*, 7–8; Maclure, *One Hundred Years*, 146–7.

28. This was the policy adopted by Middlesex after Labour lost control in 1949, though they did also open two comprehensives: Banks, *Parity and Prestige*, 201.

29. Kerckhoff et al., *Going Comprehensive*, 2–3; Wiborg, 'Scandinavian Variations'; O'Hara, *Governing Post-War Britain*, 167–8. Sweden had the advantage of more all-age schools and middle schools which could be converted to comprehensives without closing selective upper secondaries—in fact the position adopted by many Conservative authorities in England. Young, *Rise of the Meritocracy*, 51, showed a prescient appreciation of the demographic factor in suppressing new school-building after the war, in comparison here not with Sweden but with the United States.

30. Paterson and Iannelli, 'Social Class and Educational Attainment', 343, showing gains in equality in Scotland during this period as a result of higher rates of enrolment in academic courses.

31. Heath and Clifford, 'Class Inequalities', 216–19; Halsey, Heath, and Ridge, *Origins and Destinations*, 63–4, both using the 1972 Oxford Mobility Survey data on those born in the 1930s and '40s; but also perceived at the time by Floud, Halsey, and Martin, *Social Class and Educational Opportunity*, 36. All of these commentators understate the degree to which working-class as well as middle-class families benefited from this temporary expansion.

32. Brooks, 'Role of External Examinations', 455.

33. Byrne, *Planning and Educational Inequality*, 111–12, 117–26, 136; Fenwick, *Comprehensive School*, 60–1. For the operation of this constraint on Leicestershire, see Jones, 'Reorganization of Secondary Education', 23–5. In still other authorities— the West Riding, Middlesex—electoral shifts affected development plans. The civil servants' hard line against comprehensive education became increasingly controversial within the Labour party, but after Labour lost power in 1951 this source of pressure of course collapsed. See further Wann, 'Collapse of Bipartisanship'.

34. Cf. McCulloch, 'Local Education Authorities', 236, arguing that tripartism was 'deeply rooted'. I don't think the evidence of initial development plans and their fate bears out this conclusion, but in any case my point is that initial LEA positions—which were indeed often inherited from very different interwar conditions—were quickly superseded.

35. Byrne, *Planning and Educational Inequality*, 26–7; Gosden, *Education in the Second World War*, 87–9.

36. Thus Fenwick's emphasis on the 'mediators' of public opinion rather than public opinion itself, *Comprehensive School*, 150, but cf. 156–7, 163; McKenzie, *Changing Education*, 71–8; but cf. Harrison, *Seeking a Role*, 52–3, 348–9.

37. Vaizey and Sheehan, *Resources for Education*, 4. Not all of this increase came from the bulge: the first surge came with the application of universal secondary education in the late 1940s, the second from wartime fertility rates, and the third— 50% growth 1955–65—came partly from the bulge and partly from the trend.

38. O'Hara, 'Demographic Change and the British State', 246–55. As late as the 1960s, there were only three part-time demographic researchers in central government, so that even a second bulge starting in the late '50s caught the Registrar-General's department by surprise. Vaizey and Sheehan, *Resources for Education*, 23.

39. Thom, '1944 Education Act', 120–3; Jones, 'Reorganization of Secondary Education', 23–5.

40. Titmuss and Titmuss, *Parents Revolt*, 69–70.

41. Sutcliffe-Braithwaite, *Class, Politics, and the Decline of Deference*, 62, 104–5; and cf. Vincent, 'Mobility, Bureaucracy and Careers', 223–4, on the 'shadows' cast by frustrated aspiration before the war.

42. Gallup Poll of May 1948, Gallup (ed.), *Public Opinion Polls*, 177; 'Present Day Education', Aug. 1948, Mass-Observation File Report 3025.

43. Todd and Young, 'Baby-Boomers to "Beanstalkers"'; Todd, *The People*, 220–2; Lawrence, *Me, Me, Me?*, 16, 125–6, 134, 163, 179, 217; Ortolano, *Thatcher's Progress*, 52; Gambetta, *Did They Jump?*, 87–99. Contemporary psychologists doubted and/or disapproved of this: Stacey, 'Psychological Consequences of Mobility'.

44. Gallup Poll of Jan. 1955, Gallup (ed.), *Public Opinion Polls*, 341; Davis, 'Hopes of Industrial Workers', 12–13.

45. An early study found, for example, that working-class students in secondary moderns had more aspirations to upward mobility than middle-class students in grammar schools, though working-class students in grammars had more still. Himmelweit, 'Social Status and Secondary Education', 156–8; on gender differences, see also Spencer, *Gender, Work, and Education*, 53–65.

46. Pooley, 'Mobility in the Twentieth Century', 85–7; Clapson, *Invincible Green Suburbs*, 43–4, 49–50; Bott, *Family and Social Network*; Lawrence, *Me, Me, Me?*, 60–1, 71–2, 90, 129, 132–3, 193, 219, 223; and for a Scottish case study, Abrams et al., 'Aspiration and New Selves'.

47. Bukodi et al., 'Mobility Problem in Britain', 104; Bukodi, 'Education and Occupational Attainment', 13–14.

48. *Gurney-Dixon Report*, 5–6. The report was doubtful that the trend would continue. In fact demand for O-levels grew 10% p.a. 1955–8 and then 15% p.a. 1961–3. Phillips, *Changes in Subject Choice*, 37.

49. *Robbins Report*, I, 11; Jean Floud, memorandum, *Robbins Report*, XII, 53; Pissarides, 'Staying-on', 346–7; cf. this growth expressed as an absolute rate of increase (much slower) for early '50s by *Crowther Report*, 68.

50. Brooks, 'Role of External Examinations', 460–3.
51. Paterson, 'Secondary Education', 144; McPherson and Raab, *Governing Education*, 369–70; see also Paterson, 'Democracy or Intellect?', which tracks the unique Scottish 1936 birth cohort through secondary education after the war, and Paterson et al., 'Social Class, Gender and Secondary Education', which argues that Scottish bipartism was less socially selective than English bipartism in the 1950s.
52. Vernon (ed.), *Secondary School Selection*, 21. The most obvious case of wilful misinterpretation or disbelief is that of Mark Abrams, discussed further on pp. 60–1; another interesting self-contradiction can be found in *Crowther Report*, 67, which noted a pent-up demand for staying-on 'that public opinion in the past has been slow to believe existed'—i.e. demand was not counted as (respectably articulated) public opinion, but had to be 'discovered' or 'created' by opportunity.
53. Floud et al., *Social Class and Educational Opportunity*, 76–83. A very similar result was obtained from the parents of the 1946 cohort in 1954 when their children were 8 years old: 62% of mothers preferred grammar school for their children. Douglas, *Home and School*, 17–19. PEP, *Family Needs*, 178, 183 found similarly higher levels of dissatisfaction with available levels of information about schools in the lower-middle and lower social groups.
54. E.g. Boyle, 'Politics of Secondary Reorganisation', 29–30; Annan, *Our Age*, 364; Timmins, *Five Giants*, ch. 12; CCCS, *Unpopular Education*, 69, 78–9; Sandbrook, *White Heat*, 314–16; cf. Rao, 'Labour and Education', 100.
55. As acknowledged by Vernon (ed.), *Secondary School Selection*, 21, 54. This small minority would have been mostly made up of parents of children currently enrolled in modern schools, who might when younger or older have been more positive about grammar schools, but at that stage of life didn't wish to seem to be shaming their children: see further p. 46.
56. Research Services Ltd, 'A Pilot Enquiry into Some Aspects of Working-Class Life in London', 1956–7: Abrams Papers, ABMS/5/6/7, 11–14, 37.
57. Not of course true except for the top 6% of the population—most middle-class parents relied on the 11+, as did all working-class parents. Abrams might have better said that this middle-class majority would have to be the target audience for any expansion of the fee-paying sector, though that expansion did not in fact materialize.
58. Research Services Ltd, 'A Pilot Enquiry into Some Aspects of Working-Class Life in London', 1956–7: Abrams MSS., ABMS 5/6/7, 14–15. The copy in Abrams MSS., ABMS 3/78, makes clear that the survey was for Lintas Ltd, an advertising agency.
59. In general, Abrams saw a widening gap between a more materialist working class and a better educated middle class. See, e.g., Abrams, 'British Social Classes and Class Distinctions', n.d. [1958?], 'Educational Aspiration', Sep. 1960, 'Social Equality: The Class System', July 1961, 'Is There A Working Class?', n.d. [1963]: Abrams Papers, ABMS/5/6/2, 2/4/6, 5/6/3, 5/6/2. Abrams' views would bear further investigation.

60. Research Services Ltd, 'Survey of Educational Attitudes' (J.912/M.A.), Nov. 1957, 2, 6: Abrams Papers, ABMS 3/64. See pp. 60–1, for the way in which Abrams cherry-picked the single most pessimistic finding from his survey in his report to the Labour party.

61. Abrams' 1957 survey for Political and Economic Planning showed high levels of dissatisfaction with modern schools, a majority in favour of widened educational provision and more information about schools, and the usual powerful preference for grammar schools over other school types: PEP, *Family Needs*, 176–8, 180–3, 201–3. The 'affluent worker' study of Luton c. 1962 showed nearly as high a preference for grammar schools as among the middle classes: Goldthorpe et al., *Affluent Worker*, 130–3. Young and Willmott's study of Bethnal Green and Woodford showed as strong support for grammar school in the working-class as in the middle-class area: *Family and Kinship*, 28–30, 162. The Chief Inspector of Schools testified in 1960 that 'parents have become increasingly anxious for their children to enjoy the advantages associated with a grammar-school education', though he thought this anxiety could be assuaged by extending opportunities in secondary-modern schools: W. R. Elliott, 'Notes on Various Forms of Secondary School Organisation', 10 Dec. 1960: TNA, ED147/641.

62. Kogan, *Politics of Educational Change*, 32; Hughes, 'In Defence of Ellen Wilkinson', 159; Ellison, 'Consensus Here', 30–1; Timmins, *Five Giants*, ch. 12; McCulloch, 'Labour Party Education Policy', 237–45; Crook, 'Missing, Presumed Dead', 160; Marsden, *Politicians, Equality, and Comprehensives*, 10–11; Boyle et al., *Politics of Education*, 21–2; Lawton, *Education and Labour Party*, 62; Benn and Chitty, *Thirty Years On*, 27; Chitty, *Towards a New Education System*, 40–1; Jones, *Education in Britain*, 50–1; Reay, *Miseducation*, 47. Kynaston, *Modernity Britain*, gives a good account of Abrams' own views, seems to take them as documentary evidence, but then provides a raft of conflicting counter-evidence: cf. 220–1, 242–3, with 228–34; see also Marsden, *Politicians, Equality, and Comprehensives*, 9, Parkinson, *Labour Party and Secondary Education*, 81–2, Black, *Political Culture of the Left*, 174, and McCulloch, 'Labour Party Education Policy', 237–40; cf. Clapson, *Invincible Green Suburbs*, 73–5.

63. Pedley, *Comprehensive Education*, 17–18, responding to Hartley Shawcross's 1955 call for 'a comprehensive grammar school type of education for all'; for a somewhat later recognition of this popular 'common sense' in the 1950s, see Burgess, *Inside Comprehensive Schools*, 9–10.

64. Millward, 'Rise of the Service Economy', 240–5.

65. Todd, *Young Women, Work, and Family*, 134–42; Todd and Young, 'Baby-Boomers to "Beanstalkers"', 454–7; Jahoda, 'Job Attitudes and Choice', 132–3, 135, 206–7; Davis, 'Hopes of Industrial Workers', 18–20; Young and Willmott, *Family and Kinship*, 178–9; Douglas, *Home and School*, 17–19; PEP, *Family Needs*, 178; Land, 'We Sat Down', 46–9; Goldthorpe et al., *Affluent Worker*, 130–2, discusses a number of recent surveys showing variable but growing levels of aspiration for non-manual employment.

66. Lowndes, *Silent Social Revolution*, 265, 296–8.

67. McKibbin, *Classes and Cultures*, 46–7; Banks, *Parity and Prestige*, 171–85. This helps to explain the lack of interest in technical schools. Engineering apprenticeships were also taken up at lower levels by a large proportion of male secondary-modern leavers: 34% of all Youth Employment Service placements in Lincoln, 28% in Nottingham, for example. Byrne, *Planning and Educational Inequality*, 289–90, 293.

68. Ibid., 289–90; and, for Scotland, see the popularity with employers of the O-grade, Gray et al., *Reconstructions of Secondary Education*, 122–9.

69. Goldthorpe et al., *Affluent Worker*, 132–3; somewhat more parents referred to educational standards than to career prospects and only a third as many to their children's abilities, the meritocratic criterion, in the 1964 survey for Plowden, *Plowden Report*, 111. See also the range of identity-building qualities ascribed to education in Savage's reading of Goldthorpe and Lockwood's 1961 interviews, *Identities and Social Change*, 231–5.

70. Pissarides, 'Staying-on', 347–9, 354; Trow, 'Problems in the Transition', 90; Gambetta, *Did They Jump?*, 78–80. In fact, before the rise of human-capital theory in the 1960s, the default position was to take education as a consumption good, demand for which rose with income. Blaug, 'Human Capital Theory', 829–30.

71. See for example the very high approvals of children's schools in PEP, *Family Needs*, 179, and of the actual destinations of grown-up children in Abrams' 1956–7 study, Abrams Papers, ABMS/5/6/7, 38; *Crowther Report*, II, 20–4, showed that teenagers and their parents nearly always felt that they had left at the 'right' age.

72. Parents with children in secondary-modern schools were less likely to support ROSLA (which would just keep them in those schools longer): see Abrams' 1957 study of working-class parents of school-age children, ABMS/3/64, 2; Carter, *Home, School, and Work*, 81–2, a study of Sheffield secondary moderns in 1959. But even parents with children in secondary-modern schools liked the idea of post-compulsory education for their children by choice: PEP, *Family Needs*, 176–7.

73. Abrams found that parents with 'hypothetical' 17/18 year olds who had a choice preferred even more education (i.e. university): Abrams Papers, ABMS/3/64, 3; in a later survey for the sociologist W. G. Runciman, he also found that working-class and middle-class parents had nearly the same hopes for university: Runicman, *Relative Deprivation*, 230.

74. Abrams found differences between older and younger children's parents' 'aspirations' in 'Probable Age of Leaving', n.d. (*c.* 1961): Abrams Papers, ABMS/2/4/6; the Plowden Committee found that parents of primary-age children had much higher expectations of staying on: *Plowden Report*, 109–10.

75. Davis, 'Hopes of Industrial Workers', 19–20.

76. Abrams noted that unskilled parents were *more* likely to value the best education for their children, but undercut this finding by adding that they were also

more likely to 'allow' their children to leave at 15—a matter of choice for the child. 'Encyclopaedia Survey – November 1960': Abrams Papers, ABMS/2/4/6.

77. PEP, *Family Needs*, 92, 178.

78. One contemporary way of seeing education as 'positional' was to talk about 'relative deprivation', which was supposed to make suburban parents whose children failed the 11+ feel the keenest deprivation, or alternatively to highlight the 'egoistic' motives of aspirational working-class parents: Runciman, *Relative Deprivation*, 117–18; Boyle, 'Politics of Secondary Reorganisation', 29; see the response in Goldthorpe et al., *Affluent Worker*, esp. 144n. Runciman's conclusions were based on another Abrams survey, one which asked questions aimed at eliciting 'egoistic' but not 'fraternalistic' answers. Yet another Abrams survey, in 1965, claimed to have found 3–5 times as many 'individualistic' as 'collectivistic' answers, but no details were provided: Turner, 'Acceptance of Irregular Mobility', 352.

79. Trow, *Problems in the Transition*, 41.

80. Whiteside, 'Creating the Welfare State', esp. 95; Harris, 'Did British Workers Want the Welfare State?'; Lowe, *Welfare State*, 205–6, and Lowe, 'Replanning of the Welfare State', 259, 261–3, despite underlying pessimism; cf. Hayes, 'Did We Really Want a National Health Service', more pessimistic; on Scotland, Gray et al., *Reconstructions of Secondary Education*, 5–7.

81. Douglas, 'Parental Encouragement', 153–4; Lowe, *Welfare State*, 18, and 'Replanning of the Welfare State', 266–7. Edgerton, *Rise and Fall*, 243, seems to me not quite right in saying that health care was 'the only universal benefit giving services at a level the middle class would consider adequate'.

82. For example, both education and health tend to appear more frequently over time in M.P.s' local election addresses, and by the late 1950s have become almost ubiquitous: cf. Nicholas, *General Election of 1950*, 221; Butler, *General Election of 1951*, 54; Butler, *General Election of 1955*, 31–3, 36; Butler and King, *General Election of 1959*, 131; Butler and Rose, *General Election of 1964*, 140–4.

83. Edgerton, *Rise and Fall*, 459.

84. 'Survey of Educational Attitudes', Abrams Papers, ABMS/3/64, 15. These were answers to a more open-ended question about selection.

85. These were the most common responses, if you include a further 15% who said that common schools allowed better adjustment after age 11 to children's abilities. Nevertheless, Abrams interpreted these findings as more about efficiency and children's problems than about equal provision. Ibid., 13. These were answers to a more specific question about comprehensive schools.

86. PEP, *Family Needs*, 178.

87. Brooks, 'Role of External Examinations', 459; see also Heaton, 'External Examinations', 94, for another, earlier observation along the same lines.

88. PEP, *Family Needs*, 201–3, 206. The highest levels of dissatisfaction were of course felt by parents of modern-school children who had failed to pass the 11+.

89. David Eccles, 'Secondary Education', 18 Sep. 1956: TNA, ED 147/636.

90. Vernon (ed.), *Secondary School Selection*, 169–70; Stacey, 'Psychological Consequences of Mobility', 5.

91. On the scholarship boy, Hoggart, *Uses of Literacy*, 291–304; on the scholarship girl, Young and Willmott, *Family and Kinship*, 174–8; for an excellent literary analysis of the phenomenon, Robbins, *Upward Mobility and the Common Good*.

92. Simon, *Education and the Social Order*, 276, and see further Chapter 4, n. 90. Similarly most attention focuses on the pioneer LEAs crusading for a completely comprehensive system—the LCC, Middlesex, later Manchester and Liverpool—rather than on the many LEAs, including Conservative ones, finding other ways to dismantle the 11+. Surveys found little overt interest in comprehensive schools, largely because as yet few parents had any idea what they were: *Plowden Report*, 111, 122; and see pp. 60–1, for Abrams' surveys.

93. Lowndes, *Silent Social Revolution*, 296–8, a view shared even to some extent by the left-wing historian Brian Simon, *Education and the Social Order*, 288–9; see also James, *Reorganization of Secondary Education*, ch. 3, on the 'myth' of parent power.

CHAPTER 4

1. CCCS, *Unpopular Education*, 64, sees education policy to 1964 as a 'quiet' period; Kogan, *Politics of Educational Change*, 11; McCulloch, *Educational Reconstruction*, 168–9.

2. For the question of 'standards' raised by the right, see ch. 6 on the 1970s, when the issue became most acute.

3. A.A. Part, 'The Pattern of Secondary Education', 16 Nov. 1954: TNA, ED147/206. Responses to this memo by other senior civil servants suggest that, after the initial disciplining of LEAs into bipartism, the Ministry no longer took firm views on things such as the 'right' proportion of grammars to moderns, or even on comprehensives. Nor did they even have to be notified if an LEA simply shifted its policies within existing schools—adding a 'grammar' stream to a modern school, for example, or widening access to a grammar so that its intake became almost comprehensive. Reorganization in such cases took place under the radar.

4. J. R. Jameson, 'Comprehensive Schools', 16 Apr. 1959; L. R. Fletcher to Toby Weaver, 26 Mar. 1959: TNA, ED147/640; Edward Boyle to Kenneth Thompson, n.d. (Apr. 1961): TNA, ED147/641; Boyle, 'Politics of Secondary School Reorganisation', 31. On the smooth transition to comprehensive education in one area of Dorset, see Walton, 'Beaminster'.

5. In Leicestershire, some grammar schools *were* converted to 'junior' comprehensives, but many retained their academic flavour by being retained as 'senior' schools. Jones, 'Secondary Education in Leicestershire', 25–7; Kerckhoff et al., *Going Comprehensive*, 118–22. On Wiltshire's Leicestershire-style schemes, see Goodman, 'Comprehensive Re-Organisation in Wiltshire', 161, 166, and see also Fenwick and Woodthorpe, 'Secondary Education in Leeds', 21–7, for another two-tier scheme aimed at avoiding grammar-school closures.

6. The Ministry was at this early date anyway disposed to countenance later selection: 'Secondary Education', 23 Feb. 1955: TNA, ED147/206. There remained resistance to two-tier plans which proposed to offer transfer to all parents without selection. L. R. Fletcher to Toby Weaver, 29 Mar. 1960: TNA, ED147/641.

7. Two-tier models became easier after 1964 when transfer at 11 was no longer compulsory and true 'middle schools' could be created; the Conservatives legislated for this to accommodate the West Riding. Kerckhoff et al., *Going Comprehensive*, 24–5; on Stoke, see ibid., 112–16; on the West Riding, Gosden and Sharp, *Development of an Education Service*, 182–90; on Glasgow, Fife, and Renfrewshire, Gray et al., *Reconstructions of Secondary Education*, 237–9, and Watt, 'Comprehensive School in West of Scotland', 46–8, and in Scotland generally, 'Secondary School Organisation in Scotland', n.d. [Jan. 1965]: TNA, ED147/640.

8. On the Croydon model, see Donnison and Chapman, *Social Policy and Administration*, ch. 12, and for its spread, Kerckhoff et al., *Going Comprehensive*, 25; by 1992, there were 63 'tertiary' (beginning with Devon in 1970) and 116 sixth-form colleges (beginning with Luton in 1966) in England and Wales: Smithers and Robinson (eds), *Further Education*, 1–2.

9. Northumberland and Glamorgan faced less demographic pressure and so put off this transition until the 1960s. Kerckhoff et al., *Going Comprehensive*, 137–42.

10. Boyle, 'Politics of Secondary School Reorganisation', 31. Similarly, Quintin Hogg claimed retrospectively that while tripartism had been in fashion in the 1940s after that 'nobody in the country' since had adhered to that 'fashionable theory of the time which seems to me to bear no relation to any common sense at all.' *Hansard*, 5th ser., 705 (1964–5), 494–5 [21 Jan. 1965].

11. N. A. Y. Yorke-Lodge, County Education Officer, 'Warwickshire High Schools: Report by the County Education Officer', Sep. 1958: TNA, ED136/943.

12. Byrne, *Planning and Educational Inequality*, 187–207; and see also Batley et al., *Going Comprehensive*, 24–33, 40 on Darlington which first adopted a comprehensive plan in 1956 but was not able to implement it until 1963.

13. Withington, 'Brookfield School', 74–7.

14. Kerckhoff et al., *Going Comprehensive*, 87.

15. Ibid., 87–8; Fenwick and Woodthorpe, 'Secondary Education in Leeds', 18–20. See also a sizeable list of other comprehensive projects aimed at new housing areas which did not threaten grammar schools, in L. R. Fletcher to Toby Weaver, 26 Mar. 1959: TNA, ED147/640.

16. Boyle, 'Politics of Secondary School Reorganisation', 32.

17. Fenwick, *Comprehensive School*, 130–1. Bristol is the primary example where this kind of agitation seems to have had wider purchase, especially at the General Election of 1964 where Labour lost two seats (and lost control of the council in 1967). Butler and King, *General Election of 1964*, 140–1; Kerckhoff et al., *Going Comprehensive*, 92–4. Another factor as Kerckhoff et al. point out is the presence of direct-grant and independent schools, as in Leeds and Manchester, which diluted middle-class resistance because they offered alternative bolt holes: ibid., 90, 100. The opposite was the case in Croydon, where the fee-paying Whitgift

schools formed the kernel of resistance to the 'Croydon model'. Donnison and Chapman, *Social Policy and Administration*, 214–25. Otherwise, Boaden found that grammar-school defence correlated well with high concentrations of Class I and II parents; Solihull, which was a particular point of resistance after 1965, had the highest rates of transfer to grammar school in the country. Boaden, *Urban Policy-Making*, 45–6, 48, 55–6.

18. Byrne, *Planning and Educational Inequality*, 69–70; see also McPherson and Raab, *Governing Scotland*, 363–4, on a new generation of 'young Turks' in Aberdeen; Boaden, *Urban Policy-Making*, 50–2, 54–5, 57, found that political control and educational demand but not the views of CEOs correlated well with educational policy decisions.

19. Fenwick, *Comprehensive School*, 150, doubted 'any groundswell of opinion among the electorate', and held that 'the organizations which mediate between governors and governed – the teachers' organizations, associations of local authorities, and, above all, political parties – structured the attitudes of parents and ministers'; Byrne, *Planning and Educational Inequality*, 305–7, focuses on the mismatch between local needs and LEA provision, and especially on the role of CEOs; Kerckhoff et al., *Going Comprehensive*, 160–7, James, *Reorganization of Secondary Education*, and Batley et al., *Going Comprehensive*, take a similar line; Fearn, 'Politics of Local Reorganization', finds no evidence of organized 'consumer groups' and also falls back on local government officers; Simon, *Education and the Social Order*, 204–9, 271, considers 'unceasing pressures...from below' but these are Labour and Communist pressure groups—he otherwise gives a gloomy picture of LEA movement and sees the 'break-out' starting in 1963, triggered by Labour gains in local elections; Parkinson, *Labour Party and Secondary Education*, 87–90, argues that comprehensives were on the decline as 'a political issue' after 1959 while acknowledging at the same time 'a spontaneous growth at the grass roots of education'; Kynaston, *Modernity Britain*, 228–45, acknowledges 'deep dissatisfaction' with the 11+ but focuses on expert and Labour party debates, placing a lot of emphasis on Abrams' findings; Sandbrook, *White Heat*, 314–16, associates comprehensives with 'left-wing theorists', 'educationalists', and then 'most importantly, middle-class parents', but then seems to acknowledge a much broader social movement, indeed 'a tidal wave'; Jones, *Education in Britain*, 52–68, sees local developments as all about teachers and educationists, while dissatisfaction with the 11+ ('a further dynamic of change') was weaker and less ambitious; McPherson and Raab, *Governing Education*, x–xii, 24, 500–1, is best at presenting the way 'disadvantaged groups...use the state to ameliorate inequalities of access to educational opportunity' but still focuses attention on 'the common sense of the policy community' in Scotland; Jones, *Which Nation's Schools*, 176–7, does something similar for Wales.

20. Parkinson, *Labour Party and Secondary Education*, 126; McPherson and Raab, *Governing Education*, 366; Kerckhoff et al., *Going Comprehensive*, 160–9, acknowledging that outdoor pressure remains largely unexplored; Crook, 'Edward Boyle', 51; James, *Reorganization of Secondary Education*, 37–8, considers briefly

'the rule of anticipated reactions', gives evidence of it, and then moves quickly on. Talk of a '"grass-roots" revolution' in this context usually means LEA or even Ministry experiments.

21. W. R. Elliott, 'Notes on Various Forms of Secondary School Organisation', 10 Dec. 1960: TNA, ED147/641.

22. Lord Gardiner, 10 Feb. 1965, in *Hansard*, 5th ser., 263 (1964–5), 245–6. Simon, *Education and the Social Order*, 279, tells this story but misattributes it to the Conservative Lord Newton, who had opened the debate to defend, not to attack the 11+. I myself got some of the details wrong in Mandler, 'Educating the Nation I', 18.

23. W. Harte, 'Secondary Reorganisation Schemes', 25 Feb. 1964: TNA, ED147/636. This had already been achieved in swathes of Wales and Scotland by the introduction of comprehensives, the blurring of the divide between school types, and/or by very high rates of transfer at 11.

24. Jay, *Socialist Case*, 258 (from the revised edition of 1947). This notorious remark was aimed at treating both health and education not as consumption goods but as investment goods for society, which required central planning, and was not aimed against consumer choice per se—nevertheless, it did exemplify the rather breezy socialist attitude to parental choice in this period. See the discussion in Toye, '"Gentleman in Whitehall" Reconsidered', esp. 193–4, 199–200.

25. Wann, 'Collapse of Parliamentary Bipartisanship'; Butler, *General Election of 1955*, 14; Fenwick, *Comprehensive School*, 73–80.

26. Some of the historiography is surprisingly scornful about the Labour rank-and-file as a mere teachers' lobby: Barker, *Education and Politics*, 83; Francis, 'Socialist Policy for Education?', 322–3; and even Rao, 'Labour and Education', 106.

27. For this dynamic, see Black, *Political Culture of the Affluent Left*, and esp. 174 on the Abrams report. This suspicion on the part of the Labour left of 'public opinion' was shared by Abrams' own son Philip, a budding sociologist, who told his father that party policy ought to be based on ideology not market research: Abrams, 'Interview', 77–8.

28. Thus the study of early leaving undertaken in 1952 by social scientists for *Gurney-Dixon Report*, 3, 18–22; early studies of selection by F. M. Martin, Hilde Himmelweit, and Arthur Summerfield; Vernon (ed.), *Secondary School Selection*, still largely about misallocation. This approach remained significant for a long time: see Sanderson, *Educational Opportunity and Social Change*, xiii–xiv, 35, 45–54; Wooldridge, *Measuring the Mind*, 255–9, 270–1, 363–79; and for its prehistory, Renwick, 'Eugenics and Social Mobility', esp. 860–4.

29. Glass was also more interested in movement from bottom to top than from bottom to middle, and this emphasis on social leadership again put the onus on grammar schools. Glass (ed.), *Social Mobility*, 16–17, 21–4; see also Glass's BBC broadcast with Mark Abrams, 'Social Mobility', 16 Nov. 1954: Abrams Papers, ABMS 5/6/3.

30. Floud, Halsey and Martin, *Social Class and Educational Opportunity*, xv–xviii, 65, 142–9, and see also pp. 84–6; Vernon, 'Pool of Ability'. For the 'revolutionary'

implications of this sociological move, see Nuttall, *Psychological Socialism*, 109–11; Savage, *Identities and Social Change*, 205–6. Halsey for one did still seem to believe that 'innate' intelligence was randomly distributed, but then 'distorted' by home and school experiences from infancy. 'Sociological Selection', *TES*, 4 Apr. 1958.

31. Frederick Martin was less involved politically.

32. Raymond Aron, quoted in fact by Halsey, 'Provincials and Professionals', 151.

33. This may account for the attention they garnered in contrast to the work of another Glass student, Olive Banks, publishing at the same time but much less data-driven: see further McCulloch, 'Parity and Prestige', 381–4, who also points out that Banks's labour-market analysis offered less for educational reformers.

34. Cited, for example, by Alice Bacon, the long-time advocate of comprehensives, in *Hansard*, 5th ser., 568 (1956–7), 688–92 [5 Apr. 1957].

35. Jackson, *Equality and the British Left*, 163–7; Jefferys, *Crosland*, 57.

36. Crosland, *Future of Socialism*, 258–9, 266–7, 270; see also Anthony Crosland in dialogue with Donald MacRae, 'What is Wrong with Britain?', *Listener*, 5 July 1962, pp. 3–5. Crosland's Permanent Secretary Sir Herbert Andrew thought that Crosland set much more store in the opinion of his social scientists than in 'the probable views of the man in the street, the uneducated Demos': 'Aristocratic Qualities of Boyle and Crosland', *THES*, 15 Oct. 1971, 31.

37. Young appears to have picked up the term from Alan Fox who had earlier written about meritocracy in *Socialist Commentary*. Jackson, *Equality and the British Left*, 171–5.

38. Donovan, 'Chequered Career', 68–71; Dench, 'Reviewing Meritocracy', 8; see pp. 99–100.

39. Jackson, *Equality and the British Left*, 169; Wooldridge, *Measuring the Mind*, 323–4; Briggs, 'Labour Party as Crucible'; Jefferys, *Crosland*, 57. Cf. Littler, *Against Meritocracy*, 32–4, who suggests oddly that Fox and perhaps even Young were 'to the left of the Labour Party'.

40. Wooldridge, *Measuring the Mind*, 306–15; Butler, 'Young and the Politics of Kinship'.

41. Young, *Rise of the Meritocracy*, 47, on real parental opposition to tripartism in the 1950s, and 163–75, on the women's campaigns of the early twenty-first century; see also Land, 'We Sat Down', which however shares Young's view that mothers cared less about education than about family and community, 46, and Young, 'Looking Back', 74–5. Crosland seems to have got his awareness of popular hostility to the 11+ from Young as much as from Floud and Halsey.

42. Briggs, 'Labour Party as Crucible', 25; Butler, 'Young and the Politics of Kinship'.

43. Young, *Rise of the Meritocracy*, 46–55. He was particularly scathing about the Leicestershire plan, as it did *not* require 'destruction of the grammar schools'. It may have been this satirical line that caused Marris, 'Just Rewards', 158, to label Young a critic of Crosland; Young does slip Crosland in, mischievously, amongst the champions of meritocracy, though he also acknowledges his influence

(alongside Marris himself, Floud, Halsey, Tawney, and others)—*Rise of the Meritocracy*, 9, 96—and Crosland even before Young drew attention to the way in which meritocracy made most people feel like failures—*Future of Socialism*, 234–5, 266–7.

44. As Young himself noted, 'Looking Back', 73; see also Barker, 'A Tract for the Times', 38. A related text, which had very little influence, was the Socialist Union's *Education and Socialism* (1958), sharing Young's critique of meritocracy and his favouring of common schools, but decidedly soggily and for reasons of fellowship rather than equality; see Black, 'Social Democracy as a Way of Life', on 'fellowship' and the SU's ties to Young, and esp. 509–10, 538, on this text.

45. Only at the end of his tenure in late 1959 did John Vaizey persuade him to meet with 'a group of academics [who] are anxious to act as a kind of unofficial Civil Service for me on education matters', including Jean Floud and Maurice Kogan, or 'Coogan' as Stewart heard it: Stewart diary, 20, 22 Oct. 1959: Stewart Papers, STWT 8/1/1.

46. McCulloch, 'Labour Party Education Policy', 229–30, 237–41.

47. As McCulloch pointed out, there is a set of papers relating to the study group in the Stewart Papers; there is also a set of papers, not entirely overlapping, in Labour Party Archives, Box 71.

48. Speech by Hugh Gaitskell, Co-operative Day Celebrations, Morden Park, Surrey, 5 July 1958: Stewart Papers, STWT 9/2/5.

49. Abrams' work for Gaitskell from 1956 is fragmentarily documented in Abrams Papers, ABMS 2/4/2; for Abrams' contemporary surveys for Political and Economic Planning and for Lintas Ltd, see pp. 43–4, 46–7.

50. Study Group, Minutes, 19 Dec. 1957; 'Brief Summary of the Findings of the Survey on Educational Attitudes', Feb. 1958: Stewart Papers, STWT 9/2/12. This was the first question posed in the survey, which may have affected responses; also, it asked about the current system and parents were keen not to criticize their children's own schools, as another response indicated: Research Services Ltd, 'Survey of Educational Attitudes', Nov. 1957, 23.

51. Research Services Ltd, 'Survey of Educational Attitudes', Nov. 1957, 9–10, 12–13, 15–17: Abrams Papers, ABMS 3/64. See above, pp. 43–4, for the similar warping of Abrams' analysis of his Lintas Ltd survey. For high approval levels of comprehensives among those who had heard of them, see also Gallup poll of July 1958, Gallup (ed.), *Gallup International Polls*, 471.

52. See ch. 3, n. 62. An implicit contemporary criticism can be found in Goldthorpe et al., *Affluent Worker*, esp. 137.

53. E.g. Stewart diaries, 31 Jan. 1959, 16 June 1959, 17 Sep. 1959, 2 Mar. 1960: Stewart Papers, STWT 8/1/1, 2.

54. David Eccles, 'Secondary Education', 18 Sep. 1956: TNA, ED147/636. Unfortunately for the impact of this paper, Eccles told his civil servants that its principal purpose was 'to save the Public Schools', which were threatened by these democratic and technocratic forces, upon which they naturally poured scorn—the independent sector was too small to drive a major reorganization

of the state sector, and not their job to begin with. See further Dean, 'Preservation or Renovation?', 6–7, 12.

55. M. P. Roseveare to A. Thompson, 21 Sep. 1956; R. N. Heaton to A. Thompson, 2 Oct. 1956; Dennis Vosper to David Eccles, 12 Oct. 1956; memorandum by D. H. Morrell (after a meeting between Eccles and Robin Pedley), 18 Oct. 1956: TNA, ED147/636.

56. A. R. Maxwell-Hyslop to A. A. Part, 22 Jan. 1955; Toby Weaver to A. A. Part, 22 Jan. 1955: TNA, ED147/206; Minutes of a meeting, '11+ Selection and its Effects on Primary Schools', 13 Jan. 1956: TNA, ED147/635.

57. David Eccles, 'Consultation with Local Authorities', 30 July 1956; David Eccles, 'Secondary Education', 18 Sep. 1956: TNA, ED147/984, ED147/636.

58. The first, second and fourth of these enquiries (Crowther, Newsom, and Plowden) were undertaken by the Ministry's Central Advisory Council, which had been revived by Eccles for this purpose; the third, the Robbins Committee, was a prime-ministerial commission.

59. Harold Macmillan to Geoffrey Lloyd, 5 Dec. 1957; Lloyd to Macmillan, 24 Dec. 1957; Macmillan to Lloyd, 27 Dec. 1957; Lloyd to Macmillan, 1 Jan. 1958; Geoffrey Lloyd, 'A Drive in Education', 10 July 1958: TNA, ED136/941; *Secondary Education For All* (1958), 6–7.

60. *Crowther Report*, I, 5, 22–5, 54, 64, 66, 74–6, 81–2, 202–3, 407–9. Their evidence for lack of enthusiasm for post-compulsory education was lack of enthusiasm for ROSLA; it is revealing that their social survey work focused on ROSLA rather than on staying on, and cf. the brief, discouraging consideration of staying on at 64–8. Crowther's social survey of parents and teenagers focused on ROSLA. Ibid., II, 7–24.

61. *Hansard*, 5th ser., 620 (1959–60), 41–56 [21 Mar. 1960].

62. Geoffrey Lloyd to Harold Macmillan, 'Main Action to be Taken in 1960–65', 17 June 1959: TNA, ED136/945.

63. W. R. Elliott, 'Notes on Various Forms of Secondary School Organisation', 10 Dec. 1960: TNA, ED147/641.

64. J. R. Jameson, 'Comprehensive Schools', 16 Apr. 1959; L. R. Fletcher to Toby Weaver, 26 Mar. 1959: TNA, ED147/640.

65. Waiting either to become the comprehensive bottom tier of a two-tier system (dividing at 14 or 16), or, less often, waiting for grammar schools to be merged or closed, creating 'all-through' 11–18 comprehensives. G. N. Flemming to Edward Boyle, 1 Apr. 1959: TNA, ED147/640; Stewart gave the example of 1959 of a multilateral school in Swansea which was a comprehensive but had been forbidden by the Ministry to say so: Stewart diaries, 16 June 1959: Stewart Papers, STWT/8/1/1/; Middlesex was moving to offer O-levels in all its modern schools in the late '50s, as Croydon proposed, seen as comprehensivization by stealth: T. R. Weaver to D. H. Morrell, 26 Nov. 1958: TNA, ED136/943. Even a very exurban LEA like Wiltshire had developed O-level courses in most of its modern schools and by 1963 had opted for comprehensivization simply because it seemed wasteful to maintain artificial bipartite distinctions: Goodman,

"Comprehensive Re-Organisation in Wiltshire", 161. For a different model of 'comprehensives in waiting', see the case of Gateshead which was still building new bipartite schools through 1962 to replace all-age schools, which many in its ruling Labour group saw as two-tier comprehensives in waiting: Batley et al., *Going Comprehensive*, 61–7. For comprehensives in waiting in Oxfordshire, and the inevitable pressures of the bulge and the trend, see Makin, 'Policy Making', esp. 228–32, and cf. 348, where a different demographic pattern relaxed such pressures in the case of Buckinghamshire.

66. Vaizey and Sheehan, *Resources for Education*, 24. Enrolment in secondary moderns accordingly began to fall—despite the continuation of the bulge—from 1961–2.

67. L. R. Fletcher to Toby Weaver, 29 Mar. 1960; Mary Smieton to Toby Weaver, 21 Nov. 1960; W. R. Elliott, 'Notes on Various Forms of Secondary School Organisation', 10 Dec. 1960: TNA, ED147/641.

68. Mary Smieton to W. R. Elliott, 13 Feb. 1961; Mary Smieton to David Eccles, 9 Mar. 1961: TNA, ED147/641.

69. Catholic Bishop of Salford to Edward Boyle, 19 Dec. 1963; W. Harte to V. H. Stevens, 6 Jan. 1964; Stevens to Harte, 24 Jan. 1963: ED147/636. The figure reported by Harte was 92 of 129 LEAs. Other estimates included 90 of 163, 89 of 148 and 120 of 149: M.L.J., 'Reorganization of Secondary Education in England and Wales: Analysis of Local Education Authorities' current practice and future plans for secondary education', 21 Oct. 1964: TNA, T227/1604; Boyle, 'Politics of Secondary School Reorganisation', 32; 'Schools in Upheaval', *Sunday Times*, 8 Nov. 1964, 4.

70. W. Harte, 'Secondary Reorganisation Schemes: Effect on Voluntary Schools and Direct Grant Schools', 25 Feb. 1964, a briefing note for Boyle's forthcoming meeting with the Catholic Bishop of Salford: TNA, ED147/636.

71. To be fair to Boyle, he had visited many LEAs during his first stint at the Ministry, as Parliamentary Secretary under Eccles, and was certainly better informed than most MPs. But he admitted that he got his ideas about the 'pool of ability' quite late in the day, either from Crosland or from Crosland's economic adviser John Vaizey. Boyle, 'Politics of Secondary School Reorganisation', 32–3; Boyle et al., *Politics of Education*, 56, 83–4, 91–3, 115–17, 121–2; Fenwick, *Comprehensive School*, 118; Lowe, *Welfare State*, 479n29; John Vaizey, 'On the Road to James', *TES*, 21 Jan. 1972, 88. His deputy Christopher Chataway argued more forcefully that 'The impetus for change comes invariably from a desire to "get rid of the eleven plus"'. Christopher Chataway, 'Secondary Organisation', 4 May 1964: TNA, ED136/955.

72. *Newsom Report*, iv.

73. *Hansard*, 5th ser., 758 (1967–8) [14 Feb. 1968].

74. *Hansard*, 5th ser, 702 (1964–5), 1785 [27 Nov. 1964]; see also the survey in 'Schools in Upheaval', *Sunday Times*, 8 Nov. 1964, 4.

75. Crosland, *Tony Crosland*, 143–4; Michael Stewart, 'Comprehensive Secondary Education', n.d.. (18 Jan. 1965), and Cabinet Conclusions, 19 Jan. 1965: TNA,

T227/1604. See also the candid account by Wilma Harte, 'Wilma Harte on Labour's Comprehensive Policy', 2 July 1974: Crosland Papers, 5/1, and Crossman, *Diaries*, I, 132–3.

76. See some of the contributors to *Ins and Outs*, e.g. 34, 82, 108–17. The *Mail on Sunday* columnist Peter Hitchens took exception to a broadcast that I did with Alison Wolf in 2016, charting the shift to comprehensivization (including among Conservative authorities) in the 1950s, saying that he had always believed there had been little shift until Crosland compelled change in 1965; when I showed him evidence to the contrary, he chose to disbelieve it.

77. Crosland, *Tony Crosland*, 148.

78. McPherson and Raab, *Governing Education*, 373, 394, and see W. Harte, 18 Jan. 1965, on Scottish ministers' desire to align with English and Welsh practice: TNA, ED147/640.

79. M.L.J. 'Reorganization of Secondary Education in England and Wales: Analysis of Local Education Authorities' current practice and future plans for secondary education', 21 Oct. 1964: TNA, T227/1604; Evans et al., *Secondary Schools of Wales*, 120; Jones, *Which Nation's Schools*, 187, 193.

80. Gray et al., *Reconstructions of Secondary Education*, 231–2; McPherson and Raab, *Governing Education*, 373, 382.

81. T. E. Cleeve, 29 Aug. 1967: Crosland Papers, 5/2. For a case study of one LEA that had already submitted plans at the time of Circular 10/65, and proceeded smoothly to implement it despite a change of control to the Conservatives in 1967, see Fiske, *Reorganisation in Manchester*. Reorganization requiring new schools was always going to be slow—the same applied to secondary education for all after the Butler Act, as all-age schools persisted into the 1960s.

82. Kerckhoff et al., *Going Comprehensive*, 208; Boaden, *Urban Policy-Making*, 57.

83. *Hansard*, 5th ser, 702 (1964–5), 1780 [27 Nov. 1964].

84. As pointed out by Kerckhoff et al., *Going Comprehensive*, 3–5. Neither France nor Sweden introduced 11–18 comprehensives until the 1970s, so Britain's two-tier LEAs were in the European mainstream in the 1960s. In 1960 France was still only transferring half of its age cohort at 11 to any type of secondary education, access even to the lower-tier *collèges* regulated by selective exam until 1959. Phillips, *Subject Choice*, 84; Chanet, 'Mass Education in France', 132.

85. D. V. Donnison, 'Education and Opinion', *New Society*, 26 Nov. 1967, 583–7.

86. Gallup polls of Apr. 1966, Feb. 1967: Gallup (ed.), *Gallup International Polls*, 864, 911–12; Caroline Benn, 'Polling the People', *Where: The Education Magazine for Parents*, Nov. 1975, 304.

87. Caroline Benn, 'Referenda—do they help or hinder decision-making?', *Education*, 21 Apr. 1972, 374–5; Caroline Benn, 'Polling the People', *Where: The Education Magazine for Parents*, Nov. 1975, 304–5.

88. For the emergence of grammar-school 'preservationism', see Knight, *Making of Tory Education Policy*, 10–63; for a defence of Boyle against his right-wing critics, see Crook, 'Edward Boyle'.

89. E.g. Sandbrook, *Seasons in the Sun*, 196–215. Sandbrook, *White Heat*, 314–16, seems to be confusing a small number of direct-grant grammar schools which went independent much later, and the great majority of LEA or voluntary grammar schools which could not and did not. The direct-grant schools were at this stage already quasi-independent and were not much affected by comprehensivization, although LEAs were free to reduce the number of free places they bought in them.

90. E.g. Marsden, *Politicians, Equality and Comprehensives*; CCCS, *Unpopular Education*, 66–85, 127–9, 164; Spooner, 'Secondary Schools', 73–5, but somewhat belied by his own defences of comprehensive innovation, 75–7; Benn and Chitty, *Thirty Years On*, 28–9; Littler, *Against Meritocracy*, 214–15; and from a different perspective entirely, Wooldridge, *Measuring the Mind*, 360–77.

91. Marsden, *Politics, Equality, and Comprehensives*, 1–4, did not recognize the 'swell of economic and social change' lying behind comprehensivization as a 'popular movement', apparently because it was not 'roused' by the Labour party; Benn and Chitty, *Thirty Years On*, v, 8, 12, 60–1, do recognize it but regret the failure of successive governments to back it up.

92. See, for a good introduction, Burgess, *Inside Comprehensive Schools*, commissioned in 1970 by the DES; Lawton and Dufour, *New Social Studies*, including on mixed-ability experiments, 18–21; in Scotland, in a turnabout, the SED actively encouraged mixed-ability teaching: McPherson and Raab, *Governing Education*, 391–2; by the 1990s, most subjects were taught in mixed ability classes until exam preparation began at 14: Benn and Chitty, *Thirty Years On*, 255–8, 275.

93. A point well made by Byrne, *Planning and Educational Inequality*, 26–7; and, on this pent-up demand, see Spencer, *Gender, Work and Education*, Worth, 'Women, Education, and Social Mobility', 7, and Abrams, 'Mothers and Daughters', 67–8, 75–6, 77–8, 80, the latter two based on oral histories with women born in the 1940s. And see Goodman, 'Comprehensive Re-Organisation in Wiltshire', for a rare discussion of the intertwining of comprehensive and mixed-sex education.

94. Mandler, 'Two Cultures', 149–51; cf. Saint, *Towards a Social Architecture*, esp. 128, on the struggle for comprehensives 'to acquire authentic standing and expression of their own'.

95. Bridges, 'Parents and Schools', 302–9. As Scottish observers noted, comprehensives worked particularly well in small towns where they supported local identity, but much the same could be said of new suburban areas and indeed in most places where there were not long-established clusters of grammar-school clients. Gray et al., *Reconstructions of Secondary Education*, 266; Watt, 'Comprehensive School in the West of Scotland', 66, 102; and see the survey in S. E. Gunn, 'Parental Choice of Secondary School', Oct. 1974: TNA, ED213/18.

96. At a peak two-thirds of LEAs organized their secondary education on a feeder or catchment basis: Gorard et al., '"Spiral of Decline"', 368–70.

97. Crosland showed early awareness of this issue and LEAs were advised from the beginning to design catchment areas thoughtfully to maximize social diversity.

See, e.g., 'Comprehensive Schools: Bristol, Devon', n.d; 'Comprehensive Education', Speech at North of England Education Conference, 7 Jan. 1966: Crosland Papers, 5/2. For effects (or non-effects) on social mobility and equality, see p. 148.

98. A point realized by the Labour government which sought to apply 'positive discrimination' to deprived communities in a comprehensive Urban Programme, reminiscent of New Labour's later 'joined-up' policy. It may have been, however, that the Education Priority Areas, to oversee which Crosland brought A.H. Halsey into the DES (jointly funded by Michael Young at the Social Science Research Council), still put too much emphasis on the school alone. See the discussion in Shapely, *Deprivation*, ch. 4.

99. Thus even great advocates of equalization such as Marsden, *Politics, Equality and Comprehensives*, 18, disapproved of 'banding' for social integration which undermined the neighbourhood school.

100. Gorard, 'School Intake Characteristics and Segregation', 132; Gorard and Smith, 'International Comparison of Equity', 21–2, 25–6.

101. Bynner, *Parents' Attitudes*, 15–19 (a follow-up study on the Plowden enquiry four years later, in 1968, after comprehensivization had reached about 20% of the sample); and see Elder, 'Life Opportunity and Personality', 184–94, 201–2.

CHAPTER 5

1. Sanderson, *Educational Opportunity*, 130. These figures put Britain at 2% below France and Germany at 3%, but are questionable because different systems tend to define and measure 'higher education' in different ways. In contrast, the OECD put UK higher education participation rates in 1950 as the highest in Europe, at 5.2%. OECD, *Towards New Structures*, 18. Scottish rates were higher than English rates. Dyhouse, 'Going to University', 1–2. APR is often expressed as an 'index', API, but APR is used here to align with other measures such as QPR and QLR.

2. Larson, 'Production of Expertise', 41.

3. Indicator B1, OECD, *Education at a Glance 2018*, 160. These data are from 2016; OECD average was then 34%, with the UK at 42%.

4. The Barlow Report of 1945 had taken psychological advice and set the maximum at 5%. Simon, *Education and the Social Order*, 83–4.

5. For an influential contemporary estimate from an American, see Flexner, *Universities*, 253–77.

6. *Robbins Report*, I, 8.

7. In a survey of 1954, 65% of Cambridge students and 55% of Oxford students attended independent or direct-grant schools. 13% of Oxford students and 9% of Cambridge students had working-class fathers, vs. 25% for the university system as a whole. Kelsall, *Inquiry into Admissions*, Tables 11, 14.

8. Ibid., Table 14. The 21 include 6 'university colleges' given university status after the war. Keele was the anomaly, purpose-built as a university college after the

war but given degree-granting powers immediately. The under-representation of working-class students was not, however, greater in Britain than elsewhere: Halsey, 'Trends in Access and Equity', 643–4.

9. Truscot, *Redbrick University*, 153. While most graduates were teachers, however, most teachers were not yet graduates, more likely still to go from school to teacher-training colleges, which had lower entrance requirements.

10. A majority of all Birmingham graduates, even of male science graduates, in employment in 1937–8 were teachers: Schwarz, 'Professions, Elites and Universities', 950. As late as 1960, the first employment of all university graduates was most likely to be teaching—a whopping 41%—or industry—26%—the former especially for women and the latter especially for men. Kelsall et al., *Six Years After*, 33. An earlier survey found only half of graduates in teaching or industry, but this cohort had an unusual concentration of older ex-servicemen: Political and Economic Planning, *Graduate Employment*, 59.

11. Carswell, *Government and the Universities*, 1–2.

12. David Edgerton calls it the 'warfare state'—a mellifluous contrast to the welfare state—and it had certainly been driven by the demands of war up to 1945, though less so afterwards.

13. Shattock and Berdahl, 'UGC', 474.

14. Stewart, *Higher Education*, 37–8, 46–7.

15. Stewart, *Higher Education*, 47–8; Simon, *Education and the Social Order*, 92–5.

16. University Grants Committee, *University Development. Interim Report on the Years 1947 to 1951*, Cmd. 8473.

17. Moser and Layard, 'Estimating the Need for Qualified Manpower', 296.

18. James, *Education and Leadership*, 49.

19. The argument was that big capital investments in science facilities to fee-paying schools could only be made by industry, since the state confined its investments to its own schools. But this was the beginning of a major push to modernize the curriculum in independent schools. McCulloch et al., *Technological Revolution?*, 31–2, 76, 109–10, 118–19, 191.

20. Quoted in the introduction to the government's White Paper, *Technical Education*, Cmd. 9703 (1956), 4.

21. *Percy Report*, 21. In fact, many were already providing university-type courses, leading for example to external University of London degrees. 66 such technical colleges were identified as providing 'higher technological education' in a subsequent White Paper, *Higher Technological Education*, (1950–1), 3.

22. Carswell, *Government and the Universities*, 10–11; *Robbins Report*, I, 199, XII, 104–5. This growth came both through the 'block grant' awarded to the universities on a quinquennial basis, and through increased payment of student fees through LEAs.

23. Tomlinson, 'Inventing "Decline"', and see esp. the work of the OEEC (OECD's predecessor) in inciting international comparisons of national accounts, productivity levels and other measures, 738, 741–2, 744–5.

24. OECD was making forecasts of science and technology enrolments as early as 1960. OECD, *Development of Higher Education*, 206–7.

25. Halsey, 'British Universities', 504, a charge repeated by Fred Willey in Parliament, *Hansard*, 5th ser., 649 (1961–2), 50 [13 Nov. 1961], supposedly quoting Eccles; *Robbins Report*, V, 9–11. Sanderson, 'Higher Education in the Post-War Years', 420, cherry-picks only the nations with higher rates than Britain. The OECD found British growth rates in higher education (both at degree and sub-degree level) to be near average over the period 1950–67. OECD, *Development of Higher Education*, 21, 27, 34, 44.

26. Schultz, *Economic Value of Education*, 11, and higher estimate in Schultz, 'Investment in Human Capital', 12–13.

27. Becker, *Human Capital*, 7–9.

28. Field, *Blood, Sweat and Toil*, 184, 189, 213–16, 341; Renwick, 'Eugenics and Social Mobility', 852–60.

29. See, e.g., Attlee in *Hansard*, 5th ser., 418 (1945–6), 1902 [7 Feb. 1946]. Thanks to Chika Tonooka for pointing this out to me.

30. Becker, *Human Capital*, 577.

31. Blaug, 'Economics of Education', 17. The Chicago approach deprecated manpower planning—it held that well-designed markets would supply all the relevant information to individuals to direct them towards the educational outcomes that would maximize return (for individuals and society both, it was assumed).

32. Gaukroger and Schwarz, 'Student Recruitment to Birmingham', 189; *Robbins Report*, XII, 104–5.

33. Schultz, *Economic Value of Education*, 50–1; Becker, *Human Capital*, 12–13; Blaug, 'Rate of Return', 228–30.

34. Vaizey and Debauvais, 'Economic Aspects of Educational Development', 40; Goldin and Katz, *Race Between Education and Technology*, 208; Machin and Vignoles (eds), *What's the Good of Education*, 3–4.

35. For arguments that privilege the techno-state, see Sanderson, 'Higher Education in the Post-War Years', 417–18; Tight, *Development of Higher Education*, 59–63; Salter and Tapper, *State and Higher Education*, 4, 12–17; Edgerton, *Rise and Fall*, 341; King and Nash, 'Politics of Higher Education Expansion', 185–90; Shattock, *Making Policy*, cf. 3–4, 134, sees expansion as engineered by policy elites, though acknowledges demand as the wind in their sails; Kogan, 'The Political View', 70, 74, also gives a mixed picture, as does Halsey, *Decline of Donnish Dominion*, 5–17. Carswell, *Government and the Universities*, 26, is unusual in prioritising demand over technocratic drivers, perhaps because of his close involvement with Robbins; see also Halsey in an earlier, more optimistic vein, 'Expansion and Equality', 207; Harrison, *Seeking a Role*, 52–3, 349–50.

36. Whyte, *Redbrick*, chs 9–10.

37. Runciman, *Relative Deprivation*, 230–2; Research Services Ltd, 'Survey of Educational Attitudes', Nov. 1957: Abrams Papers, ABMS/3/64, 3, 18, 19; Goldthorpe et al., *Affluent Worker*, 137; Douglas et al., *All Our Future*, Table 20, 214; Abrams, reporting on his findings for Robbins, in 'Is There a Working Class?', n.d. (1963): Abrams MSS, ABMS/5/6/2.

38. Education and Employment Committee, *Access for All?*, ix.

39. Blume, 'Framework for Analysis', 10.

40. Snow claimed to be talking about the dominance of the arts in the general culture, but his educational examples were almost exclusively drawn from Oxbridge, and he claimed explicitly that the whole school system was 'dictated by the Oxford and Cambridge scholarship examinations'. Snow, *Two Cultures*, esp. 19. On the controversy, see Ortolano, *Two Cultures Controversy*.

41. Sampson, *Anatomy of Britain*, 195–7 (on the university system as a whole), 197–217 (on Oxbridge).

42. 63% of Oxbridge students took arts degrees, but only 43% of all students. *Robbins Report*, II, 24.

43. Kingsley Amis, 'Lone Voices: Views of the 'Fifties', *Encounter*, July 1960, 8–10.

44. On manpower planning, Vaizey, *Economics of Education*, 99–107; on human-capital theory, ibid., 40–5, Vaizey and Debeauvais, 'Economic Aspects of Educational Development', 40–1.

45. Halsey and Vaizey were the 'rapporteurs' for the report of a study group organised by *Socialist Commentary*, *Policy for Higher Education*, 4, heavily influenced by the thinking of Michael Young. It was where they first met. Michael Stewart was a member of this study group, too, but he found Halsey and Vaizey so rude that he almost walked out of it. Vaizey later introduced Floud to Stuart; Vaizey and Young collaborated on the Advisory Centre for Education and its publication *Where?*, which sought to educate consumer opinion on schools; Vaizey, Stewart, and Young collaborated on the Fabian Society submission to the Robbins Commission: John Vaizey, 'On the Road to James', *TES*, 21 Jan. 1972, 88; Stewart diary, 20 Oct. 1959: Stewart Papers, STWT/8/1/1; Vaizey to Crosland, 27 June 1961: Crosland Papers, 10/4; Vaizey, *Economics of Education*, 151–2; for the Fabian submission to Robbins, see Stewart Papers, STWT/18/2/148. So close was Vaizey to the sociologists that he is often virtually taken for one: Parkinson, *Labour Party and the Organization of Secondary Education*, 60–70; Annan, *Our Age*, 363; Silver and Silver, *Educational War on Poverty*, 173–7.

46. Schwarz, 'Professions, Elites, and Universities', 951–6. As late as 1960, however, the dominance of education and industry was still notable: Kelsall et al., *Six Years After*, 33–5; *Robbins Report*, II, 149–52.

47. Phillips, *Subject Choice*, 37; Robbins found some effect of higher-education entry with O-levels from secondary modern schools: *Robbins Report*, I, Appx 1, 67.

48. Perkin, 'University Planning', 116.

49. Vaizey and Sheehan, *Resources for Education*, 64, 66; Gosden, *Education System*, 169–73; Lister, 'Effects of External Examinations', 74. Despite widespread hopes for part-time further education after school-leaving age, only 1% of 15–18 year olds were enrolled in such courses in 1960. Carter, *Home, School and Work*, 257.

50. *Robbins Report*, I, 16. These calculations differ slightly from Moser and Layard's later calculations, for which see Figure 5.3, but the trend is similar.

51. *Hansard*, 5th ser., 649 (1961–2), 68 [13 Nov. 1961].

52. OECD, *Development of Higher Education*, 108–9; Pissarides, 'From School to University', 656, found a similar trend, with a turning-point in 1960–5 when qualifiers grew much more rapidly than entrants; *Robbins Report*, I, 12, estimated the drop from 75% in 1957 to 61% in 1961.

53. There was a mounting tempo of criticisms of higher rates of unsuccessful applications in the spring of 1962, especially over the call for a new university for Scotland (5 Apr.) and in the debate on the education estimates (17 May); see also Shattock, *Making Policy*, 118–19. QPR as a term of art did not arise until later, but the gap between qualified applicants and entrants had clearly been identified.

54. *Years of Crisis*, esp. 5–9. Of course, the similarity only went so far—the 11+ row was over equal provision in compulsory education, the 18+ row over equal access to a place for qualified leavers.

55. Democratic: Carswell, *Government and the Universities*, 33–5; technocratic: King and Nash, 'Politics of Higher Education', 191–2; meritocratic: Anderson, *British Universities*, 148–9; aristocratic: Scott, *Knowledge and Nation*, 113.

56. The point is usually lost that Robbins found Newman 'repellent', and that reading him was a prophylactic against rather than a driver towards Victorian elitism: Howson, *Robbins*, 862.

57. Howson, *Robbins*, 878, 889; on the liberal arts college, see particularly the exchanges between the committee and Richard Hoggart, 6 Oct. 1961, and Robbins' exchanges with Sir Charles Morris, 19 Oct. 1962: *Robbins Report*, VI, 178–80, XI, 2081, 2085.

58. *Robbins Report*, I, 54. The tone was very similar to that struck by the Taylor Report, with its own principle that 'all who are capable of benefiting from higher education must have access to it'—unsurprisingly, as Taylor had access to the written evidence submitted to Robbins. *Years of Crisis*, 6.

59. *Robbins Report*, I, 298–300; Abrams in 'Is There a Working Class?', Abrams Papers, ABMS/5/6/2.

60. *Robbins Report*, I, 300–12.

61. i.e. 'the end of the first quarter of the twenty-first century': Robbins did not expect the rate of increase to remain uniform for that long, but he did expect the 'Robbins Principle' to apply and governments to accommodate demand from qualified leavers, as they still more or less do. *Robbins Report*, I, 70–3.

62. *Robbins Report*, I, 49–54, 84. The relevant evidence was presented in Appendix I, esp. Part II, 'The Pool of Ability'. See also Floud's memoranda in *Robbins Report*, XII, 45–57, and Moser's comments on what finally committed Robbins to an ambitious programme of expansion, in Howson, *Robbins*, 876–7. LEA representatives were even more optimistic about the prospects of future expansion. Memorandum submitted by the Association of Chief Education Officers, 24 Nov. 1961: *Robbins Report*, IX, 1283–5.

63. Moser and Layard, 'Estimating the Need for Qualified Manpower', esp. 311–13 on Robbins; *Robbins Report*, I, 71–4.

64. *Robbins Report*, I, 6–8, 48, 73–4; Robbins and Ford, 'Report on Robbins', 9–10.

65. *Robbins Report*, I, 63–6, Appendix 1, 119–20, 136–43, 266–71.

66. *Robbins Report*, I, 65–6.
67. Annan, *Our Age*, 372–3; Collini, *What Are Universities For?*, 30–1; Halsey, *Decline of Donnish Dominion*, 5–7, but cf. the rather different emphasis 8–11; Willetts, *University Education*, 44–6, is unusual in stressing Robbins' impact on participation instead.
68. OECD, *Educational Situation*, 33; OECD, *Development of Higher Education*, 147.
69. *Robbins Report*, I, 16, Appx 1, 14, II, 71–2. The rate for universities in both cases was around 25%. It was also evident to Robbins that the 'pinch' on university entrance since 1958 had hit the teacher-training colleges too but not the technical and other specialist colleges.
70. Annan's claims to the contrary notwithstanding, *Our Age*, 373–4.
71. *Robbins Report*, I, 147–55, VI, 175–81.
72. Robbins and Ford, 'Report on Robbins', 6–8; Jean Floud had also advocated this policy in her memorandum, 11 Mar. 1962: *Robbins Report*, XII, 45–8; as had the Taylor Report, *Years of Crisis*, 9, 21–2, 24–7, 29–32, although Taylor was for extending university status to more institutions more rapidly. On this basis Shattock, *Making Policy*, 54–7, 65, finds Taylor's unitarism oddly to be more like Crosland's binarism, even though he also thinks Crosland's binarism aimed to protect the universities from rivals.
73. *Robbins Report*, I, 89–97, 163–5, 186–8; and see evidence in ibid., VI, 323–7 (Institute of Chartered Accountants), VII, 364 (Law Society), 575–80 (Federation of British Industries), X, 1670 (Sir Eric Ashby).
74. *Robbins Report*, XI, 2085.
75. Edward Boyle even before the Report, *Hansard*, 5th ser., 681 (1962–3), 642–3 [17 July 1963]; his junior minister Christopher Chataway after the Report, *Hansard*, 5th ser., 684 (1963–4), 595–6 [15 Nov. 1963]; see also Boyle in Kogan et al., *Politics of Education*, 91–3.
76. *Hansard*, 5th ser., 684 (1963–4), 39–40 [12 Nov. 1963]. Privately his advisers were speaking of 'a moral and social duty' to ensure 'the universal availability of higher education', but this proved a step too far, especially as it was doubted that it could be guaranteed before 1968 with 'the passing of the bulge'. 'Suggested points on the Robbins Report for inclusion in the Prime Minister's speech on the Debate on the Address', n.d.; F. G. Burrett to T. J. Bligh, 1 Nov. 1963: TNA, ED 188/12.
77. *Higher Education. Government Statement*, 3–4; cf. *Robbins Report*, I, 33, 131, 133.
78. Cf. Deer, 'Politics of Access', 106–7; Neave, 'Elite and Mass Higher Education', 351. And in fact access to A-levels proved more egalitarian than access to the *Abitur*: see Ohidy, 'Widening Participation in Germany'.
79. Wilson, 'Labour's Plan for Science', 3–4, 7.
80. See Crosland's thoughts on the social and democratic agenda for education in his memorandum to self, probably around 1966, 'Education – Politics', and his balancing up of planning and demand in Crosland to Secretary, 25 May 1966: Crosland Papers, 5/2.
81. Layard and King, 'Impact of Robbins', 24; Gannicott and Blaug, 'Scientists and Engineers', 128; Blaug, 'Rate of Return', 228–30, 242–5; Vaizey, *Education for*

Tomorrow, 29–30, 69–70, 78–80. Moser was, however, willing to cooperate with the controversial right-wing economists Peacock and Wiseman in attempting to quantify in human-capital terms the 'output' of university education, but the effort was nixed by Labour's economic advisers, led by Thomas Balogh: see TNA, ED181/12.

82. J. A. Boyd-Carpenter to Cabinet Committee on Education Policy, 'Robbins Report', 24 Sep. 1963: TNA, ED 188/12; Shattock, *Making Policy*, 110. The new public-expenditure monitoring system, PESC, so-called after the Public Expenditure Survey Committee, was inaugurated in 1961.

83. Morris, 'Investment in Higher Education', 72–3; Armytage, 'Thoughts after Robbins', 97–100; Peston, 'Economics and Administration of Education', 64, 70.

84. See e.g. Robin Pedley to Crosland, 3 May 1965: TNA, ED147/640. Robbins himself called the policy 'reactionary and half-baked': Robbins and Ford, 'Report on Robbins', 13. Crosland had signed up to the Taylor Report which had come out strongly in favour of a unitary system, with a wide range of institutions including teacher training deserving university status.

85. 'New University Institutions', 17 Nov. 1964: TNA, ED136/955; Carswell, *Government and the Universities*, 63; the text of Crosland's Woolwich speech is in Crosland Papers, 5/2.

86. Robinson, *New Polytechnics*, gives a good account of their genesis.

87. Carswell, *Government and the Universities*, 72–4; Willetts, *University Education*, 53–6; Stewart, *Higher Education*, 138–44; Anderson, *British Universities*, 155; Harrison and Weightman, 'Academic Freedom', 36–7. These commentaries also ignore the fact that the Labour party's official position, agreed by Crosland in the Taylor Report, was for a firmly unitary system with a wide range of institutions gaining university status.

88. Godwin, 'Origin of the Binary System', gives a good blow-by-blow account; Boyle's paper to the Education and Research Committee of the Cabinet, 'The Future of Non-University Higher Education', 25 Mar. 1964, uses the language of 'social control' in respect to teacher training and 'other needed technical occupations': TNA, ED136/955. The same policy was presented to the Cabinet Social Services Committee after the election. 'New University Institutions', 17 Nov. 1964: TNA, ED136/955. See also Crosland's retrospective in Kogan et al., *Politics of Education*, 195, and his notes in Crosland Papers, 5/2; on the LEAs' alliance with the DES, see Sharp, *Creation of the Local Authority Sector*, 18–26, 38–45, 168–72; and on the UGC, Shattock, *Making Policy*, 49–50, Godwin, 'Origin of the Binary System', 184–5.

89. On these new middle-class identities, see Savage, *Identities and Social Change*, 19, 67, 76, 83–5, 221–35; Dyhouse, *Students*, 101, points out that Sussex started out with a good gender balance because it had not yet opened its science faculties.

90. *Anderson Report*.

91. Willetts, *University Education*, 41–4, 51–2; Carswell, *Government and the Universities*, 24–5. See also the exchange between Hillman, 'From Grants for All', and David Malcolm, 'Anderson Appreciated', *Wonkhe*, 2 June 2014 (https://wonkhe.com/

blogs/anderson-appreciated/), with response from Hillman, *HEPI Blog*, 2 June 2014 (https://www.hepi.ac.uk/2014/06/02/grants/).

92. *Anderson Report*, 46–7, 118, 119–22; Gaukroger and Schwarz, 'Student Recruitment to Birmingham', 189–90; Hillman, 'From Grants for All', 253.

93. *Anderson Report*, 57–8; Magnussen, 'Cost and Finance of Post-Secondary Education', 215–23, an OECD report of 1974 which nevertheless endorsed the British approach. This approach also built on a longstanding tradition of providing means-tested maintenance allowances for post-compulsory schooling.

94. The Anderson Report cited Crowther on the 'new family pattern' as a rationale for providing grants: *Anderson Report*, 53. On the emergence of 'student life' in the new universities, and national catchments, see Vernon, 'New Universities and their Communities'; Paterson, *Scottish Education*, 159, 169; and see also Whyte, *Redbrick*, e.g. 247. The trend to live away from home had actually begun immediately after the war. Cf. Abbott, *Student Life in a Class Society*, the most famous contemporary study of 'student life', which portrayed it as a straightforward perpetuation of older bourgeois norms, was a study of Edinburgh, Durham and Newcastle in 1962–5, based on a cohort born before the postwar bulge.

95. The Universities Central Council for Admissions also served as another growing centre for higher-education statistics which monitored widening participation; see Andy Youell, 'A Brief History of Higher Education Data', *Wonkhe Blog*, http://wonkhe.com/blogs/a-brief-history-of-higher-education-data/.

96. Pratt, *Polytechnic Experiment*, 77–9. One later estimate put universities at 58% from classes I and II, polytechnics at 46%, though with 10% unclassified: Williams and Blackstone, *Response to Adversity*, 31. On this basis, universities may have had 25% working-class students, polytechnics 30%, teacher-training colleges 40%. It was not necessarily the case, as per Whyte, *Redbrick*, 239–40, 246, that universities were becoming *more* middle-class, only that more middle-class children were going to them (as were more working-class children, in pretty much the same proportions as before), although a study of Scotland in this period did find that the growth of middle-class women's participation reduced the relative share of working-class men: Hutchison and McPherson, 'Sex and Social Class Structure'.

97. Robinson, *New Polytechnics*, offers a good contemporary introduction to the colleges that formed the basis for the polytechnic sector, though firmly committed to the binary divide and differentiation; but see 37–8 on degree hunger, 38 on national catchments, 43 on convergence with universities. Pratt, who with Tyrrell Burgess developed the critique of 'academic drift' in the early '70s, partially recanted later: see Pratt, *Polytechnic Experiment*, 11–12, 105–7, though cf. 305–9.

98. Layard and King, 'Impact of Robbins', 20. This article was a kite for their subsequent Penguin Special, Layard, King, and Moser, *Impact of Robbins*.

99. Pellegrin, 'Quantitative Trends in Post-Secondary Education', 23–7. The exception was the United States, where the bulge accounted for 60% of growth, though of course the US was operating at much higher participation rates already.

100. Voters also prioritized Robbins over the contemporaneous Newsom Report on less academic children, for which see Gallup polls of Nov. and Dec. 1963: Gallup (ed.), *Gallup International Opinion Polls*, 715, 718. For Robbins' high profile in the general election of 1964, see Carswell, *Government and the Universities*, 38, 52; Butler and King, *General Election of 1964*, 140–4. Both health and education peaked in 1964 as issues identified as the 'most important problem facing the country': King (ed.), *British Public Opinion*, 262–73.

101. All of these statistics have to be taken with a grain of salt. Even something as simple as APR or QPR can vary greatly depending on how you count 'qualified' or indeed 'higher education'. The longitudinal graphs relied upon later by the DES and its successors say that APR rose from about 5% to 14% (see Figure 6.1). For different calculations of QPR by OECD, Robbins and Pissarides, see n. 52; the 1970 calculations can be found in DES, *Report on Education* 99 (Apr. 1983), and DES, *Statistical Bulletin* 9/85 (July 1985), the latter showing some QPR rates over 100% in 1970 if you include teacher-training entrants with fewer than two A-levels. Layard and King, 'Impact of Robbins', 20–2, 27–8, 34–6, show different figures still, but the trends are similar. Pissarides, 'Overview of the Demand', 155–6, thought there were no supply constraints at all after 1963 and that QPR (which he measured as qualified entrants to 'degree-granting institutions') remained level at 70%, actually below Robbins' predictions. On O-levels, see Wright, *Progress in Education*, 70–1.

CHAPTER 6

1. Pissarides, 'Staying-on at School', 346–7. But see pp. 111 for subsequent fluctuations after 1973.
2. Education, Science and Arts Committee, *Funding and Organisation of Courses*, lxvi.
3. *What Has Happened?*.
4. Beckett, *When the Lights Went Out*, 406–7, briefly mentions Callaghan's Ruskin speech but apart from an appreciation of his own cousin's Marxist period at Middlesex Polytechnic offers no further reflection; Turner, *Crisis? What Crisis?*, 260–1, acknowledges education as a 'key battleground' but gives it only a single page; Black et al., *Reassessing 1970s Britain*, doesn't even give it that; Sandbrook, *Seasons in the Sun*, 196–216, 289–300, is the signal exception. In contrast, a very influential contemporary analysis took higher education as paradigmatic for the 1970s crisis of governance: King, 'Overload', 163. Accounts of this period in higher education portray it against all the evidence as one of expansion: Sandbrook, *Seasons in the Sun*, 293–4, Anderson, *British Universities*, 158–9, Scott, 'British Universities' (but cf. his gloomier view a decade later, positing 1973 as the peak of the 'golden age': 'Higher Education', 127–31), Harrison, *Finding a Role*, 391 (conflating slackening demand until the late 1980s with the sudden jump thereafter), Whyte, *Redbrick*, 272–5 (similarly conflating the two periods), and even Paterson, *Secondary Education*, 164–5, usually very alive to such things.

5. On the decline of optimism and the rise of competitive individualism, see Lawrence, *Me, Me, Me?*, 193–4, 205–6.

6. Goldin and Katz, *Race Between Education and Technology*, 290–1, 301–2; Acemoglu and Autor, 'What Does Human Capital Do?', 455–8; OECD, *Educational Situation*, 32, noticed slackening of growth from 1968 in some but not all OECD countries (1974); OECD, *Employment Prospects*, 2, 6–7, on the spread of graduate employment difficulties (1981). The slackening of participation in the US spanned a similar period from *c.* 1970 to *c.* 1985.

7. On the former, see e.g. Hodgson, 'Inequality'; on the latter, Blaug, 'Economics of Education', 17. Two American books, one from the right and the one from the left, came to similar conclusions about the limited effects of education on social class: the Coleman Report of 1966 (*Equality of Educational Opportunity*), and Jencks et al., *Inequality*, in 1972. Both were influential on the British right in informing renewed arguments for meritocracy: see Joseph and Sumption, *Equality*, 34–5; Wooldridge, 'Education', 164–6; Wooldridge, *Meritocracy*, 27–9.

8. Tomlinson, 'Retrospect on Ruskin', 44.

9. Driver, *Schoolhouse Gate*, 156, 180–1. 'Discipline' was the top concern of British parents in the 1974 sweep of the 1958 birth cohort, though cited by only 6%; 'standards' were cited by only 3%; and two-thirds were generally satisfied with their children's secondary school: Fogelman (ed.), *Britain's 16-Year-Olds*, 50.

10. At first in England and Wales, but a few years later an even more dramatic amalgamation of local authorities in Scotland, leading to 'regionalization': Watt, 'Comprehensive School in the West of Scotland', 229–38; see also Sharp, 'Surviving not Thriving', 200–2.

11. Blackburn and Jarman, 'Changing Inequalities in Access', 203.

12. Knight, *Making of Tory Education Policy*, 16–18; Cox, *Great Betrayal*, 145–7.

13. Cox, *Great Betrayal*, 150, 156–7, 164–5, 170–2; Cox and Dyson (eds), *Black Papers*, 26–31, 33; Szamuely, 'Comprehensive Inequality', 123–5.

14. Cox and Dyson (eds), *Black Papers*, 26–31; Goldthorpe and Jackson, 'Education and Meritocracy', 94. As Dean Blackburn points out, in an as yet unpublished paper 'From Merit to the Market? John Vaizey and the Rise of Thatcherism', among these born-again meritocrats were prominent intellectuals moving from Labour to Conservatism such as John Vaizey and C. P. Snow.

15. Crook, 'Edward Boyle', 59–62; Knight, *Tory Education Policy*, 22–5, 42–50.

16. Of the Black Papers authors, Burt, 'Mental Differences', and Lynn, 'Streaming', certainly believed that social elites were largely formed by heredity.

17. This was particularly true of Angus Maude—see his contribution to the Black Papers, 'The Egalitarian Threat'.

18. For an early exception, see John O'Sullivan, 'The Direction of Conservatism', *Swinton Journal*, Spring 1970, 33–4, with its critique of Maude's tripartism as 'paternalistic'.

19. Davis, 'Tyndale Affair', now offers the best historical account.

20. Jacka, Cox, and Marks, *Rape of Reason*. Caroline Cox, no relation to Brian Cox, was made a Conservative peer in 1982. John Marks would also play an

important role later in debates over standards in comprehensive schools, for
which see p. 298 n. 3.

21. Although there is not to my knowledge a good historical account, see the
intense exploration of the legal issues in Bull, 'Tameside Revisited'.

22. Again there appears to be no full historical account; but see Chris Jeppesen's
discussion at https://sesc.hist.cam.ac.uk/2017/12/08/best-days-panorama-
21st-march-1977/ and a Radio 4 retrospect, 'Panorama Broke My School', 20
Sep. 2019, https://www.bbc.co.uk/programmes/m0008pfw, in which he features.

23. Simon, *Education and the Social Order*, 433–5, 443–4; Timmins, *Five Giants*, ch. 15;
Knight, *Tory Education Policy*, 95–6, 99–100.

24. These were the findings of a study of 6 LEAs undertaken in 1973–4: Jennings,
Education and Politics, 13–26, 42; see also James, *Reorganization of Secondary
Education*, ch. 3, though depreciating the responsiveness of LEAs to such pressures. On the role of the LEA in the Tyndale affair, see Davis, 'Tyndale Affair',
276–83, 288–9, 293, and in the Tameside affair, Bull, 'Tameside Revisited', esp.
314–22; for the 'how to' guide for parents' action groups issued by the
Conservatives in 1975, see St John-Stevas and Brittan, *How to Save Your Schools*,
and DES responses in TNA, ED207/119.

25. The *locus classicus* is CCCS, *Unpopular Education*, 65–114 for the historical critique, 133–41 for the Bernsteinian analysis; see also Lowe, *Schooling and Social
Change*, 21–8 (with a whiff of technocracy added for good measure), and 118–22
on effects on ethnic minorities; Ranson, 'Towards a Tertiary Tripartism', 240–3;
Watt, 'Comprehensive School in the West of Scotland', chs 4–5. For an unusual
critique of the CCCS position on the left, see Benn and Chitty, *Thirty Years On*,
60–1.

26. E.g. Bernstein, 'Elaborated and Restricted Codes', 62, 66–7. For some endorsements in sociology of the long 1970s, see Abbott, *Student Life in a Class Society*,
56; Ashton, 'Transition from School to Work', 107–18; Paterson, 'Incubus and
Ideology', 203.

27. Quoted by Silver and Silver, *Educational War on Poverty*, 179.

28. Willis, *Learning to Labour*, 2–3, 14–15, 52, 62–3, 102–4, 127–8, and see the gentle
critique in Robbins, *Upward Mobility*, 219–22; Basil Bernstein, 'Education
Cannot Compensate for Society', *New Society*, 26 Feb. 1970, 344–7. For a different approach, taking evidence of the counter-school culture in Scotland as
demands for respect and more equal provision, see Gow and McPherson (eds),
Tell Them From Me.

29. See e.g. Heald and Wybrow, *Gallup Survey of Education*, 238–40; also CCCS,
Unpopular Education, 209–13, Benn and Chitty, *Thirty Years On*, 40.

30. The SESC project has been working closely with this cloudburst of educational ethnography, beginning with the 'Manchester School' studies commissioned by the Ministry of Education in 1962–6. Willis's was one such
ethnography, of 'Hammerton' in the West Midlands, conducted 1972–5.

31. Halsey, 'Towards Meritocracy?', 174–6, 184; for the head-on radical critique of
Halsey, see CCCS, *Unpopular Education*, 79–87.

32. Pearson, *Life Project*, 79–80, 127–8, 130, 135.

33. The full text of the speech can be found at http://www.educationengland.org. uk/documents/speeches/1976ruskin.html, from which text all quotations here are taken. See also Callaghan's reflections 25 years later in Callaghan, 'Education Debate I'.

34. See e.g. Lawton, *Education and Labour Party Ideologies*, 91; Chitty, *Towards a New Education System*, 60–3; Gray et al., *Reconstructions of Secondary Education*, 105–6.

35. He did not mention 'choice', though this would enter Labour discourse under his Education Secretary Shirley Williams. 'Choice' was more conducive to selection than 'standards', but it proved something of a damp squib.

36. For the Ruskin speech as the 'turning point' in an inexorable rightward shift, leading even to 'the end of comprehensive education', see e.g. Chitty, *Towards a New Education System*, 134–5; Benn and Chitty, *Thirty Years On*, 12; Morris and Griggs (ed.), *Education, the Wasted Years*, 6–9; Salter and Tapper, 'Reversing the Rachet', 63–6; Jones, *Education in Britain*, 73–4, 94–6.

37. See e.g. Simon, *Education and the Social Order*, 446–51; Knight, *Tory Education Policy*, 95–102, 121–3; Scott, *Knowledge & Nation*, 154; Wright, *Progress in Education*, 190, unusual in acknowledging the Black Papers for raising the issue of standards; Batteson, 'Education in the Moment of 1976', makes the most positive case for Callaghan's policy. The Conservative manifesto in 1974 talked up 'parents' rights' without specifically playing on selection.

38. Arnott, 'Thatcher and Educational Reform in Scotland', 185–6; Jones, 'Education in Wales'; though cf. Watt, 'Comprehensive School in the West of Scotland', 354–61, on the mid-1970s 'crisis of confidence' there too.

39. The only explicit policy outcome was a Green Paper in July 1977 emphasizing accountability and standards; in some respects it also led to growth of sentiment for a national curriculum, finally realised in the late 1980s. See Williams, 'Ruskin in Context'.

40. Quoted by Ranson, 'Towards a Tertiary Tripartism', 167.

41. Robinson et al., 'Popular Individualism and the "Crisis" of the 1970s', 271–2, 277–8, 282–3; Sutcliffe-Braithwaite, *Class, Politics, and the Decline of Deference*, 17, 19, 29–30, 53, 60–1, 88, 132–3; Lawrence, *Me, Me, Me?*, 205–6, 229, 233–4; Ortolano, *Thatcher's Progress*, 28, 33, 52–3, 102–3; Black and Pemberton, 'Reassessing the 1970s', esp. 14–17.

42. Taylor-Gooby, *Public Opinion, Ideology and State Welfare*, 2, 29, 32–3, 38–47, 51–2, 61–6, 111–14; Taylor-Gooby, *Social Change*, 113–15, 133–5. The DES came to the same conclusions at the time. DES Planning Unit, 'DOE Seminar on Long-Term Trends: Thesis Paper', 25 Jan. 1980: TNA, ED181/373/1.

43. Edgerton, *Rise and Fall of the British Nation*, 244, 459; Glennerster and Hills (eds), *State of Welfare*, 36–41, giving a more mixed but still stable picture. The total fertility rate peaked around 1965, so that the secondary school population began to drop in the late 1970s, and dropped rapidly in the 1980s. Smith, 'Schools', 202–3, shows that expenditure as proportion of GDP changed little across 1970–90; a surge in the mid-1970s had more to do with GDP than with

educational expenditure; and per capita expenditure on secondary schools rose considerably in the 1980s.

44. To some extent picked up in the historiography: Sanderson, *Educational Opportunity and Social Change*, 8; Stevens, *University to Uni*, 29–30, 79–83; Edgerton, *Rise and Fall of the British Nation*, 464. The OECD predicted in 1974 an international surge in the private sector which didn't happen. *Educational Situation*, 18–19.

45. The 1958 cohort study found that 6% of that cohort (in secondary school 1969–74) were in independent schools, more or less the long-term average. Smith, 'Schools', 187, shows a decline to below 6% in the 1970s, and then a rise to 7% in the 1980s—much of this must be due to assisted places (see Taylor-Gooby, *Social Change*, 125–6)—and a decline again after 1990.

46. O'Hara, *Governing Post-War Britain*, 174–5; Sutcliffe-Braithwaite, *Class, Politics, and the Decline of Deference*, 17–20; O'Hara, 'Complexities of "Consumerism"', on participation in health services; Fielding, '"Participation" in the 1960s', 141–6, on participation in social services; cf. Kefford, 'Housing and the Citizen-Consumer', on the impact of consumerism in the private marketplace on public services; and see Goldthorpe, 'The Current Inflation', on the 'pushfulness' of a mature working class and its scepticism about 'meritocracy', 200, 203. Thanks to Florence Sutcliffe-Braithwaite for pointing out the relevance of this latter paper.

47. This is a still poorly understood phenomenon that deserves closer study. Efforts to achieve greater social and ethnic integration by 'banding' or bussing proved short-lived and unpopular; sometimes, as in the Tyndale affair (for which see Davis, 'Tyndale Affair', 288–9), to avoid integration, but more often I think because the neighbourhood catchment was held to be so valuable. In 1981 the Race Relations Board ruled that bussing for racial integration was discriminatory and the practice largely ceased. See Bebber, 'Bussing and South Asians in London', 645–8, 650–2, 655 on South-Asian community organising against bussing in Ealing.

48. Wragg and Jarvis, 'Perceptions of Education', 123.

49. S. E. Gunn, 'Parental Choice of Secondary School', Oct. 1974, on the broad acceptance of the catchment principle and the limited (though growing) desire for parental choice; Jennings, *Education and Politics*, 96; Tomlinson, 'Retrospect on Ruskin', 50–1; Allen, 'Allocating Pupils', on the limited desire for choice even after 1980s legislation which facilitated it. Attachment to the neighbourhood school as a community institution was probably almost as strong in most areas of England and Wales as in Scotland: Arnott, 'Thatcher and Educational Reform in Scotland', 193–5; but cf. the pessimism in Benn and Chitty, *Thirty Years On*, 35–8.

50. As observed, cynically, by Wooldridge, *Measuring the Mind*, 400; see also Simon, *Education and the Social Order*, 499; Kerckhoff et al., *Going Comprehensive*, 41–2; Benn and Chitty, *Thirty Years On*, 23–4nn8–9. This despite the fact that Solihull

had had the highest rate of grammar-school participation of any LEA in the 1960s. Boaden, *Urban Policy-Making*, 45–6.

51. Bridges, 'Relation Between Parents and Schools', 302–11; Bridges, 'Parents', 65–71; Deem et al., *Active Citizenship*, 32–3. All of these studies worried about the tendency to turn parents into mere consumers by offering them 'choice', but most parents had a neighbourhood school and most did not seek a choice, at least at this point.

52. See again the remarkable scorn for parents in CCCS, *Unpopular Education*, 202–7, construing them (in the words of Tory propaganda) as '*petit bourgeois*' and a 'parvenu elite' anxious to distance themselves from the working class, and again offering as an alternative only counter-school radicalism, and similar in Lowe, *Schooling and Social Change*, 68–9. On middle-class participation, see Bagnall et al., 'PTA and Middle-Class Narratives'; on parental involvement more generally, Reid et al., *A Matter of Choice*, a study of 5 outer London comprehensives in 1974, ch. 11. The 1974 sweep of the 1958 birth cohort found that 63% of the 16-year-olds' parents had access to a PTA and two-thirds had one or more meetings with teachers to discuss their children's progress: Fogelman (ed.), *Britain's 16-Year-Olds*, 42, 47.

53. On the effects of parental education, see OECD, *Post-Secondary Education*, 20; based on the 1958 cohort, Fogelman, 'Educational and Career Aspirations', 51; Burnhill et al., 'Social Change and Entry to Higher Education', 70–4, 79; on the 'sense of class well-being' of the 1970s and '80s resulting from continued upward mobility into non-manual occupations, see Payne and Roberts, 'Opening and Closing the Gates'; a DES report pointed out that nearly half of 18-year-olds in 1981 whose parents were then in Class II (the rapidly growing lower-managerial classes) had been born into lower classes at birth: DES, *Report on Education* 100 (1984). This important realization showed how useless it was to project future demand without allowing for occupational change.

54. Some of these uncertainties are discussed in Cebulla and Tomaszewski, 'The Demise of Certainty', esp. 141–3, 147, 154, and in Savage and Flemmen, 'The End of Linear Mobility', drawing on the 'jagged' life courses of the 1958 cohort.

55. Murtin and Viarengo, 'Compulsory Schooling', 508.

56. Gamoran, 'Scottish Secondary Education', 2–3. Access to O-grade was further facilitated by recognizing lower grades as passes from 1972. McPherson and Willms, 'Equalisation and Improvement', 515, 530.

57. Heath and Clifford, 'Class Inequalities and Educational Reform', 220–2. Wales, however, was now lagging behind England by this measure, as its industrial areas were performing poorly: Rees and Rees, 'Educational Inequality in Wales', 75–9.

58. See further Woodin et al., *Secondary Education and ROSLA*, 148–50, on growth of certification in the 1970s; and for Scotland McPherson and Willms, 'Equalisation and Improvement', showing improvements in attainment at 16 for the 1970–84 cohorts. Attainment levels at 16 in Wales were becoming more

problematic, probably as a result of social and economic stagnation: Rees and Delamont, 'Education in Wales', 240–3.

59. Gray et al., *Reconstructions of Secondary Education*, 7.

60. Britain had very low rates of enrolment at 16 in secondary education (35%, well below France, Germany and Italy for example) in the late 1970s in comparison to most leading OECD countries, but it had average rates of enrolment at 16 in all forms of education (61% or 80% including part-time, still below Germany but not far behind France and above Italy): OECD, *Access to Higher Education*, 79–80. This may have been because Britain had above average takeup of apprenticeships and other forms of technical education by European standards: Green et al., *Convergence and Divergence*, 181–7; Walker, *IEA Six Subject Survey*, 277.

61. Woods, 'Myth of Subject Choice'; Neave, 'Elite and Mass Higher Education', 353; Chitty, *Towards a New Education System*, 40–4. Critics who applied this diagnosis initially to Welsh schools—to explain the poor average performance at 16 but high staying-on rates—later argued that the underlying problem was a general 'underperformance' of schools. Rees and Delamont, 'Education in Wales', 241–2.

62. Ranson, 'Towards a Tertiary Tripartism', 222–4, 238–40.

63. Sanderson, *Educational Opportunity and Social Change*, 7, 122–3, 126; Aldcroft, *Education, Training and Economic Performance*, 31–3, 54, 61. However, both in Germany and in the UK, 16-year-olds who stayed on in vocational education had little chance of upward mobility into non-manual jobs: Heath and Cheung, 'Education and Occupation', 90–1, based on the 1958 cohort.

64. Shattock, 'Demography and Social Class', 390–1, almost immediately belied by the surge in participation later in the 1980s.

65. Pissarides, 'Staying-on at School', 357, and (for the comparison with the U.S.) 360; Pissarides, 'Demand for Post-Compulsory Education', 151, 154; Pissarides, 'From School to University', taking the longer view.

66. Pissarides, 'Staying-on at School', 357, 360, and (for girls) 358; Pissarides, 'Demand for Post-Compulsory Education', 154.

67. Lindley, 'Challenge of Market Imperatives', 149–52; Aldcroft, *Education, Training, and Economic Performance*, 7–8, 18, 26, 87, and esp. 161; but cf. Peston, 'Higher Education Policy', 127–8, defending consumption, and Kogan and Boys, 'Expectations of Higher Education', 53, showing both consumption and investment clearly weighing in students' minds in 1980.

68. See ch. 8.

69. Pissarides, 'Staying-on at School', 357 (but cf. 358, where the decline in the graduate premium for girls seemed to matter more); Pissarides, 'From School to University', 665.

70. Though, paradoxically, he did think they were influenced by graduate wage rates, albeit deeply discounted as lying farther in the future: Pissarides, 'Post-Compulsory Education', 151, 155.

71. Girls' staying-on rates rose throughout the decade, though only slowly 1975–8, whereas boys' rates were stable 1969–72 and dropped 1975–8: Pissarides,

'Staying-on at School', 346–7; and see the critique by Whitfield and Wilson, 'Staying-on in Full-Time Education', 395.

72. Contemporaries were aware that non-manual employment was overtaking manual employment in the 1980s: Shattock, 'Demography and Social Class', 390–1; 'Demand for Higher Education in Great Britain, 1984–2000', DES, *Report on Education* 100 (July 1984).

73. Clark et al., 'Post-Compulsory Education', 71–2, 76–82, 86; Whitfield and Wilson, 'Staying-on in Full-Time Education', 395, 400–1; see also McIntosh, 'Demand for Post-Compulsory Education', 70, 72, concluding that no policy interventions made any difference until the advent of GCSE in the late 1980s, for which see pp. 134–5, and McVicar and Rice, 'Participation in Further Education', 63, on the 'role model effects' of greater female participation.

74. A. Thompson for Policy Steering Group, 'Policy Planning for Non-Advanced Further Education', 30 May 1980: TNA, ED181/373/2; McIntosh, 'Demand for Post-Compulsory Education', 77–80; McVicar and Rice, 'Participation in Further Education', 47–8, 50; Gosling et al., 'Male Wages in the UK', 642; Benn and Chitty, *Thirty Years On*, 96–106; Pratt, *Polytechnic Experiment*, 28–33, 43–51; Sanderson, 'Education and the Labour Market', 284; Gosden, *Education System*, 185.

75. As concluded by Clark et al., 'Post-Compulsory Education', 75–7, 79–81, 86.

76. One additional obstacle might have been 'rationing' of high O-level grades, during a period in which O-levels may still have been 'norm-referenced', i.e. high grades limited to a fixed quota: see Stobart and Gipps, *Assessment*, 44–5, and pp. 134–5, on Keith Joseph's surprising opposition to norm-referencing.

77. Cf. Pissarides, 'From School to University', 656, 665; Machin and Vignoles, 'Education Policy', 1–2; Policy Group A, 'Higher Education into the 1990s', Annex B, Sep. 1978, suggesting that QLR had risen even in the 1970s from 13.2% 1969 to 15.5% 1977: TNA, ED181/497. Some of the differences may arise from the difference between measuring attainment of 5 'good' O-levels, usually seen as the qualifier for A-levels, and A-levels themselves, as there were now more ways of accessing A-levels than through O-levels.

78. Burnhill et al., 'Social Change and Entry to Higher Education', 70–1; Policy Group A, 'Higher Education into the 1990s', Annex B, Sep. 1978: TNA, ED181/497

79. Green et al., *Convergence and Divergence*, 89–90; Neave, 'Elite and Mass Higher Education', 353–4.

80. Observed for example in the 1958 cohort by Fogelman (ed.), *Growing Up*, 274.

81. Shattock, 'Demography and Social Class', 389.

82. Tight, *Development of Higher Education*, 74; Brennan, 'Access Courses', 54–60; Pratt, *Polytechnic Experiment*, 142–4.

83. See pp. 69–70; an influential survey in 1966 argued that married women graduates were 'captives by choice'—satisfied with their fate and protected by convention— but that even these married graduates' levels of dissatisfaction rose in mid-life. Kelsall et al., *Graduates*, 140–1, 158, 162 (the relevant chapter by Annette Kuhn).

84. Blackburn and Jarman, 'Changing Inequalities', 208–10; Egerton and Halsey, 'Trends by Social Class and Gender', 183; Dyhouse, *Students*, 97–9, 113–16; Pratt, *Polytechnic Experiment*, 56–62; Griffiths, 'Women in Higher Education'; Worth, 'Women, Education and Social Mobility'. This trend too was international: see e.g. Kett, *Pursuit of Knowledge*, 437, 447.

85. Robbins' 1980 target of 14% had already been met; the White Paper now aimed for 22%: *Framework for Expansion*, 1, 34–6. Carswell (who at the time was about to become Secretary to the UGC), *Government and the Universities*, 139–41, sees this as the high-water mark of Robbins-era expansion. In fact, a new cost-benefit element being built into the higher-education planning system in advance of the White Paper, as part of the 'policy analysis and review' (PAR) process, was already challenging the sanctity of the Robbins Principle: Morris, 'Investment in Higher Education', 72–4; J. M. Forsyth, 'Mr. Mayne's paper on education', 6 Aug. 1971, and 'Review of Government Strategy', 5 Oct. 1971: TNA, T227/3924.

86. Gosden, *Education System*, 48–9; Carswell, *Government and the Universities*, 141–3; Planning Unit for Policy Group A, 'Implications of the Moratorium for Places in Higher Education', 16 Nov. 1973; Statistics Branch, 'Possible Developments of Demand for Higher Education in the Light of Recent Trends', (Nov. 1973): TNA, ED181/273; Williams, 'Events of 1973–1974', 39–42.

87. The term was apparently coined by a 1977 report from the Central Policy Review Staff, 'Population and the Social Services': Shattock, *Making Policy*, 147–8. But the policy goal was already in evidence in 1974; see Planning Unit for Policy Group A, 'Higher Education Numbers to 1985 in Great Britain', 5 Sep. 1974: TNA, ED181/274.

88. Robbins' adjutant Richard Layard was partly responsible for recruiting the academic Gareth Williams to tackle this question: Gareth L. Williams to J. R. Jameson, 8 Jan. 1974: TNA, ED181/273. The results of Williams' study were published in 1975 as '16 and 19 Year Olds'.

89. Policy Group A, 'Higher Education Numbers to 1981 and Beyond', 8 Jan. 1974: TNA, ED181/273; see further on the 'pool of ability', Williams, 'Events of 1973–1974', 43, and Statistics Branch, 15 July 1977: TNA, ED 181/424; on eugenic speculations, Policy Group A, Minutes, 27 May 1977; Policy Group A, 'Higher Education into the 1990s', Sep. 1978: TNA, ED 181/424, ED 181/497. These latter speculations had been definitively dropped by the early 1980s, when staying on rates resumed their upward trend: NAB, 'Trends in Full-Time Higher Education', 26 Apr. 1983: TNA, T494/75; 'Demand for Higher Education in Great Britain, 1984–2000', DES, *Report on Education* 100 (July 1984); and see Royal Society, 'Demographic Trends and Future University Candidates: A Working Paper', 1983: TNA, T494/75. So it is not right really to pin them on Keith Joseph, as do Watson and Bowden, *New University Decade*, 11.

90. Crowther-Hunt and Forecast in *What Has Happened?*, 1, 4–10. Forecast had been very nervous before the conference about the effects of publicizing his reduced projections. Planning Unit for Policy Group A, Minutes, 18 Oct. 1974: TNA, ED181/321.

91. Williams and Gordon, '16 and 19 Year Olds', 31–6, but concluding that more research was needed. Note Crowther-Hunt's wise comment appended to this report that decisions by 16-year-olds (whether to stay on) and by 18-year-olds (whether to proceed to higher education) might follow quite different pathways: Williams and Gordon, '16 and 19 Year Olds', 36–7.

92. See discussion of Forecast's presentation by Eric Robinson, John Pratt, and John Randall among others in *What Has Happened?*, 11–27.

93. Hencke, *Colleges in Crisis*, esp. 50–72, 80–1, 99–100, 111–16.

94. 'Higher Education Numbers', 31 Apr. 1974; E. H. Simpson, 'Higher Education Numbers', 4 June 1974; E. H. Simpson, 'HFE Numbers and 1974 PESC', 2 Aug. 1974; Policy Group A, Minutes, 27 May, 15 July 1977; Policy Group A, 'Higher Education in the 1990s', Sep. 1978: TNA, ED181/274, 424, 497.

95. Whereas in 1972–4 'willingness' was mostly seen to be a matter of demand, by late 1974 successive reductions in the planning target had made the DES more sensitive to its role as supplier. Planning Unit, Policy Group A, 'Higher Education Numbers to 1985 in Great Britain', 5 Sep. 1974; Minutes, 18 Oct. 1974: TNA, ED181/274, 321. In reality, of course, QPR represented a compound of supply and demand—the demand for places at 18 amongst qualified leavers, and the number of places made available in higher education.

96. Council of Local Education Authorities, 'Planning of Higher Education Numbers in 1981', Dec. 1974: TNA, ED181/274; Williams and Gordon, '16 and 19 Year Olds'. This 5/6th-1/6th formula became orthodox and by 1977 no further research was deemed necessary into 'willingness', although there was interest in making use of the 1958 cohort. Policy Group A, Minutes, 15 July, 31 Oct. 1977: TNA, ED181/424.

97. See Crowther-Hunt's post mortem on the whole bruising experience in 'Policy Making and Accountability'. His range of concerns seems to me to have gone well beyond mere 'manpower planning', as has sometimes been alleged: e.g. Premfors, *Politics of Higher Education*, 110; David Lane in *Hansard*, 5th ser., 911 (1975–6), 1230–2.

98. *Government's Expenditure Plans* (1976–77), 70–1.

99. The stimulus was the need to chart a longer-term government course, which resulted in a paper, 'Higher Education into the 1990s', released in February 1978, and in public consultations thereafter.

100. Policy Group A, 'Higher Education into the 1990s', Sep. 1978: TNA, ED181/497.

101. Ibid., and especially Annexes B and E; A. Thompson, 'Responses to "Higher Education into the 1990s": A Future Policy for Higher Education', 9 Oct. 1978; Note, 'Responses to "Higher Education into the 1990s": A Future Policy for Higher Education', 20 Nov. 1978.

102. As APR showed no signs of budging, the DES was already backing off the targeted upticks in January 1979. Policy Group A, Minutes, 24 Jan. 1979: TNA, ED181/429.

103. DES estimated in 1978 that QPR (which they were calling opportunity/willingness rate at this point, including non-qualified participants, mostly women in teacher training with fewer than 2 A-levels) had dropped from 103.7% in

1969 to 94% in 1973 to 84% in 1977. Policy Group A, 'Higher Education into the 1990s', Sep. 1978, Annex B, Table 2: TNA, ED181/497. This rate for women fell from 110% to 80%, 1969–79, but only from 100% to 90% for men. DES, *Statistical Bulletin* 12/80 (Sep. 1980). Somewhat different figures for true QPR (excluding non-qualified leavers) but with a similar trend appear in DES, *Statistical Bulletin* 9/85 (July 1985).

104. In earlier work, I placed more emphasis on this factor; see Mandler, 'Educating the Nation II', 13–14. It still seems possible to me that alienation from higher education played a role in depressing QPR (more than staying on or QLR), though it must have been a waning force after the mid-1970s. It did not after all put off mature women, who might be thought to have been more rather than less allergic to 'student life'.

105. See the observations in Planning Unit, Policy Group A, Minutes, 11 June 1974: TNA, ED181/321; also the Oct. 1974 mission statement by the Committee of Directors of Polytechnics, *Many Arts, Many Skills*, 4–5, 16–17, 24; by 1978, the UGC had seemed to accept ceding share to the public sector. Policy Group A, 'Higher Education into the 1990s', Sep. 1978: TNA, ED181/497.

106. Shattock, *UGC and British Universities*, 11–14, 145.

107. Pratt, *Polytechnic Experiment*, 28–31. Some of this uneven growth came from the absorption of the teacher-training colleges, so did not represent overall growth in the HE sector, but some of it also came from growth in mature students who (as explained above) did not factor in any of the statistical measures, QLR, QPR or APR.

108. 'Academic drift' was first diagnosed in 1974 by the polytechnic pioneers John Pratt and Tyrrell Burgess (both at North East London Polytechnic) in *Polytechnics*; it was embraced both by polytechnic advocates and by manpower planners who wanted more 'social' (or government) control of higher education. See e.g. Burgess, 'Autonomous and Service Traditions', 70–3; Sanderson, 'Education and the Labour Market', 287–9; Neave, 'Elite and Mass Higher Education', 352.

109. On changing participation by class in this period, see Williams and Blackstone, *Response to Adversity*, 30; Pratt, *Polytechnic Experiment*, 77–9. Somewhat different results derive from analysis of the cohorts—between the 1946 and 1958 cohorts, the fastest growth in any tertiary participation is in the top two social classes, especially women, and white-collar women only: Makepeace et al., 'From School to the Labour Market', 42–3. This data is analysed further below, ch. 8.

110. For contemporary hand-wringing about the static working-class share, see e.g. Neave, 'Elite and Mass Higher Education', 356–7; for a claim, not so far as I can tell supported by the evidence cited, that working-class share was increasing in the 1970s (particularly unlikely in a period of no or slow growth), see Todd, *Golden Age of the Grammar School*, 6.

111. For rare acknowledgement of declining working-class share in the general population, see N. Scott in *Whatever Happened?*, 18, and Glennerster and Hills (eds), *State of Welfare*, 59.

112. This is the subject of ch. 9.

113. Women grew from 12% of all part-time students at polytechnics in 1970 to 40% in 1987; and from 16% of all full-time students in 1970 to 46% in 1991. Pratt, *Polytechnic Experiment*, 63–5.

114. For this more benign view of academic drift, see e.g. Scott, 'Has the Binary Policy Failed?', 182, 186–9; Scott, *Meanings of Mass Higher Education*, 56–9; Watson and Bowden, *New University Decade*, 20. For Pratt's revision of his earlier views, *Polytechnic Experiment*, 105–7.

115. Jacka et al., *Rape of Reason*, 24–7.

116. This compresses a highly complex negotiation, for which see Kogan with Kogan, *Attack on Higher Education*, chs 4, 7 (which however almost entirely ignores the public sector).

117. The immediate change of tone can be tracked in Policy Group A Minutes, e.g., 4 June, 18 July, 11 Oct., 7 Nov. 1979: TNA, ED181/429; see Sir James Hamilton's public defence of the Robbins Principle in Committee of Public Accounts, 1979–80, Minutes of Evidence, 7 May 1980, 13; but cf. DES assumptions in 1980 that government's cash limits required either 'driving down demand' or ignoring it. Statistics Branch, 'The Demand for and Supply of Places in GB Higher Education during the 1980s' (June 1980); A. Thompson to R. H. Bird, 20 June 1980; D. M. Forrester to J. R. Jameson, 2 July 1980; A. Thompson, 'Entry Prospects in Higher Education under Present and Possible Future Expenditure Plans', 2 July 1980: TNA, ED181/385.

118. Boyson had served as Parliamentary Under-Secretary to Joseph's predecessor Mark Carlisle since 1979, but he welcomed Joseph's appointment as 'a breath of fresh air': Denham and Garnett, *Keith Joseph*, 369.

119. Ibid., 368; Bird, 'Reflections on Government and Higher Education', 75–6; Kogan and Hanney, *Reforming Higher Education*, 72–3, 89; Kogan with Kogan, *Attack on Higher Education*, 33–4; Keith Joseph to Leon Brittan, 6 Dec. 1982: TNA, T494/74.

120. Cf. *Government's Expenditure Plans* (1980–1), 106, and (1981–2), 40.

121. See Joseph's presentation of the reformulation of Robbins to Parliament in *Hansard*, 6th ser., 65 (1983–4), 915, and also George Walden (964) and Peter Brooke (974) [26 Oct. 1984]. This interpretation was then embedded in the 1985 Green Paper, *Development of Higher Education*.

122. See the debates around the projections offered in DES, *Report on Education* 99 (Apr. 1983). One civil servant suggested that upwardly-mobile people were less devoted to education than traditional social elites and that ethnic minorities less devoted than the older white working class. I. A. S. Jones to E. Thoms, 12 May 1983: TNA, T494/75.

123. Kogan and Hanney, *Reforming Higher Education*, 73–4.

124. Ibid., 88–90.

125. M. Faulkner to Sir A. Rawlinson, 26 Nov. 1982; Keith Joseph to Leon Brittan, 6 Dec. 1982: TNA, T494/74.

126. NAB, 'Trends in Full-Time Higher Education in Great Britain', 26 Apr. 1983: TNA, T494/75; Note, 'Higher Education Demand to the Year 2000', 7 Mar. 1983: TNA, ED 261/206.

127. N. R. Sallnow-Smith to M. J. Faulkner, 19 Nov. 1982; M. J. Faulkner to J. A. Gilbey, 17 Oct. 1983: TNA, T494/74, 75. The same applied to mandatory awards for tuition until 1982, when the funding system was adjusted to put cash limits on tuition as well, but it proved impossible to do the same to maintenance grants which were funded through LEAs. University Grants Committee, *Annual Survey, Academic Year 1981–82*, Cmnd. 8965 (1983–4), 53–5.

128. Memorandum submitted by DES, 19 July 1982: Education, Science and Arts Committee, *Second Scrutiny Session*, HC 480 (1981–82), 3; J. R. Jameson, 'Expenditure on Higher Education into the 1990s', 18 Feb. 1983: TNA, ED261/206.

129. R. L. Smith, 'Public Expenditure on Higher Education to the Year 2000', 3 Mar. 1983: TNA, ED261/206; Draft Minute, Keith Joseph to Margaret Thatcher, 17 Mar. 1983: TNA, T494/60.

130. *Hansard*, 6th ser., 20 (1981–2), 188–9 [16 Mar. 1982]; ibid., 28 (1981–2), 1331–41 [29 July 1982].

131. 'Future Demand for Higher Education in Great Britain', DES, *Report on Education* 99 (Apr. 1983); cf. J. R. Jameson to E. H. Simpson, 21 Nov. 1973: TNA, ED 181/273.

132. DES, *Report on Education* 100 (July 1984), in part a response to criticism of the more pessimistic projections from the year before, from the Royal Society, the Royal Statistical Society, the universities and the teachers' unions; see also Burnhill *et al.*, 'Social Change and Entry to Higher Education', 68.

133. Cf. Silver, *Higher Education and Opinion Making*, 216, which argues in contrast for 'growing government ascendancy over policy, action and argument' in this period.

134. *The Development of Higher Education into the 1990s*, Cmnd. 9524 (1984–5), 3–5, 8, 10, 11, 39–42. This was based on the most pessimistic of the projections in DES, *Report on Education* 100 (July 1984), which had left this escape-hatch for Joseph and also conveniently reminded him that 'demand...adjusts to the characteristics of the system available and to the economic and social conditions at the time', giving him perhaps too much reason to over-value his own interventions.

135. Even among moderate commentators such as Shattock, *Making Policy*, 97; Stewart, *Higher Education*, 315; Kogan and Hanney, *Reforming Higher Education*, 74; see also the review of the press reception in Giles Radice's speech, *Hansard*, 6th ser., 80 (1984–5), 206–9 [4 June 1985].

136. Thatcher had initially been supportive, favouring loans as part of a CPRS review of higher education in 1982–3, but by March 1983 Joseph felt he had to retreat to a 'minimal scheme' only. M. J. C. Faulkner to Leon Brittan, 17 Mar. 1983; Keith Joseph to Geoffrey Howe, 21 Mar. 1983: TNA, T494/60, PREM19/1728, and see ED 261/206 for the CPRS review.

137. Denham and Garnett, *Keith Joseph*, 390–4; Hillman, 'From Grants for All', 256–7; Whyte, 'Student Funding', 69–70. This despite the fact that there had always been a degree of means-testing for grants, and for tuition as well until 1977.

138. Oliver Letwin to Margaret Thatcher, 23 May, 4 Oct. 1985; Mark Addison to Margaret Thatcher, 10 July 1985: TNA, PREM19/1728.

CHAPTER 7

1. Shattock, 'Demography and Social Class', 385–9, 390–1 (citing Pissarides' work); Stewart, *Higher Education*, 160.
2. Policy Group A, Minutes, 27 May 1977: TNA, ED 181/424; Policy Group A, 'Higher Education into the 1990s', Sep. 1978: TNA, ED 181/497; Kogan and Hanney, *Reforming Higher Education*, 49, Watson and Bowden, *Ends Without Means*, 2, and even HEPI, *Demand for Higher Education*, appear to take a parallel view, attributing rising participation rates in the 1980s to middle-class fertility rather than to changes in the occupational structure.
3. Lowe, *Schooling and Social Change*, 44; Scott, *Knowledge & Nation*, 159–60; McKenzie, *Changing Education*, 6. For an unusually prescient prediction of how the wheel would actually turn, see Perkin, 'University Planning', 119.
4. Wagner, 'National Policy', 155–6. This low-expectations model suffuses the many seminars and volumes sponsored by the Society for Research into Higher Education and funded by the Leverhulme Trust from May 1981; see e.g. Williams and Blackstone, *Response to Adversity*, 19–20; Fowler, 'Past Failure', 80–2; discussion of Crowther-Hunt, 'Policy Making and Accountability', 66–7; Taylor, 'Change Within a Contracting System', 101; and see Gareth Williams' prospectus for the series, 'The Main Policy Issues Facing Institutions of Higher Education in Britain in the 1980s and 1990s', Nov. 1980: TNA, ED181/373/2.
5. Minutes, Policy Steering Group, 18 June 1980; A. Thompson to R. Bird, 20 June 1980; A. Thompson to Mark Carlisle, 'Entry Prospects in Higher Education under Present and Possible Future Expenditure Plans', 2 July 1980; 'Population Trends and the Demand for Higher Education to the Year 1999–2000', 26 Aug. 1982: TNA, ED181/373/1; ED181/385; ED261/202.
6. This political narrative naturally does not come from left-wing educationists, who tend to skate over the expansion (or, for which see pp. 144–5, to emphasize its means—'cuts', markets—rather than its ends). But for some examples, see Willetts, *University Education*, 57; Shattock, *UGC and Management of British Universities*, 134–5; Shattock, *Making Policy*, 97, 148–9, 152; Sanderson, 'Higher Education in the Post-War Years', 427–8; Stevens, *University to Uni*, 57; and, of course, Baker, *Turbulent Years*, 233–42.
7. Contemporaries were better at estimating the effects of growing gender equality, but that trend had been evident for some time; Robbins proved quite prescient on that front. Interestingly, to judge by the frequency of the term in British books (as measured by the Google n-gram software), 'learning society' first came into mild vogue in the 1960s, went out of fashion in the 1970s, and then soared from 1988.
8. Scott, '1992–2002', 71–2; Kogan and Hanney, *Reforming Higher Education*, 73–4; King and Nash, 'Politics of Higher Education Expansion', 197–200; Garnett, *From Anger to Apathy*, 207–8. Scott knew, however, that 'absent-mindedness' only provided the starting gun for the racers (i.e. demand) to take off.
9. On this there is a huge literature, but Vinen, *Thatcher's Britain*, usefully emphasizes the often neglected anti-permissive current, and Jackson and Saunders (eds), *Making Thatcher's Britain*, does a good job of laying out Thatcherism's 'varieties'.

10. Education plays little role in ibid., but see Dale, 'Thatcherism and Education', and for a similar neo-conservative/neo-liberal divergence in schools policy, Whitty, 'New Right and the National Curriculum'.

11. In addition to the sources cited below, I am very grateful for interviews and emails with politicians—Lord (Kenneth) Baker, Robert Jackson—and civil servants—Peter Syme, Michael Jubb, Bahram Bekhradnia—for sharing their experiences of the shift in policy in the late 1980s and early 1990s.

12. *Croham Report*, 10–11, 15, 18, 30. At this point (Feb. 1987) government was only modestly more optimistic about the prospects for future growth. On the impact of Croham and the advent of the new funding regime, see further Shattock, *UGC and Management of British Universities*, 138–41; Zellick, 'Universities and the Law', 7–8; Kogan and Hanney, *Reforming Higher Education*, 153–8, 167–8, 170; Scott, *Knowledge & Nation*, 114–18; Williams, 'Market Route', 282–8. Initially the university and the public sectors had different funding councils, with the latter supposed to be much more directive (and industrial), but they were soon merged and became much more cost-focused, in part at Treasury insistence.

13. *Meeting the Challenge*, iv, 5–6.

14. Interview with Lord (Kenneth) Baker, 30 Oct. 2014.

15. *Meeting the Challenge*, iv, 9.

16. Note of a meeting between Baker and Thatcher, 18 Sep. 1986: TNA, PREM19/1724. At this meeting Baker mooted a target of 20% APR by 2000, even higher than the White Paper's most positive projection. See also Baker's speech to the CVCP, 23 Sep. 1986: TNA, PREM19/1725.

17. See further discussion of Baker's policy on schools, pp. 144–5. Baker's proudest achievement was not in fact his market reforms but his establishment of a network of city technology colleges, to which he has continued to bend his efforts in retirement.

18. Brown with Coldstream, *A Successful Partnership*, 2, 5; for an example of CIHE's divided loyalties, see Smithers and Robinson, *Trends in Higher Education*, 3, 15, both a celebration of ever-expanding demand and a conventional re-assertion of 'actual employer needs'.

19. Brown with Coldstream, *A Successful Partnership*, 6.

20. Note that in 1978 the CBI was still taking the view that Robbins had gone too far on participation. Policy Group A, 'Higher Education into the 1990s', Annex A, Sep. 1978: TNA, ED 181/497. The term 'knowledge economy' was put into play in the late 1960s by the American commentator Peter Drucker, correctly foreseeing a transition away from an economy of goods: Drucker, *Age of Discontinuity*, 247, 250.

21. Kogan and Hanney, *Reforming Higher Education*, 61–4, 76–8.

22. BBC News, 'Conservative MP Defects to Labour', 15 Jan. 2005: http://news.bbc.co.uk/1/hi/uk_politics/4178309.stm. For a good statement of Jackson's views on market forces in higher education, see Jackson to Kenneth Baker, 10 Mar. 1989: TNA, PREM19/2643.

23. Benn and Fieldhouse, 'Government Policies on Expansion', 307–8, and see Jackson's contributions to the Ministerial Priorities Review in 1987: TNA, ED181/529. In contrast, Jackson's predecessor in the portfolio, George Walden, had been only a reluctant advocate of expansion and came to believe that 'more is worse': Walden, *Lucky George*, 270, 285–6.

24. *Government's Expenditure Plans* (1988–9), 13; Education, Science and Arts Committee, *Higher Education*, Minutes, 14 Dec. 1988, 7. As Baker revealed in May 1989, APR had already hit 15.1 % that year. *Hansard*, 6th ser., 152 (1988–9), 3 [2 May 1989].

25. See the extracts published in *THES*, 13 Jan. 1989, 7, and the partial text of the speech on the HEPI website, https://www.hepi.ac.uk/2016/09/01/last-time-conservative-government-set-higher-education-targets/.

26. *THES*, 13 Jan. 1989, 6–7, 29 Dec. 1989, 6. See also the contributors to Fulton (ed.), *Access and Institutional Change*, who acknowledged the commitment to widening participation in the 1987 White Paper but still doubted that government would be able to find the money or the bodies to meet Baker's Lancaster projections, and to Schuller (ed.), *Future of Higher Education*, still apart from Andrew McPherson gloomy or uncertain about the potential demand, in 1991.

27. *New Framework*, 2, 8–11, 41.

28. The popular but rather bizarre 'explanation' emphasizing differential birth rates between social classes (rather than the much more direct and obvious shift in the balance between social classes) is still evident as late as HEPI, *Demand for Higher Education* (2006).

29. Dilnot and Emmerson, 'Economic Environment', 332.

30. The claim was repeated in *New Framework*, 10.

31. Swinnerton-Dyer, 'Policy on Higher Education', 213–14.

32. Williams, 'Market Route', 282–5; and see Brown, *Everything for Sale?*, 76–80, on the mechanisms by which rapid growth was facilitated, especially recruitment of 'fees only' students who now carried fees substantially higher than their marginal cost.

33. Hillman, 'From Grants for All', 258; for Jackson's work on tuition fees, linked to the legislation for the maintenance loans, see TNA, ED261/240; and see his unusual appeal in Robert Jackson to John Major, 12 Apr. 1991: TNA, PREM19/3295.

34. This was MASN—Maximum Aggregate Student Numbers. Watson and Bowden, *New University Decade*, 33; Williams, 'Market Route', 285; Kogan and Hanney, *Reforming Higher Education*, 91–3; and see the longer-term perspective on 'student number controls' in general by Mike Ratcliffe in his blog, https://moremeansbetter.wordpress.com/2017/10/08/whats-wrong-with-a-student-number-cap/, 8 Oct. 2017.

35. Kogan and Hanney, *Reforming Higher Education*, 46, 49.

36. See nn. 6, 8, for some politically-focused explanations; the only work solely devoted to explaining growth is almost entirely about Conservative policy: Watson and Bowden, 'Why Did They Do It?'.

37. C. H. K. Williams, 'Higher Education: Demand to 2000', 17 Jan. 1983: TNA, CAB184/713.

38. I. A. S. Jones to E. Thoms, 12 May 1983: TNA, T494/75; Bennett et al., 'Investing in Skill', 137–8; Gambetta, *Were They Pushed?*, 132–4.

39. Glennerster, 'Education', 46; Blanden et al., *Intergenerational Mobility*, 10–12; Paterson, *Scottish Education*, 145.

40. David (ed.), *Widening Participation*, 33–4; Tight, *Development of Higher Education*, 110; Pratt, *Polytechnic Experiment*, 78–85. For government plans to use BTEC and Access to expand higher education, see TNA, ED192/223, which interestingly began as a file on special efforts to attract ethnic minorities.

41. Ertl et al., 'Learners' Transition', 78; Brennan, 'Access Courses'.

42. OU courses were not disproportionately female or disadvantaged, but they were disproportionately mature: Woodley, 'Wider and Still Wider', 52–6, 60–1.

43. Weedon, 'Widening Access in Sweden'; Paterson, *Scottish Education*, 166–7. Though behind the curve, other European countries were also moving in the direction of converting vocational qualifications to 'general' qualifications that gave access to higher education: Green et al., *Convergence and Divergence*, 157–9, 161, 163–4.

44. Ertl et al., 'Learners' Transition', 78; Paterson, *Scottish Education*, 166, 168. A growing number of entrants also now held both vocational and academic qualifications, especially as both were available at FE colleges and also increasingly in schools.

45. Sandra Ashman's paper for a seminar on widening participation organized by the Dearing Inquiry, 27 Mar. 1997: TNA, ED266/11; Pratt, *Polytechnic Experiment*, 84–5.

46. Pratt, *Polytechnic Experiment*, 56–65; Brian Ramsden's paper at the Dearing seminar, 27 Mar. 1997: TNA, ED266/11; Dyhouse, *Students*, 99; David Robertson and Josh Hillman, 'Widening Participation in Higher Education for Students from Lower Socio-Economic Groups', May 1997, 7: TNA, ED266/11.

47. Callaghan, *Conservative Party Education Policies*, esp. 56–9.

48. Keith Joseph to Margaret Thatcher, 17 May 1984, 6 Mar. 1986; Kenneth Baker to Margaret Thatcher, 2 June 1986: TNA, PREM19/1214, 1722, 1724.

49. Arnott, 'Thatcher and Educational Reform in Scotland', 185–6; Gamoran, 'Scottish Secondary Education', 3–5, 14; Burnhill et al., 'School Attainment and Higher Education'.

50. McVicar and Rice, 'Participation in Further Education', 49–50, 56–7, 61; McIntosh, 'Demand for Post-Compulsory Education', 72, 80, 85.

51. For an illustration of this integration in one discipline, see Cannadine et al., *Right Kind of History*, 185–93.

52. HEPI, *Demand for Higher Education*; McVicar and Rice, 'Participation in Further Education', 63.

53. Gamoran, 'Scottish Secondary Education', 16–18; Blanden et al., 'Educational Inequality', 110–11, but cf. Blanden et al., 'Intergenerational Mobility', 13.

54. Cited in this context by Mayhew et al., 'Move to Mass Higher Education', 70. The politics- and policy-centred explanations tend to assume (without always being explicit about this) that supply created its own demand.

55. That is, distinct from the politics- and policy-centred explanations in nn. 6 and 8; for demand-centred explanations that specify more-or-less rational investment decisions, see e.g. Marginson, 'Anglo-American University', 68 (though blurring credentialist and investment explanations), Aldcroft, *Education, Training and Economic Performance*, 86–7 (concerned that it's not all that rational), Glennerster, 'Education', 47 (while admitting the difficulty of disentangling multiple causes), and the economists' arguments in nn. 56, 57, 59.

56. SBTC originated in a body of work after 2000 by the American economists David Autor, Claudia Goldin and Lawrence Katz. See Hacker and Pierson, *Winner-Take-All Politics*, 34–40, for an exegesis and a critique, and Berman et al., 'Implications of Skill-Biased Technological Change', for international comparisons.

57. Walker and Zhu, 'College Wage Premium', 700–2; Harkness and Machin, 'Graduate Earnings'; Machin and Vignoles, 'Education Policy', 16–17; Blundell, 'UK Wage Premium Puzzle', 4–5, 8–9, 11, 29, 32–4; and for international comparisons, Harmon et al. (eds), *Education and Earnings*, 8–9.

58. Gambetta, *Were They Pushed?*, for the earlier period; Tholen, *Graduate Work* and *Graduate Labour Market*, for the more recent period.

59. Machin and Vignoles (eds), *What's the Good?*, 3–4; Mayhew et al., 'Move to Mass Higher Education', 70–4; Bennett et al., 'Investing in Skill', 140–1; Dearden et al., 'Impact of Higher Education Finance', 3–5, 24; Walker and Zhu, 'Impact of University Degrees', 5–6, 60; Belfield et al., 'Relative Labour Market Returns', 11–12; Blundell et al., 'Returns to Higher Education', F83 (simply abandoning attempt to assess social returns); and see Willetts, *University Education*, 131, 135–7, for one policymaker's endorsement. Cf. Whitfield and Wilson, 'Staying On', which puts rate of return alongside other factors including consumption and occupational structure.

60. See Marginson, *Education and Public Policy*, 45–51, on this turn in economics and policy-making.

61. See p. 229 n. 9.

62. Blundell, 'UK Wage Premium Puzzle'; see also Salvatori, 'Job Polarisation in the UK', 13–18; Bynner et al., 'Benefits of Higher Education', 57–8; Willetts, 'Robbins Revisited', 18–19, 22–3.

63. Wolf, *Does Education Matter?*, 27; *Wolf Report*, 31.

64. McIntosh, 'Demand for Post-Compulsory Education', 81, 85. McIntosh found that in all four of these countries prior attainment was the most important factor, so that the supply of qualified leavers (in England and Wales, thanks to GCSE) rather than labour-market considerations really prevails.

65. Harmon et al. (eds), *Education and Earnings*, 8–9; Harkness and Machin, 'Graduate Earnings'; Teichler and Bürger, 'Student Enrolments and Graduation Trends', 169.

66. Liu and Grusky, 'Payoff to Skill', 1336, 1359–60, 1368–9; McIntosh and Morris, 'Labour Market Returns', 25–6; *Wolf Report*, 35–6; Tholen, *Graduate Labour Market*, 54–5.

67. Salvatori, 'Job Polarisation in the UK', 2–4.

68. See pp. 192–3, and for the way in which screening moves upward from 16 to 18 to 21, Wolf, *Does Education Matter?*, 29–30, 196–7, and cf. 262–3n33.

69. Pratt, *Polytechnic Experiment*, 111–13; Tholen, *Graduate Labour Market*, 32–4; Tholen, *Graduate Work*, 73–5; Green et al., *Convergence and Divergence*, 163–8.

70. Jackson et al., 'Education, Employers and Class Mobility', 13; Goldthorpe, 'Role of Education', 272–5.

71. Tholen, *Graduate Work*, 61, 67–70; Liu and Grusky, 'Payoff to Skill', 1336–40, 1367.

72. Liu and Grusky, 'Payoff to Skill', 1337, 1351–4; Goldthorpe, 'Role of Education', 275–9; and for an unusual recognition of screening for this purpose, by an economist, in a government report, *Wolf Report*, 30, 33. Blaug, 'Economics of Education', 18–26, made many of the same points in 1985, but the intellectual tide was then turning against him.

73. Kogan and Boys, *Expectations of Higher Education*, 13–26; Tholen, *Graduate Work*, 61, 67–8, 71, 73–5; Jackson et al., 'Education and Class Mobility', 19–27; Institute of Student Employers, *Annual Survey 2018*, 31. These studies are all based on scrutiny of employers' actual selection processes. UK employers appear to screen in this way more than employers in other countries; see Simon Baker, 'University Reputation "Less Important" for Recruiters', *THES*, 21 Nov. 2019, 22–3.

74. For the argument against screening, see e.g. Chevalier and Walker, 'United Kingdom', 315–6, though cf. the less certain Chevalier et al., 'Does Education Raise Productivity?', F506–10; for a policymaker's argument against screening, Willetts, *University Education*, 144–6.

75. Holmes and Mayhew, *Changing Shape of the UK Job Market*; see also Gosling et al., 'Changing Distribution of Male Wages', 661; Green and Zhu, 'Overqualification and Increasing Dispersion', 744–5; Tholen, *Graduate Labour Market*, 46–54, 62–4; and cf. Lindley and McIntosh, 'Growth in Within Wage Inequality'.

76. Dolton and Vignoles, 'Overeducation', gives an unusually thoughtful account of these possibilities; and see also Connor, 'Different Graduates', in the same volume.

77. Sociologists are, predictably, sceptical about economic growth as the motor for educational expansion—see e.g. Meyer et al., 'World Expansion of Mass Education', 130, Schofer and Meyer, 'Worldwide Expansion', 900—but even economists go back and forth about the connection—see Cohen and Soto, 'Growth and Human Capital', 51–2.

78. Goldthorpe, 'Role of Education', 270–1. Cf. Gareth Williams, 'Events of 1973–1974', 54–5: 'It is not of course being claimed that they *do* estimate rates of return, merely that a statistical estimate of rates of return is quite a good summary of many of the factors . . . that make higher education seem worthwhile to young people deciding what they are going to do with their lives.'

79. Gambetta, *Were They Pushed?*, 32.
80. At last as evidenced in the Google n-gram for British books, which shows the two phrases taking off at the same time but with 'learning society' about twice as prevalent by 2000. The term got its widest currency in the 1997 Dearing Report, *Higher Education in the Learning Society*, esp. 9–12, which however used it as a virtual synonym for 'knowledge economy'.
81. But see Glennerster and Hills (eds), *State of Welfare*, 35–67. Historians of education prefer to see this period as one of decline or even the 'death' of state education, for which see p. 143.
82. Taylor-Gooby, *Social Change*, 113–14; King (ed.), *British Political Opinion*, 76–9, 262–73; Wragg and Jarvis, 'Perceptions of Education', 110–13, 118, 123–4, 126; Purcell and Pitcher, *Great Expectations*, 39; Mountford-Zimdars et al., 'Framing Higher Education', 809–10.
83. Butler and Kavanagh, *General Election of 1992*, 126; Butler and Kavanagh, *General Election of 1997*, 110–11, 220; and see also Kavanagh and Butler, *General Election of 2005*, 176.
84. McCulloch, *Failing the Ordinary Child?*, 152–7; Callaghan, *Conservative Education Policies*, 169–70; Crook et al., *Grammar School Question*, 16–18; Exley and Ball, 'Conservative Education Policy', 98–9.
85. Blair's leader's speech at the Labour party conference in 1996, full text available at http://www.britishpoliticalspeech.org/speech-archive.htm?speech=202.
86. As we have seen in previous chapters, this drift to office-work applied also to the industrial sector; what was unusual about Britain, as David Edgerton has pointed out recently, was its heavy reliance on the industrial sector for so long and its sudden and late collapse: *Rise and Fall*, 484.
87. Sanderson, 'Education and the Labour Market', 284; Wolf, *Does Education Matter?*, 58–9, 87–9, 145–7.
88. Apprenticeships reached their nadir in the 1990s, since when they have been redesigned around a wider variety of service-sector jobs (law, business, health and social services), taken up mostly by women, and have benefited both from the requirement for 17 and 18 year olds who have left school to remain in training as well as from the growing tendency to combine vocational and academic qualifications: see Machin and Vignoles, 'Education Policy', 10–14; Mirza-Davies, *Apprenticeships Policy*; Powell, *Apprenticeship Statistics*.
89. Wragg and Jarvis, 'Perceptions of Education', 121, 128; Wolf, *Does Education Matter?*, 82–6; *Wolf Report*, 51; Willetts, *University Education*, 247–8. As noted by Green et al., *Convergence and Divergence*, 157–61, this trend was spreading across Europe, including the German-speaking nations where vocational tracks had seemed most firmly entrenched. When acquired later in life, academic qualifications are still more valuable in the labour market than vocational qualifications, as shown by Bukodi and Goldthorpe, *Social Mobility*, 171–80.
90. As noted as early as 2011 by *Wolf Report*, 25–8.
91. The transition was smoothed by including training as an alternative to schooling.

92. Although observable in popular culture, not yet an object much of close study; though note Sutcliffe-Braithwaite, *Class and the Decline of Deference*, 128.

93. Wolf, *Does Education Matter?*, 167, 242–3; Willetts, *University Education*, 5.

94. Trow, 'Problems in the Transition', 90, though cf. 63–4 where Trow also gives a conventional technocratic explanation for this transition; Green et al., *Convergence and Divergence*, 37–9, giving a wider menu of explanations.

95. McVicar and Rice, 'Participation in Further Education', 53; *Wolf Report*, 28.

96. 'Millennium mothers want university education for their children', 20 Oct. 2010: https://cls.ucl.ac.uk/millennium-mothers-want-university-education-for-their-children/; Mountford-Zimdars et al., 'Framing Higher Education', 800–3, though see also comments on how recent surveys have tended to be pitched to elicit emphasis on private benefit, 799–801, 808–10; Huchet-Bodet et al., *Attitudes to Education*, 14.

97. Purcell and Pitcher, *Great Expectations*, 11; and see similar results in a parallel survey 10 years later, with surprisingly little variation by social class, Purcell et al., *Applying for Higher Education*, 35, 39, 60–2, 99, 108–9, 111, and Purcell et al., *Transitions into Employment*, 133–4.

98. Dolton and Vignoles, 'Over-Education', 118–20; and see Manski, 'Measuring Expectations', 1331, on economists' growing awareness under the influence of behavioural economics that 'observed choice behaviour may be consistent with many alternative specifications of preferences and expectations'.

99. Franklin and McCulloch (eds), *Death of the Comprehensive?*; Gewirtz et al., *Markets, Choice and Equity*, 187–9; Ball, *Education Debate*, 85–7, 95–6; Reay, *Miseducation*, 42, 176–8; Chitty, *Towards a New Education System*, 178, 197, 220; Jones, *Education in Britain*, 130–7; Pring, *Life and Death of Secondary Education*, 156–7, 187–90. For a more balanced assessment, see Whitty, 'Twenty Years of Progress?'; from the right, Wooldridge, *Meritocracy*, 7–9, 34–5, 41–4, characterized Thatcher's educational policy as in practice overly democratic, and called in the 1990s for a shift back to meritocracy.

100. McKenzie, *Changing Education*, 4–6.

101. Green, *Education and State Formation*, vii-viii, much cited, e.g. by McCulloch, *Educational Reconstruction*, 14–15, 21, 169, Reay and Ball, '"Spoilt for Choice"', 93, Lloyd and Payne, 'Political Economy of Skill', 95–6, Reay, *Miseducation*, 30; and see Lowe, *Schooling and Social Change*, 147–53.

102. Educationist critics complained that this national system was the wrong kind—GCSE not really as common an exam as it might be, the national curriculum not a 'professional' but a 'bureaucratic' one. Chitty, *Towards a New Education System*, 106, 161–3; Nuttall, 'Doomsday or a New Dawn?', 173–5; Simon, *Education and the Social Order*, 458, 450, 485, 504–10, and cf. 483–4; Pring, *Life and Death*, 155–6, 189–90; and cf. Chitty, *New Labour and Secondary Education*, 131–4, criticizing the erosion of a national curriculum he hadn't liked in the first place. Whitty, 'New Right and the National Curriculum', 339, unfashionably defends the national curriculum as 'the one remaining symbol of a common education system and specifiable entitlement'.

103. Tomlinson, 'The Schools', 186–7; Ball, *Education Debate*, 75–83; Pring, 'Liberal Education', 59; Salter and Tapper, 'Politics of the Ratchet', 67–9; Green, *Education and State Formation*, 315.

104. 'Responsibility' could have both disciplinary and liberating aspects: cf. Oliver Letwin to Margaret Thatcher, 23 Apr. 1985, 21 Feb. 1986, Kenneth Baker to Bishop of London, 2 Nov. 1987: TNA, PREM19/1470, 1722, 2123; *Choice and Diversity*, the 1992 White Paper, 1–5; Wooldridge, *Meritocracy*, 7–9, 34–7, 43–4.

105. Cf. Whitty, 'Twenty Years of Progress', 170–1, arguing that such competition always has losers as well as winners, apparently denying that the result could be higher standards for all.

106. McCulloch, *Educational Reconstruction*, 169; Chitty, *Towards a New Education System*, 178, 197, 220.

107. For example, in pioneering mixed-sex comprehensives, 'progressive education' (though courting trouble as in the Tyndale affair), multicultural education, social studies and Access courses; it was also a pioneer in local management of schools.

108. Glennerster and Hills (eds), *State of Welfare*, 31–2; Chitty, *Towards a New Education System*, 142; Crook, 'What Happened to the Comprehensive School?', 155–6; Gorard et al., 'School Choice', 368–70; Echols et al., 'Parental Choice in Scotland', 208–9; Limond, 'Locality, Education and Authority in Scotland', 366.

109. Chitty, *Towards a New Education System*, 157–8; Bridges, 'Parents', 65–6. On LEA resistance to parental choice, see J. A. Hudson, 'Choice of School', 17 Feb. 1976: TNA, ED207/119.

110. Jones, *Education in Britain*, 138, arguing against the influence of parents 'as individuals, rather than as a group of voters'; Pring, *Life and Death*, 155, praising 'responsiveness to local opinion' but only through LEAs; Lowe, *Schooling and Social Change*, 140–5, 160; Whitty et al., *Devolution and Choice*, 94–101, and Deem et al., *Active Citizenship*, esp. 37–41, 168–70, struggling with alternatives; but cf. Lawton, *Education and Labour Party Ideologies*, 102–3, and a rare defence of choice (as incompatible with selection) from the left, Wright, *Progress in Education*, 84–5, 190–1, 199–200.

111. Sharp, 'Surviving Not Thriving', 204, 206.

112. Whitty et al., *Devolution and Choice*, 100; Halsey and Lievesley, 'Reactions to Reform', 99–100; Deem et al., *Active Citizenship*, 7, 43 72, 87, 156–7. Even in Scotland, where local-authority responsibility remains intact, the Scottish Parliament legislated in 2006 to ensure parental representation at school level.

113. Black et al., *Reassessing 1970s Britain*, 2, 14–15, 17.

114. Ranson, 'Towards a Tertiary Tripartism', claiming that tripartism had simply been moved forward to the 16–19 age group; Lowe, 'Secondary Education', 14–16; McCulloch, *Failing the Ordinary Child?*, 158–9.

115. Chitty, *Towards a New Education System*, 222; Chitty, *New Labour and Secondary Education*, 54; Benn and Chitty, *Thirty Years On*, 54–6; Lawton, *Education and Labour Party Ideologies*, 137–9; Wooldridge, 'Education', 176–8.

116. Morris and Griggs, 'Thirteen Wasted Years', 23. To Baker's horror, Thatcher herself did raise the possibility of fee-paying for opted-out schools, but as with tuition fees for higher education this 'gaffe' was widely seen as electoral poison at the time: see David Norgrove to Rob Smith, 25 Sep. 1986: TNA, PREM 19/1724; Baker, *Turbulent Years*, 182, 194–5.

117. As pointed out by Chitty, *New Labour and Secondary Education*, 58–9, though he calls this 'selection by specialization'; and see Knight, *Making of Tory Education Policy*, 157–62, on what he calls 'the new selection'.

118. Wooldridge, 'Education', 176–8. I myself have heard investors ask a Conservative Education Secretary when they would be free to buy schools (though the minister deflected the question).

119. Edwards and Whitty, 'Specialisation and Selection', 12; Coldron et al., 'Selection by Attainment', 257.

120. Conversely, there was one referendum held under the terms of the 1998 School Standards and Framework Act to end selection in Ripon in March 2000, which failed. Chitty, *New Labour and Secondary Education*, 90–2.

121. Uneasily granted by Whitty and Wisby, 'Education in England', 318–21; see further pp. 204–5.

122. Benn and Chitty, *Thirty Years On*, 52–3; Tomlinson, 'The Schools', 191, 194–5; Whitty, 'Twenty Years of Progress', 170–1, 179; Ball, *Education Debate*, 93; Reay, *Miseducation*, 46–9, 189–91; Whitty et al., *Devolution and Choice*, 112–22.

123. Gewirtz et al., *Markets, Choice and Equity*, esp. 22–52, based on 137 parent interviews in London LEAs between 1991 and 1994, was the pioneer; Reay and Ball, '"Spoilt for Choice"', uses a working-class subset of the same interviews; see also Reay, *Class Work*, on two schools in 1993–4, Reay et al., *Degrees of Choice*, on 6 schools in 1998–2000, and Reay et al., *White Middle-Class Identities*, on 125 middle-class families in London comprehensives.

124. Reay, *Miseducation*, 7, says the working class are still a majority because 60% self-identify as working class, and cf. 49, granting that there is 'little evidence either way in relation to segregation'; Thompson, 'Social Class and Participation', 38, acknowledges the growth of the middle class alongside growing middle-class participation but calls this only 'apparent egalitarianism'. Manual occupations in reality had shrunk from 2/3 of the total in 1951 to 1/3 in 1991, fewer among the younger workers who were parents in the 1990s. Halsey, 'Social Change', 16.

125. Allen, 'Allocating Pupils', 753, 758–62; and for Scotland, Paterson, 'Secondary Education', 148, Echols et al., 'Parental Choice in Scotland', 212, Arnott, 'Thatcher and Educational Reform in Scotland', 199–200; for Wales, Rees and Delamont, 'Education in Wales', 238, Jones, 'Education in Wales', 103–4, Power, 'Misrecognition of Wales', 286–90.

126. Gorard, 'School Intake Characteristics and Segregation', 136, 138–40; Gorard et al., 'School Choice', 380–1; cf. Walford, 'School Choice', 79–81, and Allen and Vignoles, 'School Segregation', 664, for critiques of these measures, but in the latter case agreement that there was no substantial increase in segregation after 1988.

127. Allen et al., 'Changes in School Admissions', 351–3, 357.

128. Burgess et al., 'School Choice in England', 7–8, 10, 12.

129. A full discussion of the 'attainment gap' in this period can be found in Chapter 9.

130. Atkinson, *Inequality*, 72–3, 104–7; and see the range of measures in Fig. 3, https://www.ons.gov.uk/peoplepopulationandcommunity/personaland-householdfinances/incomeandwealth/bulletins/householdincomeinequality-financial/yearending2018.

131. Burgess et al., 'School Choice in England', 4.

132. Wragg and Jarvis, 'Perceptions of Education', 122; Exley, 'Parental Freedom to Choose'; and for international comparisons, Plank and Sykes, 'Why School Choice?', x–xii.

133. Or a single funding council for each nation, as England, Wales, Scotland and Northern Ireland each got their own higher-education funding council.

134. Dearing patterned himself after Robbins, but his ambitions were in reality much narrower: *Dearing Report*, 13–15, 51, and cf. verdicts in Wolf, *Does Education Matter?*, 254–5; King and Nash, 'Politics of Higher Education Expansion', 203–5; Mountford-Zimdars et al., 'Framing Higher Education', 795; Hillman, 'From Grants for All', 259.

135. Dearing, 'Dearing on Dearing', 69–70; Dearing's afterword to Watson and Amoah (eds), *Dearing Report*, 175–6, 179. On the progress of fees, see Shattock, *Making Policy*, 162–6; Hubble and Bolton, 'Higher Education Tuition Fees'. And note Dearing's tendency to define 'demand' as demand *for* students *from* employers, rather than demand *from* students: *Dearing Report*, 87–96, cf. 96–7, 100.

136. Willetts, *University Education*, 65–6; Shattock, 'Public Expenditure and Tuition Fees', 27–9; Scott, 'Coalition Government', 33, 36–7.

137. It is hard to make direct comparisons because we can't know in advance how much British debtors will end up paying off under a relatively new and still highly volatile scheme, but one study showed that the nominal debt was higher even than in the U.S.: Kirby, *Degrees of Debt*.

138. David Willetts, 'You Are What You Earn?', *THES*, 11 Apr. 2019, 38–9. The data project is called Longitudinal Educational Outcomes (LEO). A Green Paper in 2015 also proposed to link variable fees to institutions' graduate premia through the misleadingly-named Teaching Excellence Framework (TEF), although this proposal was later suspended; a 'subject-level' TEF is still in preparation which would also allegedly measure 'teaching excellence' in part in terms of subject premia.

139. Willetts, *University Education*, 70, 78–9, 83–5, 249–52; Hillman, 'From Grants for All', 265; and see the critique in Williams, 'Economic Critique of Marketization', esp. 66–70.

140. Scott, 'Coalition Government', 38; Willetts, the architect of LEO, says in *University Education*, 83–5, that he nevertheless now hopes that students will *not* make decisions on this basis; and cf. ibid., 123–6, 139–41, sensibly setting out non-economic benefits, with 127–38, 147–9, economic benefits getting the much greater share of his interest.

141. Since choice was not new in higher education, there has been less written on its effects here than on schooling, though some of the same assumptions about the effects of choice on stratification have been applied: see e.g. Crozier et al., 'Working-Class Students'; Brown, *Everything for Sale?*, 135–8; Callender and Dougherty, 'Student Choice', 9–11, 18–19, balancing up reductions of part-time enrolments with rises in full-time and some narrowing of participation gaps; on narrowing of the participation gap, see Lupton et al., 'Education: New Labour's Top Priority', 87–8; Heath et al., 'Education under New Labour', 239–40; Whitty and Anders, 'How Did New Labour?', 35.

142. As rightly argued by Willetts, *University Education*, 71–2. Cf. Callender and Dougherty, 'Student Choice', 9–10, focusing on declines in part-time and (inevitably, given high leaver participation rates) mature entrants.

143. Widespread belief in non-pecuniary benefits of higher education was revealed in the single piece of opinion research commissioned by Browne, but not released until a Freedom of Information request in 2011. McGettigan, *Great University Gamble*, 21, 24.

144. *Patterns and Trends 2018*, 9. The new fee regime may however have affected not the decision whether to participate but the decision about what subjects to study, for which see the next chapter.

145. Willetts' interview with Timmins, *Five Giants*, ch. 24; Willetts, *University Education*, 66–8, 87, 149, 156, 177–8 (where tables 7.1 and 7.2 do not support the argument that students were previously being 'turned away' before the lifting of controls released 'pent-up demand'); David Willetts, 'You Are What You Earn?', *THES*, 11 Apr. 2019, 41; Hillman, 'Coalition's Higher Education Reforms', 338–41, again without evidence that lifting controls led to 'an improvement in social mobility'.

146. Willetts, *University Education*, 131.

147. See Mike Ratcliffe's defence of student-number controls in his blog, https://moremeansbetter.wordpress.com/2017/10/08/whats-wrong-with-a-student-number-cap/, 8 Oct. 2017, Watson and Bowden, *New University Decade*, 32–4, on homogenizing rather than constraining effects of controls, and Parry, 'Policy Contexts', 36–7, on the ability of the funding regime before high fees to cater to part-time and mature students. If anything, government has given itself *more* control over student numbers with the new loan regime, the terms of which can be manipulated to affect demand without the need for consultation with students or providers.

148. Gorard et al., '"Spirals of Decline"', 374, 379–81, found that there was an average variance of less than 10% in the size of schools under open enrolment and only one school had entered a 'spiral of decline'.

149. Lupton et al., 'Education: New Labour's Top Priority', 77–8, 81–2, though cf. 85–6, rather underestimating progress towards the 50% target; Heath et al., 'Education under New Labour', 238–40; Whitty and Anders, 'How Did New Labour?', 11, 18–19.

150. As Bolton points out, these figures need to be viewed in the light of demographics and economic growth. As far as the former goes, the chief distortions are the bulge until the early '70s followed by the trough in '80s, but with little variation since. With these corrections, the 2000s still represent a remarkable period of growth and the years since 2010 a remarkable period of decline. Bolton, 'Education Spending in the UK', 3, 13, 20–2.

151. Public expenditure on health followed roughly the same trajectory as education: a bumpy road between the mid-'70s and the mid-'90s, rapid growth from the late '90s to 2010, but with even more rapid growth in this latter period than education. A roughly comparable graph to that in Bolton, 'Education Spending in the UK', can be found at https://www.ukpublicspending.co.uk/uk_national_healthcare_analysis. On health and education as electoral issues, see Butler and Kavanagh, *British General Election of 1992*, 126; Butler and Kavanagh, *British General Election of 1997*, 22, 110–11, 220; Kavanagh and Butler, *British General Election of 2005*, 176. But cf. Scott, *Meanings of Mass Higher Education*, 80–2, still in the shadow of Thatcherism, arguing that higher education at least was only 'peripheral' to the welfare state while health, pensions and social security formed its 'core'.

CHAPTER 8

1. That is, in England and Wales until GCSE subjects were selected, which increasingly takes place at 13. Formally the national curriculum no longer applies at all to the bulk of secondary schools, which are academies.

2. *Crowther Report*, I, 223–4; White, *Secondary Curriculum*, 102; Edwards, *Changing Sixth Form*, x-xi; cf. Peterson, 'Myth of Subject-Mindedness'.

3. Woods, 'Myth of Subject Choice'; cf. Hammersley, 'Myth of a Myth'.

4. PEP, *Graduate Employment*, 28–9; by 1963, however, Robbins found that the Oxbridge arts share had dropped to 61%, still well above the national average of 43%: *Robbins Report*, II, 21–4.

5. Duckworth, *Continuing Swing?*, 22–3.

6. *Robbins Report*, II, 31; Phillips, *Changes in Subject Choice*, 24–7.

7. A. A. Part, 'The Pattern of Secondary Education', 16 Nov. 1954: TNA, ED147/206; Phillips, *Changes in Subject Choice*, 37–9; Duckworth, *Continuing Swing?*, 22–3.

8. Phillips, *Changes in Subject Choice*, 33–4.

9. Kelsall et al., *Six Years After*, 34.

10. *Robbins Report*, II-I, 151–9.

11. OECD, *Development of Higher Education*, 125–6. Edgerton, *Science, Technology and 'Decline'*, 54–6, was one of the first historians to pick up on this postwar swing to science; he also cites McCrensky, *Scientific Manpower*, who showed awareness in 1958 of British superiority at some levels though ch. 5 bore down on alleged deficiencies in engineering, which were also being made up at the

time, and still argued, 97–105, that while Britain was superior at sub-degree levels Germany was superior at higher levels.

12. Phillips, *Changes in Subject Choice*, 58, 69, 106–11. The exception was France, where a higher proportion of *baccalauréat* candidates did science, though still fewer progressed to university.

13. Gosden, *Education System*, 168–73, 185.

14. Lowe, *Education in the Post-War Years*, 170.

15. Quoted in UGC, *University Development 1967–1972*, 25.

16. E.g. SED, *Grants to Students*, 50.

17. Moser and Layard, 'Estimating the Need for Qualified Manpower', 296–301, 313–14.

18. Banks, *Parity and Prestige*, 164–93, still provides the best overview; on the 'swing to science and technology' in postwar London grammar schools, see Campbell, *Eleven-Plus and All That*, ch. 6.

19. McCulloch et al., *Technological Revolution*, 30–2; Jeppesen, 'Worthwhile Career', 146–8.

20. Despite the protracted discussion of the Dainton swing in government and the media, it hasn't been well covered in the secondary literature, apart from the excellent McCulloch et al., *Technological Revolution*, esp. 165–6. Harrison, *Seeking a Role*, 363–4, says there was 'no striking shift in the balance of studies'; Boys et al., *Higher Education*, 12–13, says that there was no public concern about it until the advent of Thatcherism.

21. *Robbins Report*, II, 30.

22. *Robbins Report*, 170–1.

23. McCulloch et al., *Technological Revolution*, 63–6, 71, 74–7, 191–3; Hailsham, *Science and Politics*, 13–14.

24. A point made by Willetts, *University Education*, 36.

25. For a survey of these studies, beginning before Dainton with a DES-funded working party on subject choice organized by the Royal Statistical Society, see Barnard and McCreath, 'Subject Commitments', 358–9.

26. I am grateful to Celia Phillips for talking to me about her role in the Dainton Enquiry and about subject-choice research more generally.

27. *Dainton Report*, 68–70, 74–5, 84–6; interview with Celia Phillips, 5 May 2017.

28. Layard and King, 'Impact of Robbins', 29–30; Morris, 'Investment in Higher Education', 73; Lindley, 'Education, Training and the Labour Market', 22; cf. UGC, *University Development 1962–7*, 94–5.

29. McPherson, '"Swing from Science"', 30–2, 35–6; McPherson, 'Dainton Report', 261–2, 264–5; Pont and Butcher, 'Choice of Course', 15; Butcher, '"Swing from Science"', 56. McPherson was arguing not only with Dainton and Phillips but also with A. D. C. Peterson, who had asserted that early specialization *was* the cause of the swing. Peterson was an advocate of the International Baccalaureate, a broader curriculum based on some European models. See Peterson, 'Britain's Missing Scientists', *New Statesman*, 5 Mar. 1965, 358.

30. OECD, 'Development of Higher Education in OECD Member Countries: Quantitative Trends', 3 Apr. 1969; UGC, 'Student Numbers: International Comparisons', 23 July 1970: TNA, UGC7/1245; Bryan Silcock, 'The Great Scientist Fallacy', *Sunday Times*, 14 Apr. 1968; Pellegrin, 'Quantitative Trends', 39.

31. McPherson, '"Swing from Science"', 36–41.

32. Duckworth, *Continuing Swing?*, 13–17, 45, 56–7; Entwistle and Duckworth, 'Choice of Science Courses', 66–7.

33. Dyhouse, *Students*, 82; Duckworth and Entwistle, 'Swing from Science', 49–50; Duckworth, *Continuing Swing?*, 43–4. On school as well as social effects on girls' subject choices, see the contemporary research by Harding, 'Sex Differences'.

34. For example, see the interesting case study of a crisis of faith in medical science that led to a moratorium on heart transplants in 1969: Nathoo, *Hearts Exposed*, esp. ch. 4.

35. *Dainton Report*, 80; Dainton, 'A Note on Science', 37–9.

36. Quoted by Entwistle and Duckworth, 'Choice of Science Courses', 68; and see similar views from teachers in Butcher, '"Swing from Science"', 42–3.

37. See e.g. Hoggart, 'Higher Education and Personal Life', 218–19; Esnault and Le Pas, 'Post-Secondary Education and Employment', 157–8; Entwistle and Duckworth, 'Choice of Science Courses', 72–3.

38. Duckworth, *Continuing Swing?*, 32; on General Studies, see Edwards, *Changing Sixth Form*, 83–4, Lowe and Worboys, 'Teaching of Social Studies', 179–81.

39. Duckworth and Entwistle, 'Swing from Science', 51–3, based on a study of grammar schools in Lancashire; Duckworth, *Continuing Swing?*, 13; Redpath and Harvey, *Young People's Intentions*, 25. Psychologists tended to argue that enjoyment was conditioned by personality type, more fixed, though working on this model it was difficult to explain the swing except by reference to bio-logically determined gender. Pitt, 'Choice of Subjects'; Alan Smithers, 'Occupational Values of Students', *Nature*, 24 May 1969, 725–6; Butcher, '"Swing from Science"', 56; Entwistle and Duckworth, 'Choice of Science Courses', 74, and cf. 76–7 for a more fluid understanding of subject choice and identity formation.

40. Trow, *Problems in the Transition*, 41; Trow, 'Problems in the Transition', 90; Peston, 'Higher Education Policy', 127–8, 133; Kogan and Boys, 'Expectations of Higher Education', 53; and see further Marginson, *Education and Public Policy*, 52–3.

41. Mandler, 'Rise of the Social Sciences', gives a more comprehensive account of what follows.

42. Worth, 'Women, Education and Social Mobility', 4–6.

43. Statistics for this period are taken from DES, *Statistics of Education*, vol. 2 (for A-levels, 1962–79).

44. Statistics for this period are taken from DES, *Statistics of Education* (for degrees, 1967–78). On subject choice in the polytechnics, see Pratt, *Polytechnic Experiment*, 51–6; Lowe and Worboys, 'Teaching of Social Studies'; Jary, *Sociology in the Polytechnics*.

45. On the traditional career path, see Banks, 'Employment of Sociology Graduates', Rodgers, *Careers of Social Science Graduates* and *Social Administration Students*.

46. On new career paths, see Ball and Bourner, 'Employment of Psychology Graduates', esp. 39; Van Laar and Sherwood, 'Destinations of Psychology Graduates', esp. 44.

47. See the studies by Ben Schmidt on gender and subject choice in the US: 'Gender and the long-term decline in humanities enrollments', http://sappingattention.blogspot.co.uk/2013/06/some-long-term-perspective-on-crisis-in.html, 'Crisis in the humanities, or just women in the workplace?', http://sappingattention.blogspot.co.uk/2013/06/crisis-in-humanities-or-just-women-in.html. There is a swing to social science amongst women in the U.S., too, but the strongest swing is to business, journalism and communications. See further for the UK, Worth, 'Women, Education and Social Mobility', 4; Dyhouse, *Students*, 115–16; and for European comparisons, OECD, *Employment Prospects*, 13–16.

48. For observations to this effect, see Blaug, 'Empirical Status', 846–8, and 'Economics of Education', 18–22; Williams, 'Events of 1973–74', 53–4; Hunter, 'Employers' Perceptions', 20–2; Gray et al., *Reconstructions of Secondary Education*, 110–29, 138; Kogan and Boys, 'Expectations of Higher Education', 13–15; Blackburn and Jarman, 'Changing Inequalities', 200–2.

49. Hunter, 'Employers' Perceptions', 18, 20–2.

50. Kogan and Boys, 'Expectations of Higher Education', 9–11; Gray et al., *Reconstructions of Secondary Education*, 122, 126–7.

51. Lindley, 'Education, Training and the Labour Market', 22, writing in 1981, said as yet little was known on this subject, but see Hunter, 'Employers' Perceptions', 38–9; C. H. K. Williams to Michael Elliott, 10 Dec. 1982: TNA, CAB184/712; Williams and Blackstone, *Response to Adversity*, 42–4; Kogan and Boys, 'Expectations of Higher Education', 19–23; and, later, Wolf, 'Comparative Perspective', 28–9.

52. Hunter, 'Employers' Perceptions', 15; OECD, *Employment Prospects*, 27.

53. Kelsall et al., *Graduates*, 69; *Robbins Report*, II, 175–6; Alan Smithers, 'Occupational Values of Students', *Nature*, 24 May 1969, 725–6, found that technological students at a technological university were very focused on career and income, but others much less so. Butcher, '"Swing from Science"', 54, found very low priorities given to career and income at Edinburgh University.

54. On the one hand, Abbott, *Student Life in a Class Society*, 188–90; Kogan and Boys, 'Expectations of Higher Education', 42–5; on the other, Boys and Kirkland, *Degrees of Success*, 18–19; Boys et al., *Higher Education and Work*, 203–4.

55. OECD, *Access to Higher Education*, 22–4. Even counting sub-degree qualifications, in the early 1980s Britain remained just ahead of Germany and Italy and well ahead of the USA, France, Netherlands and Japan: DES, *Statistical Bulletin* 4/87 (Mar. 1987).

56. Policy Group A, Minutes, 10 Mar. 1978: TNA, ED181/426.

57. Gannicott and Blaug, 'Scientists and Engineers', 141–3; OECD, *Educational Situation*, 36–7; UGC, *University Development 1967–72*, 25–6; Morris, 'Investment in Higher Education', 86–90; Williams, 'Events of 1973–4', 54.

58. DES and UGC, 'Note of a meeting', 26 Oct. 1977; 'HE Planning Numbers to 1981–82 and Beyond', 28 Oct. 1977; 'Secretary of State's Meeting with University Grants Committee', 18 Nov. 1977: TNA, ED181/423.

59. Shattock, *UGC and the Management of British Universities*, 145; Stevens, *University to Uni*, 35.

60. Policy Group A, Minutes, 11 Oct. 1979: TNA, ED181/429.

61. A. Thompson, 'Entry Prospects in Higher Education', 2 July 1980; Unit for Manpower Studies, 'Higher Education and the Employment of Graduates', Oct. 1980: TNA, ED181/385, 373/2.

62. R. H. Bird, 'Steering Higher Education: Some Notes as a Basis for Discussion', Oct. 1980: TNA, ED181/373/2; and see the assessment by Gareth Williams and Oliver Fulton, 'Playing the USSR Numbers Game', *THES*, 25 July 1980, and by Williams, 'The Main Policy Issues Facing Institutions of Higher Education', Nov. 1980: TNA, ED181/373/2. Labour also supported a 'shift to science and technology', but even more unrealistically as part of a policy of expansion. *Hansard*, 6th ser., 65 (1983–4), 924–5 [26 Nov. 1984].

63. Wiener, *British Culture*, was a key text making this argument for Thatcherites; a left-wing version appeared in the essays collected into Anderson, *English Questions*. For contemporary applications to education, see Aldcroft, *Education, Training and Economic Performance*, Lowe, *Schooling and Social Change*, 25–44, Sanderson, *Educational Opportunity*, 5–7, 14–16, 136–7; and see also Whyte, *Redbrick*, 272–7, on declinism in educational discourse in the 1980s and '90s.

64. Kogan and Hanney, *Reforming Higher Education*, 89.

65. Ibid., 61–4.

66. UGC, *Annual Survey 1980–81*, 6–7, actually uses 'social demand' in a way redolent of 'social return'.

67. M. J. Elliott to C. H. K. Williams, 25 Oct., 4 Nov. 1982; M. J. Elliott to John Sparrow, 5 Nov. 1982; see also John Sparrow to Keith Joseph, 'Draft CPRS Remit, Higher Education', 19 Oct. 1982, M. J. Elliott to HE Team, 7 Dec. 1982: TNA, CAB184/172; J. H. Thompson to I. Wilde, 'CPRS Work Programme', 2 Nov. 1982: TNA, ED261/206.

68. Kogan and Hanney, *Reforming Higher Education*, 73–4, 110–11, 137–8.

69. J. H. Thompson to I. Wilde, 'Mid-Term Financial Options', 14 Dec. 1982: TNA, ED261/206.

70. See e.g. Halsey, *Decline of Donnish Dominion*, 180–4; Stewart, *Higher Education*, 176–81; Simon, *Education and the Social Order*, 494–5.

71. UGC, 'The Future of the University System: Some Implications from External Factors', 11 Sep. 1980: TNA, UGC1/143; UGC, *Annual Survey 1980–81*, 607. This position was endorsed by a report of the Education, Science and Arts Committee, *Funding and Organisation of Courses*, xx–xxii, which affirmed that 'the ultimate arbiter of our higher education system ... is the demand made on it by individual school leavers'; and see also the paragraph about 'student preference' at lxxvii omitted from the final report, a gibe at Thatcher.

72. Keith Joseph to Edward Parkers, 14 July 1982; Parkes to Joseph, 24. Nov. 1982: UGC, *Annual Survey 1981–82*, 32–3, 38.

73. J. H. Thompson to I. Wilde, 'Mid-Term Financial Options', 14 Dec. 1982: TNA, ED261/206.

74. G. L. Williams and Oliver Fulton, 'Higher Education and Manpower Planning', in Education, Science and Arts Committee, *Funding and Organisation of Courses*, 444–7; see also Williams and Fulton, 'Playing the USSR Numbers Game', *THES*, 25 July 1980, and Williams, 'Economic Approach', 82–3, on resurgence of economists' interest in private rates of return.

75. Green and Zhu, 'Overqualification and Dispersion in Returns', fig. 1; Walker and Zhu, 'Impact of University Degrees', 32.

76. M. Faulkner to Sir A. Rawlinson, 26 Nov. 1982: TNA, T494/74.

77. Already in the 1985 Green Paper Joseph acknowledged that market signals had *not* had the desired effect on young people's subject choices: *Development of Higher Education*, 7–8, and see similar uncertainty in *Croham Report*, 18.

78. See pp. 126–7, and the 1987 White Paper, *Higher Education: Meeting the Challenge*, 7, and the new realism at DES, e.g. Economics Division, 'Assessing the Future Demand for Graduates', Sep. 1987: TNA, ED261/240.

79. https://www.hepi.ac.uk/2016/09/01/last-time-conservative-government-set-higher-education-targets/, 7–8, 14–16; *Higher Education: A New Framework*, 9.

80. Marginson, *Education and Public Policy*, 45–51, 125–6; Paterson, *Scottish Education*, 174–5; Connor, 'Different Graduates', 100–2.

81. McIntosh, 'Demand for Post-Compulsory Education', 70.

82. Williams, 'Market Route', 277–8, 281–2, 288.

83. Dearing did point to the negative impact on apprenticeships and technical education from the rush to higher education, but hoped this would be addressed at sub-degree rather than at university level: Dearing, 'Dearing on Dearing', 65–6, 70; *Dearing Report*, 11, 26–8, 58, 68, 79, 82, 90–3, 96, 107–11.

84. Dyhouse, *Students*, 82; cf. Smithers and Robinson, *Trends in Higher Education*, 8, putting the proportion of women at 52% already in 1995.

85. In a 2006 survey an astonishing 44% of Pharmacy applicants were of Asian background: Purcell et al., *Applying for Higher Education*, 55–6, 165.

86. Walker, 'Why Do Students Choose Psychology?'; Jarvis, *Teaching Psychology*, 2–4; see further Mandler, 'Rise of Social Sciences'.

87. Pratt, *Polytechnic Experiment*, 111–13; Smithers and Robinson, *Trends in Higher Education*, 5–6; Purcell et al., *Applying for Higher Education*, 163–4. In 2018 men and women are almost equally represented in business degrees.

88. J. H. Thompson to I. Wilde, 'Mid-Term Financial Options', 14 Dec. 1982: TNA, ED261/206; see also Edward Parkes in Education, Science and Arts Committee, *University Funding*, I, 29.

89. Alan Thompson, 'Entry Prospects in Higher Education', 2 July 1980: TNA, ED181/385; Brown with Coldstream, *Successful Partnership*, 7; Fulton and Ellwood, 'Admissions, Access and Institutional Change', 32–3; Gibbons et al., *New Production of Knowledge*, 80; Marginson, *Education and Public Policy*, 127; Belfield et al., 'Relative Labour Market Returns', 37; Iannelli and Smyth, 'Curriculum Choices in Scotland', 736.

90. Purcell and Pitcher, *Great Expectations*, 6–7, 11–12.
91. Ibid., 11.
92. Institute of Student Employers, *Annual Survey 2018*, 31.
93. Stables and Wikeley, 'Changes in Preference', 397, 401, found no increase in 'career intentions' as a factor in subject choice between 1984 and 1996; Wikeley and Stables, 'Changes in Approaches', 289–90, finding few differences in class or gender; Stables, *Subjects of Choice*, 88–9, 94, 101, 105; Kogan and Boys, 'Expectations of Higher Education', 27, 44–5, 53; Purcell et al., *Applying for Higher Education*, 38–9, 61–2, 99, 108–9, 111; Purcell et al., *Transitions to Employment*, 133–6, 194; Purcell and Pitcher, *Great Expectations*, 23; Blenkinsop et al., 'How Do Young People Make Choices?', 47, 52–4; Vidal Rodeiro, *A Level Subject Choice*, 6–7, 9–10, 18–19, 30, 42; Cebulla and Tomaszewski, 'Demise of Certainty', 150–1, 143; but cf. Reay et al., *Degrees of Choice*, 44, and Montmarquette et al., 'How Do Young People Choose?', a 1979 study of US youth. On gender, see Wiswall and Zafar, 'Preference for the Workplace', 457, 459–60, a US study.
94. For studies of the structural factors in subject choice, see Sullivan et al., 'Social Structure of the Curriculum', Henderson et al., 'Class, Gender and Ethnic Differences', and Anders et al., 'Role of Schools'; cf. Vidal Rodeiro, *A Level Subject Choice*, 36–7, 42, 45–6, finding less differentiation by class for most subjects but more by school type.
95. Smith, 'Is There a Crisis?'; Smith and Gorard, 'Is There a Shortage?'; Smith and White, 'Where Do All the STEM Graduates Go?', surveying all cohorts from 1958 onwards; for American critiques, see Teitelbaum, *Falling Behind*, and Hacker, *Math Myth*.
96. On a global scale, see Schofer and Meyer, 'Worldwide Expansion', 903; for a balanced assessment of the UK, Dolton and Vignoles, 'Overeducation'; Wolf, *Does Education Matter?*, 51–2, 196–7; Lindley and McIntosh, 'Growth in Within Wage Inequality', 109. Most of these assessments accepted that even where there was no graduate premium there was other value (e.g. consumption).
97. Watson, 'New Attack'.
98. *Dearing Report*, 89–93, 100; *Augar Report*, 35, 37, 40, but cf. 123, granting that the decline in sub-degree qualifications was 'partly caused by the growth in undergraduate degrees'. This is not to dispute the charge that FE had been under-funded, 46, but it doesn't seem necessary to argue at the same time that HE had been over-funded, 63, 66–7, 80.
99. *Augar Report*, 23–4, 26.
100. *Augar Report*, 25–6, 50, 145–7, 149, 152–3. Although Alison Wolf sat on the Augar Committee, her earlier report on vocational education prescribed 'fairly general, rather than highly specific, vocational qualifications' as well as more academic qualifications combined with workplace experience: *Wolf Report*, 11, 33–4, 42–3, 69, 74–5, 82–3, 141–2, 148–9, 173–4; she had also pointed to the rapid growth in demand not for STEM skills but for sales, care, office work, cleaning, and marketing (the largest occupational groups), with educational and care assistants showing the greatest absolute levels of growth: ibid., 36.

101. This was the conclusion of the *Wolf Report*, 10, 30, 33–4, 42. And see above, ch. 7, esp. n. 73.

102. Thus not by any means a novelty of the early twenty-first century, though now fortified by new data sources driving human-capital arguments; neither does its ubiquity guarantee that it was the actual driver of policy, still less of behaviour; cf. Woodin et al., *Secondary Education*, 167–8, King and Nash, 'Continuity of Ideas', esp. 185–8, 202–7.

103. *Roberts Report*, 2, 21, 26–8.

104. Initially with the creation of the Department of Innovation, Universities and Skills (DIUS), later as a unit within the Business department, and since 2016 shared between Business and Education.

105. See Appendix, Figs. 8.1 and 8.2, for sources for degree and A-level statistics; the time series for A-levels now extended to 2018 from the same site.

106. Homer et al., 'Participation Rates in School Science', esp. 259–60; Bennett et al., 'Schools that Make a Difference', 686.

107. Homer et al., 'Participation Rates in School Science' 249. There was also a Higher Education Funding Council 'rescue plan' in 2008 to boost STEM, noted by Regan and Dillon, 'A Place for STEM', 122.

108. Marginson, 'International Comparisons', 25–8; Teitelbaum, *Falling Behind?*, 3–5.

109. Teitelbaum, *Falling Behind?*, 180–1.

110. The latest, and most comprehensive evidence for the UK can be found in Smith and White, 'Where Do All the STEM Graduates Go?'.

111. Walker and Zhu, 'Differences by Degree', 1183–4; and see some similar findings in Belfield et al., 'Relative Labour Market Returns', 37, 41.

112. Teitelbaum, *Falling Behind?*, 22–3, 180–1, 185; Ramirez et al., 'Student Achievement', 14–15, 20–1.

113. See, for example, Google's Eric Schmidt calling for 10,000 more Computer Science lecturers (despite the fact that Computer Science graduates have one of the highest unemployment rates and there are only enough high-level computer science jobs to absorb about a quarter of them). 'Eric Schmidt: UK Needs 10,000 Computer Science Academics', *THES*, 27 Nov. 2016; HESA, *Destination of Leavers 2012/13*, Chart 4; Smith and White, 'Where Do All the STEM Graduates Go?', 30.

114. E.g. OECD, 'A Brave New World', *Trends Shaping Education Spotlight* 15 (2018): https://www.oecd.org/education/ceri/Spotlight-15-A-Brave-New-World-Technology-and-Education.pdf; Marie-Helene Doumet, 'Where Will Tomorrow's Graduates Come From?', *OECD Education Today*, 24 May 2018: https://oecdedutoday.com/where-will-tomorrows-graduates-come-from/.

115. Hillman, 'From Grants for All', 263; Willetts, *University Education*, 66–7, rebutting charge that the new funding regime hurt the humanities; McGettigan, *Great University Gamble*, 58.

116. 'Nicky Morgan Speaks at Launch of Your Life Campaign', DfE, 10 Nov. 2014: https://www.gov.uk/government/speeches/nicky-morgan-speaks-at-launch-of-your-life-campaign.

117. *Augar Report*, 9, 10, 25, 26, 81; and see the *Wakeham Report* of 2016, which sought more finely to identify those STEM subjects with the highest graduate returns (finding incidentally that many had very low returns).

118. Marginson, *Education and Public Policy*, 51, 122–9, 180–1; Freeman, 'STEM Policies'; Lyons and Quinn, 'Declining Science Participation'. Australian economists were also in the vanguard in making wage premium calculations for subject choices: Daly et al., 'Private Rate of Return'; Healy et al., 'STEM Labour Market', 6–7.

119. Willetts' claim that 60% of students were on vocational courses rests on the dubious inclusion of all students in subjects allied to medicine, engineering, education and business studies (54% in total), without reference to students' stated motivations for studying these subjects or their actual employment outcomes: Willetts, *University Education*, 6, 232–3. In 2011 testimony to the Business Select Committee, he defended student choice by asserting that students' greater vocationalism would naturally align student and employer demand, while repudiating manpower planning, rebuffing queries about what would happen if they did not so align: BIS S.C., Oral Evidence, 18 July 2011.

120. Quoted by McGettigan, 'The Treasury View of HE', 2–3.

121. As predicted, e.g., by Chevalier, 'Subject Choice and Earnings', 1188; similar concerns in Collini, *Speaking of Universities*, 196–7, 215, 273, where a graduate tax is preferred because it works in the opposite direction.

122. For initial ventures, see Conlon and Patrignani, 'Returns to HE Qualifications', a 2011 paper for the Business department aimed at calculating the benefits to the Treasury of subject choices; Walker and Zhu, 'Impact of University Degrees', a 2013 paper for the Business department which found it difficult to develop robust data on the impact of subject choice. Another initiative was the Social Mobility Transparency Board set up in 2010 which began the linkage of educational and tax data that led to LEO. I am grateful to John Goldthorpe and Anna Vignoles for talking to me about these initiatives.

123. Belfield et al., 'Relative Labour Market Returns', esp. 12–15, 20–1, 36, 38–9, 45–6; cf. a preliminary study based on a 10% sample, which found even less variation between subjects at the median, but which is difficult to compare with the later study because the data are presented differently, Britton et al., 'How English Graduate Earnings Vary', 26–7, and cf. 37, again showing rather more variation by institution than by subject. Curiously, Willetts, *University Education*, 83–5, asserts the opposite, that subjects show more variation than institutions.

124. Belfield et al., 'Relative Labour Market Returns', 11–12, 48, 62; cf. Willetts, *University Education*, 136–8, 144–6, struggling a little to refute Alison Wolf with whom he usually agrees.

125. See Zachary Bleemer, 'Wage-by-Major Statistics: Transparency to What End?', *Inside Higher Ed*, 24 June 2019: https://www.insidehighered.com/blogs/just-visiting/guest-post-wage-major-statistics-transparency-what-end; also Smith and Gorard, 'Is There a Shortage?', 173–4, on the irony that human-capital

theory itself warns against over-recruitment to 'difficult' subjects, especially as late as 18.

126. David Willetts, 'The Economic Value of Going to University is Not Declining', *THES*, 16 May 2019, 26–7.

127. BIS, *Students at the Heart of the System*.

128. *Hansard*, 3 Nov. 2010, col. 941: https://publications.parliament.uk/pa/cm201011/cmhansrd/cm101103/debtext/101103–0001.htm#10110358000955. The Browne Report, however, had specifically recommended this subsidy on the grounds that STEM met national needs rather than student demand: *Browne Report*, 47, and cf. 15, 23 where it continues to wrestle with the contradictions between student demand, employer demand and national needs.

129. Recognized when the exercise was renamed Teaching Excellence and Student Outcomes Framework, though still abbreviated as TEF.

130. David Willetts, 'You Are What You Earn?', *THES*, 11 Apr. 2019.

131. *Augar Report*, 101–5; and see Williams, 'A Bridge Too Far', 66–70, on the trade-offs involved in such steering, and Collini, *Speaking of Universities*, 103–4, 183.

132. E.g. by Ben Schmidt at https://twitter.com/benmschmidt/status/804066577368944640.

133. I discuss this further in a contribution to a symposium in *THES*, 15 Feb. 2018.

134. UUK, *Patterns and Trends 2018*, 10–11, 19.

135. Mountford-Zimdars et al., 'Framing Education', 803–5, 808–10.

136. McGettigan, *Great University Gamble*, 21, 24; *Browne Report*, 21, and for its low estimates of the actual private contribution based on the disproved assumption of variable fees, 42–4. The proportion fluctuates because government can change the terms of the loan retrospectively and because private contributions depend on changing labour-market conditions over the very long term.

CHAPTER 9

1. Lucas, 'Effectively Maintained Inequality'.

2. As noted by Glass in his BBC radio discussion with Mark Abrams, 16 Nov. 1954: Abrams Papers, ABMS 5/6/3; and still in 1961 by Floud, 'Social Class Factors', 92.

3. Thus the opportunity for a 'natural experiment' with the 1958 birth cohort, which could be divided into sub-cohorts exposed to bipartite and comprehensive systems and compared, was not widely taken up until the 1980s (when academic attainment could be compared) and didn't flourish until a good deal later (when employment outcomes could be compared): for the 1980s, see the bitter debates on the effects of comprehensivization in England, e.g. Marks and Cox, 'Educational Attainment', Gray et al., 'Predicting Differences', the symposium on 'Assessment of Performance', and summed up in Crook et al., *Grammar School Question*, 27–40, and, for Scotland, McPherson and Willms, 'Equalisation and Improvement' and Burnhill et al., 'School Attainment'; for later studies, see Heath and Cheung, 'Education and Occupation', Glaesser and Cooper, 'Educational Achievement', and Boliver and Swift, 'Do Comprehensive Schools?'.

4. For the history and structure of NS-SEC, see https://www.ons.gov.uk/ methodology/classificationsandstandards/otherclassifications/thenational statisticssocioeconomicclassificationnssecrebasedonsoc2010#structure-and- flexibility.

5. Glass and Hall, 'Social Mobility'. Only men were sampled on the assumption that only men (and their fathers) would all have occupations.

6. Halsey et al., *Origins and Destinations*; a somewhat different sample from the same study was made for Goldthorpe et al., *Social Mobility and Class Structure*.

7. Election surveys were used by Anthony Heath (e.g. Heath and Payne, 'Social Mobility', Heath and Clifford, 'Class Inequalities'); the BHPS has been used to create 'quasi-cohorts' to fill in the gap between the 1970 and 2000 birth-cohort surveys (e.g. Blanden and Machin, 'Educational Inequality', Blanden et al., 'Intergenerational Persistence', Devine and Li, 'Changing Relationship', Li and Devine, 'Is Social Mobility Declining?', Paterson and Iannelli, 'Social Class'). Other studies such as the GHS and the LFS are less useful for this purpose because they don't consistently ask about social origins.

8. The birth-cohort studies were not much used before 2000 to track long-term mobility across cohorts, but Gray et al., *Reconstructions of Secondary Education*, as early as 1983, unusually used the earlier Scottish birth-cohort study of 1936 alongside the Scottish cohorts in the 1946 and 1958 British studies.

9. The basic model was laid out (though not in this form) in the late 1960s by the American sociologists Blau and Duncan, *American Occupational Structure*.

10. Glass (ed.), *Social Mobility*, 4–5, 22–4; Hall and Glass, 'Education and Social Mobility', 296–7; Floud et al., *Social Class and Educational Opportunity*, xvi–xviii, 36–8, 51; and see the interesting retrospective analysis by Heath and Clifford, 'Class Inequalities', esp. 213–16.

11. Glass (ed.), *Social Mobility*, 22–3; Glass and Abrams, 'Social Mobility', 16 Nov. 1954: Abrams MSS, ABMS 5/6/3. See also Campbell, *Eleven-Plus*, esp. 129–31.

12. Cf. Floud et al., *Social Class and Educational Opportunity* (1956), 144–9, still focused on meritocracy, but observing that intellectual disadvantage was already being developed in the home environment in early years, with Halsey (ed.), *Ability and Educational Opportunity* (1961), 23–5, 33–4, 36, still asserting the random distribution of ability but insisting now on 'a wider equalization of "the social environment of the child"' to bring it out, and Floud's testimony to Robbins (1962) casting doubt on 'ability' and indeed on any limits to 'the educational potential of the population': *Robbins Report*, XII, 50–3.

13. Already evident in Glass (ed.), *Social Mobility*, 25–7, and strongly so in Glass's BBC radio talk, 25 Jan. 1957: Abrams MSS, ABMS 5/6/3, and Glass, 'Education and Social Change', 403–5.

14. Halsey et al., *Origins and Destinations*, 1–7, 12–13. Halsey admitted that the omis- sion of women was 'quite unjustifiable', but justified it nonetheless, both on the ground that male occupations were the 'major articulation' of class and status, and also because he was seeking to reproduce the Blau and Duncan study, which considered only men. Ibid., 20.

15. Ibid., 63–4, 110, 146, 185, 188.

16. Ibid., 205, 218; the thesis was formulated by Raftery and Hout as 'Maximally Maintained Inequality' (a study of Ireland), esp. 56 (crediting Halsey), 60, and refined by Lucas as 'Effectively Maintained Inequality' (a study of the US), 1652–3.

17. On stable OE association over time, see Kerckhoff and Trott, 'Educational Attainment', 148–9, Heath and Clifford, 'Class Inequalities', 216–19, Iannelli and Paterson, 'Does Education Promote Social Mobility?', Paterson and Iannelli, 'Social Class and Educational Attainment', 349–51 (comparing the four nations of the UK), Blanden and Machin, 'Educational Inequality', 237, 245–6, Goldthorpe and Jackson, 'Education-Based Meritocracy', 99–100, cf. 104; for strengthening OE association, see Machin and Vignoles, 'Educational Inequality', 108.

18. Shavit and Blossfeld (eds), *Persistent Inequality*, and see e.g. Blossfeld and Shavit, 'Persisting Barriers', 15; but cf. Breen et al., 'Non-Persistent Inequality', arguing for some weakening OE association in Britain as well, and in general a degree of convergence across Europe; Jonsson et al., 'Increasing Educational Openness?', 190–5, arguing for weakening OE in Sweden and Germany but not Britain; Breen and Jonsson, 'Inequality of Opportunity', 226–8, a more mixed view. Shavit later conceded that there may have been a modest weakening of OE associations, but only at the lower levels of education (which had reached saturation) and mostly just after the war: Shavit et al., 'Persistence of Persistent Inequality', 52–3.

19. Blossfeld and Shavit, 'Persisting Barriers', 19, 21–2.

20. Paterson and Iannelli, 'Social Class and Educational Attainment', 350–1; Goldthorpe, 'Problems of "Meritocracy"', 262–5; Breen and Goldthorpe, 'Explaining Educational Differentials', 277–8, 283, 286, 294–6; Goldthorpe, 'Role of Education', 275–9; Bukodi and Goldthorpe, 'Educational Attainment', 7–8, 13–14.

21. Jonsson et al., 'Increasing Educational Openness?', 197–9, 202–4; Ganzeboom et al., 'Comparative Stratification', 284, 290; Breen and Jonsson, 'Inequality of Opportunity', 226–7; Müller and Shavit, 'Stratification Process', 37; cf. Breen and Luijkx, 'Social Mobility and Education', 112–13, though with the disparity diminishing over time. These findings contrast strongly with the widespread belief in the British educated classes that the German system, being 'better' for skilled workers and manufacturing, must also be 'better' for social mobility. For an unusual admission that social-scientific research shows otherwise, see David Goodhart, 'More Mobile than We Think', *Prospect*, Oct. 2008.

22. Breen and Jonsson, 'Inequality of Opportunity', 228; Müller and Shavit, 'Stratification Process', 39; Kerckhoff and Trott, 'Educational Attainment', 149–52; Weedon, 'Widening Access in Sweden'.

23. Goldthorpe et al., *Social Mobility and Class Structure*, 76, 83–5; Goldthorpe, 'Problems of "Meritocracy"', 262–5; Jackson et al., 'Education and Class Mobility', 6–7; Goldthorpe and Jackson, 'Education-Based Meritocracy', 104–8; Goldthorpe, 'Role of Education', 267–8, 274–5; Bukodi and Goldthorpe, 'Class

Origins and Occupational Attainment', 349; Bukodi and Goldthorpe, 'Educational Attainment', 9.

24. Bukodi and Goldthorpe, *Social Mobility and Education*, 91–4, 143–5; and see also Marshall et al., *Against the Odds?*, 92–5, on the significance of OD associations across Europe.

25. Goldthorpe, 'Understanding Social Mobility', 444.

26. Friedman and Laurison, *Class Ceiling*, 38–9.

27. Bukodi and Goldthorpe, *Social Mobility and Education*, 163–5, 167, 221–2; cf. Major and Machin, *Social Mobility*, 195–9.

28. Goldthorpe, 'Understanding Social Mobility', 443–5; Bukodi and Goldthorpe, *Social Mobility and Education*, 68–70; Werfhorst, 'Role of Education', 410–11, 435.

29. And see also Paterson and Iannelli, 'Social Class and Educational Attainment', 349–51, arguing for a more fluctuating level of inequality during educational expansion in Scotland.

30. Boliver and Swift, 'Do Comprehensive Schools?', 98–100; Sullivan et al., 'School Type and Higher Education', 757; Burgess et al., 'Access to Grammar Schools', 1382–4.

31. Halsey et al., *Origins and Destinations*, 1–3; and see Halsey, 'Towards Meritocracy', 182–4, reporting on the results of the 1972 study, acknowledging absolute mobility but emphasizing the lack of relative mobility.

32. Goldthorpe et al., *Social Mobility and Class Structure*, 69–71. Each successive cohort of births between 1908 and 1937 had a higher rate of movement from the working class to higher classes, from 53% to 60%. The youngest cohort, born 1938–47, also the first to benefit from universal secondary education, had not yet reached occupational maturity, but Goldthorpe correctly expected it to continue this upward trajectory.

33. Goldthorpe, 'Understanding Social Mobility', 441.

34. Ibid., 70. About a third of the men of intermediate origin dropped down into the working class, as did 13% of men of salariat origin. But these rates of downward mobility remained stable across cohorts.

35. Goldthorpe et al., *Social Mobility and Class Structure*, 59, 76. Blau and Duncan, *American Occupational Structure*, 66, 77–8, 426–31, had drawn attention as early as 1967 to 'an excess of upward mobility' due to 'the demand for manpower at the top', which they considered to be not a feature of American exceptionalism but of 'advanced industrial societies' in general.

36. Heath and Payne, 'Social Mobility', 260, 265. These figures were based on the British Election Surveys of 1964–97 and give a somewhat higher level for the salariat than the 1958 birth cohort study, which found 38% in the salariat: Bukodi and Goldthorpe, 'Social Class Returns', 189. Much depends on when the survey is taken; the 1958 figure was taken at age 34, probably before cohort members reached their highest levels.

37. Bukodi and Goldthorpe, *Social Mobility and Education*, 40, 42, 60–3; Heath and Payne, 'Social Mobility', 266–7; Goldthorpe et al., *Social Mobility and Class Structure*, 58–9 had noted this already in 1980.

38. Kelsall, *Applications for Admission*, 12 (25%), Halsey et al., *Origins and Destinations*, 183, 188 (20%), Pratt, *Polytechnic Experiment*, 77–9 (16–18% universities, 25–8% polytechnics); in 1981, Shattock, 'Demography and Social Class', 386–9 (19%), took this declining proportion as evidence of 'a decline in working–class interest in higher education', and similar in 1987 from Neave, 'Elite and Mass Education', 356–7; and, since the 1980s, McKibbin, *Classes and Cultures*, 268, Whyte, 'Student Funding', 73, but see Reay et al., *Degrees of Choice*, 5, recognizing that 'the class landscape of Britain has changed radically'. Glennerster, 'Education and Inequality', 91, showed an unusually early (1972) appreciation of the decline of working–class share, and see also Glennerster and Hills (eds), *State of Welfare*, 59.

39. 'Demand for Higher Education in Great Britain, 1984–2000', DES, *Report on Education* 100 (July 1984), after criticism of its previous estimates in April 1983. See p. 121. By the time of Dearing, there was more awareness of the impact of social change in determining the social origins of students, and the proportion of students from a working–class background was dropped as a measure and an index measuring OE association, i.e. differential participation between social classes or an 'attainment gap', employed instead: David Robertson and Josh Hillman, 'Widening Participation in Higher Education for Students from Lower Socio-Economic Groups', May 1997, 7–8, 11: TNA, ED266/11; *Dearing Report*, 22–3, but cf. 79, showing persistence of Robbins-era assumptions.

40. Savage, *Identities and Social Change*, 176–8, 216; Lawrence, 'Class, "Affluence", and the Study of Everyday Life', esp. 282–4; Lawrence, 'Inventing the "Traditional Working Class"'. These re-readings take in Goldthorpe's earlier 'affluent worker' studies, which recognized social change but sought to fit it within pre-existing class schemas. See, further, Lawrence, 'Social-Science Encounters'.

41. Heath and Payne, 'Social Mobility', 265, 267.

42. Goldthorpe et al., *Social Mobility and Class Structure*, 52, 143–5. Of the initial 20% who joined the intermediate classes, 6% continued their journey upwards to the salariat, and 6% subsequently fell back down into the working class.

43. Bukodi and Goldthorpe, 'Social Class Returns', 192; Bukodi, 'Education and Later Occupational Attainment', 7–8, 13–14.

44. Bukodi and Goldthorpe, *Social Mobility and Education*, 140–2.

45. Tampubolon and Savage, 'Intragenerational Social Mobility', 120–3.

46. Heath and Payne, 'Social Mobility', 262–3, 265–7; Worth, 'Women, Education and Social Mobility', 10–12; Payne, *New Social Mobility*, 114, 118, 133. Todd, *The People*, 234, argues that there was no golden age of mobility but only a shift to 'routine clerical work', but this again exaggerates the importance of mobility to the very top and minimizes the general upward trend to 'clean' jobs which in previous work she had shown to be widely desired.

47. Goldthorpe et al., *Social Mobility and Class Structure*, 248; see further Friedman, 'Price of the Ticket', 354–6.

48. Payne and Roberts, 'Opening and Closing the Gates'; though cf. Miles and Leguina, 'Narratives of Class Mobility', who found more dislocation amongst

the 'doubly mobile' in the 1958 cohort, i.e. those who were geographically as well as socially mobile, such as children of the northern working-class who moved to the south-east to escape deindustrialization.

49. Most clearly illustrated by Paterson and Iannelli, 'Patterns of Absolute Mobility'; see also Bukodi and Goldthorpe, 'Class Origins and Occupational Attainment', 360–1, 365–6, Goldthorpe, 'Understanding Social Mobility', 441–3.

50. Kerckhoff and Trott, 'Educational Attainment', 149–52.

51. Jonsson et al., 'Educational Openness?', 197–9, 202–4; Ganzeboom et al., 'Comparative Stratification Research', 290; Heath and Cheung, 'Education and Occupation', 90–1; Müller and Shavit, 'Institutional Embeddedness', 37, 39–40; Breen and Luijkx, 'Social Mobility', 54, 60; Breen and Jonsson, 'Inequality of Opportunity', 226–34; Wolf, *Does Education Matter?*, 71, 88–9, 145.

52. This raises the question of the interaction between income inequality and occupational structure, discussed pp. 198–204.

53. Paterson and Iannelli, 'Patterns of Absolute and Relative Mobility'.

54. Goldthorpe et al., *Affluent Worker*, 123, 130–40, 144n, challenging the thesis of Runciman, *Relative Deprivation*.

55. Blossfeld and Shavit, 'Persisting Barriers', 22; see also Halsey et al., *Origins and Destinations*, 218–19.

56. Savage, *Identities and Social Change*, 218–23; Savage et al., *Social Class*, 25–6, 38, 369–71.

57. Lawrence, *Me, Me, Me?* , 14, 38, 75, 90, 125–6, 134, 179, 217–19, 223–4. The role of schooling in community formation remains seriously under-studied: the emphasis has long been on workplace or neighbourly sociability or at best on associational life through voluntary organizations, community centres and the like.

58. Ibid., 99–100, 159.

59. Bukodi and Goldthorpe, *Social Mobility and Education*, 36; but cf. Payne, *New Social Mobility*, 114, using a slightly different classification, who found very rapid growth in Class II and shrinkage in I and III.

60. Payne and Roberts, 'Opening and Closing the Gates'.; Payne, 'Labouring under a Misapprehension', 231, 233–4; Li and Devine, 'Is Social Mobility Declining?'; Sandberg, *Lean In*.

61. As noted by *Wolf Report*, 35–6, Liu and Grusky, 'Payoff to Skill', 1349–54, 1359–60, 1362–4, which points to the difference between changing occupational distribution and changing distribution of rewards (thus 'payoff to skill' is not necessarily a sign of growing demand for skill), and Goos et al., 'Job Polarization', noting growing demand for both high-paying and low-paying jobs.

62. Paterson and Iannelli, 'Patterns of Absolute and Relative Mobility'; Bynner et al., 'Benefits of Higher Education', 17, 20; Miles and Leguina, 'Socio-Spatial Mobilities', 1074. Goos et al., 'Job Polarization', 61, found lower growth in high-paying jobs in Britain than the European average, confirmed recently by Montresor, 'Job Polarization', 200, which however blames greater competition amongst a better educated workforce for reducing the wage levels of high-paying jobs.

63. Bukodi and Goldthorpe, *Social Mobility and Education*, 48–9, 212–14; Payne, 'Labouring under a Misapprehension', 239.

64. Paterson and Iannelli, 'Patterns of Absolute and Relative Mobility', illustrate this effect by showing how parents' non-manual occupation rates catch up over time with their children's.

65. Li and Devine, 'Is Social Mobility Declining?'; Payne, 'Labouring under a Misapprehension', 236–7; Payne, 'A New Social Mobility', 67–8.

66. Blanden and Machin, 'Educational Inequality', 235; Blanden et al., *Intergenerational Mobility*, 7; Crawford et al., 'Social Mobility', 8; Major and Machin, *Social Mobility*, 37–41.

67. Blanden et al., *Intergenerational Mobility*, 4–9.

68. Blanden et al., 'Educational Inequality', 99–101.

69. Ibid., 10–12, but cf. 10 on the larger non-educational effects; Blanden and Machin, 'Educational Inequality', 237, 247; also d'Addio, 'Intergenerational Transmission', 33, 36–8, but cf. 62, summing up for the OECD a number of studies.

70. See esp. Erikson and Goldthorpe, 'Has Social Mobility Decreased?'; Goldthorpe, 'Understanding Social Mobility', 435–6, 438; Bukodi and Goldthorpe, *Social Mobility and Education*, ch. 1.

71. Jäntti et al., 'American Exceptionalism', 17–19; and, later, Jerrim, 'Family Background and Lifetime Income', 5–6, 8, 18–19.

72. Bukodi and Goldthorpe, *Education and Social Mobility*, esp. 68–9, 203–4.

73. Paterson and Iannelli, 'Patterns of Absolute and Relative Mobility'; Payne, *New Social Mobility*, 1–3, 139, 148, 157–8; Bukodi and Goldthorpe, *Education and Social Mobility*, 212–14.

74. Blanden and Machin, 'Recent Changes in Intergenerational Mobility', 14–19.

75. Blanden, 'Cross-Country Rankings', 55, 61–2; see also Black and Devereux, 'Recent Developments', 16; Bukodi and Goldthorpe, 'Class Origins and Educational Attainment', 370, make a similar concession.

76. Major and Machin, *Social Mobility*, 87.

77. Wakeling and Savage, 'Entry to Elite Positions', 314–15; Devine and Li, 'Changing Relationship', 783–4; Li and Devine, 'Is Social Mobility Declining?'.

78. Heath et al., 'Education under New Labour', 239–40; Lupton et al., 'Education', 77–8; Blanden et al., 'Intergenerational Mobility', 10–12. Consistent with effectively maintained equality, advantaged groups kept their edge during a period of widening participation by moving further up, e.g. into the 'best' universities and into postgraduate qualifications: Goldthorpe, 'Understanding Social Mobility', 443–5; Lindley and Machin, 'More and More Education', 277, 283; cf. Wakeling and Savage, 'Entry to Elite Positions', Boliver, 'How Fair is Access?', Belfield et al., 'Relative Labour Market Returns', esp. 48, on the extent to which the 'best' universities enhance or create advantage.

79. Crawford et al., 'Social Mobility', 8–9; D'Addio, 'Intergenerational Transmission', 45, 69; Payne, *New Social Mobility*, 173; Goldthorpe, 'Understanding Social

Mobility', 445–7; Bukodi and Goldthorpe, *Education and Social Mobility*, 51, 212–16. Economists are more likely to argue that investment in education would also upgrade the labour market, following human capital theory—see e.g. Belfield et al., 'Relative Labour Market Returns', 11–12—while sociologists tend to prioritize investment in workplace skills—see e.g. Liu and Grusky, 'Payoff to Skill', 1367; for both, Atkinson, *Inequality*, 84–9.

80. Uses of the term 'social mobility' show a distinct upturn in both *The Times* newspaper and in *Hansard's Parliamentary Debates* around 1990.

81. Payne, *New Social Mobility*, 73–5; David Goodhart, 'More Mobile than We Think', *Prospect*, Oct. 2008; Friedman and Laurison, *Class Ceiling*, 7–8.

82. For the connection made between education and social mobility in New Labour thinking, see Adonis and Pollard, *A Class Act*, 36, 61–2; Adonis, *Education*, xiv, 118, 210, 214.

83. Payne, *New Social Mobility*, 68–70, 96; Major and Machin, *Social Mobility*, 200; Goldthorpe and Jackson, 'Education-Based Meritocracy', 95.

84. Lupton et al., 'Education'; Heath et al., 'Education under New Labour'.

85. Goldthorpe, 'Understanding Social Mobility', 431–4, holds that there was no resurgence of interest in social mobility until the 'entry of the economists'; Payne, *New Social Mobility*, 100–4.

86. See the arguments assembled in de Waal (ed.), *Ins and Outs*, e.g. Brady, 'Case for Selection', and Smithers, 'Dilemma of Selection', esp. 195. For an interesting discussion comparing grammar-school arguments of the 1950s with their recent revival, see Ware, 'Grammar Schools'.

87. For example, already in the 2003 White Paper *The Future of Higher Education*, 67–74. Initiatives such as Educational Maintenance Allowances, Aimhigher, and Access agreements with higher-education institutions were all aimed at narrowing the attainment gap. See further Parry, 'Policy Contexts', 36–9, and Whitty et al., 'Who You Know', 28–31, but also the more realistic report, not for the Education but for the Work and Pensions Department, Nunn et al., 'Factors Influencing Social Mobility', 15, 43, 45, 47, 73–4.

88. *New Opportunities*, 1–2, 4, claiming that social mobility had already improved under its aegis, though cf. 16–20. The White Paper was followed by a Panel on Fair Access to the Professions chaired by the New Labour MP Alan Milburn.

89. E.g. Andrews et al., 'Closing the Gap', 6, 11; 'Trends in Compulsory Education', *POSTnote* 506 (Sep. 2015); Hutchinson et al., *Education in England*, 10–11; and see Lupton et al., 'Education', 87–8, Heath et al., 'Education under New Labour', 239–42, Whitty and Anders, 'Did New Labour Narrow?', 18–19, Whitty et al., 'Who You Know', 33–4, Lupton and Thomson, 'Inequalities under the Coalition', 15–16.

90. On Scottish efforts to close the attainment gap, see McCluskey, 'Closing the Attainment Gap', and Riddell, 'Wider Access'; on Wales, Blackburn, 'Student Support in Wales'; on continuing similarity between the four nations of the UK, see Machin et al., 'Educational Attainment'. 'Trends in Compulsory

Education', *POSTnote* 506 (Sep. 2015), found a short-term closure of the gap in Scotland but not England, Wales or Northern Ireland, while admitting that the data were not strictly comparable.

91. Educational Maintenance Allowances and Aimhigher were terminated at this point, and efforts concentrated on measures to shrink the attainment gap in higher education: Whitty et al., 'Who You Know', 38–40.

92. Willetts, *University Education*, 152–65, 199–201, and cf. 365, acknowledging in fact that 'disadvantaged students' *do* 'fall further behind' at every prior stage.

93. Note, for example, Breen and Jonsson, 'Inequality of Opportunity', 233–4, 236–7, considering possibility of weakening OE association at higher levels of education, but also possibility they are cancelled out by strengthening OD associations.

94. Chowdry et al., 'Widening Participation', 449, 452, 454–5; Crawford et al., 'Social Mobility', 1–4, 8–9, 11–12; Crawford et al., 'Higher Education and Intergenerational Inequality', 555–6, 564–5; see also Major and Machin, *Social Mobility*, 92–4, and, from a sociologist, Stephen Gorard, 'How to Overcome the Stratification of Higher Education', https://wonkhe.com/blogs/how-to-overcome-the-stratification-of-higher-education/#comments, 16 Mar. 2018.

95. Wooldridge, *Meritocracy*, esp. 26–32, 43–6; Phillips, *All Must Have Prizes*, 138, 334–5; Saunders, *Social Mobility Delusions*, iii, 16, 18; Hitchens, 'Selection by Wealth', 170–2.

96. Adonis and Pollard, *A Class Act*, 39, 45–6, 61–2.

97. Michael Young, 'Down with Meritocracy', *Guardian*, 29 June 2001.

98. See pp. 149–50, but also note doubts about meritocracy from perhaps unlikely quarters: Dominic Lawson, 'Stuck Fast in the Myth of Social Immobility', *Sunday Times*, 18 Jan. 2009; Elizabeth Truss, 'Academic Rigour and Social Mobility: How Low Income Students Are Being Kept Out of Top Jobs', *Centre:Forum* (Mar. 2011), 5; Mahoney and Knox, 'Selection by House Price'.

99. Kavanagh and Butler, *General Election of 2005*, 41.

100. Ball, 'Risks of Social Reproduction', Reay, 'Social Mobility', Reay, *Miseducation*, 96–8, 102, 112, 180, Snee and Devine, 'Fair Chances and Hard Work'; on disidentification, see Skeggs, *Formations of Class and Gender*, but cf. Crozier et al., 'Experiences of Working-Class Students', 71–4, and Loveday, 'Working-Class Participation', 580–2.

101. Stefan Collini, 'Blahspeak', *London Review of Books*, 8 Apr. 2010; Lawrence, *Me, Me, Me?*, 208, 229, but cf. 233–4; Littler, *Against Meritocracy*, 86–93; Bloodworth, *Myth of Meritocracy*, 133–4. See also the report of the Panel on Fair Access to the Professions, *Unleashing Aspiration*, which is one of the subjects of Collini's indictment.

102. Noted early on, e.g. in Himmelweit, 'Social Status', 156–8, Floud et al., *Social Class and Educational Opportunity*, 78, 80, 147, Young and Willmott, *Family and Kinship*, 162 (though preferring the urban to the suburban brand of aspiration), Lowndes, *Silent Social Revolution*, 265, 296–8.

103. Runciman, *Relative Deprivation*, 9–11, 49–50, 77–85, 116–18, 280, detected a shift already in the early '60s from 'fraternalistic' to 'egoistic' aspirations, but this was contested by Goldthorpe and others, for which see pp. 79–81, 194.

104. Savage, *Social Mobility*, 211–12, 403–4.

105. Atkinson, *Inequality*, 104–6.

106. See the discussion in Littler, *Against Meritocracy*, 117, 212–14, 217–21, 224; Savage, *Social Mobility*, attempts to develop a typology that distinguishes better the top fractions of Class I and the bases of their advantage; Friedman and Laurison, *Class Ceiling*, 5, 9–10 on the 'hidden mechanisms' at work in 'elite recruitment'.

107. Snee and Devine, 'Fair Chances and Hard Work', 1148.

108. E.g. YouGov surveys in Aug.-Sep. 2016, reported at https://yougov.co.uk/topics/politics/articles-reports/2016/08/15/two-thirds-people-would-send-their-child-grammar-s and https://yougov.co.uk/topics/politics/articles-reports/2016/09/15/grammar-school-fans-know-theyre-worse-for-less-abl.

109. Sutton Trust, *What the Polling Says*, 5–6.

110. See for example 2019 Ipsos MORI Survey for Sutton Trust: https://www.suttontrust.com/wp-content/uploads/2019/08/Aspirations-polling-2019.pdf.

EPILOGUE

1. As noted above, Goldin and Katz, *Race Between Technology and Education*, e.g. 164, 194, 197, 217, moves from one explanation to another: the 'central driving force' was 'substantial pecuniary returns' to individuals, but 'other matters' including non-economic 'demand' and 'community' support keep intruding.

2. But note the work of Daron Acemoglu and his colleagues who have a more institutional analysis of the 'joint evolution' of education, democracy and economic growth, without asserting a clear causal flow from one to the other: e.g. Acemoglu and Autor, 'What Does Human Capital Do?', and Acemoglu et al., 'From Education to Democracy?', 48.

3. Willetts, *University Education*, 131.

4. Goldthorpe, 'Role of Education', 270–1.

5. Gambetta, *Did They Jump?*, 168–9.

6. Trow, *Problems in the Transition*, 41.

7. McPherson and Raab, *Governing Education*, 14–15.

8. Holland et al., 'Graduates and Economic Growth', 51.

9. Flynn, *Are We Getting Smarter?*, 15, 36–40, 95–6, 102–3, 156–7, 186.

10. Among those I have found most helpful are two by Stefan Collini, *What Are Universities For?*, esp. ch. 5, and *Speaking of Universities*.

11. *Speaking of Universities*, 58–9, 66–7, 78–82, 156.

12. E.g., in the UK, Bate (ed.), *Public Value of the Humanities*, Small, *Value of the Humanities*, and in the US, Menand, *Marketplace of Ideas*, and Nussbaum, *Not for Profit*. I discuss successive waves of 'crisis of the humanities' talk in Mandler,

'Rise of the Humanities', though my primary focus was on charting the humanities' fortunes in the US, UK, and Australia, rather than making an argument for them; see also Mandler, 'Two Cultures Revisited', and for the US, Ben Schmidt, 'A Crisis in the Humanities?', 10 June 2013, http://chronicle.com/blognetwork/edgeofthewest/2013/06/10/the-humanities-crisis/, and his updates (when humanities enrolments did take a tumble) on his blog 'Sapping Attention', http://sappingattention.blogspot.co.uk/, and his Twitter feed, e.g. https://twitter.com/benmschmidt/status/804066577368944640.

13. Layard, *Happiness*, 6–8, 62–3, 200–1, 228, 255, 269–70.
14. Bynner et al., 'Revisiting the Benefits', 23, 35, 27, 40, 44–7, 49–50, and Bynner et al., 'Wider Benefits', 348–53; cf. Paterson, 'Comprehensive Education', 18–19, 29–30, using the 1958 cohort only, but comparing comprehensively educated to other students, which found little independent effect of comprehensivization in making 'a tolerant and socially conscious society'.
15. Whitty et al., 'Who You Know', 30.
16. The book was primarily an argument for the psychological and physiological benefits of greater social equality, but greater social equality and more education were seen to be correlated (though only weakly so for Britain): Wilkinson and Pickett, *Spirit Level*, 103, 105–10, and see also 159–61 for an endorsement of Blanden's correlation between income inequality and low social mobility, as so often making a link with education that Blanden did not herself necessarily make.
17. McMahon, *Higher Learning, Greater Good*, 96, 128–9, 145–6, 173, 182–5, 205–6, 243, 254.
18. King and Ritchie, 'Benefits of Higher Education'; Willetts, *University Education*, 123–41.
19. *Augar Report*, 81, 84 (but cf. 97), 101–2.
20. Clark with Heath, *Hard Times*, 144–5, 168–9.
21. 2019 Ipsos MORI Survey for Sutton Trust: https://www.suttontrust.com/wp-content/uploads/2019/08/Aspirations-polling-2019.pdf.
22. 'The Whythitt Report on Comprehensive Universities', *Times Educational Supplement*, 13 Dec. 1963.

Bibliography

ARCHIVES

Mark Abrams Papers, Churchill Archives Centre, Churchill College, Cambridge
Anthony Crosland Papers, London School of Economics
Labour Party Archives, People's History Museum, Manchester
Mass Observation Archive, University of Sussex
National Archives (TNA)
    CAB   Papers of the Cabinet Office
    ED   Papers of the Board of Education and its successors
    PREM Papers of the Prime Minister's Office
    T   Treasury Papers
    UGC   Papers of the University Grants Committee
Michael Stewart Papers, Churchill Archives Centre, Churchill College, Cambridge

INTERVIEWS

Mark Abrams, by Dominic Abrams, 19 Sep. 1984: https://surveyresearch.weebly.com/uploads/2/9/9/8/2998485/markabrams_interview_damainfeb22nd2012w97versionclean.pdf
Lord (Kenneth) Baker, 30 Oct. 2014
Dr Celia Phillips, 5 May 2017

OFFICIAL PUBLICATIONS

Board of Education, *Education in 1938*, Cmd. 6013 (1938–39)
Board of Education, *The Education of the Adolescent* (London, 1927) [*Hadow Report*]
Business, Innovation and Skills Select Committee, Oral Evidence, 18 Jul. 2011: https://publications.parliament.uk/pa/cm201012/cmselect/cmbis/885/110718.htm
Choice and Diversity: A New Framework for Schools, Cm. 2021 (1992–3)
Committee on Higher Education, *Higher Education*, Cmnd. 2154 (1962–3) [*Robbins Report*]
Council for Scientific Policy, *Enquiry into the Flow of Candidates in Science and Technology into Higher Education*, Cmnd. 3541 (1967–8) [*Dainton Report*]
Curriculum and Examinations in Secondary School (London, 1943) [*Norwood Report*]
Department for Business, Innovation and Skills, *Higher Education: Students at the Heart of the System*, Cm. 8122 (2011)

Department for Education, 'A-level and Other Level 3 Results': https://webarchive.
nationalarchives.gov.uk/20110906154901/http://www.education.gov.uk/rsgateway/
DB/SFR/s000986/index.shtml, published 21 Jan. 2016

Department for Education, 'GCE/Applied GCE A/AS and Equivalent Examination
Results': https://webarchive.nationalarchives.gov.uk/20110906154901/http://www.
education.gov.uk/rsgateway/DB/SFR/s000986/index.shtml, archived 6 Sep. 2011

Department for Education, 'Nicky Morgan Speaks at Launch of Your Life
Campaign', 10 Nov. 2014: https://www.gov.uk/government/speeches/nicky-
morgan-speaks-at-launch-of-your-life-campaign

Department for Education, *Participation Rates in Higher Education* (London, 2018)

Department for Education and Skills, *The Future of Higher Education*, Cm. 5735
(2002–03)

Department of Education and Science, *Children and their Primary Schools* (London,
1967) [*Plowden Report*]

Department of Education and Science, *Education Statistics for the United Kingdom*

Department of Education and Science, *Future Trends in Higher Education* (London,
1979)

Department of Education and Science, *Reports on Education*

Department of Education and Science, *Statistical Bulletins*

Department of Education and Science, *Statistics of Education*

The Development of Higher Education into the 1990s, Cmnd. 9524 (1984–5)

Education: A Framework for Expansion, Cmnd 5174 (1972–3)

Education and Employment Committee, *Access for All? A Survey of Post-16
Participation*, HC57 (1998–9)

Education, Science and Arts Committee, *The Funding and Organisation of Courses in
Higher Education*, HC787 (1979–80)

Education, Science and Arts Committee, *University Funding*, HC449 (1980–1)

Education, Science and Arts Committee, *The Second Scrutiny Session 1982; Minutes of
Evidence*, HC480 (1981–2)

Education, Science and Arts Committee, *Higher Education*, HC87 (1988–9)

The Government's Expenditure Plans, Cmnd. 6271 (1976–7)

The Government's Expenditure Plans 1981–82 to 1983–84, Cmnd. 8175 (1980–1)

The Government's Expenditure Plans 1982–83 to 1984–85, Cmnd. 8494 (1981–2)

The Government's Expenditure Plans 1989–90 to 1991–92, Cm. 612 (1988–9)

Hansard's Parliamentary Debates [*Hansard*]

Higher Education: A New Framework, Cm. 1541 (1990–1)

*Higher Education: Government Statement on the Report of the Committee Under the
Chairmanship of Lord Robbins 1961–63*, Cmnd. 2165 (1963–4)

Higher Education: Meeting the Challenge, Cm. 114 (1986–7)

Higher Education Statistics Agency: https://www.hesa.ac.uk/data-and-analysis/
releases

Higher Education Statistics Agency, *Destination of Leavers from Higher Education
2012/13*: https://www.hesa.ac.uk/intros/dlheintro1213

Higher Education Statistics Agency, *Higher Education Statistics for the United Kingdom*

Higher Technological Education, Cmd. 8357 (1950–1)

Independent Panel Report to the Review of Post-18 Education and Funding, CP117 (2019) [*Augar Report*]

Ministry of Education, *15 to 18* (London, 1959) [*Crowther Report*]

Ministry of Education, *Early Leaving* (London, 1954) [*Gurney-Dixon Report*]

Ministry of Education, *Half Our Future* (London, 1963) [*Newsom Report*]

Ministry of Education, *Higher Technological Education* (1945) [*Percy Report*]

Ministry of Education, *The New Secondary Education* (London, 1947)

Ministry of Education and Scottish Education Department, *Grants for Students*, Cmnd. 1051 (1959–60) [*Anderson Report*]

National Committee of Inquiry into Higher Education, *Higher Education in the Learning Society* (London, 1997) [*Dearing Report*]

New Opportunities: Fair Chances for the Future, Cm. 7533 (2009)

Office of National Statistics: http://www.ons.gov.uk

Parliamentary Office of Science and Technology, *POSTnotes*

Review of the University Grants Committee, Cm. 81 (1986–7) [*Croham Report*]

Review of Vocational Education (2011) [*Wolf Report*]

Scottish Education Department, *Grants to Students*, Cmnd. 1051 (1960)

Securing a Sustainable Future for Higher Education: An Independent Review of Higher Education Funding and Student Finance (2010) [*Browne Report*]

SET for Success: The Supply of People with Science, Technology, Engineering and Mathematics Skills: The Report of Sir Gareth Roberts' Review (2002) [*Roberts Report*]

Secondary Education For All: A New Drive, Cmnd. 604 (1958)

Technical Education, Cmd. 9703 (1955–6)

University Grants Committee, *Annual Survey, Academic Year 1980–81*, Cmnd. 8663 (1981–2)

University Grants Committee, *Annual Survey, Academic Year 1981–82*, Cmnd. 8965 (1983–4)

University Grants Committee, *University Development: Interim Report on the Years 1947 to 1951*, Cmd. 8473 (1951–2)

University Grants Committee, *University Development 1962–1967*, Cmnd. 3820 (1968–9)

University Grants Committee, *University Development 1967–1972*, Cmnd. 5728 (1974)

Universities' Statistical Record, *University Statistics*

Unleashing Aspiration: The Final Report of the Panel on Fair Access to the Professions (London, 2009)

Wakeham Review of STEM Degree Provision and Graduate Employability (2016) [*Wakeham Report*]

NEWSPAPERS AND MAGAZINES

Centre:Forum

Education

Encounter

The Listener
London Review of Books
(Manchester) Guardian
Nature
New Society
New Statesman
OECD Education Today
OECD Trends Shaping Education
Prospect
Sunday Times
Swinton Journal
The Times
Times Educational Supplement (TES)
Times Higher Education Supplement (THES)
Where: The Education Magazine for Parents

BOOKS AND ARTICLES

Abbott, Joan, *Student Life in a Class Society* (Oxford, 1971)

Abrams, Lynn, 'Mothers and Daughters: Negotiating the Discourse on the "Good Woman" in 1950s and 1960s Britain', in Michael Gauvreau and Stephen J. Heathorn (eds), *The Sixties and Beyond: Dechristianization in North America and Western Europe, 1945–2000* (Toronto, 2012), 60–83

Abrams, Lynn and Callum G. Brown (eds), *A History of Everyday Life in Twentieth-Century Scotland* (Edinburgh, 2010)

Abrams, Lynn, Barry Hazley, Valerie Wright, and Ade Kearns, 'Aspiration, Agency, and the Production of New Selves in a Scottish New Town, c.1947–c.2016', *Twentieth-Century British History* 29 (2018), 576–604

Acemoglu, Daron and David Autor, 'What Does Human Capital Do? A Review of Goldin and Katz's *The Race between Education and Technology*', *Journal of Economic Literature* 50 (2012), 426–63

Acemoglu, Daron, Simon Johnson, James A. Robinson, and Pierre Yared, 'From Education to Democracy?', *American Economic Review* 95 (2005), 44–9

Adonis, Andrew, *Education, Education, Education: Reforming England's Schools* (London, 2012)

Adonis, Andrew and Stephen Pollard, *A Class Act: The Myth of Britain's Classless Society* (London, 1997)

Aldcroft, Derek H., *Education, Training and Economic Performance* (Manchester, 1992)

Allen, Rebecca, 'Allocating Pupils to Their Nearest Secondary School: The Consequences for Social and Ability Stratification', *Urban Studies* 44 (2007), 751–70

Allen, Rebecca and Anna Vignoles, 'What Should an Index of School Segregation Measure?', *Oxford Review of Education* 33 (2007), 643–68

Allen, Rebecca, John Coldron, and Anne West, 'The Effect of Changes in Published Secondary School Admissions on Pupil Composition', *Journal of Education Policy* 27 (2012), 349–66

Anders, Jake, Morag Henderson, Vanessa Moulton, and Alice Sullivan, 'The Role of Schools in Explaining Individuals' Subject Choices at Age 14', *Oxford Review of Education* 44 (2018), 75–93

Anderson, Perry, *English Questions* (London, 1992)

Anderson, Robert, *British Universities Past and Present* (London, 2006)

Annan, Noel, *Our Age: Portrait of a Generation* (London, 1990)

Ansell, Ben W., *From the Ballot to the Blackboard: The Redistributive Political Economy of Education* (Cambridge, 2010)

Armytage, W. H. G., 'Thoughts after Robbins', in John Lawlor (ed.), *The New University* (London, 1968), 77–100

Arnott, Margaret A., ' "The More Things Change…?": The Thatcher Years and Educational Reform in Scotland', *Journal of Educational Administration and History* 43 (2011), 181–202

Ashton, D. N., 'The Transition from School to Work: Notes on the Development of Different Frames of Reference Among Young Male Workers', *Sociological Review*, n.s., 21 (1973), 101–25

'Assessment of Examination Performance in Different Types of Schools', *Journal of the Royal Statistical Society, Ser. A (General)* 147 (1984), 569–81

Atkinson, Anthony B., *Inequality: What Can Be Done?* (Cambridge MA, 2015)

Bagnall, Gaynor, Brian Longhurst, and Mike Savage, 'Children, Belonging and Social Capital: The PTA and Middle Class Narratives of Social Involvement in the North-West of England', *Sociological Research Online* 8:4 (2003), http://www. socresonline.org.uk/8/4/bagnall.html

Bailey, Bill, 'James Chuter Ede and the 1944 Education Act', *History of Education* 24 (1995), 209–20

Baines, Dudley and Paul Johnson, 'In Search of the "Traditional" Working Class: Social Mobility and Occupational Continuity in Interwar London', *Economic History Review*, n.s., 52 (1999), 692–713

Baker, Kenneth, *The Turbulent Years: My Life in Politics* (London, 1993)

Ball, Ben and Tom Bourner, 'The Employment of Psychology Graduates', *Bulletin of the British Psychological Society* 37 (1984), 39–40

Ball, Stephen J., *The Education Debate* (Bristol, 2008)

Ball, Stephen J., 'The Risks of Social Reproduction: The Middle Class and Education Markets', *London Review of Education* 1 (2003), 163–75

Banks, J. A., 'Employment of Sociology and Anthropology Graduates: Final Report', *British Journal of Sociology* 9 (1958), 271–83

Banks, Olive, *Parity and Prestige in English Secondary Education: A Study in Educational Sociology* (London, 1955)

Bantock, G. H., 'Education in an Industrial Society' (1963), in Harold Silver (ed.), *Equal Opportunity in Education: A Reader in Social Class and Educational Opportunity* (London, 1973), 208–16

Barber, Michael, *The Making of the 1944 Education Act* (London, 1994)

Barker, Paul, 'A Tract for the Times', in Geoff Dench (ed.), *The Rise and Rise of Meritocracy* (Oxford, 2006), 36–44

Barker, Rodney, *Education and Politics 1900–1951: A Study of the Labour Party* (Oxford, 1972)

Barnard, G. A. and M. D. McCreath, 'Subject Commitments and the Demand for Higher Education', *Journal of the Royal Statistical Society, Ser. A (General)* 133 (1970), 358–408

Barron, Hester, 'Parents, Teachers and Children's Well-being in London, 1918-1939', in Hester Barron and Claudia Siebrecht (eds), *Parenting and the State in Britain and Europe, c. 1870–1950: Raising the Nation* (Basingstoke, 2017)

Bate, Jonathan, *The Public Value of the Humanities* (London, 2011)

Batley, Richard, Oswald O'Brien, and Henry Parris, *Going Comprehensive: Educational Policy-Making in Two County Boroughs* (London, 1970)

Batteson, Charles, 'A Review of Politics of Education in the "Moment of 1976"', *British Journal of Educational Studies* 45 (1997), 363–77

Becker, Gary S., *Human Capital: A Theoretical and Empirical Analysis, with Special Reference to Education*, 3rd ed. (Chicago, 1993)

Bebber, Brett, ' "We Were Just Unwanted": Bussing, Migrant Dispersal, and South Asians in London', *Journal of Social History* 48 (2015), 635–61

Beckett, Andy, *When the Lights Went Out: What Really Happened to Britain in the Seventies* (London, 2009)

Beers, Laura, *Red Ellen: The Life of Ellen Wilkinson, Socialist, Feminist, Internationalist* (Cambridge MA, 2016)

Belfield, Chris, Jack Britton, Franz Buscha, Lorraine Dearden, Matt Dickson, Laura van der Erve, Luke Sibieta, Anna Vignoles, Ian Walker, and Yu Zhu, 'The Relative Labour Market Returns to Different Degrees', Institute for Fiscal Studies, Research Report (2018)

Benn, Caroline, 'Comprehensive School Reform and the 1945 Labour Government', *History Workshop Journal* 10:1 (1980), 197–204

Benn, Caroline and Clyde Chitty, *Thirty Years On: Is Comprehensive Education Alive and Well or Struggling to Survive?* (London, 1996)

Benn, R. and R. Fieldhouse, 'Government Policies on University Expansion and Wider Access, 1945–51 and 1985–91 Compared', *Studies in Higher Education* 18 (1993), 299–313

Bennett, Judith, Fred Lubben, and Gillian Hampden-Thompson, 'Schools That Make a Difference to Post-Compulsory Uptake of Physical Science Subjects: Some Comparative Case Studies in England', *International Journal of Science Education* 35 (2013), 663–89

Bennett, Robert, Howard Glennerster, and Douglas Nevison, 'Investing in Skill: To Stay On or Not to Stay On?', *Oxford Review of Economic Policy* 8 (1992), 130–45

Bentwich, Helen C., 'Two Views on the Future of Secondary Education', *Political Quarterly* 23 (1952), 134–46

Berg, Ellen L., '"To Become Good Members of Civil Society and Patriotic Americans": Mass Education in the United States, 1870–1930', in Laurence Brockliss and Nicola Sheldon (eds), *Mass Education and the Limits of State Building, c. 1870–1930* (Basingstoke, 2012), 177–201

Berman, Eli, John Bound, and Stephen Machin, 'Implications of Skill-Biased Technological Change: International Evidence', *Quarterly Journal of Economics* 113 (1998), 1245–79

Bernstein, Basil, 'Elaborated and Restricted Codes: Their Social Origins and Some Consequences', *American Anthropologist* 66:6 (1964), supp., 55–69

Bird, Richard, 'Reflections on the British Government and Higher Education', *Higher Education Quarterly* 48 (1994), 73–85

Black, Lawrence, *The Political Culture of the Left in Affluent Britain, 1951–64* (Basingstoke, 2003)

Black, Lawrence, 'Social Democracy as a Way of Life: Fellowship and the Socialist Union, 1951–9', *Twentieth Century British History* 10 (1999), 499–539

Black, Lawrence, Hugh Pemberton, and Pat Thane (eds), *Reassessing 1970s Britain* (Manchester, 2013)

Black, Lawrence and Hugh Pemberton, 'Introduction: The Benighted Decade? Reassessing the 1970s', in Lawrence Black, Hugh Pemberton, and Pat Thane (eds), *Reassessing 1970s Britain* (Manchester, 2013), 1–24

Black, Sandra E. and Paul J. Devereux, 'Recent Developments in Intergenerational Mobility', IZA Discussion Paper 4866 (Apr. 2010)

Blackburn, Lucy Hunter, 'Student Support in Wales: A Case of Progressive Universalism?', in Sheila Riddell, Sarah Minty, Elisabet Weedon, and Susan Whittaker (eds), *Higher Education Funding and Access in International Perspective* (Bingley, 2018), 13–37

Blackburn, Robert M. and Jennifer Jarman, 'Changing Inequalities in Access to British Universities', *Oxford Review of Education* 19 (1993), 197–215

Blanden, Jo, 'Cross-Country Rankings in Intergenerational Mobility: A Comparison of Approaches from Economics and Sociology', *Journal of Economic Surveys* 27 (2013), 38–73

Blanden, Jo, Paul Gregg, and Stephen Machin, 'Educational Inequality and Intergenerational Mobility', in Stephen Machin and Anna Vignoles (eds), *What's the Good of Education? The Economics of Education in the UK* (Princeton, 2005), 99–114

Blanden, Jo, Paul Gregg, and Stephen Machin, *Intergenerational Mobility in Europe and North America: A Report Supported by the Sutton Trust* (London, 2005)

Blanden, Jo, Paul Gregg, and Lindsey Macmillan, 'Intergenerational Persistence in Income and Social Class: The Effect of Within-Group Inequality', *Journal of the Royal Statistical Society, Ser. A* 176 (2013), 541–63

Blanden, Jo and Stephen Machin, 'Educational Inequality and the Expansion of UK Higher Education', *Scottish Journal of Political Economy* 51 (2004), 230–49

Blanden, Jo and Stephen Machin, *Recent Changes in Intergenerational Mobility in Britain: A Report for the Sutton Trust* (London, 2007)

Blaug, Mark, 'The Empirical Status of Human Capital Theory: A Slightly Jaundiced Survey', *Journal of Economic Literature* 14 (1976), 827–55

Blaug, Mark, 'The Rate of Return on Investment in Education' (1965), in M. Blaug (ed.), *Economics of Education 1: Selected Readings* (Harmondsworth: Penguin, 1968), 215–59

Blaug, Mark, 'Where Are We Now in the Economics of Education?', *Economics of Education Review* 4 (1985), 17–25

Blenkinsop, Sarah, Tamaris McCrone, Pauline Wade, and Marian Morris, 'How Do Young People Make Choices at 14 and 16?', Research Report RR773, Department for Education and Skills (2006)

Blume, Stuart S., 'A Framework for Analysis', in Geoffrey Oldham (ed.), *The Future of Research* (Guildford, 1982), 5–47

Boaden, Noel, *Urban Policy-Making: Influences on County Boroughs in England and Wales* (Cambridge, 1971)

Bolton, Paul, 'Education: Historical Statistics', Standard Note SG/4252, House of Commons Library (2012)

Bolton, Paul, 'Education Spending in the UK', Briefing Paper SN01078, House of Commons Library (Jul. 2019)

Bloodworth, James, *The Myth of Meritocracy: Why Working-Class Kids Get Working-Class Jobs* (London, 2016)

Blossfeld, Hans-Peter and Yossi Shavit, 'Persisting Barriers: Changes in Educational Opportunities in Thirteen Countries', in Yossi Shavit and Hans-Peter Blossfeld (eds), *Persistent Inequality: Changing Educational Attainment in Thirteen Countries* (Boulder CO, 1993), 1–23

Blundell, Richard, David A. Green, and Wenchao Jin, 'The UK Wage Premium Puzzle: How Did a Large Increase in University Graduates Leave the Education Premium Unchanged?', IFS Working Paper W16/01, Institute for Fiscal Studies (2016)

Boli, John, Francisco O. Ramirez, and John W. Meyer, 'Explaining the Origins and Expansion of Mass Education', *Comparative Education Review* 29 (1985), 145–70

Boliver, Vikki, 'How Fair is Access to More Prestigious UK Universities?', *British Journal of Sociology* 64 (2013), 344–64

Boliver, Vikki and Adam Swift, 'Do Comprehensive Schools Reduce Social Mobility?', *British Journal of Sociology* 62 (2011), 89–110

Bott, Elizabeth, *Family and Social Network* (London, 1957)

Boyle, Edward, 'The Politics of Secondary School Reorganisation: Some Reflections', *Journal of Educational Administrative and History* 4:2 (1972), 28–38

Boyle, Edward, Anthony Crosland, and Maurice Kogan, *The Politics of Education* (Harmondsworth, 1971)

Boys, C. J. et al., *Higher Education and the Preparation for Work* (London, 1988)

Boys, C. J. and John Kirkland, *Degrees of Success: Career Aspirations and Destinations of College, University and Polytechnic Graduates* (London, 1988)

Brady, Graham, 'The Twenty-First Century Case for Selection', in Anastasia de Waal (ed.), *The Ins and Outs of Selective Secondary Schools: A Debate* (London, 2015), 29–54

Breen, Richard and John H. Goldthorpe, 'Explaining Educational Differentials: Towards a Formal Rational Action Theory', *Rationality and Society* 9 (1997), 275–305

Breen, Richard and Jan O. Jonsson, 'Inequality of Opportunity in Comparative Perspective: Recent Research on Educational Attainment and Social Mobility', *Annual Review of Sociology* 31 (2005), 223–43

Breen, Richard and Ruud Luijkx, 'Social Mobility in Europe Between 1970 and 2000', in Richard Breen (ed.), *Social Mobility in Europe* (Oxford, 2004), 38–76

Breen, Richard and Ruud Luijkx, 'Social Mobility and Education: A Comparative Analysis of Period and Cohort Trends in Britain and Germany', in Stefani Scherer, Reinhard Pollak, Gunnar Otte, and Markus Gangl (eds), *From Origin to Destination: Trends and Mechanisms in Social Stratification* (Frankfurt, 2007), 102–24

Breen, Richard, Ruud Liujkx, Walter Müller, and Reinhard Pollak, 'Non-Persistent Inequality in Educational Attainment: Evidence from Eight European Countries', *American Journal of Sociology* 114 (2009), 1475–1521

Brennan, John, 'Access Courses', in Oliver Fulton (ed.), *Access and Institutional Change* (Milton Keynes, 1989), 51–63

Bridges, David, 'Government's Construction of the Relation between Parents and Schools in the Upbringing of Children in England: 1963–2009', *Educational Theory* 60 (2010), 299–324

Bridges, David, 'Parents: Customers or Partners?', in David Bridges and Terence H. McLaughlin (eds), *Education and the Market Place* (London, 1994), 65–79

Briggs, Asa, 'The Labour Party as Crucible', in Geoff Dench (ed.), *The Rise and Rise of Meritocracy* (Oxford, 2006), 17–26

Britton, Jack, Lorraine Dearden, Neil Shephard, and Anna Vignoles, 'How English Domiciled Graduate Earnings Vary with Gender, Institution Attended, Subject and Socio-Economic Background', IFS Working Paper W16/06, Institute for Fiscal Studies (2016)

Brockliss, Laurence and Nicola Sheldon (eds), *Mass Education and the Limits of State Building, c. 1870–1930* (Basingstoke, 2012)

Brooks, Val, 'The Role of External Examinations in the Making of Secondary Modern Schools in England 1945–65', *History of Education* 37 (2008), 447–67

Brown, Richard A. with Patrick Coldstream, *A Successful Partnership* (London, 2008)

Brown, Roger with Helen Carasso, *Everything for Sale? The Marketisation of UK Higher Education* (Abingdon, 2013)

Bukodi, Erzsébet, 'Education, First Occupation and Later Occupational Attainment: Cross-cohort Changes among Men and Women in Britain', Working Paper 2009/4, CLS Cohort Studies, Centre for Longitudinal Studies (Dec. 2009)

Bukodi, Erzsébet and John H. Goldthorpe, 'Class Origins, Education and Occupational Attainment in Britain', *European Societies* 13 (2011), 347–75

Bukodi, Erzsébet and John H. Goldthorpe, 'Educational Attainment—Relative or Absolute—as a Mediator of Intergenerational Class Mobility in Britain', *Research in Social Stratification and Mobility* 43 (2016), 5–15

Bukodi, Erzsébet and John H. Goldthorpe, 'Social Class Returns to Higher Education: Chances of Access to the Professional and Managerial Salariat for Men in Three British Birth Cohorts', *Longitudinal and Life Course Studies* 2 (2011), 185–201

Bukodi, Erzsébet and John H. Goldthorpe, *Social Mobility and Education in Britain: Research, Politics and Policy* (Cambridge, 2019)

Bukodi, Erzsébet, John H. Goldthorpe, Lorraine Waller, and Jouni Kuha, 'The Mobility Problem in Britain: New Findings from the Analysis of Birth Cohort Data', *British Journal of Sociology* 66 (2015), 93–117

Bull, David, '*Tameside* Revisited: Prospectively "Reasonable" Retrospective "Maladministration"', *Modern Law Review* 50 (1987), 307–40

Burgess, Simon, Claire Crawford, and Lindsey Macmillan, 'Access to Grammar Schools by Socio-Economic Status', *Environment and Planning A: Economy and Space* 50 (2018), 1381–5

Burgess, Simon, Ellen Greaves, and Anna Vignoles, 'School Choice in England: Evidence from National Administrative Data', *Oxford Review of Education* 45 (2019), 690–710

Burgess, Tyrrell, 'Autonomous and Service Traditions', in Leslie Wagner (ed.), *Agenda for Institutional Change in Higher Education* (Guildford, 1982), 70–9

Burgess, Tyrrell, *Inside Comprehensive Schools* (London, 1970)

Burnhill, Peter, Catherine Garner, and Andrew McPherson, 'Social Change, School Attainment and Entry to Higher Education 1976-1986', in David Raffe (ed.), *Education and the Youth Labour Market: Schooling and Scheming* (London, 1988), 66–99

Burt, Cyril, 'The Mental Differences between Children', in C. B. Cox and A. E. Dyson (eds), *The Black Papers on Education* (London, 1971), 45–63

Butcher, H. J., 'An Investigation of the "Swing from Science"', *Research in Education* 1 (May 1969), 38–57

Butler, D. E., *The British General Election of 1951* (London, 1952)

Butler, D. E., *The British General Election of 1955* (London, 1955)

Butler, D. E. and Dennis Kavanagh, *The British General Election of 1992* (Basingstoke, 1992)

Butler, D. E. and Dennis Kavanagh, *The British General Election of 1997* (Basingstoke, 1997)

Butler, D. E. and Anthony King, *The British General Election of 1964* (London, 1965)

Butler, D. E. and Richard Rose, *The British General Election of 1959* (London, 1960)

Butler, Lise, 'Michael Young, the Institute of Community Studies, and the Politics of Kinship', *Twentieth Century British History* 26 (2015), 203–24

Bynner, J. M., *Parents' Attitudes to Education* (London, 1972)

Bynner, John, Thomas Schuller, and Leon Feinstein, 'Wider Benefits of Education: Skills, Higher Education and Civic Engagement', *Zeitschrift für Pädagogik* 49 (2003), 341–61

Bynner, John, Peter Dolton, Leon Feinstein, Gerry Makepeace, Lars Malmberg, and Laura Woods, 'Revisiting the Benefits of Higher Education', Report by the Bedford Group for Lifecourse and Statistical Studies, Institute of Education (2003)

Byrne, Eileen M., *Planning and Educational Inequality: A Study of the Rationale of Resource-Allocation* (Windsor, 1974)

Callaghan, Daniel, *Conservative Party Education Policies 1976–1997: The Influence of Politics and Personality* (Brighton, 2006)

Callaghan, Lord (James), 'The Education Debate I', in Michael Williams, Richard Daugherty, and Frank Banks (eds), *Continuing the Education Debate* (London, 1992), 11–16

Callender, Claire and Kevin J. Dougherty, 'Student Choice in Higher Education— Reducing or Reproducing Social Inequalities?', *Social Sciences* 7:10 (2018), 1–28

Campbell, Flann, *Eleven-Plus and All That: The Grammar School in a Changing Society* (London, 1956)

Cannadine, David, Jenny Keating, and Nicola Sheldon, *The Right Kind of History: Teaching the Past in Twentieth-Century Britain* (Basingstoke, 2011)

Carpentier, Vincent, 'Public Expenditure on Education and Economic Growth in the UK, 1833–2000', *History of Education* 32 (2003), 1–15

Carpentier, Vincent, 'Public Expenditure on Education and Economic Growth in the USA in the Nineteenth and Twentieth Centuries in Comparative Perspective', *Paedagogica Historica* 42 (2006), 683–706

Carswell, John, *Government and the Universities in Britain: Programme and Performance 1960–1980* (Cambridge, 1985)

Carter, M. P., *Home, School and Work: A Study of the Education and Employment of Young People in Britain* (Oxford, 1962)

Cebulla, Andreas and Wojtek Tomaszewski, 'The Demise of Certainty: Shifts in Aspirations and Achievement at the Turn of the Century', *International Journal of Adolescence and Youth* 18 (2013), 141–57

Centre for Contemporary Cultural Studies Education Group, *Unpopular Education: Schooling and Social Democracy in England since 1944* (London, 1981)

Chevalier, Arnaud, Colm Harmon, Ian Walker, and Yu Zhu, 'Does Education Raise Productivity, or Just Reflect It?', *Economic Journal* 114 (2004), F499–517

Chevalier, Arnaud and Ian Walker, 'United Kingdom', in Colm Harmon, Ian Walker, and Niels Westergaard-Nielsen (eds), *Education and Earnings in Europe: A Cross Country Analysis of the Returns to Education* (Cheltenham, 2001), 302–30

Chitty, Clyde, *New Labour and Secondary Education, 1994–2010* (Basingstoke, 2013)

Chitty, Clyde, *Towards a New Education System: The Victory of the New Right?* (London, 1989)

Chowdry, Haroon, Claire Crawford, Lorraine Dearden, Alissa Goodman, and Anna Vignoles, 'Widening Participation in Higher Education: Analysis Using Linked Administrative Data', *Journal of the Royal Statistical Society, Ser. A* 176 (2013), 431–57

Clapson, Mark, *Invincible Green Suburbs, Brave New Towns: Social Change and Urban Dispersal in Postwar England* (Manchester, 1998)

Clark, Damon, Gavan Conlon, and Fernando Galindo-Rueda, 'Post-Compulsory Education and Qualification Attainment', in Stephen Machin and Anna Vignoles (eds), *What's the Good of Education? The Economics of Education in the UK* (Princeton, 2005), 71–97

Clark, Tom with Anthony Heath, *Hard Times: Inequality, Recession, Aftermath* (New Haven CT, 2014)

Cohen, Daniel and Marcelo Soto, 'Growth and Human Capital: Good Data, Good Results', *Journal of Economic Growth* 12 (2007), 51–76

Coldron, John, Ben Willis, and Claire Wolstenholme, 'Selection by Attainment and Aptitude in English Secondary Schools', *British Journal of Educational Studies* 57 (2009), 245–64

Collini, Stefan, *Speaking of Universities* (London, 2017)

Collini, Stefan, *What Are Universities For?* (London, 2012)

Conlon, Gavan and Pietro Patrignani, 'The Returns to Higher Education Qualifications', Research Paper 45, Department for Business, Innovation and Skills (2011)

Coleman, James S. et al., *Equality of Educational Opportunity* (Washington, 1966)

Connor, Helen, 'Different Graduates, Different Labour Market: Is There A Mismatch In Supply-Demand?', in Mary Henkel and Brenda Little (eds), *Changing Relationships between Higher Education and the State* (London, 1999), 90–104

Cox, Brian, *The Great Betrayal* (London, 1992)

Cox, C. B. and A. E. Dyson (eds), *The Black Papers on Education* (London, 1971)

Crawford, Claire, Paul Gregg, Lindsey Macmillan, Anna Vignoles, and Gill Wyness, 'Higher Education, Career Opportunities, and Intergenerational Inequality', *Oxford Review of Economic Policy* 32 (2016), 553–75

Crawford, Claire, Paul Johnson, Steve Machin, and Anna Vignoles, 'Social Mobility: A Literature Review', Department for Business, Innovation and Skills, March 2011

Crook, David, 'Edward Boyle: Conservative Champion of Comprehensives?', *History of Education* 22 (1993), 49–62

Crook, David, 'Missing, Presumed Dead? What Happened to the Comprehensive School in England and Wales?', in Barry M. Franklin and Gary McCulloch (eds), *The Death of the Comprehensive High School? Historical, Contemporary, and Comparative Perspectives* (Basingstoke, 2007), 147–67

Crook, David, Sally Power, and Geoff Whitty, *The Grammar School Question: A Review of Research on Comprehensive and Selective Education* (London, 1999)

Crosland, C. A. R., *The Future of Socialism* (London, 1956)

Crosland, Susan, *Tony Crosland* (London, 1982)

Crossman, Richard, *The Diaries of a Cabinet Minister, Vol. I: 1964–1966* (New York, 1976)

Crowther-Hunt, Lord (Norman), 'Policy Making and Accountability in Higher Education', in Michael Shattock (ed.), *The Structure and Governance of Higher Education* (Guildford, 1983), 46–67

Crozier, Gill, Diane Reay, and John Clayton, 'The Socio-Cultural and Learning Experiences of Working-Class Students in Higher Education', in Miriam David (ed.), *Improving Learning by Widening Participation in Higher Education* (London, 2010), 62–74

Cuin, Charles-Henry, 'Durkheim et la mobilité sociale', *Revue française de sociologie* 28 (1987), 43–65

D'Addio, Anna Cristina, 'Intergenerational Transmission of Disadvantage: Mobility or Immobility across Generations? A Review of the Evidence for OECD Countries', *OECD Social, Employment and Migration Working Papers* 52 (2007)

Daglish, Neil, *Education Policy-Making in England and Wales: The Crucible Years, 1895–1911* (London, 1996)

Dainton, Frederick, 'A Note on Science in Higher Education', in W. Roy Niblett (ed.), *The Sciences, the Humanities and the Technological Threat* (London, 1975), 36–41

Dale, Roger, 'Thatcherism and Education', in John Ahier and Michael Flude (eds), *Contemporary Education Policy* (London, 1983), 233–55

Daly, Anne, Phil Lewis, Michael Corliss, and Tiffany Heaslip, 'The Private Rate of Return to a University Degree in Australia', *Australian Journal of Education* 59 (2015), 97–112

David, Miriam (ed.), *Improving Learning by Widening Participation in Higher Education* (London, 2010)

Davies, Wynford, *The Curriculum and Organization of the County Intermediate Schools 1880–1926* (Cardiff, 1989)

Davis, Angela, *Modern Motherhood: Women and Family in England, 1945–2000* (Manchester, 2012)

Davis, John, 'The Inner London Education Authority and the William Tyndale Junior School Affair, 1974–1976', *Oxford Review of Education* 28 (2002), 275–98

Davis, Norah M., 'The Hopes of Industrial Workers for their Children', *Occupational Psychology* 27 (1953), 11–22

Dean, Dennis W., 'Circular 10/65 Revisited: The Labour Government and the "Comprehensive Revolution" in 1964–1965', *Paedagogica Historica* 34 (1998), 63–91

Dean, Dennis W., 'Consensus or Conflict? The Churchill Government and Educational Policy 1951–55', *History of Education* 21 (1992), 15–35

Dean, Dennis W., 'Conservatism and the National Education System 1922–40', *Journal of Contemporary History* 6 (1971), 150–65

Dean, Dennis W., 'Conservative Governments, 1951–64, and Their Changing Perspectives on the 1944 Education Act', *History of Education* 24 (1995), 247–66

Dean, Dennis W., 'The Dilemmas of an Academic Liberal Historian in Lloyd George's Government: H.A.L. Fisher at the Board of Education, 1916–1922', *History* 79 (1994), 57–81

Dean, Dennis W., 'Preservation or Renovation? The Dilemmas of Conservative Educational Policy 1955–1960', *Twentieth Century British History* 3 (1992), 3–31

Dearden, Lorraine, Emla Fitzsimons, and Gill Wyness, 'The Impact of Higher Education Finance on University Participation in the UK', Research Paper No. 11, Department for Business, Innovation and Skills (2010)

Dearing, Lord (Ron), 'Dearing on Dearing and the 2003 White Paper', *Perspectives: Policy & Practice in Higher Education* 7 (2003), 62–70

Deem, Rosemary, Kevin Brehony, and Sue Heath, *Active Citizenship and the Governing of Schools* (Buckingham, 1995)

Deer, Cécile, 'The Politics of Access to Higher Education: A Comparison between France and England', *Perspectives: Policy & Practice in Higher Education* 7 (2003), 105–9

Delamont, Sara, 'No Such Thing as a Consensus: Olive Banks and the Sociology of Education', *British Journal of Sociology* 29 (2008), 391–402

Dench, Geoff, 'Introduction: Reviewing Meritocracy', in Geoff Dench (ed.), *The Rise and Rise of Meritocracy* (Oxford, 2006), 1–14

Denham, Andrew and Mark Garnett, *Keith Joseph* (London, 2001)

Devine, Fiona and Yaojun Li, 'The Changing Relationship between Origins, Education and Destinations in the 1990s and 2000s', *British Journal of Sociology of Education* 34 (2013), 766–91

Dilnot, Andrew and Carl Emmerson, 'The Economic Environment', in A. H. Halsey with Josephine Webb (eds), *Twentieth-Century British Social Trends* (Basingstoke, 2000), 324–47

Dolton, Peter J. and Anna Vignoles, 'Overeducation: Problem Or Not?', in Mary Henkel and Brenda Little (eds), *Changing Relationships between Higher Education and the State* (London, 1999), 105–24

Donnison, D. V. and Valerie Chapman, *Social Policy and Administration: Studies in the Development of Social Services at the Local Level* (London, 1965)

Donovan, Clare, 'The Chequered Career of a Cryptic Concept', in Geoff Dench (ed.), *The Rise and Rise of Meritocracy* (Oxford, 2006), 61–72

Douglas, J. W. B., *The Home and the School: A Study of Ability and Attainment in the Primary School* (London, 1964)

Douglas, J. W. B., 'Parental Encouragement', in Maurice Craft (ed.), *Family, Class and Education: A Reader* (London, 1970), 151–7

Douglas, J. W. B., J. M. Ross, and H. R. Simpson, *All Our Future: A Longitudinal Study of Secondary Education* (London, 1968)

Driver, Justin, *The Schoolhouse Gate: Public Education, the Supreme Court, and the Battle for the American Mind* (New York, 2018)

Drucker, Peter, *The Age of Discontinuity: Guidelines to Our Changing Society*, 1st ed. 1968 (London, 1969)

Duckworth, Derek, *The Continuing Swing? Pupils' Reluctance to Study Science* (Windsor, 1978)

Duckworth, Derek and N. J. Entwistle, 'The Swing from Science: A Perspective from Hindsight', *Educational Research* 17 (1974), 48–53

Dyhouse, Carol, 'Going to University Between the Wars: Access and Funding', *History of Education* 31 (2002), 1–14

Dyhouse, Carol, *Students: A Gendered History* (Abingdon, 2006)

Echols, Frank, Andrew McPherson, and J. Douglas Willms, 'Parental Choice in Scotland', *Journal of Education Policy* 5 (1990), 207–22

Edgerton, David, *The Rise and Fall of the British Nation: A Twentieth-Century History* (London, 2018)

Edgerton, David, *Science, Technology and the British Industrial 'Decline', 1870–1970* (Cambridge, 1996)

Edwards, A. D., *The Changing Sixth Form in the Twentieth Century* (London, 1970)

Edwards, Tony and Geoff Whitty, 'Specialisation and Selection in Secondary Education', *Oxford Review of Education* 23 (1997), 5–15

Egerton, Muriel and A. H. Halsey, 'Trends by Social Class and Gender in Access to Higher Education in Britain', *Oxford Review of Education* 19 (1993), 183–96

Elder, Glen H., Jr., 'Life Opportunity and Personality: Some Consequences of Stratified Secondary Education in Great Britain', *Sociology of Education* 38 (1964–5), 173–202

Eliot, T. S., *Notes towards the Definition of Culture* (London, 1948)

Ellison, Nick, 'Consensus Here, Consensus There…but not Consensus Everywhere: The Labour Party, Equality and Social Policy in the 1950s', in Harriet Jones and Michael Kandiah (eds), *The Myth of Consensus: New Views on British History, 1945–64* (Basingstoke, 1996), 17–39

Entwistle, N. J. and D. Duckworth, 'Choice of Science Courses in Secondary School: Trends and Explanations', *Studies in Science Education* 4 (1977), 63–82

Erikson, Robert and John H. Goldthorpe, 'Has Social Mobility in Britain Decreased? Reconciling Divergent Findings on Income and Class Mobility', *British Journal of Sociology* 61 (2010), 211–30

Ertl, Hubert, Geoff Hayward, and Michael Hölscher, 'Learners' Transition from Vocational Education and Training to Higher Education', in Miriam David (ed.), *Improving Learning by Widening Participation in Higher Education* (London, 2010), 75–94

Esnault, Eric and Jean Le Pas, 'New Relations between Post-Secondary Education and Employment', in OECD, *Towards Mass Higher Education: Issues and Dilemmas* (Paris, 1974), 105–69

Evans, W. Gareth, Robert Smith, and Gareth Elwyn Jones, *Examining the Secondary Schools of Wales 1896–2000* (Cardiff, 2008)

Exley, Sonia, 'Parental Freedom to Choose and Educational Equality', *British Social Attitudes* 28 (2012), 53–76

Exley, Sonia and Stephen J. Ball, 'Something Old, Something New: Understanding Conservative Education Policy', in Hugh Bochel (ed.), *The Conservative Party and Social Policy* (Bristol, 2011), 97–117

Fearn, Edward, 'The Politics of Local Reorganization', in Roy Lowe (ed.), *The Changing Secondary School* (Lewes, 1989), 36–51

Fenwick, I. G. K., *The Comprehensive School 1944–1970: The Politics of Secondary School Reorganization* (London, 1976)

Fenwick, I. G. K. and A. J. Woodthorpe, 'The Reorganisation of Secondary Education in Leeds: The Role of Committee Chairmen and Political Parties', *Aspects of Education* 22 (1980), 18–28

Fidler, Geoffrey C., 'Labour and "Secondary Education for All" in Liverpool, c. 1902–1932', *Transactions of the Historic Society of Lancashire and Cheshire* 133 (1984), 89–111

Field, Geoffrey G., *Blood, Sweat, and Toil: Remaking the British Working Class, 1939–1945* (Oxford, 2011)

Fielding, Steven, 'The British Labour Party and "Participation" in the 1960s', in John Callaghan and Ilaria Favretto (eds), *Transitions in Social Democracy: Cultural and Ideological Problems of the Golden Age* (Manchester, 2006), 135–48

Finn, Mary E., 'Social Efficiency, Progressivism and Secondary Education in Scotland, 1885–1905', in Walter M. Humes and Hamish M. Paterson (eds), *Scottish Culture and Scottish Education 1800–1980* (Edinburgh, 1983), 175–96

Flexner, Abraham, *Universities: American, English, German*, 1st pub. 1930 (London, 1968)

Floud, J. E., 'Social Class Factors in Educational Achievement', in A. H. Halsey (ed.), *Ability and Educational Opportunity* ([Paris], 1961), 91–109

Floud, J. E., A. H. Halsey, and F. M. Martin, *Social Class and Educational Opportunity* (London, 1956)

Flynn, James R., *Are We Getting Smarter? Rising IQ in the Twenty-First Century* (Cambridge, 2012)

Fogelman, Ken (ed.), *Britain's Sixteen-Year-Olds* (London, 1976)

Fogelman, Ken (ed.), *Growing Up in Great Britain: Papers from the National Child Development Study* (London, 1983)

Fowler, Gerald, 'Past Failure and the Imperative for Change', in Leslie Wagner (ed.), *Agenda for Institutional Change in Higher Education* (Guildford, 1982), 80–99

Francis, Martin, *Ideas and Policies under Labour, 1945–1951: Building a New Britain* (Manchester, 1997)

Francis, Martin, 'A Socialist Policy for Education? Labour and the Secondary School, 1945–51', *History of Education* 24 (1995), 319–35

Franklin, Barry M. and Gary McCulloch (eds), *The Death of the Comprehensive High School? Historical, Contemporary, and Comparative Perspectives* (Basingstoke, 2007)

Freeman, Brigid, 'Federal and State STEM Policies and Programmes Spanning Australian Education, Training, Science and Innovation', in Brigid Freeman, Simon Marginson, and Russell Tytler (eds), *The Age of STEM: Educational Policy and Practice Across the World in Science, Technology, Engineering and Mathematics* (London, 2015), 178–200

Friedman, Sam, 'The Price of the Ticket: Rethinking the Experience of Social Mobility', *Sociology* 48 (2014), 352–68

Friedman, Sam and Daniel Laurison, *The Class Ceiling: Why It Pays to Be Privileged* (Bristol, 2019)

Gallup, George H. (ed.), *The Gallup International Public Opinion Polls: Great Britain 1937–1975* (New York, 1976)

Gambetta, Diego, *Were They Pushed or Did They Jump? Individual Decision Mechanisms in Education* (Cambridge, 1987)

Gamoran, Adam, 'Curriculum Standardization and Equality of Opportunity in Scottish Secondary Education, 1984–1990', *Sociology of Education* 69 (1996), 1–21

Gannicott, Kenneth and Mark Blaug, 'Scientists and Engineers in Britain' (1973), in Carolyn Baxter, P. J. O'Leary, and Adam Westoby (eds), *Economics and Education Policy: A Reader* (London, 1977), 128–46

Ganzeboom, Harry B. G., Donald J. Treiman, and Wout C. Ultee, 'Comparative Intergenerational Stratification Research: Three Generations and Beyond', *Annual Review of Sociology* 17 (1991), 277–302

Garnett, Mark, *From Anger to Apathy: The British Experience since 1975* (London, 2007)

Gaukroger, Alison and Leonard Schwarz, 'A University and Its Region: Student Recruitment to Birmingham, 1945–1975', *Oxford Review of Education* 23 (1997), 185–202

Gewirtz, Sharon, Stephen J. Ball, and Richard Bowe, *Markets, Choice and Equity in Education* (Buckingham, 1995)

Gibbons, Michael, Camille Limoges, Helga Nowotny, Simon Schwartzman, Peter Scott, and Martin Trow, *The New Production of Knowledge: The Dynamics of Science and Research in Contemporary Society* (London, 1994)

Glass, D. V. (ed.), *Social Mobility in Britain* (London, 1954)

Glaesser, Judith and Barry Cooper, 'Educational Achievement in Selective and Comprehensive Local Education Authorities: A Configurational Analysis', *British Journal of Sociology of Education* 33 (2012), 223–44

Glennerster, Howard and John Hills (eds), *The State of Welfare: The Economics of Public Spending*, 2nd ed. (Oxford, 1998)

Glennerster, Howard, 'Education and Inequality', in Peter Townsend and Nicholas Bosanquet (eds), *Labour and Inequality* (London, 1972), 83–107

Glennerster, Howard, 'Education: Reaping the Harvest?', in Howard Glennerster and John Hills (eds.), *The State of Welfare: The Economics of Public Spending*, 2nd ed. (Oxford, 1998), 27–74

Godwin, C.D., 'The Origin of the Binary System', *History of Education* 27 (1998), 171–91

Goldin, Claudia and Lawrence F. Katz, *The Race Between Education and Technology* (Cambridge MA, 2008)

Goldman, Lawrence, *The Life of R.H. Tawney: Socialism and History* (London, 2013)

Goldman, Peter, 'Opportunity in Education', in *The Future of the Welfare State: Seven Oxford Lectures* (London, 1958), 76–87

Goldthorpe, John H., 'The Current Inflation: Towards a Sociological Account', in Fred Hirsch and John H. Goldthorpe (eds), *The Political Economy of Inflation* (London, 1978), 186–214

Goldthorpe, John H., 'Problems of "Meritocracy"', in Robert Erikson and Jan O. Jonsson (eds), *Can Education Be Equalized? The Swedish Case in Comparative Perspective* (Boulder CO, 1996), 255–87

Goldthorpe, John H., 'The Role of Education in Intergenerational Social Mobility: Problems from Empirical Research in Sociology and Some Theoretical Pointers from Economics', *Rationality and Society* 26 (2014), 265–89

Goldthorpe, John H., 'Understanding—and Misunderstanding—Social Mobility in Britain: The Entry of the Economists, the Confusion of Politicians and the Limits of Educational Policy', *Journal of Social Policy* 42 (2013), 431–50

Goldthorpe, John H. with Catriona Llewellyn and Clive Payne, *Social Mobility and Class Structure in Modern Britain* (Oxford, 1980)

Goldthorpe, John H. and Michelle Jackson, 'Education-Based Meritocracy: The Barriers to its Realization', in Annette Lareau and Dalton Conley (eds), *Social Class: How Does it Work?* (New York, 2008), 93–117

Goldthorpe, John H., David Lockwood, Frank Bechhofer, and Jennifer Platt, *The Affluent Worker in the Class Structure* (Cambridge, 1969)

Goodman, Joyce, 'Comprehensive Re-Organisation: Debating Single-Sex and Mixed Education in Wiltshire 1967–1985', *Journal of Educational Administration and History* 36 (2004), 159–69

Goos, Maarten, Alan Manning, and Anna Salomons, 'Job Polarization in Europe', *American Economic Review* 99:2 (2009), 58–63

Gorard, Stephen, 'The Complex Determinants of School Intake Characteristics and Segregation, England 1989 to 2014', *Cambridge Journal of Education* 46 (2016), 131–46

Gorard, Stephen and Emma Smith, 'An International Comparison of Equity in Education Systems', *Comparative Education* 40 (2004), 15–28

Gorard, Stephen, Chris Taylor, and John Fitz, 'Does School Choice Lead to "Spirals of Decline"?', *Journal of Education Policy* 17 (2002), 367–84

Gordon, Peter and John White, *Philosophers as Educational Reformers: The Influence of Idealism on British Educational Thought and Practice* (London, 1979)

Gosden, Peter, *Education in the Second World War: A Study in Policy and Administration* (London, 1976)

Gosden, Peter, *The Education System since 1944* (Oxford, 1983)

Gosden, Peter and P. R. Sharp, *The Development of an Education Service: The West Riding 1889–1974* (Oxford, 1978)

Gosling, Amanda, Stephen Machin, and Costas Meghir, 'The Changing Distribution of Male Wages in the U.K.', *Review of Economic Studies* 67 (2000), 635–66

Gow, Lesley and Andrew McPherson (eds), *Tell Them From Me: Scottish School Leavers Write about School and Life Afterwards* (Aberdeen, 1980)

Gray, John, David Jesson, and Ben Jones, 'Predicting Differences in Examination Results between Local Education Authorities: Does School Organisation Matter?', *Oxford Review of Education* 28 (1984), 45–68

Gray, J., A. F. McPherson and D. Raffe, *Reconstructions of Secondary Education: Theory, Myth and Practice Since the War* (London, 1983)

Green, Andy, *Education and State Formation: The Rise of Education Systems in England, France and the USA* (Basingstoke, 1990)

Green, Andy, Alison Wolf, and Tom Leney, *Convergence and Divergence in European Education and Training Systems* (London, 1999)

Green, Francis and Yu Zhu, 'Overqualification, Job Dissatisfaction, and Increasing Dispersion in the Returns to Graduate Education', *Oxford Economic Papers* 62 (2010), 740–63

Green, S. J. D., *The Passing of Protestant England: Secularisation and Social Change, c. 1920–1960* (Cambridge, 2010)

Griffiths, Moira, 'Women in Higher Education: A Case Study of the Open University', in Rosemary Deem (ed.), *Schooling for Women's Work*, 1st pub. 1980 (Abingdon: Routledge, 2012), 126–41

Griggs, Clive, *The Trade Union Congress and the Struggle for Education 1868–1925* (Lewes, 1983)

Hacker, Jacob S. and Paul Pierson, *Winner-Take-All Politics*, 1st pub. 2010 (New York, 2011)

Hailsham, Viscount, *Science and Politics* (London, 1963)

Hall, J. R. and D. V. Glass, 'Education and Social Mobility', in D. V. Glass (ed.), *Social Mobility in Britain* (London, 1954), 291–307

Halsey, A. H., 'British Universities and Intellectual Life' (1958), in A. H. Halsey, Jean Floud, and C. Arnold Anderson (eds), *Education, Economy, and Society* (New York, 1961), 502–12

Halsey, A. H., *Decline of Donnish Dominion: The British Academic Professions in the Twentieth Century* (Oxford, 1992)

Halsey, A.H., 'Expansion and Equality', in Harold Silver (ed.), *Equal Opportunity in Education: A Reader in Social Class and Educational Opportunity* (London, 1973), 205–8

Halsey, A. H., 'A Hundred Years of Social Change', *Social Trends* 30 (2000), 15–20

Halsey, A. H., 'Provincials and Professionals: The British Post-War Sociologists', *European Journal of Sociology* 23 (1982), 150–75

Halsey, A. H., 'Towards Meritocracy? The Case of Britain', in Jerome Karabel and A.H. Halsey (eds), *Power and Ideology in Education* (New York, 1977), 173–86

Halsey, A. H., 'Trends in Access and Equity in Higher Education: Britain in International Perspective' (1993), in A. H. Halsey, Hugh Lauder, Phillip Brown, and Amy Stuart Wells (eds), *Education: Culture, Economy, and Society* (Oxford, 1997), 638–45

Halsey, A. H. and Denise Lievesley, 'Education: Reaction to Reform', in Roger Jowell et al. (eds.), *British Social Attitudes: The 11th Report* (Aldershot, 1994), 95–106

Halsey, A. H. (ed.), *Ability and Educational Opportunity* ([Paris], 1961)

Halsey, A. H., A. F. Heath and J. M. Ridge, *Origins and Destinations: Family, Class, and Education in Modern Britain* (Oxford, 1980)

Hammersley, Martyn, 'A Myth of a Myth? An Assessment of Two Ethnographic Studies of Option Choice Schemes', *British Journal of Sociology* 42 (1991), 61–94

Harding, Jan, 'Sex Differences in Performance in Science Examinations', in Rosemary Deem (ed.), *Schooling for Women's Work* (London, 1980), 87–97

Harkness, Susan and Stephen Machin, 'Graduate Earnings in Britain, 1974-95', Department for Education and Employment, Research Brief No. 95 (1999)

Harmon, Colm, Ian Walker and Niels Westergaard-Nielsen (eds), *Education and Earnings in Europe: A Cross Country Analysis of the Returns to Education* (Cheltenham, 2001)

Harris, Jose, 'Did British Workers Want the Welfare State? G.D.H. Cole's Survey of 1942', in Jay Winter (ed.), *The Working Class in Modern British History* (Cambridge, 1983), 200–14

Harrison, Brian, *Finding a Role? The United Kingdom, 1970–1990* (Oxford, 2010)

Harrison, Brian, *Seeking a Role: The United Kingdom, 1951–1970* (Oxford, 2009)

Harrison, M.J. and Keith Weightman, 'Academic Freedom and Higher Education in England', *British Journal of Sociology* 25 (1974), 32–46

Hayes, Nick, 'Did We Really Want a National Health Service? Hospitals, Patients and Public Opinions before 1948', *English Historical Review* 127 (2012), 625–61

Haxey, Simon, *Tory M.P.* (London, 1941)

Heald, Gordon and Robert J. Wybrow, *The Gallup Survey of Education* (London, 1986)

Healy, Josh, Kostas Mavromaras, and Rong Zhu, 'The STEM Labour Market in Australia', Australian Council of Learned Academies (2013): https://acola.org/wp-content/uploads/2018/12/Consultant-Report-Australian-Labour-Market.pdf

Heath, Anthony and Sin Yi Cheung, 'Education and Occupation in Britain', in Yossi Shavit and Walter Müller (eds), *From School to Work: A Comparative Study of Educational Qualifications and Occupational Destinations* (Oxford, 1998), 71–101

Heath, Anthony and Peter Clifford, 'Class Inequalities and Educational Reform in Twentieth-Century Britain', in David J. Lee and Bryan S. Turner (eds), *Conflicts About Class: Debating Inequality in Late Industrialism* (London, 1996), 209–24

Heath, Anthony and Clive Payne, 'Social Mobility', in A. H. Halsey and Josephine Webb (eds), *Twentieth-Century British Social Trends* (Basingstoke, 2000), 254–78

Heath, Anthony, Alice Sullivan, Vikki Boliver, and Anna Zimdars, 'Education under New Labour, 1997–2010', *Oxford Review of Economic Policy* 29 (2013), 227–47

Heaton, P. R., 'External Examinations in the Secondary Modern School', in G. B. Jeffery (ed.), *External Examinations in Secondary Schools: Their Place and Function* (London, 1958) 93–111

Hencke, David, *Colleges in Crisis: The Reorganization of Teacher Training 1971–7* (Harmondsworth, 1978)

Henderson, Morag, Alice Sullivan, Jake Anders, and Vanessa Moulton, 'Social Class, Gender and Ethnic Differences in Subjects Taken at Age 14', *Curriculum Journal* 29 (2018), 298–318

Higher Education Policy Institute (HEPI), *Demand for Higher Education to 2020* (London, 2006)

Hillman, Nicholas, 'The Coalition's Higher Education Reforms in England', *Oxford Review of Education* 42 (2016), 330–45

Hillman, Nicholas, 'From Grants for All to Loans for All: Undergraduate Finance from the Implementation of the Anderson Report (1962) to the Implementation of the Browne Report (2012)', *Contemporary British History* 27 (2013), 249–70

Hillman, Nicholas, 'Public Schools and the Fleming Report of 1944: Shunting the First-Class Carriage on to an Immense Siding', *History of Education* 41 (2012), 235–55

Himmelweit, H.T., 'Social Status and Secondary Education since the 1944 Act: Some Data for London', in D.V. Glass (ed.), *Social Mobility in Britain* (London, 1954), 141–59

Hitchens, Peter, 'Why is Selection by Wealth Better than Selection by Ability?', in Anastasia de Waal (ed.), *The Ins and Outs of Selective Secondary Schools: A Debate* (London, 2015), 167–82

Hobsbawm, Eric, *Age of Extremes: The Short Twentieth Century, 1914–1991* (London, 1994)

Hodgson, Godfrey, 'Inequality: Do Schools Make a Difference?' (1973), in Harold Silver (ed.), *Equal Opportunity in Education: A Reader in Social Class and Educational Opportunity* (London, 1973), 352–67

Hoggart, Richard, 'Higher Education and Personal Life: Changing Atittudes', in W. R. Niblett (ed.), *Higher Education: Demand and Response* (London, 1969), 211–30

Hoggart, Richard, *The Uses of Literacy*, 1st pub. 1957 (Harmondsworth, 1958)

Holland, Dawn, Iana Liadze, Cinzia Rienzo, and David Wilkinson, 'The Relationship between Graduates and Economic Growth Across Countries', Research Paper No. 110, Department for Business, Innovation and Skills (Aug. 2013)

Holmes, Craig and Ken Mayhew, *The Changing Shape of the UK Job Market and its Implications for the Bottom Half of Earners* (London, 2012)

Homer, Matt, Jim Ryder, and Jim Donnelly, 'Sources of Differential Participation Rates in School Science: The Impact of Curriculum Reform', *British Educational Research Journal* 39 (2013), 248–65

Howson, Susan, *Lionel Robbins* (Cambridge, 2011)

Hubble, Sue and Paul Bolton, 'Higher Education Tuition Fees in England', Briefing Paper Number 8151, House of Commons Library (2018)

Huchet-Bodet, Aimee, Muslihah Albakri, and Neil Smith, *Attitudes to Education: The British Social Attitudes Survey 2017* (London, 2019)

Hughes, Billy, 'In Defence of Ellen Wilkinson', *History Workshop Journal* 7:1 (1979), 157–60

Humes, Walter M., 'State: The Governance of Scottish Education 1872–2000', in Heather Holmes (ed.), *Institutions of Scotland: Education* (East Linton, 2000), 84–105

Hunter, Laurence C., 'Employers' Perceptions of Demand', in Robert Lindley (ed.), *Higher Education and the Labour Market* (Guildford, 1981), 4–48

Hutchinson, Jo, Sara Bonett, Whitney Crenna-Jennings, and Avinash Askhal, *Education in England: Annual Report 2019* (London, 2019)

Hutchison, Dougal and Andrew McPherson, 'Competing Inequalities: The Sex and Social Class Structure of the First Year Scottish University Student Population 1962–1972', *Sociology* 10 (1976), 111–16

Iannelli, Cristina and Lindsay Paterson, 'Does Education Promote Social Mobility?', *Briefing* 35, Centre for Educational Sociology, University of Edinburgh (2005)

Iannelli, Cristina and Emer Smyth, 'Curriculum Choices and School-to-Work Transitions Among Upper-Secondary School Leavers in Scotland and Ireland', *Journal of Education and Work* 30 (2017), 731–40

Institute of Student Employers, *Annual Student Recruitment Survey 2018* (London, 2018)

Jacka, Keith, Caroline Cox, and John Marks, *Rape of Reason: The Corruption of the Polytechnic of North London* (Enfield, 1975)

Jackson, Ben, *Equality and the British Left: A Study in Progressive Political Thought, 1900–64* (Manchester, 2007)

Jackson, Ben and Robert Saunders (eds), *Making Thatcher's Britain* (Cambridge, 2012)

Jackson, Brian and Dennis Marsden, *Education and the Working Class*, rev. ed. (Harmondsworth, 1966)

Jackson, Michelle, John H. Goldthorpe, and Colin Mills, 'Education, Employers and Class Mobility', *Research in Social Stratification and Mobility* 23 (2005), 3–33

Jahoda, Gustav, 'Job Attitudes and Job Choice among Secondary Modern School Leavers' (I and II), *Occupational Psychology* 26 (1952), 125–40, 206–24

James, Eric, *Education and Leadership* (London, 1951)

James, Philip H., *The Reorganization of Secondary Education: A Study of Local Policy Making* (Windsor, 1980)

Jäntti, Markus et al., 'American Exceptionalism in a New Light: A Comparison of Intergenerational Earnings Mobility in the Nordic Countries, the United Kingdom and the United States', IZA Discussion Paper 1938 (January 2006)

Jarvis, Matt, *Teaching Psychology 14–19: Issues and Techniques* (London, 2011)

Jary, David, *The Development of Sociology in the Polytechnics* (Oxford, 1979)

Jay, Douglas, *The Socialist Case*, rev. ed. (London: Faber and Faber, 1947)

Jefferys, Kevin, *Anthony Crosland*, 1st pub. 1999 (London, 2000)

Jefferys, Kevin, 'R.A. Butler, The Board of Education and the 1944 Education Act', *History* 69 (1984), 415–31

Jencks, Christopher et al., *Inequality: A Reassessment of the Effect of Family and Schooling in America* (New York, 1972)

Jennings, Robert E., *Education and Politics: Policy-Making in Local Education Authorities* (London, 1977)

Jeppesen, Chris, '"A Worthwhile Career for a Man who is Not Entirely Self-Seeking": Service, Duty and the Colonial Service During Decolonization', in Andrew W. M. Smith and Chris Jeppesen (eds), *Britain, France and the Decolonization of Africa* (London, 2017), 133–55

Jerrim, John, 'The Link Between Family Background and Later Lifetime Income: How Does the UK Compare to Other Countries?', Working Paper No. 14–02, Department of Quantitative Social Science, Institute of Education (Feb. 2014)

Jones, Ben, *The Working Class in Mid-Twentieth Century England* (Manchester, 2012)

Jones, Donald K., 'The Reorganization of Secondary Education in Leicestershipre, 1947–1984', in Roy Lowe (ed.), *The Changing Secondary School* (Lewes, 1989), 20–35

Jones, Gareth Elwyn, *Which Nation's Schools? Direction and Devolution in Welsh Education in the Twentieth Century* (Cardiff, 1990)

Jones, Ken, *Education in Britain: 1944 to the Present* (Cambridge, 2003)

Jonsson, Jon O., Colin Mills, and Walter Müller, 'A Half Century of Increasing Educational Openness? Social Class, Gender and Educational Attainment in Sweden, Germany and Britain', in Robert Erikson and Jan O. Jonsson (eds), *Can Education Be Equalized? The Swedish Case in Comparative Perspective* (Boulder CO, 1996), 183–206

Joseph, Keith and Jonathan Sumption, *Equality* (London, 1979)

Kavanagh, Dennis and David Butler, *The British General Election of 2005* (Basingstoke, 2005)

Kefford, Alistair, 'Housing the Citizen-Consumer in Post-war Britain: The Parker Morris Report, Affluence and the Even Briefer Life of Social Democracy', *Twentieth Century British History* 29 (2018), 225–58

Kelsall, R.K., *Report on an Inquiry into Applications for Admission to Universities* (London, 1957)

Kelsall, R.K., Anne Poole, and Annette Kuhn, *Graduates: The Sociology of an Elite* (London, 1972)

Kelsall, R.K., Anne Poole, and Annette Kuhn, *Six Years After* (Sheffield, 1970)

Kerckhoff, Alan and Jerry M. Trott, 'Educational Attainment in a Changing Educational System: The Case of England and Wales', in Yossi Shavit and Hans-Peter Blossfeld (eds), *Persistent Inequality: Changing Educational Attainment in Thirteen Countries* (Boulder CO, 1993), 133–53

Kerckhoff, Alan, Ken Fogelman, David Crook, and David Reeder, *Going Comprehensive in England and Wales: A Study of Uneven Change* (London, 1996)

Kett, Joseph F., *The Pursuit of Knowledge Under Difficulties* (Stanford, 1994)

King, Anthony, 'Overload: Problems of Governing in the 1970s', *Political Studies* 23 (1975), 284–96

King, Anthony (ed.), *British Political Opinion 1937–2000: The Gallup Polls* (London, 2001), 262–73

King, Desmond and Victoria Nash, 'Continuity of Ideas and the Politics of Higher Education Expansion in Britain from Robbins to Dearing', *Twentieth Century British History* 12 (2001), 185–207

King, Janette and Charles Ritchie, 'The Benefits of Higher Education Participation for Individuals and Societies: Key Findings and Reports, "The Quadrants"', Research Paper No. 146, Department for Business, Innovation and Skills (Oct. 2013)

Kirby, Philip, *Degrees of Debt: Funding and Finance for Undergraduates in Anglophone Countries* (London, 2016)

Knight, Christopher, *The Making of Tory Education Policy in Post-War Britain 1950–1986* (Lewes, 1990)

Kogan, Maurice, 'The Political View', in Burton R. Clark (ed.), *Perspectives on Higher Education: Eight Disciplinary and Comparative Views* (Berkeley, 1984), 56–78

Kogan, Maurice, *The Politics of Educational Change* (London, 1978)

Kogan, Maurice, Edward Boyle, and Anthony Crosland, *The Politics of Education* (Harmondsworth, 1971)

Kogan, Maurice and C. J. Boys, 'Expectations of Higher Education: A Synopsis and Commentary on its Main Findings', Brunel University, Expectations of Higher Education Project, Paper No. 2 (May 1984)

Kogan, Maurice and Stephen Hanney, *Reforming Higher Education* (London, 2000)

Kogan, Maurice with David Kogan, *The Attack on Higher Education* (London, 1983)

Kynaston, David, *Modernity Britain: Opening the Box, 1957–59* (London, 2013)

'Labour and Secondary Education', *Political Quarterly* 22 (1951), 317–22

Labour Party, *The Years of Crisis: Report of the Labour Party's Study Group on Higher Education* (London, n.d. [1962])

Land, Hilary, 'We Sat Down at the Table of Privilege and Complained about the Food', in Geoff Dench (ed.), *The Rise and Rise of Meritocracy* (Oxford, 2006), 45–60

Larson, Magali Sarfatti, 'The Production of Expertise and the Constitution of Expert Power', in Thomas L. Haskell (ed.), *The Authority of Experts: Studies in History and Theory* (Bloomington, 1984), 28–80

Lawrence, Jon, 'Class, "Affluence" and the Study of Everyday Life in Britain, *c.* 1930–64', *Cultural and Social History* 10 (2013), 273–99

Lawrence, Jon, 'Inventing the "Traditional Working Class": A Re-Analysis of Interview Notes from Young and Willmott's *Family and Kinship in East London*', *Historical Journal* 59 (2016), 567–93

Lawrence, Jon, *Me, Me, Me? The Search for Community in Post-War England* (Oxford, 2019)

Lawrence, Jon, 'Social-Science Encounters and the Negotiation of Difference in Early 1960s England', *History Workshop Journal* 77 (2014), 215–39

Lawson, John and Harold Silver, *A Social History of Education in England* (London, 1973)

Lawton, Denis, *Education and Labour Party Ideologies 1900–2001 and Beyond* (Abingdon, 2005)

Lawton, Denis and Barry Dufour, *The New Social Studies* (London, 1973)

Layard, Richard, *Happiness: Lessons from a New Science*, 2nd ed. (London, 2011)

Layard, Richard and John King, 'The Impact of Robbins' (1968), in Carolyn Baxter, P. J. O'Leary, and Adam Westoby (eds), *Economics and Education Policy: A Reader* (London, 1977), 20–38

Layard, Richard, John King, and Claus Moser, *The Impact of Robbins* (Harmondsworth, 1969)

Li, Yaojun and Fiona Devine, 'Is Social Mobility Really Declining? Intergenerational Class Mobility in Britain in the 1990s and the 2000s', *Sociological Research Online* (2011), http://www.socresonline.org.uk/16/3/4.html

Limond, David, 'Locality, Education and Authority in Scotland: 1902–2002 (Via 1872)', *Oxford Review of Education* 28 (2002), 359–71

Lindley, Joanne and Stephen Machin, 'The Quest for More and More Education: Implications for Social Mobility', *Fiscal Studies* 33 (2012), 265–86

Lindley, Joanne and Steven McIntosh, 'Growth in Within Wage Inequality: The Role of Subjects, Cognitive Skill Dispersion and Occupational Concentration', *Labour Economics* 37 (2015), 101–11

Lindley, Robert M., 'Education, Training, and the Labour Market in Britain', *European Journal of Education* 16 (1981), 7–27

Lindley, Robert M., 'The Challenge of Market Imperatives', in Robert Lindley (ed.), *Higher Education and the Labour Market* (Guildford, 1981), 148–71

Lindsay, Kenneth, *Social Progress and Educational Waste* (London, 1926)

Lister, H., 'The Effects of External Examinations on the School', in G. B. Jeffery (ed.), *External Examinations in Secondary Schools: Their Place and Function* (London, 1958), 55–77

Littler, Jo, *Against Meritocracy: Culture, Power and Myths of Mobility* (London, 2018)

Liu, Yujia and David B. Grusky, 'The Payoff to Skill in the Third Industrial Revolution', *American Journal of Sociology* 118 (2013), 1330–74

London Economics, 'Review of Student Support Arrangements in Other Countries', Research Paper 10, Department for Business, Innovation and Skills (2010)

Loveday, Vik, 'Working-Class Participation, Middle-Class Aspiration? Value, Upward Mobility and Symbolic Indebtedness in Higher Education', *Sociological Review* 63 (2015), 570–88

Lowe, Philip D. and Michael Worboys, 'The Teaching of Social Studies of Science and Technology in British Polytechnics', *Social Studies of Science* 5 (1975), 177–92

Lowe, Rodney, 'The Replanning of the Welfare State, 1957–1964', in Martin Francis and Ina Zweiniger-Bargielowska (eds), *The Conservatives and British Society, 1880–1990* (Cardiff, 1996), 255–73

Lowe, Rodney, *The Welfare State in Britain since 1945*, 3rd ed. (Basingstoke, 2005)

Lowe, Roy, *Education in the Post-War Years: A Social History* (London, 1988)

Lowe, Roy, *Schooling and Social Change 1964–1990* (London, 1997)

Lowe, Roy, 'Secondary Education since the Second World War', in Roy Lowe (ed.), *The Changing Secondary School* (Lewes, 1989), 3–19

Lowe, Roy (ed.), *The Changing Secondary School* (Lewes, 1989)

Lowndes, G.A.N., *The Silent Social Revolution: An Account of the Expansion of Public Education in England and Wales 1895–1965* (Oxford, 1969)

Lucas, Samuel R., 'Effectively Maintained Inequality: Education Transitions, Track Mobility, and Social Background Effects', *American Journal of Sociology* 106 (2001), 1642–90

Lupton, Ruth and Stephanie Thomson, 'Socio-Economic Inequalities in English Schooling Under the Coalition Government 2010–15', *London Review of Education* 13 (2015), 4–20

Lupton, Ruth, Natalie Heath, and Emma Salter, 'Education: New Labour's Top Priority', in John Hills, Tom Sefton, and Kitty Stewart (eds), *Towards a More Equal Society? Poverty, Inequality and Policy since 1997* (Bristol, 2009), 71–90

Lynn, Richard, 'Streaming: Standards or Equality', in C. B. Cox and A. E. Dyson (eds), *The Black Papers on Education* (London, 1971), 77–84

Lyons, Terry and Frances Quinn, 'Understanding Declining Science Participation in Australia: A Systemic Perspective', in Brigid Freeman, Simon Marginson, and Russell Tytler (eds), *The Age of STEM: Educational Policy and Practice Across the World in Science, Technology, Engineering and Mathematics* (London, 2015), 153–68

Machin, Stephen and Anna Vignoles, 'Education Policy in the UK', Centre for the Economics of Education, Discussion Paper 57 (2006)

Machin, Stephen and Anna Vignoles, 'Educational Inequality: The Widening Socio-Economic Gap', *Fiscal Studies* 25 (2004), 107–28

Machin, Stephen and Anna Vignoles (eds), *What's the Good of Education? The Economics of Education in the UK* (Princeton, 2005)

Machin, Stephen, Sandra McNally, and Gill Wyness, 'Educational Attainment across the UK Nations: Performance, Inequality and Evidence', *Educational Research* 55 (2013), 139–64

Maclure, Stuart, *One Hundred Years of London Education 1870–1970* (London, 1970)

Magnussen, Olav, 'The Cost and Finance of Post-Secondary Education', in OECD, *Towards Mass Higher Education: Issues and Dilemmas* (Paris, 1974), 171–227

Mahoney, Daniel and Tim Knox, 'How to Overcome Selection by House Price', Economic Bulletin 93, Centre for Policy Studies (5 Apr. 2017)

Major, Lee Elliot and Stephen Machin, *Social Mobility and Its Enemies* (London, 2018)

Makepeace, Gerry, Peter Dolton, Laura Woods, Heather Joshi, and Fernando Galinda-Rueda, 'From School to the Labour Market', in Elsa Ferri, John Bynner, and Michael Wadsworth (eds), *Changing Britain, Changing Lives: Three Generations at the Turn of the Century* (London, 2003), 29–70

Makin, Dorothy, 'Policy Making in Secondary Education: Evidence from Two Local Authorities, 1944–1972', Ph.D. dissertation, University of Oxford, 2015

Mandler, Peter, 'Educating the Nation: I. Schools', *Transactions of the Royal Historical Society*, 6th ser., 24 (2014), 5–28

Mandler, Peter, 'Educating the Nation: II. Universities', *Transactions of the Royal Historical Society*, 6th ser., 25 (2015), 1–26

Mandler, Peter, 'Educating the Nation: III. Social Mobility', *Transactions of the Royal Historical Society*, 6th ser, 26 (2016), 1–23

Mandler, Peter, 'Educating the Nation: IV. Subject Choice', *Transactions of the Royal Historical Society*, 6th ser., 27 (2017), 1–27

Mandler, Peter, 'Rise of the Humanities', *Aeon*, 17 Dec. 2015, https://aeon.co/essays/the-humanities-are-booming-only-the-professors-can-t-see-it

Mandler, Peter, 'The Rise of the Social Sciences in British Education, 1960–2016', in Plamena Panayotova (ed.), *The History of Sociology in Britain: New Research and Revaluation* (London, 2019), 281–99

Mandler, Peter, 'Social Mobility and the Historians', *Cultural and Social History* 16 (2019), 103–7

Mandler, Peter, 'Two Cultures—One—or Many?', in Kathleen Burk (ed.), *The Short Oxford History of the British Isles: The British Isles since 1945* (Oxford, 2003), 127–55

Mandler, Peter, 'The Two Cultures Revisited: The Humanities in British Universities Since 1945', *Twentieth Century British History* 26 (2015), 400–23

Manski, Charles F., 'Measuring Expectations', *Econometrica* 72 (2004), 1329–76

Marginson, Simon, 'The Anglo-American University at Its Global High Tide', *Minerva* 44 (2006), 65–87

Marginson, Simon, *Education and Public Policy in Australia* (Cambridge, 1993)

Marginson, Simon, 'What International Comparisons Can Tell Us', in Brigid Freeman, Simon Marginson and Russell Tytler (eds), *The Age of STEM: Educational Policy and Practice Across the World in Science, Technology, Engineering and Mathematics* (London, 2015), 22–32

Marks, John and Caroline Cox, 'Educational Attainment in Secondary Schools', *Oxford Review of Education* 10 (1984), 7–31

Marris, Peter, 'Just Rewards: *Meritocracy* Fifty Years Later', in Geoff Dench (ed.), *The Rise and Rise of Meritocracy* (Oxford, 2006), 157–62

Marsden, Dennis, *Politicians, Equality and Comprehensives* (London, 1971)

Marshall, Gordon, Adam Swift, and Stephen Roberts, *Against the Odds? Social Class and Social Justice in Industrial Societies* (Oxford, 1997)

Marshall, T. H., 'Citizenship and Social Class' (1949), in *Citizenship and Social Class and Other Essays* (Cambridge, 1950), 1–85

Maude, Angus, 'The Egalitarian Threat', in C. B. Cox and A.E. Dyson (eds), *The Black Papers on Education* (London, 1971), 37–40

Mayhew, Ken, Cécile Deer, and Mahek Dua, 'The Move to Mass Higher Education in the UK: Many Questions and Some Answers', *Oxford Review of Education* 30 (2004), 65–82

Mazower, Mark, *Dark Continent: Europe's Twentieth Century* (London, 1998)

McCluskey, Gillean, 'Closing the Attainment Gap in Scottish Schools: Three Challenges in an Unequal Society', *Education, Citizenship and Social Justice* 12 (2017), 24–35

McCrensky, Edward, *Scientific Manpower in Europe* (London, 1958)

McCulloch, Gary, 'British Labour Party Education Policy and Comprehensive Education: From Learning to Live to Circular 10/65', *History of Education* 45 (2016), 225–45

McCulloch, Gary, *Educational Reconstruction: The 1944 Education Act and the Twenty-First Century* (Ilford, 1994)

McCulloch, Gary, *Failing the Ordinary Child? The Theory and Practice of Working-Class Secondary Education* (Buckingham, 1998)

McCulloch, Gary, 'Local Education Authorities and the Organisation of Secondary Education, 1943–1950', *Oxford Review of Education* 28 (2002), 235–46

McCulloch, Gary, 'Parity and Prestige in English Secondary Education Revisited', *British Journal of Sociology* 29 (2008), 381–9

McCulloch, Gary, Edgar Jenkins, and David Layton, *Technological Revolution? The Politics of School Science and Technology in England and Wales since 1945* (London, 1985)

McDermid, Jane, 'Education and Society in the Era of the School Boards', in Robert Anderson, Mark Freeman, and Lindsay Paterson (eds), *The Edinburgh History of Education in Scotland* (Edinburgh, 2015)

McGettigan, Andrew, *The Great University Gamble: Money, Markets and the Future of Higher Education* (London, 2013)

McGettigan, Andrew, 'The Treasury View of HE: Variable Human Capital', PERC Papers Series 6, Political Economy Research Centre, Goldsmiths, University of London (2015)

McIntosh, Steven, 'The Demand for Post-Compulsory Education in Four European Countries', *Education Economics* 9 (2001), 69–90

McIntosh, Steven and Damon Morris, 'Labour Market Returns to Vocational Qualifications in the Labour Force Survey', Research Discussion Paper 002, Centre for Vocational Education Research (2016)

McKenzie, Janet, *Changing Education: A Sociology of Education since 1944* (Harlow, 2001)

McKibbin, Ross, *Classes and Cultures: England 1918–1951* (Oxford, 1998)

McMahon, Walter W., *Higher Learning, Greater Good: The Private and Social Benefits of Higher Education* (Baltimore, 2009)

McPherson, Andrew, 'An Angle on the Geist: Persistence and Change in the Scottish Educational Tradition', in Walter M. Humes and Hamish M. Paterson (eds), *Scottish Culture and Scottish Education 1800–1980* (Edinburgh, 1983), 216–43

McPherson, Andrew, 'The Dainton Report—A Scottish Dissent', *Universities Quarterly* 22 (1967–8), 254–73

McPherson, Andrew, '"Swing from Science" or Retreat from Reason?', *Universities Quarterly* 24 (1969–70), 29–43

McPherson, Andrew and Charles D. Raab, *Governing Education: A Sociology of Policy since 1945* (Edinburgh, 1988)

McPherson, Andrew and J. Douglas Willms, 'Equalisation and Improvement: Some Effects of Comprehensive Reorganisation in Scotland', *Sociology* 21 (1987), 509–39

McVicar, Duncan and Patricia Rice, 'Participation in Further Education in England and Wales: An Analysis of Post-War Trends', *Oxford Economic Papers* 53 (2001), 47–66

Menand, Louis, *The Marketplace of Ideas* (New York, 2010)

Meyer, John W., Francisco O. Ramirez, and Yasemin Nuhoglu Soysal, 'World Expansion of Mass Education, 1870–1980', *Sociology of Education* 65 (1992), 128–49

Miles, Andrew and Adrian Leguina, 'Socio-Spatial Mobilities and Narratives of Class Identity in Britain', *British Journal of Sociology* 69 (2018), 1063–95

Millward, Robert, 'The Rise of the Service Economy', in Roderick Floud and Paul Johnson (eds), *The Cambridge Economic History of Modern Britain: Vol. III* (Cambridge, 2004), 238–66

Mirza-Davies, James, 'Apprenticeships Policy, England Prior to 2010', Briefing Paper Number 07266, House of Commons Library (2015)

Montmarquette, Claude, Kathy Cannings, and Sophie Mahseredjian, 'How Do Young People Choose College Majors?', *Economics of Education Review* 21 (2002), 543–56

Montresor, Giulia, 'Job Polarization and Labour Supply Changes in the UK', *Labour Economics* 58 (2019), 187–203

Morris, Max and Clive Griggs, 'Thirteen Wasted Years?', in Max Morris and Clive Griggs (eds), *Education, The Wasted Years? 1973–1986* (Lewes, 1988), 1–27

Morris, Max and Clive Griggs (eds), *Education, The Wasted Years? 1973–1986* (Lewes, 1988)

Morris, Vera, 'Investment in Higher Education in England and Wales: A Subject Analysis' (1973), in Carolyn Baxter, P. J. O'Leary, and Adam Westoby (eds), *Economics and Education Policy: A Reader* (London, 1977), 72–91

Moser, C. A. and P. R. G. Layard, 'Estimating the Need for Qualified Manpower in Britain', in M. Blaug (ed.), *Economics of Education 1: Selected Readings* (Harmondsworth, 1968), 287–317

Moses, Julia, 'Social Citizenship and Social Rights in an Age of Extremes: T.H. Marshall's Social Philosophy in the *Longue Durée*', *Modern Intellectual History* 16 (2019), 155–84

Mountford-Zimdars, Anna, Steven Jones, Alice Sullivan, and Anthony Heath, 'Framing Higher Education: Questions and Responses in the British Social Attitudes Survey, 1983–2010', *British Journal of Sociology of Education* 34 (2013), 792–811

Müller, Walter and Yossi Shavit, 'The Institutional Embeddedness of the Stratification Process: A Comparative Study of Qualifications and Occupations in Thirteen Countries', in Yossi Shavit and Walter Müller (eds), *From School to Work: A Comparative Study of Educational Qualifications and Occupational Destinations* (Oxford, 1998), 1–48

Murtin, Fabrice and Martina Viarengo, 'The Expansion and Convergence of Compulsory Schooling in Western Europe, 1950–2000', *Economica* 78 (2011), 501–22

Nathoo, Ayesha, *Hearts Exposed: Transplants and the Media in 1960s Britain* (Basingstoke, 2009)

Neave, Guy R., 'Elite and Mass Higher Education in Britain: A Regressive Model?', *Comparative Education Review* 29 (1985), 347–61

Nicholas, H. G., *The British General Election of 1950* (London, 1951)

Nunn, Alex, Steve Johnson, Surya Monro, Tim Bickerstaffe, and Sarah Kelsey, 'Factors Influencing Social Mobility', Research Report No. 450, Department for Work and Pensions (2007)

Nussbaum, Martha, *Not for Profit: Why Democracy Needs the Humanities* (Princeton, 2010)

Nuttall, Desmond L., 'Doomsday or a New Dawn? The Prospects for a Common System of Examining at 16+', in Patricia Broadfoot (ed.), *Selection, Certification and Control: Social Issues in Educational Assessment* (London, 1984), 163–77

Nuttall, Jeremy, *Psychological Socialism: The Labour Party and Qualities of Mind and Character, 1931 to the Present* (Manchester, 2006)

OECD, *Intergovernmental Conference on Policies for Higher Education in the Eighties: Working Group 1—Access to Higher Education* (Provisional Text) (Paris, 1981)

OECD, *Development of Higher Education 1950–1967* (Paris, 1971)

OECD, *Education at a Glance 2018*: https://www.oecd-ilibrary.org/education/education-at-a-glance-2018_eag-2018-en

OECD, *The Educational Situation in OECD Countries* (Paris, 1974)

OECD, *Employment Prospects for Higher Education Graduates* (Paris, 1981)

OECD, *Towards New Structures of Post-Secondary Education* (Paris, 1971)

O'Hara, Glen, 'The Complexities of "Consumerism": Choice, Collectivism and Participation within Britain's National Health Service, c. 1961–c. 1979', *Social History of Medicine* 26 (2013), 288–304

O'Hara, Glen, *Governing Post-War Britain: The Paradoxes of Progress, 1951–1973* (Basingstoke, 2012)

O'Hara, Glen, '"We are Faced Everywhere with a Growing Population": Demographic Change and the British State, 1955–64', *Twentieth Century British History* 15 (2004), 243–66

Ohidy, Andrea, 'Widening Participation in Higher Education: Policies and Outcomes in Germany', in Sheila Riddell, Sarah Minty, Elisabet Weedon, and Susan Whittaker (eds), *Higher Education Funding and Access in International Perspective* (Bingley, 2018), 163–83

Ortolano, Guy, *Thatcher's Progress: From Social Democracy to Market Liberalism through an English New Town* (Cambridge, 2019)

Ortolano, Guy, *The Two Cultures Controversy: Science, Literature and Cultural Politics in Postwar Britain* (Cambridge, 2009)

Parkinson, Michael, *The Labour Party and the Organization of Secondary Education 1918–65* (London, 1970)

Parry, Gareth, 'Policy Contexts: Differentiation, Competition and Policies for Widening Participation', in Miriam David (ed.), *Improving Learning by Widening Participation in Higher Education* (London, 2010), 31–46

Paterson, Hamish M., 'Incubus and Ideology: The Development of Secondary Schooling in Scotland, 1900-1939', in Walter M. Humes and Hamish M. Paterson (eds), *Scottish Culture and Scottish Education 1800–1980* (Edinburgh, 1983), 197–215

Paterson, Hamish M., 'Secondary Education', in Heather Holmes (ed.), *Institutions of Scotland: Education* (East Linton, 2000), 136–53

Paterson, Lindsay, 'Comprehensive Education, Social Attitudes and Civic Engagement', *Longitudinal and Life Course Studies* 4 (2013), 17–32

Paterson, Lindsay, 'Democracy or Intellect?: The Scottish Educational Dilemma of the Twentieth Century', in Robert Anderson, Mark Freeman, and Lindsay Paterson (eds), *The Edinburgh History of Education in Scotland* (Edinburgh, 2015), 226–45

Paterson, Lindsay, 'The Reinvention of Scottish Liberal Education: Secondary Schooling, 1900–30', *Scottish Historical Review* 90 (2011), 96–130

Paterson, Lindsay, *Scottish Education in the Twentieth Century* (Edinburgh, 2003)

Paterson, Lindsay and Cristina Iannelli, 'Patterns of Absolute and Relative Social Mobility: A Comparative Study of England, Wales and Scotland', *Sociological Research Online* (2007), http://www.socresonline.org.uk/12/6/15.html

Paterson, Lindsay and Cristina Iannelli, 'Social Class and Educational Attainment: A Comparative Study of England, Wales, and Scotland', *Sociology of Education* 80 (2007), 330–58

Paterson, Lindsay, Alison Pattie, and Ian J. Deary, 'Social Class, Gender and Secondary Education in Scotland in the 1950s', *Oxford Review of Education* 37 (2011), 383–401

Payne, Geoff, 'Labouring Under a Misapprehension: Politicians' Perceptions and the Realities of Structural Social Mobility in Britain, 1995–2010', in Paul Lambert, Roxanne Connelly, Robert M. Blackburn, and Vernon Gayle (eds), *Social Stratification: Trends and Processes* (Farnham, 2012), 224–42

Payne, Geoff, 'A New Social Mobility? The Political Redefinition of a Sociological Problem', *Contemporary Social Science* 7 (2012), 55–71

Payne, Geoff, *The New Social Mobility: How the Politicians Got It Wrong* (Bristol, 2017)

Payne, Geoff and Judy Roberts, 'Opening and Closing the Gates: Recent Developments in Male Social Mobility in Britain', *Sociological Research Online* (2002), http://www.socresonline.org.uk/6/4/payne.html

Pearson, Helen, *The Life Project* (London, 2016)

Pedley, Robin, *Comprehensive Education: A New Approach* (London, 1956)

Pellegrin, Jean-Pierre, 'Admission Policies in Post-Secondary Education', in OECD, *Towards Mass Higher Education: Issues and Dilemmas* (Paris, 1974), 63–103

Pellegrin, Jean-Pierre, 'Quantitative Trends in Post-Secondary Education', in OECD, *Towards Mass Higher Education: Issues and Dilemmas* (Paris, 1974), 9–61

Perkin, Harold, 'University Planning in Britain in the 1960's', *Higher Education* 1 (1972), 111–20

Percy, Eustace, *Some Memories* (London, 1958)

Peston, Maurice, 'Economics and Administration of Education', in George Baron and William Taylor (eds), *Educational Administration and the Social Sciences* (London, 1969), 60–71

Peston, Maurice, 'Higher Education Policy', in Robert Lindley (ed.), *Higher Education and the Labour Market* (Guildford, 1981), 120–47

Peterson, A. D. C., 'The Myth of Subject-Mindedness', *Universities Quarterly* 14 (1959–60), 223–32

Phillips, Celia M., *Changes in Subject Choice at School and University* (London, 1969)

Phillips, Melanie, *All Must Have Prizes* (London, 1996)

Pissarides, Christopher A., 'From School to University: The Demand for Post-Compulsory Education in Britain', *Economic Journal* 92 (1982), 654–67

Pissarides, Christopher A., 'An Overview of the Demand for Post-Compulsory Education by British Men, 1955–77', in Burton Weisbrod and Helen Hughes (eds), *Human Resources, Employment and Development, Vol. 3: The Problems of Developed Countries and the International Economy* (London, 1983), 147–56

Pissarides, Christopher A., 'Staying-on at School in England and Wales', *Economica* 48 (1981), 345–63

Pitt, A. W. H., 'A Review of the Reasons for Making a Choice of Subjects at the Secondary School Level', *Educational Review* 26 (1973), 3–15

Plank, David N. and Gary Sykes, 'Why School Choice?', in David N. Plank and Gary Sykes (eds), *Choosing Choice: School Choice in International Perspective* (New York, 2003), vii–xxi

Political and Economic Planning, *Family Needs and the Social Services* (London, 1961)

Political and Economic Planning, *Graduate Employment: A Sample Survey* (London, 1956)

Pont, H. B. and H. J. Butcher, 'Choice of Course and Subject Specialisation in Seventeen Scottish Secondary Schools', *Scottish Educational Studies* 1:2 (May 1968), 9–15

Pooley, Colin G., 'Mobility in the Twentieth Century: Substituting Commuting for Migration?', in David Gilbert, David Matless, and Brian Short (eds),

Geographies of British Modernity: Space and Society in the Twentieth Century (Oxford, 2003), 80–96

Power, Sally, 'The Politics of Education and the Misrecognition of Wales', *Oxford Review of Education* 42 (2016), 285–98

Powell, Andrew, 'Apprenticeship Statistics: England', Briefing Paper 06113, House of Commons Library (2019)

Pratt, John, *The Polytechnic Experiment 1965–1992* (Buckingham, 1997)

Pratt, John and Tyrrell Burgess, *Polytechnics: A Report* (London, 1974)

Premfors, Rune, *The Politics of Higher Education in a Comparative Perspective: France, Sweden, United Kingdom* (Stockholm, 1980)

Pring, Richard, *The Life and Death of Secondary Education for All* (London, 2013)

Purcell, Kate and Jane Pitcher, *Great Expectations: The New Diversity of Graduate Skills and Aspirations* (Warwick, 1996)

Purcell, Kate et al., *Applying for Higher Education: The Diversity of Career Choices, Plans and Expectations* (Warwick, 2008)

Purcell, Kate et al., *Transitions into Employment, Further Study and Other Outcomes* (Warwick, 2012)

Raftery, Adrian E. and Michael Hout, 'Maximally Maintained Inequality: Expansion, Reform, and Opportunity in Irish Education, 1921–75', *Sociology of Education* 66 (1993), 41–62

Ramirez, Francisco O. and John Boli, 'The Political Institutionalization of Compulsory Education: The Rise of Compulsory Schooling in the Western Cultural Context', in J.A. Mangan (ed.), *A Significant Social Revolution: Cross-Cultural Aspects of the Evolution of Compulsory Education* (London, 1994), 1–20

Ramirez, Francisco O., Xiaowei Luo, Evan Schofer, and John W. Meyer, 'Student Achievement and National Economic Growth', *American Journal of Education* 113 (2006–7), 1–29

Ranson, Stewart, 'Towards a Tertiary Tripartism: New Codes of Social Control and the 17+', in Patricia Broadfoot (ed.), *Selection, Certification and Control: Social Issues in Educational Assessment* (London, 1984), 221–44

Rao, N., 'Labour and Education: Secondary Reorganisation and the Neighbourhood School', *Contemporary British History* 16 (2002), 99–120

Reay, Diane, *Class Work: Mothers' Involvement in their Children's Primary Schooling* (London, 1998)

Reay, Diane, *Miseducation: Inequality, Education and the Working Classes* (Bristol, 2017)

Reay, Diane, 'Social Mobility, a Panacea for Austere Times: Tales of Emperors, Frogs, and Tadpoles', *British Journal of Sociology of Education* 34 (2013), 660–77

Reay, Diane and Stephen J. Ball, '"Spoilt for Choice": The Working Classes and Educational Markets', *Oxford Review of Education* 23 (1997), 89–101

Reay, Diane, Gill Crozier, and David James, *White Middle-Class Identities and Urban Schooling* (Basingstoke, 2011)

Reay, Diane, Miriam E. David, and Stephen Ball, *Degrees of Choice: Class, Race, Gender and Higher Education* (Stoke on Trent, 2005)

Redpath, Bob and Barbara Harvey, *Young People's Intentions to Enter Higher Education* (London, 1987)

Rees, Gareth and Sara Delamont, 'Education in Wales', in David Dunkerley and Andrew Thompson (eds), *Wales Today* (Cardiff, 1999), 233–49

Rees, Gareth and Teresa L. Rees, 'Educational Inequality in Wales: Some Problems and Paradoxes', in Rees and Rees (eds), *Poverty and Social Inequality in Wales* (London, 1980), 71–92

Reeves, Rachel, *Alice in Westminster: The Political Life of Alice Bacon* (London, 2016)

Regan, Elaine and Justin Dillon, 'A Place for STEM: Probing the Reasons for Undergraduate Course Choice', in Ellen Karoline Henriksen, Justin Dillon, and Jim Ryder (eds), *Understanding Student Participation and Choice in Science and Technology Education* (Dordrecht, 2015), 119–34

Reid, Margaret I., Bernard R. Barnett, and Helen A. Rosenberg, *A Matter of Choice: A Study of Guidance and Subject Options* (Windsor, 1974)

Renwick, Chris, 'Eugenics, Population Research and Social Mobility Studies in Early and Mid-Twentieth Century Britain', *Historical Journal* 59 (2016), 845–67

Richardson, William, 'Historians and Educationists: The History of Education as a Field of Study in Post-War England. Part II: 1972–96', *History of Education* 28 (1999), 109–41

Riddell, Sheila, 'Can the Techniques of New Public Management be Used to Promote Wider Access to Higher Education?', in Sheila Riddell, Sarah Minty, Elisabet Weedon, and Susan Whittaker (eds), *Higher Education Funding and Access in International Perspective* (Bingley, 2018), 61–79

Robbins, Bruce, *Upward Mobility and the Common Good: Toward a Literary History of the Welfare State* (Princeton, 2007)

Robbins, Lord (Lionel) and Boris Ford, 'Report on Robbins', *Universities Quarterly* 20 (1965–6), 5–15

Robinson, Emily, Camilla Schofield, Florence Sutcliffe-Braithwaite, and Natalie Thomlinson, 'Telling Stories about Post-War Britain: Popular Individualism and the "Crisis" of the 1970s', *Twentieth-Century British History* 28 (2017), 268–304

Robinson, Eric, *The New Polytechnics* (Harmondsworth, 1968)

Rodgers, Barbara N., *Careers of Social Science Graduates* (Welwyn, 1964)

Rodgers, Barbara N., *A Follow-Up Study of Social Administration Students of Manchester University 1940–60* (Manchester, 1963)

Rogan, Tim, *The Moral Economists: R.H. Tawney, Karl Polanyi, E.P. Thompson, and the Critique of Capitalism* (Princeton, 2017)

Rose, Jonathan, *The Intellectual Life of the British Working Classes* (New Haven and London, 2001)

Rubinstein, David, 'Ellen Wilkinson Re-considered', *History Workshop Journal* 7:1 (1979), 161–9

Runciman, W. G., *Relative Deprivation and Social Justice: A Study of Attitudes to Social Inequality in Twentieth-Century England* (London, 1966)

Saint, Andrew, *Towards a Social Architecture: The Role of School Building in Post-War England* (New Haven and London, 1987)

St John-Stevas, Norman and Leon Brittan, *How to Save Your Schools* (London, 1975)

Salter, Brian and E. R. Tapper, 'The Politics of Reversing the Ratchet in Secondary Education, 1969–1986', *Journal of Educational Administration and History* 20 (1988), 57–70

Salter, Brian and Ted Tapper, *The State and Higher Education* (Ilford, 1994)

Salvatori, Andrea, 'The Anatomy of Job Polarisation in the UK', IZA Discussion Paper 9193 (2015)

Sampson, Anthony, *Anatomy of Britain* (London, 1962)

Sandberg, Sheryl, *Lean In: Women, Work, and the Will to Lead* (New York, 2013)

Sandbrook, Dominic, *Seasons in the Sun: The Battle for Britain, 1974–1979* (London, 2012)

Sandbrook, Dominic, *State of Emergency: The Way We Were: Britain, 1970–1974* (London, 2010)

Sandbrook, Dominic, *White Heat: A History of Britain in the Swinging Sixties* (London, 2006)

Sanderson, Michael, 'Education and the Labour Market', in Nicholas Crafts, Ian Gazeley, and Andrew Newell (eds), *Work and Pay in Twentieth-Century Britain* (Oxford, 2007), 264–300

Sanderson, Michael, *Educational Opportunity and Social Change in England* (London, 1987)

Sanderson, Michael, 'Higher Education in the Post-War Years', *Contemporary Record* 5 (1991), 417–31

Savage, Mike, *Identities and Social Change in Britain since 1940* (Oxford, 2010)

Savage, Mike, *Social Class in the 21st Century* (London, 2015)

Savage, Mike and Magne Flemmen, 'Life Narratives and Personal Identity: The End of Linear Social Mobility', *Cultural and Social History* 16 (2019), 85–101

Schuller, Tom (ed.), *The Future of Higher Education* (Buckingham, 1991)

Schultz, Theodore W., *The Economic Value of Education* (New York, 1963)

Schultz, Theodore W., 'Investment in Human Capital', *American Economic Review* 51 (1961), 1–17

Schwarz, Leonard, 'Professions, Elites, and Universities in England, 1870–1970', *Historical Journal* 47 (2004), 941–62

Scott, Peter, '1992–2002: Where Next?', *Perspectives: Policy & Practice in Higher Education* 7 (2003), 71–5

Scott, Peter, 'British Universities 1968–1978', *Paedagogica Europaea* 13 (1978), 29–43

Scott, Peter, 'The Coalition Government's Reform of Higher Education: Policy Formation and Political Process', in Claire Callender and Peter Scott (eds), *Browne and Beyond: Modernizing English Higher Education* (London, 2013), 32–56

Scott, Peter, 'Has the Binary Policy Failed?', in Michael Shattock (ed.), *The Structure and Governance of Higher Education* (Guildford, 1983), 166–97

Scott, Peter, 'Higher Education', in Max Morris and Clive Griggs (ed.), *Education, The Wasted Years? 1973–1986* (Lewes, 1988), 127–44

Scott, Peter, *Knowledge & Nation* (Edinburgh, 1990)

Scott, Peter, *The Meanings of Mass Higher Education* (Buckingham, 1995)

Secondary Education for All: A Policy for Labour, ed. for the Education Advisory Committee of the Labour Party by R. H. Tawney (London, n.d. [1922])

Searle, G. R., *A New England? Peace and War 1886–1918* (Oxford, 2005)

Sharp, Paul, *The Creation of the Local Authority Sector of Higher Education* (London, 1987)

Sharp, Paul, 'Surviving, Not Thriving: LEAs since the Education Reform Act of 1988', *Oxford Review of Education* 28 (2002), 197–215

Shattock, Michael, 'Demography and Social Class: The Fluctuating Demand for Higher Education in Britain', *European Journal of Education* 16 (1981), 381–92

Shattock, Michael, *Making Policy in British Higher Education 1945–2011* (Maidenhead, 2012)

Shattock, Michael, 'Public Expenditure and Tuition Fees: The Search for Alternative Ways to Pay for Higher Education', in Claire Callender and Peter Scott (eds), *Browne and Beyond: Modernizing English Higher Education* (London, 2013), 15–31

Shattock, Michael, *The UGC and the Management of British Universities* (Buckingham, 1994)

Shattock, Michael and Robert O. Berdahl, 'The British University Grants Committee 1919-83: Changing Relationships with Government and the Universities', *Higher Education* 13 (1984), 471–99

Shavit, Yossi, Meir Yaish, and Eyal Bar-Haim, 'The Persistence of Persistent Inequality', in Stefani Scherer, Reinhard Pollak, Gunnar Otte and Markus Gangl (eds), *From Origin to Destination: Trends and Mechanisms in Social Stratification* (Frankfurt, 2007), 37–57

Shavit, Yossi and Hans-Peter Blossfeld (eds), *Persistent Inequality: Changing Educational Attainment in Thirteen Countries* (Boulder CO, 1993)

Sherington, Geoffrey, *English Education, Social Change and War 1911–20* (Manchester, 1981)

Silver, Harold, *Higher Education and Opinion Making in Twentieth-Century England* (London, 2003)

Silver, Harold and Pamela Silver, *An Educational War on Poverty: American and British Policy-Making 1960–1980* (Cambridge, 1991)

Simon, Brian, *Education and the Social Order 1940–1990* (London, 1991)

Simon, Brian, *The Politics of Educational Reform 1920–1940* (London, 1974)

Skeggs, Beverley, *Formations of Class and Gender: Becoming Respectable* (London, 1997)

Smith, Emma, 'Is There A Crisis in School Science Education in the UK?', *Educational Review* 62 (2010), 189–202

Smith, Emma and Stephen Gorard, 'Is There a Shortage of Scientists? A Re-Analysis of Supply for the UK', *British Journal of Educational Studies* 59 (2011), 159–77

Smith, Emma and Patrick White, 'Where Do All the STEM Graduates Go? Higher Education, the Labour Market and Career Trajectories in the UK', *Journal of Science Education and Technology* (2018), https://doi.org/10.1007/s10956-018-9741-5

Smith, George, 'Schools', in A. H. Halsey and Josephine Webb (eds), *Twentieth-Century British Social Trends* (Basingstoke, 2000), 179–220

Smithers, Alan, 'The Dilemma of Selection in Schools', in Anastasia de Waal (ed.), *The Ins and Outs of Selective Secondary Schools: A Debate* (London, 2015), 194–205

Smithers, Alan and Pamela Robinson (eds), *Further Education Re-formed* (London, 2000)

Smithers, Alan and Pamela Robinson, *Trends in Higher Education* (London, 1996)

Snee, Helen and Fiona Devine, 'Fair Chances and Hard Work? Families Making Sense of Inequality and Opportunity in 21st-Century Britain', *British Journal of Sociology* 69 (2018), 1134–54

Snow, C. P., *The Two Cultures*, 1st pub. 1959 (Cambridge, 1998)

Socialist Commentary, *A Policy for Higher Education: A Group Study* (London, 1959)

Spencer, Stephanie, *Gender, Work and Education in Britain in the 1950s* (Basingstoke, 2005)

Spooner, Robert, 'Secondary Schools', in Max Morris and Clive Griggs (ed.), *Education, The Wasted Years? 1973–1986* (Lewes, 1988), 72–88

Stables, Andrew, *Subjects of Choice: The Process and Management of Pupil and Student Choice* (London, 1996)

Stables, Andrew and Felicity Wikeley, 'Changes in Preference for and Perceptions of Relative Importance of Subjects during a Period of Educational Reform', *Educational Studies* 23 (1997), 393–403

Stacey, Barrie, 'Some Psychological Consequences of Inter-Generation Mobility', *Human Relations* 20 (1967), 3–12

Stevens, Robert, *University to Uni: The Politics of Higher Education in England since 1944* (London, 2004)

Stewart, W. A. C., *Higher Education in Postwar Britain* (Basingstoke, 1989)

Stobart, Gordon and Caroline Gipps, *Assessment: A Teacher's Guide to the Issues*, 3rd ed. (London, 1997)

Sullivan, Alice, Anna Zimdars, and Anthony Heath, 'The Social Structure of the 14–16 Curriculum in England', *International Studies in the Sociology of Education* 20 (2010), 5–21

Sullivan, Alice, Samantha Parsons, Richard Wiggins, Anthony Heath, and Francis Green, 'Social Origins, School Type and Higher Education Destinations', *Oxford Review of Education* 40 (2014), 739–63

Sutcliffe-Braithwaite, Florence, *Class, Politics, and the Decline of Deference in England, 1968–2000* (Oxford, 2018)

Sutton Trust, *What the Polling Says* (London, 2017)

Sutherland, Gillian, *Ability, Merit and Measurement: Mental Testing and English Education 1880–1940* (Oxford, 1984)

Swinnerton-Dyer, Peter, 'Policy on Higher Education and Research: The Rede Lecture 1991', *Higher Education Quarterly* 45 (1991), 204–18

Szamuely, Tibor, 'Russia and Britain: Comprehensive Inequality', in C. B. Cox and A. E. Dyson (eds), *The Black Papers on Education* (London, 1971), 121–38

Tampubolon, Gindo and Mike Savage, 'Intergenerational and Intragenerational Social Mobility in Britain', in Paul Lambert, Roxanne Connelly, Robert M. Blackburn, and Vernon Gayle (eds), *Social Stratification: Trends and Processes* (Farnham, 2012), 115–31

Tawney, R. H., 'An Experiment in Democratic Education' (1914), in Rita Hinden (ed.), *The Radical Tradition: Twelve Essays on Politics, Education and Literature by R.H. Tawney* (Harmondsworth, 1966), 74–85

Tawney, R. H., *Some Thoughts on the Economics of Public Education* (London, 1938)

Taylor, Richard and Tom Steele, *British Labour and Higher Education, 1945 to 2000: Ideologies, Policies and Practice* (London, 2011)

Taylor, William, 'Change within a Contracting System', in Leslie Wagner (ed.), *Agenda for Institutional Change in Higher Education* (Guildford, 1982), 100–12

Taylor-Gooby, Peter, *Public Opinion, Ideology and State Welfare* (London, 1985)

Taylor-Gooby, Peter, *Social Change, Social Welfare and Social Science* (Hemel Hempstead, 1991)

Teichler, Ulrich and Sandra Bürger, 'Student Enrolments and Graduation Trends in the OECD Area: What Can We Learn from International Statistics?', in OECD, *Higher Education to 2030: Vol. 1—Demography* (Paris, 2008), 151–72

Teitelbaum, Michael S., *Falling Behind? Boom, Bust, and the Global Race for Scientific Talent* (Princeton, 2014)

Tholen, Gerbrand, *The Changing Nature of the Graduate Labour Market: Media, Policy and Political Discourses in the UK* (Basingstoke, 2014)

Tholen, Gerbrand, *Graduate Work: Skills, Credentials, Careers, and Labour Markets* (Oxford, 2017)

Thom, Deborah, 'The 1944 Education Act: The "Art of the Possible"?', in Harold L. Smith (ed.), *War and Social Change: British Society in the Second World War* (Manchester, 1986), 101–28

Thompson, Joan, *Secondary Education Survey: An Analysis of L.E.A. Development Plans for Secondary Education* (London, 1952)

Thompson, Ron, 'Social Class and Participation in Further Education: Evidence from the Youth Cohort Study of England and Wales', *British Journal of Sociology of Education* 30 (2009), 29–42

Tight, Malcolm, *The Development of Higher Education in the United Kingdom since 1945* (Maidenhead, 2009)

Timmins, Nicholas, *The Five Giants: A Biography of the Welfare State*, 3rd ed. (London, 2017)

Titmuss, Richard and Kathleen, *Parents Revolt: A Study of the Declining Birth-Rate in Acquisitive Societies* (London, 1942)

Todd, Selina, *The Golden Age of the Grammar School: Exploding the Myth* (London, 2014)

Todd, Selina, *The People: The Rise and Fall of the Working Class, 1910–2010* (London, 2014)

Todd, Selina, *Young Women, Work, and Family in England 1918–1950* (Oxford, 2005)

Todd, Selina and Hilary Young, 'Baby-Boomers to "Beanstalkers"', *Cultural and Social History* 9 (2012), 451–67

Tomlinson, Jim, 'Inventing "Decline": The Falling Behind of the British Economy in the Postwar Years', *Economic History Review* 49 (1996), 731–57

Tomlinson, John, 'Retrospect on Ruskin: Prospect on the 1990s', in Michael Williams, Richard Daugherty, and Frank Banks (eds), *Continuing the Education Debate* (London, 1992), 43–53

Tomlinson, John, 'The Schools', in Dennis Kavanagh and Anthony Seldon (eds), *The Thatcher Effect: A Decade of Change* (Oxford, 1989), 183–97

Tonooka, Chika, 'Reverse Emulation and the Cult of Japanese Efficiency in Edwardian Britain', *Historical Journal* 60 (2017), 95–119

Toye, Richard, '"The Gentleman in Whitehall" Reconsidered: The Evolution of Douglas Jay's Views on Economic Planning and Consumer Choice, 1937–47', *Labour History Review* 67 (2002), 187–204

Trow, Martin, *Problems in the Transition from Elite to Mass Higher Education* (Berkeley, 1973)

Trow, Martin, 'Problems in the Transition from Elite to Mass Higher Education', in OECD, *Conference on Future Structures of Post-Secondary Education, General Report, Policies for Higher Education* (Paris, 1974), 51–101

'Truscot, Bruce' (E. A. Peers), *Redbrick University* (London, 1943)

Turner, Alwyn W., *Crisis? What Crisis? Britain in the 1970s*, 1st pub. 2008 (London, 2009)

Turner, Ralph H., 'Acceptance of Irregular Mobility in Britain and the United States', *Sociometry* 29 (1966), 334–52

Turner, Ralph H., 'Modes of Social Ascent through Education: Sponsored and Contest Mobility' (1960), in A. H. Halsey, Hugh Lauder, Phillip Brown, and Amy Stuart Wells (eds), *Education, Economy, and Society* (New York, 1961), 121–47

Universities UK, *Patterns and Trends in UK Higher Education 2018* (London, 2018)

Vaizey, John, *The Economics of Education* (London, 1962)

Vaizey, John, *Education for Tomorrow*, rev. ed. (Harmondsworth, 1967)

Vaizey, John and Michael Debeauvais, 'Economic Aspects of Educational Development', in A. H. Halsey, Jean Floud and C. Arnold Anderson (eds), *Education, Economy, and Society* (New York, 1961), 37–49

Vaizey, John and John Sheehan, *Resources for Education: An Economic Study of Education in the United Kingdom, 1920–1965* (London, 1968)

Van Laar, D. L. and S. J. Sherwood, 'Where Do All the Psychologists Go? First Destinations of Psychology Graduates 1989–1991', *Psychology Teaching Review* 4 (1995), 40–51

Vernon, P. E., 'The Pool of Ability', *Sociological Review* 7 (1959), suppl., 45–57

Vernon, P. E. (ed.), *Secondary School Selection* (London, 1957)

Viarengo, Martina, 'An Historical Analysis of the Expansion of Compulsory Schooling in Europe After the Second World War', Working Paper 97/07, Department of Economic History, London School of Economics (2007)

Vidal Rodeiro, Carmen L., *A Level Subject Choice in England: Patterns of Uptake and Factors Affecting Subject Preferences* (Cambridge, 2007)

Vincent, David, 'Mobility, Bureaucracy and Careers in Early Twentieth-Century Britain', in Andrew Miles and David Vincent (eds), *Building European Society: Occupational Change and Social Mobility in Europe 1840–1940* (Manchester, 1993), 217–39

Vinen, Richard, *Thatcher's Britain: The Politics and Social Upheaval of the 1980s* (London, 2009)

Waal, Anastasia de (ed.), *The Ins and Outs of Selective Secondary Schools: A Debate* (London, 2015)

Wagner, Leslie, 'National Policy and Institutional Development', in Oliver Fulton (ed.), *Access and Institutional Change* (Milton Keynes, 1989), 149–62

Wakeling, Paul and Mike Savage, 'Entry to Elite Positions and the Stratification of Higher Education in Britain', *Sociological Review* 63 (2015), 290–320

Walden, George, *Lucky George: Memoirs of an Anti-Politician* (London, 1999)

Walford, Geoffrey, 'School Choice and Educational Change in England and Wales', in David N. Plank and Gary Sykes (eds), *Choosing Choice: School Choice in International Perspective* (New York, 2003), 68–91

Walker, David A., *The IEA Six Subject Survey: An Empirical Study of Education in Twenty-One Countries* (New York, 1976)

Walker, Ian and Yu Zhu, 'The College Wage Premium and the Expansion of Higher Education in the UK', *Scandinavian Journal of Economics* 110 (2008), 695–709

Walker, Ian and Yu Zhu, 'Differences by Degree: Evidence of the Net Financial Rates of Return to Undergraduate Study for England and Wales', *Economics of Education Review* 30 (2011), 1177–86

Walker, Ian and Yu Zhu, 'The Impact of University Degrees on the Lifecycle of Earnings: Some Further Analysis', Research Paper 112, Department for Business, Innovation and Skills (2013)

Walker, Kevin, 'Why Do Sixth Form Students Choose Psychology? A Report of Research in One Institution', *Psychology Teaching*, Summer 2004, 29–35

Walton, J., 'Beaminster School, Dorsetshire', in Elizabeth Halsall (ed.), *Becoming Comprehensive: Case Histories* (Oxford, 1970), 18–36

Wann, Peter, 'The Collapse of Parliamentary Bipartisanship in Education 1945–52', *Journal of Educational Administration and History* 3:2 (1971), 24–34

Ware, Alan, 'Grammar Schools, A Policy of Social Mobility and Selection—Why?', *Political Quarterly* 88 (2017), 280–90

Watson, David, 'The New Attack on Higher Education', *Perspectives: Policy and Practice in Higher Education* 4 (2000), 90–4

Watson, David and Michael Amoah (eds), *The Dearing Report Ten Years On* (London, 2007)

Watson, David and Rachel Bowden, *Ends without Means: The Conservative Stewardship of UK Higher Education 1979–1997* (Brighton, 1997)

Watson, David and Rachel Bowden, David, *The New University Decade 1992–2001* (Brighton, 2002)

Watson, David and Rachel Bowden, 'Why Did They Do It? The Conservatives and Mass Higher Education, 1979–97', *Journal of Education Policy* 14 (1999), 243–56

Watt, John, 'The Introduction and Development of the Comprehensive School in the West of Scotland 1965–80', Ph.D. dissertation, Glasgow University, 1989

Weedon, Elisabet, 'Widening Access to Higher Education in Sweden: Changing Political Ideologies, Changing Tactics?', in Sheila Riddell, Sarah Minty, Elisabet Weedon, and Susan Whittaker (eds), *Higher Education Funding and Access in International Perspective* (Bingley, 2018), 143–62

Weisz, George, 'The Republican Ideology and the Social Sciences: The Durkheimians and the History of Social Economy at the Sorbonne', in Philippe Besnard (ed.), *The Sociological Domain: The Durkheimians and the Founding of French Sociology* (Cambridge, 1983), 90–119

Werfhorst, Herman G. van de, 'A Detailed Examination of the Role of Education in Intergenerational Social-Class Mobility', *Social Science Information* 41 (2002), 407–38

What Has Happened to the Students? Proceedings of the Autumn Conference on 26 November 1974 at the Royal Festival Hall, London organized by the North East London Polytechnic (London, 1974)

White, John, *The Invention of the Secondary Curriculum* (Basingstoke, 2011)

Whiteside, Noel, 'Creating the Welfare State in Britain, 1945–1960', *Journal of Social Policy* 25 (1996), 83–103

Whitfield, Keith and R. A. Wilson, 'Staying on in Full-Time Education: The Educational Participation Rate of 16-Year-Olds', *Economica* 58 (1991), 391–404

Whitty, Geoff, 'The New Right and the National Curriculum: State Control or Market Forces?', *Journal of Education Policy* 4 (1989), 329–41

Whitty, Geoff, 'Twenty Years of Progress? English Education Policy 1988 to the Present', *Educational Management Administration & Leadership* 36 (2008), 165–84

Whitty, Geoff and Jake Anders, '(How) Did New Labour Narrow the Achievement and Participation Gap?', Research Paper 46, Centre for Learning and Life Chances in Knowledge Economies and Societies, Institute of Education (2014)

Whitty, Geoff, Annette Hayton, and Sarah Tang, 'Who You Know, What You Know and Knowing The Ropes: A Review of Evidence about Access to Higher Education Institutions in England', *Review of Education* 3 (2015), 27–67

Whitty, Geoff and Emma Wisby, 'Education in England—A Testbed for Network Governance?', *Oxford Review of Education* 42 (2016), 316–29

Whyte, William, 'Private Benefit, Public Finance? Student Funding in Late Twentieth-Century Britain', in Lawrence Goldman (ed.), *Welfare and Social Policy in Britain since 1870* (Oxford, 2019), 60–78

Whyte, William, *Redbrick: A Social and Architectural History of Britain's Civic Universities* (Oxford, 2015)

Wiborg, Susanne, 'The Formation of Comprehensive Education: Scandinavian Variations', in Barry M. Franklin and Gary McCulloch (eds), *The Death of the Comprehensive High School? Historical, Contemporary, and Comparative Perspectives* (Basingstoke, 2007), 131–45

Wiener, Martin J., *English Culture and the Decline of the Industrial Spirit 1850–1980* (Cambridge, 1981)

Wikeley, Felicity and Andrew Stables, 'Changes in School Students' Approaches to Subject Option Choices: A Study of Pupils in the West of England in 1984 and 1996', *Educational Research* 41 (1999), 287–99

Wilkinson, Richard and Kate Pickett, *The Spirit Level: Why More Equal Societies Almost Always Do Better* (London, 2009)

Willetts, David, *A University Education* (Oxford, 2017)

Williams, Gareth, 'A Bridge Too Far: An Economic Critique of Marketization of Higher Education', in Claire Callender and Peter Scott (eds), *Browne and Beyond: Modernizing English Higher Education* (London, 2013), 57–72

Williams, Gareth, 'The Economic Approach', in Burton R. Clark (ed.), *Perspectives on Higher Education: Eight Disciplinary and Comparative Views* (Berkeley, 1984), 79–105

Williams, Gareth, 'The Events of 1973–1974 in a Long-Term Planning Perspective' (1974), in Carolyn Baxter, P. J. O'Leary, and Adam Westoby (eds), *Economics and Education Policy: A Reader* (London, 1977), 39–56

Williams, Gareth, 'The Market Route to Mass Higher Education: British Experience 1979–1996', *Higher Education Policy* 10 (1997), 275–89

Williams, Gareth and Tessa Blackstone, *Response to Adversity: Higher Education in a Harsh Climate* (Guildford, 1983)

Williams, Gareth and Alan Gordon, '16 and 19 Year Olds: Attitudes to Education', *Higher Education Bulletin* 4 (1975), 23–37

Williams, Michael, 'Ruskin in Context', in Michael Williams, Richard Daugherty, and Frank Banks (eds), *Continuing the Education Debate* (London, 1992), 1–6

Willis, Paul, *Learning to Labour: How Working Class Kids Get Working Class Jobs*, 1st pub. 1977 (Aldershot, 1993)

Wilson, Harold, *Labour's Plan for Science* (London, 1963)

Willetts, David, *A University Education* (Oxford, 2017)

Wiswall, Matthew and Basit Zafar, 'Preference for the Workplace, Investment in Human Capital, and Gender', *Quarterly Journal of Economics* 133 (2018), 457–507

Withington, P. H., 'Brookfield School, Kirkby, Liverpool', in Elizabeth Halsall (ed.), *Becoming Comprehensive: Case Histories* (Oxford, 1970), 73–94

Wolf, Alison, 'A Comparative Perspective on Educational Standards', in Harvey Goldstein and Anthony Heath (eds), *Educational Standards* (Oxford, 2000), 9–37

Wolf, Alison, *Does Education Matter? Myths about Education and Economic Growth* (London, 2002)

Woodin, Tom, Gary McCulloch and Steven Cowan, *Secondary Education and the Raising of the School-Leaving Age: Coming of Age?* (Basingstoke, 2013)

Woodley, Alan, 'Wider and Still Wider? A Historical Look at the "Open-ness" of the Open University of the United Kingdom', in Tamsin Hinton-Smith (ed.), *Widening Participation in Higher Education* (Basingstoke, 2012), 51–70

Woods, Peter, 'The Myth of Subject Choice', *British Journal of Sociology* 27 (1976), 130–49

Wooldridge, Adrian, 'The English State and Educational Theory', in S. J. D. Green and R. C. Whiting (eds), *The Boundaries of the State in Modern Britain* (Cambridge, 1996), 231–57

Wooldridge, Adrian, *Measuring the Mind: Education and Psychology in England, c. 1860–c. 1990* (Cambridge, 1994)

Wooldridge, Adrian, *Meritocracy and the 'Classless Society'* (London, 1995)

Woolf, Leonard, 'Equality', in Mary Adams (ed.), *The Modern State* (London, 1933), 40–5

Worth, Eve, 'Women, Education and Social Mobility during the Long 1970s', *Cultural and Social History* 16 (2019), 67–83

Wragg, Ted and Lindsey Jarvis, 'Pass or Fail? Perceptions of Education', in Alison Park et al. (eds), *British Social Attitudes: Continuity and Change over Two Decades* (London, 2003), 109–29

Wright, Nigel, *Progress in Education: A Review of Schooling in England and Wales* (London, 1977)

Wright, Susannah, 'Citizenship, Moral Education and the English Elementary School', in Laurence Brockliss and Nicola Sheldon (eds), *Mass Education and the Limits of State Building, c. 1870–1930* (Basingstoke, 2012), 21–45

Young, Michael, *Labour's Plan for Plenty* (London, 1947)

Young, Michael, 'Looking Back on *Meritocracy*', in Geoff Dench (ed.), *The Rise and Rise of Meritocracy* (Oxford, 2006), 73–7

Young, Michael, *The Rise of the Meritocracy 1870–2033: An Essay on Education and Equality*, 1st pub. 1958 (Harmondsworth, 1961)

Young, Michael and Peter Willmott, *Family and Kinship in East London*, 1st pub. 1957 (Harmondsworth, 1962)

Zellick, Graham, *Universities and the Law: The Erosion of Institutional Autonomy* (London, 2000)

BLOGS AND WEBSITES

BBC News: news.bbc.co.uk

British Political Speech: http://www.britishpoliticalspeech.org/index.htm

Centre for Longitudinal Studies: cls.ucl.ac.uk

Chronicle of Higher Education: http://chronicle.com/blognetwork

Education in England: http://www.educationengland.org.uk/index.html

Higher Education Policy Institute: http://www.hepi.ac.uk

Inside Higher Ed: https://www.insidehighered.com/blogs/

Mike Ratcliffe: https://moremeansbetter.wordpress.com/

Ben Schmidt: http://sappingattention.blogspot.co.uk/

Secondary Education and Social Change in the United Kingdom since 1945: sesc.hist.cam.ac.uk/blog

Sutton Trust: http://www.suttontrust.com

UK Public Spending: https://www.ukpublicspending.co.uk/

Wonkhe: wonkhe.com/blogs

YouGov: https://yougov.co.uk/topics/politics

Index

Note: Figures are indicated by an italic "f" and notes are indicated by "n" following the page numbers.

For the benefit of digital users, indexed terms that span two pages (e.g., 52–53) may, on occasion, appear on only one of those pages.